Seeing Young Children

A Guide to Observing and Recording Behavior

Sixth Edition

I want to dedicate this sixth edition of Seeing Young Children to my late niece Melanie Riemersma, MD, who, after a long, valiant battle against a malignant brain tumor, finally lost that battle on September 30, 2007. She was an intelligent, caring, compassionate human being who will be sorely missed. I also dedicate this edition to her husband and children, and to her parents, Robert and Martyne Freed, all of whose grief I deeply share.

Join us on the web at
EarlyChildEd.delmar.cengage.com

Seeing Young Children

A Guide to Observing and Recording Behavior

SIXTH EDITION

Warren R. Bentzen, Emeritus

State University
of New York
at Plattsburgh

DELMAR
CENGAGE Learning

Australia • Brazil • Japan • Korea • Mexico • Singapore • Spain • United Kingdom • United States

DELMAR
CENGAGE Learning™

Seeing Young Children: A Guide to Observing and Recording Behavior, Sixth Edition
Warren R. Bentzen, Emeritus

Vice President, Career Education
   Strategic Business Unit: Dawn Gerrain
Director of Learning Solutions: John Fedor
Managing Editor: Robert L. Serenka, Jr.
Acquisitions Editor: Christopher Shortt
Product Manager: Philip Mandl
Editorial Assistant: Alison Archambault
Director of Production: Wendy A. Troeger
Production Manager: Mark Bernard
Content Project Manager: Jeffrey Varecka
Technology Project Manager: Sandy Charette
Director of Marketing: Wendy E. Mapstone
Channel Manager: Kristin McNary
Marketing Coordinator: Scott A. Chrysler
Marketing Specialist: Erica S. Conley
Art Director: David Arsenault

For product information and technology assistance, contact us at
Cengage Learning Customer & Sales Support, 1-800-354-9706

For permission to use material from this text or product, submit all requests online at **www.cengage.com/permissions**

Further permissions questions can be e-mailed to **permissionrequest@cengage.com.**

Library of Congress Control Number: 2007042715
ISBN-13: 978-1-4180-7378-7
ISBN-10: 1-4180-7378-4

Delmar
10 Davis Drive
Belmont, CA 94002-3098
USA

Cengage Learning is a leading provider of customized learning solutions with office locations around the globe, including Singapore, the United Kingdom, Australia, Mexico, Brazil, and Japan. Locate your local office at: **international.cengage.com/region**

Cengage Learning products are represented in Canada by Nelson Education, Ltd.

For your lifelong learning solutions, visit **delmar.cengage.com**

Visit our corporate website at **cengage.com**

Join us on the Web at **EarlyChildEd.delmar.cengage.com**

Printed in the United States of America
5 6 7 8 11

C O N T E N T S

PART ONE

OVERVIEW

CHAPTER 1 Introduction / 3

CHAPTER 2 An Introduction to Growth and Development / 19

PART TWO

**THE ELEMENTS
OF
OBSERVATION**

PART THREE

OBSERVATION EXERCISES

PART FOUR

MIDDLE CHILD-HOOD—THE SCHOOL-AGE YEARS

CHAPTER 18 The School-Age Years:
The Seven- and Eight-Year-Old Child / 434

PREFACE TO THE SIXTH EDITION

When writing the preface to the sixth edition of *Seeing Young Children*, it was my contention that one of the problems with book prefaces is that very often they do not get read. I believed this despite all the reasons I gave for why one *should* read any book's preface. Perhaps the most cogent reasons are that it gives an author the opportunity to explain at least some of what the reader will encounter in the rest of the book, and it provides the author a rationale for what he or she has or has not written. I argued further that to judge a book without having read it is dishonest. On the other hand, most of us do not have time to read an entire book in order to decide whether it was worth reading. Therefore, even though no preface will provide all the information that would be useful in making such a decision, I hope you will deem reading this one a reasonable beginning.

The Text's Intended Reading Audiences

With regard to Seeing Young Children's intended reading audiences, nothing has changed since its first publication in 1985. *Seeing Young Children* has always been written for anyone who is interested in, or works with, children in any capacity, and for whom the ability to observe and record children's behavior is a valuable skill. This use defines a broad spectrum of individuals ranging from physicians, professional child care providers and early childhood educators, students, schoolteachers, parents, grandparents, child protection agency staff, and anyone else who needs to understand how children change over time and to meaningfully document such change.

Although *Seeing Young Children* apparently has found its predominant market in the two- and four-year colleges and universities, the text's market and usefulness are not restricted to those settings. Indeed, even the casual reader can find very useful information within its pages, information that runs the gamut from discovering what observation is, to developmental theory, to exercises or practical applications of various observation and recording techniques.

Why I Wrote This Book

I initially wrote *Seeing Young Children* to replace a text that I was using in my child development classes at the State University College in Plattsburgh, New York. The text I had been using went out of print, and the heavy emphasis on the observational component of my child development class mandated that I find a new text. I felt that in order to meet the requirements I imposed on such a text, I needed to write it myself. As I became more and more involved in the writing process, I came to the realization that there is more to observing children's behavior than meets the eye, and that all the physical senses by which we gather information from our environment are merely pathways to a brain that gives meaning to this sensory information. I also quickly realized that observing children's behavior, as I was to conceptualize it, involved far more than casually watching them play. Consequently, observing children is not merely a pastime engaged in only to satisfy one's casual or transient interest. Indeed, in order to watch children play, for example, you must know what play is and whether or not play is what you are seeing. Thus, what might begin as casual interest can be transformed and result in something meaningful if the individual is an informed, skilled observer.

The Book's Conceptual Foundation

The basic conceptual foundation of *Seeing Young Children* still rests on the idea that meaningful observation, as opposed to casual watching, is a far more complicated activity than that involved in taking a picture with a camera. The camera captures images but is impervious to their meanings. The human eye also captures images, but the eye is connected to a brain that can make sense out of those images and give them meaning. The human being is endowed with other faculties—hearing, smell, touch, and taste—that also receive sensory information to which the brain gives meaning. Observation, therefore, as it is defined and practiced in this text, involves purposefully capturing information contained in children's behavior and giving that information meanings that can be used to foster their growth, development, and overall well-being. *Seeing Young Children* was expressly written to enable the reader to acquire and implement the necessary knowledge and skill to observe, record, and interpret the informational images that children exhibit in their everyday behavior.

Organization of the Text and What Is New to the Sixth Edition

The basic organization of the sixth edition differs slightly from that of the previous editions. This difference is the result of eliminating Chapter 13, "Application: Recording Methods in Action." Now some possible applications, as well as other content, are presented in each method's respective chapter. What are now the text's 18 chapters still cover the period from birth through eight years of age, which is the age span that the National Association for the Education of Young Children (NAEYC) defines as early childhood. Some reviewers wanted me to extend the book's coverage through age 12 years (through the sixth grade). I have resisted this suggestion for several reasons. Perhaps the least important reason is that, for me, at least, covering yet four more years of the lifespan contradicts the meaning of "young" in this book's title. Secondly, my primary emphasis has always been the observation of young children in a general and developmental environment that is less regimented and more spontaneous than what you will typically encounter in a public school classroom, especially when you get into the third, fourth, fifth, and sixth grades. There undoubtedly are exceptions, of course, but I don't believe there are enough of them to invalidate the rule. The focus of *Seeing Young Children* is on observing and making sense out of behavior that I like to call "natural and free-ranging." Finally, and what might conceptually be the most significant reason, is that the skills that one acquires observing and recording the behavior of "young" children are essentially the same skills one would need to observe and record the behavior of 9-, 10-, 11-, and 12-year-olds. Perhaps the major difference is that one would have to have whatever knowledge is necessary for understanding the meaning of the observed behavior. Such knowledge would be equivalent to the background information presented in chapters 15 through 18.

Even without any extended coverage, some reviewers of the fifth edition felt that covering only the first eight years of life made the book too long and presented far more material than was covered in the courses they teach. This was not a problem then, and it is not a problem now: Simply omit the chapters that are not relevant to your situation or needs. Each of the developmental periods discussed in this text can stand alone, and except for the fact that the earlier stages of the life span serve as the foundation for the later stages, the newborn can be studied and observed independent of the infant, the infant independent of the toddler, and so on.

I believe the changes incorporated into this sixth edition of *Seeing Young Children* make the text significantly more informative than it was in the fifth edition. There is a considerable amount of new material that deals with potential uses or applications of each of the recording methods. Adding this new material was the rationale for eliminating Chapter 13 and was done at the request of some of the reviewers who felt that this topic should not be confined to a single chapter. I also did what could be called minor grammatical/syntactical housekeeping: I tightened up sentences that I noticed needed tightening, recast sentences from the passive voice to the active voice, and substituted words that for some reason I didn't like for ones I did. I don't know if these word changes will make the text more readable, but they satisfy my perception of what constitutes respectable writing.

One other new feature has been added to this sixth edition—a running glossary. This addition was suggested by the reviewers who apparently reasoned that it is much more convenient not to have to turn to the glossary in the back of the book in order to learn the meanings of the various terms and concepts discussed in the text. The reviewers' reasoning is sound, and I am a little embarrassed that I didn't reach the same conclusion very early on.

As I wrote in the preface to the fifth addition, observing and recording children's behavior, as these activities are viewed in this text, are not influenced by rapidly advancing technology. The fundamental requirements for this activity remain the same— your eyes, your ears, your brain, and pencil and paper, all essentially held together and rendered useful by your knowledge and skill. This eliminates any need to revise in any significant way the observation exercises and the content that accompanies them. Consequently, other than bibliographic updates and the same kind of "housekeeping" I performed on other chapters, 15 through 18 will remain the same as in the fifth edition.

Unlike observation as defined and practiced in this text, technology has made significant advances since the fifth edition came onto the market. Now digital video cameras are popular, and I'm sure that some believe these devices could or even should play a major role in observing and recording children's behavior and, by logical extension, also in the daily operation of a child care facility. If I subscribed to this point of view, I would be obliged to expand my discussion of video cameras as a means of gathering observation data. But let me reiterate my previous position on this issue. I have not been dissuaded from my belief that a video camera is no better or more useful than the person using it, and whatever is viewed from a videotape still has to be understood and interpreted by a human being with a brain. The major advantage of a video recording is that it captures and freezes in time a segment from an ongoing stream of behavior. Unfortunately for those who are strong advocates of videotaping children's behavior, it is unfeasible to follow children around for several hours with a camera pressed up against your eye. Very often, meaningful observation occurs on the run and must be flexible enough to accomplish under sometimes widely varying circumstances. Admittedly, however, videotaped segments of children's behavior can be a useful teaching tool in the hands of a teacher who is also a skilled observer. As things presently stand, instruction is the primary purpose for which I would recommend the use of video cameras.

Observation Exercises

As with the fifth edition, recording forms for the Observation Exercises discussed in Chapters 15 through 18 are at the end of the corresponding chapters. These forms are intended only as examples of recording instruments and should not be taken as the final word on how such forms should look. I am sure that some readers would like to be able to tear out the forms and record their observations on them directly. That option would not be feasible, especially in the case of observations that preserve raw data and require fairly extensive writing; the amount of space allotted to these sample forms would be too restrictive and would limit the amount of information you could record. As a much better alternative, the publisher provides access to all the recording forms on the web as part of the student Online Companion supplement, available at earlychilded.delmar.cengage.com.

Supplemental Material

Instructor's e-Resource CD

The sixth edition of *Seeing Young Children* is accompanied by an instructor's e-Resource CD. Instructors will find that this resource provides them with a turnkey solution to help them teach. The new e-Resource supplement provides instructors with all the tools they need in one convenient CD:

- An electronic manual with study questions and suggestions for lecture topics.
- Chapter by chapter Powerpoints for use during class lectures and seminars.
- A computerized testbank with multiple question types correlated to each chapter.

Student Online Companion

The sixth edition of *Seeing Young Children* is also accompanied by an Online Companion™ that contains the forms mentioned earlier, as well as supplemental content for students to engage in further study and research. The Online Companion™ is available at earlychilded.delmar.cengage.com.

Professional Enhancement Text

A new supplement to accompany this text is the Observation & Assessment Professional Enhancement handbook for students. This resource, which is part of Delmar Learning's Early Childhood Education Professional Enhancement series, focuses on key topics of interest for future early childhood directors, teachers, and caregivers. Becoming a teacher is a process of continuing to grow, learn, reflect, and discover through experience. The Professional Enhancement text helps tomorrow's teachers along their way. Students will keep this informational supplement and use it for years to come in their early childhood practices.

The *Observation & Assessment Professional Enhancement* text provides you with:

- Child development stages and developmental alerts
- Explanation of the difference between watching and observing
- Reasons for why each child is different from another
- Awareness of yourself and its impact on observation
- Common methods used to record/document what you observe
- Uses for what you have observed and recorded that assist in advancing each child's development
- Uses of classroom documentation and assessment for reporting and accountability
- Information on how to manage all the paperwork you collect on each child
- Reminders about the ethics of gathering information on children

ACKNOWLEDGMENTS

The author would like to thank the following reviewers, enlisted by Delmar Learning, for their helpful suggestions and constructive criticism

- Toni A. Campbell, MEd, PhD, San José State University, California
- Wenju Shen, Ed.D, Valdosta State University, Georgia
- Beverlyn Cain, Ed.D, Elizabeth City State University, North Carolina
- Irene Cook, MA, California State University, Bakersfield
- Tisha Bennett Sanders, Ed.D., Vanderbilt University, Tennessee
- Jill E. Fox, PhD, University of Texas at Arlington
- Gail Goldstein, M.Ed., Albuquerque TVI Community College, New Mexico
- Tracy Keys, M.S., Kutztown University, Pennsylvania
- Susan S. Johnston, Ph.D., CCC-SLP, University of Utah
- Ann B. Watts, M.Ed., Forsyth Technical Community College, North Carolina

PART ONE

OVERVIEW

CHAPTER 1

Introduction

OBJECTIVES

After reading this chapter, you should be able to

- Describe the differences between seeing in a physiological way and seeing in an observational way.
- Analyze the importance of observation to early education.
- Analyze the importance of observation to science and to an individual.
- Examine the relationship between observation and the observer's personal and theoretical perspectives.
- Discuss in general terms what observation is and what it involves.

KEY TERMS

observe

perception

raw stimuli

empirical

OBSERVATION: SOME PRELIMINARY THOUGHTS

If you were unable to see, hear, feel, touch, and taste, you would be totally helpless, unable to move, unable to perceive or understand anything of what is happening in the world around you. Probably most of us cannot even imagine such a condition, yet there are those who are blind, deaf, or have some neurological disability that interferes with their sense of touch, smell, or taste. These individuals are unable to take in or perceive certain aspects of their environment. The blind cannot see colors, shapes, objects, or other people. The deaf cannot hear speech, music, bird songs, or traffic noises. Without taste sensations, what enjoyment would we get from eating, or how could we know when we were putting something harmful into our mouths? Without a sense of touch, how could we ever know when we had cut ourselves or had come into contact with another person? If we didn't have a sense of smell, smoke from a fire could not alert us to danger, nor could we savor the odors of good food. We can do the things we must do to survive and to enjoy life because we have the ability to **observe**.

observe
The ability to take in information through one or more of the five physical senses and to make sense of that information so that it can be used in meaningful ways.

perception
Taking in information through one or more of the five physical senses and organizing it in a meaningful way.

raw stimuli
Stimuli such as perceptions and data acquired through observation that have not been interpreted or processed in any way, thus the term *raw*. When using the narrative description method of recording behavior, for example, one is gathering raw data or stimuli that must subsequently be interpreted and given some meaning if the observation is to have any significance.

Most of us take in more information through our eyes than through any of the other senses, and hearing is next in importance, generally speaking. In this text, therefore, visual **perception** or "seeing" will be emphasized, although hearing also plays an important role in understanding children's behavior.

We need to distinguish seeing in a psychological sense from seeing in a physiological sense. Seeing physiologically requires, at minimum, an intact retina in the back of the eye and reasonable visual acuity so that we can make out the objects we are looking at. In this way, the eye acts something like a camera, but instead of a visual image being imposed onto film, as with a camera, the visual image is imposed on the retina. This is the minimal information needed to see in this most basic meaning of seeing. Unfortunately, we humans would be as limited as the camera if we saw only in the way just described. What we have that the camera does not is a brain, and it is the brain that allows us to see in a psychological sense.

Therefore, observation depends upon our ability to make sense of and give meaning to what our eyes (and our ears, and all of the other senses) bring to us as **raw** (uninterpreted) **stimuli** from the outside world.

And so it is really our brains that do any meaningful, useful seeing.

Why Observation Is Important: Some General Considerations

The most basic answer to why observation is important is that it enables us to survive. But we can move beyond that most basic answer to another issue that is especially relevant to working with young children. Without the ability to observe—to "see" and to "hear"—in meaningful ways, we could not interact effectively with the children in our care. We could not understand how they grow and develop and how to assist them in their growth and development. We would be unable to protect them from harm. In short, we would be ineffective, if not useless, in our roles as caregivers, child care providers, early childhood educators, parents, or students learning about children and learning how eventually to assume one or more of these roles. Let us look at a hypothetical example of an observation that could very well take place in an actual child care center or early education facility:

You are a trained child care provider, and you are watching some four-year-olds playing in the big block area. With you is Mrs. Garcia, mother of four-year-old Carlos, one of the children playing with the big blocks. Mrs. Garcia is complaining that she doesn't feel her son is learning anything by simply stacking blocks one on top of another. You ask her to watch more closely and especially to look for examples of social interactions such as sharing blocks or cooperating with another child in lifting a heavy block to put on the pile. You ask her to listen to what the children are saying to one another as they move around the block area and participate in a cooperative building venture. "Do they give instructions to one another?" you ask Mrs. Garcia. She nods and says, "I think so."

You then point out to Mrs. Garcia how the children are gaining a sense of size and weight as they select blocks of a particular size so that they fit appropriately into the structure they are designing and building "on the run." Just then, Carlos shouts, "Hey, this little block is harder to pick up than this big block." Jonathan replies, "Yeah, I know, but we need three more blocks to finish this tower." Carlos says, "OK, but we can't put this big block on top of that little one; it won't stay."

During play, children can learn many things that go unnoticed by the untrained observer.

In all likelihood, Mrs. Garcia and you, our trained observer, would have described what occurred in pretty much the same language as far as general behavior or overt actions are concerned. However, you saw things that Mrs. Garcia simply missed. You were able to make interpretations and draw conclusions regarding other things that were happening "below the surface." You saw skills and concepts being expressed or in the process of being developed. Carlos learned, for example, that size and weight are not necessarily directly related. He knew, probably from previous experience, that putting a big block on top of a much smaller block results in an unstable tower that is likely to fall over. Jonathan indicated at least some understanding of number when he commented that they needed "three more blocks."

Our brains enable us to see in ways that far exceed the camera's ability to "see." But observation becomes complicated precisely because we do more with sensory information than the camera is able to do. As the example illustrates, what and how much information we perceive varies from person to person, and even within the same person from one time to another. So it is that two individuals can be visually aware of the same object or event but visually aware in quite different ways—for example, Mrs. Garcia and our trained observer (see also Hansen, 1958).

The crucial point of the example is that Carlos's mother and the trained observer saw essentially the same overt behaviors as they watched Carlos playing in the big block area. However, what we have depicted is Mrs. Garcia seeing only play going on. She does not fully understand the value of play and the many kinds of learning that are taking place. You, the trained observer, do see learning taking place during play. Mrs. Garcia does not see spatial relationship or arithmetic skills being acquired and practiced, nor does she see Carlos learning social interaction skills.

One very important conclusion to be drawn from this is that all of us look at and organize the objects and events in our world according to our past experiences, what we know, and what we believe. These factors make up what we shall call our personalities or frames of reference. This idea deserves further explanation.

Each of us brings to any situation our own personalities, experiences, and even personal theories about how the world operates. What we observe is filtered or processed through our theories and beliefs, and we draw conclusions based on what gets through the filter. Each of us notices different information (stimuli, events) because each of us is sensitive to different aspects of our environment. Brandt (1972) indicates that observation is dependent on attention, and attention is necessarily selective. Or, to put it into another context, teachers (child care providers) are more likely to see those aspects of children's behavior that fit into, let us say, their professional interests or training than those that do not. For instance, if a teacher is particularly interested in children's social development, she might tend to overlook, not to see, or at least to deemphasize motor behavior. Or perhaps more likely, she will see motor behavior as a means to promote social skills—she will see those behaviors in terms of their relevance to social behavior. In contrast, a teacher whose special interests or concerns lie with children's physical/motor development is more apt to overlook social behaviors in favor of observing how children walk, run, jump, tumble, use their hands, and so on.

On a more general level, a teacher trained in the Montessori method will likely see many opportunities for children to experience self-discovery learning. Another teacher whose approach to early childhood education (or beyond) is based on behavioral analysis will see occasions where structure and teacher-directed activities are required. Yet, if in the same classroom with the same children, both teachers will have access to what are objectively the same situations and information, but each will simply attend to different aspects of the situation.

Why Observation Is Important: Some Specific Considerations

To make sense of the observation process as it pertains to you, we should look at some reasons that observation is important. Some of these reasons will be particularly relevant in a formal child care setting such as an early childhood education center or professional child care facility.

Almost three decades ago, Goodwin and Driscoll (1980) argued for three reasons that observation is important in early childhood education. First, observation allows for the measuring of many behaviors that otherwise may not be measurable. Many tests performed on adults rely on their ability to speak, write, or in some other manner communicate rather complex ideas or feelings. However, young children still have immature language and conceptual skills, and they cannot always express awareness and understanding of what is transpiring around them. Interviews or pencil-and-paper tests would therefore be useless with very young children. Emotions, Goodwin and Driscoll claim, are especially suitable to observational methods. The observer can see children as they actually behave, without the shortcomings of limited test-taking ability, unreliable understanding of test instructions, and eagerness to please adults by responding in the way they think the adults want them to respond.

In more recent scholarship, Morrison (1995) speaks to this characteristic by also referring to the ability of observation to "gather data that cannot be gleaned by conducting paper-and-pencil tests or questioning a young child" (p. 45). Morrison comments on the overall importance of observation, noting that

> Professionals recognize that children are more than just what is measured by a particular test. Utilizing more "authentic" means for assessing children, professionals realize that observation is one of the most authentic means of learning about children and what they know and are able to do, especially when it occurs in *naturalistic settings* such as classrooms, child care centers, playgrounds, and homes. (p. 45, italics original)

He states further that "observation enables professionals to gain information directly that could otherwise be gathered only indirectly" (p. 45).

Critical to all of this is Morrison's view that when looking at children, professionals and parents sometimes "do not really see what they [the children] are doing or understand why they are engaging in a particular behavior or activity.... This is why it is important for early childhood professionals to understand the importance of and how to use observation to gather data about young children" (p. 45).

Second, children do not typically view formal testing procedures as seriously as do adults. Goodwin and Driscoll (1980) believe that young children do not take to heart adults' advice that the test is serious business and that they should try as hard as they can, an attitude that formal testing relies on for its success. There are other criticisms leveled against the formal testing of young children. It is argued, for example, that formal testing is developmentally inappropriate for young children. Some also contend that rather than not taking testing seriously, as Goodwin and Driscoll claim, children in fact become severely stressed under formal testing conditions. The National Association for the Education of Young Children (NAEYC), for example, cites as a developmentally inappropriate practice the evaluation of children "only against a predetermined measure, such as a standardized group norm or adult standard of behavior. All are expected to perform the same tasks and achieve the same narrowly defined, easily measured skills" (cited in *Early Childhood Education 88/89*, Annual Editions, p. 111).

In the context of assessment, Morrison (1995) cites the value of observation for assessing children's abilities, which in turn "determines areas in which they need additional support and help" (p. 45). He mentions that observation is used to assess children's "performance over time" and that observation enables professionals to gather information that can be used in parent conferences and in reports to parents about their children (p. 45).

Spodeck and Saracho (1994) also discuss the issue of the standardized testing of young children, and they essentially take the perspective of NAEYC: "While some form of assessment is important as an indicator of the effectiveness of programs, standardized tests may be the wrong instrument for this purpose" (p. 240). It is not our purpose to become embroiled in the controversy regarding such tests. Nonetheless, the fact that standardized testing is coming under serious scrutiny, together with the resulting emphasis on the importance and appropriateness of naturalistic observation, makes refining one's skills in observing young children's behavior all the more critical.

Fortunately, naturalistic observation shares none of these disadvantages with formal testing. The observer wants to see children's behavior as it occurs without adult

Some argue against the formal, standardized testing of young children.

interference. The observer does not want to generate anxiety or other emotions that might inappropriately affect the children's behavior.

Finally, Goodwin and Driscoll's third reason is that even when young children know they are being observed, they feel less threatened or anxious than do older children and adults. Presumably, young children are also less likely than older children or adults to change their behavior in response to being observed. The assumption here is that, in the case of older children and adults, if someone knows he is being watched, it is harder for him to behave normally than if he thinks he is alone. It has been said that if we were observed behaving in what we thought were private moments, most of us would be judged insane. Observation of young children supposedly yields behavior that is relatively unaffected by the process of observing it.

This belief or argument notwithstanding, its underlying assumption should be subjected to empirical verification or refutation in any given situation and with any given child or group of children. Perhaps the wisest course of action is not to take it for granted that young children do not react adversely to being observed. This admonition is really related to the general principle of remaining as inconspicuous as possible when in the observation setting (see Chapter 3). However, it is an irrefutable fact that it is impossible to remain invisible to the children or to keep them ignorant of your presence under all circumstances. Consequently, the children will see you, and they either may come to know what you are doing on their "turf" or develop a perception or belief about what you are doing. This must be handled carefully, most importantly for the sake of the children's well-being, and secondarily for the sake of the successful and "honest" completion of your observation.

OBSERVATION AND THEORY

Aside from these reasons, there are others that give importance to the observation process. You may find yourself observing children who are in a variety of settings (e.g., in preschool classrooms, playgrounds, the home, or public school classrooms). Our knowledge of children and how they change over time ultimately depends on many people studying children: observing them doing various things in various situations at various ages. There are two aspects to the relationship between theory and observation. First, theories that attempt to explain development have to be tested and shown to be useful or not useful in understanding the developmental process. In this case, such testing must ultimately involve observation. Although it is unlikely that you will have to test a theory in any formal or official manner, we think it is accurate to say that observing and interpreting children's behavior does result in theory testing of a sort. Let us look at an example.

Piaget's theory of cognitive development has given rise to a huge amount of research, both for its own sake and for the sake of developing such things as preschool curricula and programs. Piaget argued that egocentrism, which essentially is defined as the inability to take another person's point of view or perspective, is a basic characteristic of the young child. His "mountain view" task is a classic in the field of egocentrism research, and it's from children's performances on tasks such as the mountain view that Piaget derived his essential conclusions about the extent of children's egocentrism. (Most simply put, in at least one version of the mountain view task, the child is shown a three-dimensional model of a mountain landscape. The child is then shown a set of photographs taken from different positions around the model. A doll is placed at these various positions, and the child is asked to select the photograph that best represents what the doll "sees.") Nonetheless, for some time now researchers have been finding evidence that young children are not as egocentric as Piaget thought. Murray Krantz (1994), a writer and researcher, reports that when materials and situations that are familiar to the children are substituted for Piaget's essentially unfamiliar mountain task, their responses are consistently nonegocentric (p. 295). Laura Berk (2005) offers a general statement regarding Piaget's conclusions: "Research indicates that Piaget underestimated the competencies of infants and preschoolers. When young children are given tasks scaled down in difficulty, their understanding appears closer to that of the older child and adult than Piaget assumed" (p. 22). She further states, "This discovery has led many investigators to conclude that the maturity of children's thinking may depend on their familiarity with the task presented and the complexity of knowledge sampled" (p. 22). The point here is that if you are looking for examples of egocentrism in preschoolers' typical behavior, you may instead observe instances of nonegocentric behavior, an event that would in effect put Piaget's conclusions and theory to the test.

Jean Piaget's theory plays a very important role in our understanding of children's intellectual development.

The second aspect of the relationship between theory and observation has to do with the fact that your observations can help you better understand the theories you may be studying. There is a relationship between what you learn from books, for example, and your observation experiences. On the one hand, involvement with real children can help you understand what you read and hear about them; on the other hand, what you are learning about children and their development will influence what you see as you complete the observation exercises. For example, what you know in general about language development will affect what you learn and understand about a particular child's language development. The nature of your understanding, and how you explain what you see, will depend on your knowledge, your observation skills, and the theoretical and personal perspective(s) from which you view growth, development, and even people in general. This is also true in areas other than early childhood education.

For instance, a Freudian therapist is very likely to see a client's problem as involving psychic conflict, whereas a behavioral therapist is more likely to see the same problem in terms of the client's reinforcement history. Each therapist, because of his professional training, sees that behavior from a different point of view and is sensitive to different aspects of the individual's behavior. If you work with children in a professional capacity, your particular training will incline you to see children in certain ways and to interpret their behavior in a way that agrees with your point of view or theory. This text is designed to help you sharpen your observation skills. It also emphasizes the need for a conceptual framework from which to observe and make sense out of what is seen.

The need for a conceptual or theoretical framework cannot be emphasized too strongly. Let us illustrate with a hypothetical scenario:

The scene is a preschool classroom, and you have come simply to visit and to watch. You notice a small boy sitting at a table playing with a piece of clay. He is alone, and you want to get closer to see what he is doing. The boy (we will call him Robby) smiles as you approach and asks you if you want to play with him. You say "yes," and he gives you his clay. As Robby watches very closely, you roll the clay into one large ball and then break it into two, roughly equal parts. You hand him his portion of the clay and tell him, "Now we both have just as much to play with." Robby nods and smiles again, takes his ball of clay, and rolls it around on the surface of the table. You take your part of the clay and proceed to flatten it out like a pancake. Robby is now very interested; he looks intently at your flattened piece and then shouts, "Hey, your piece is bigger! I want that one!" Because you are, after all, a guest, and you certainly do not want to quarrel with a three-year-old over a piece of clay, you trade your piece for his. He smiles once more and goes back to his playing.

You have just observed a child's behavior in a particular situation. You have received information through your eyes and ears. How could you explain what you have just seen using a theoretical or conceptual framework? One possible explanation could be based on Piaget's theory of cognitive development. You might have "seen" Robby functioning intellectually in Piaget's preoperational stage of cognitive development. From that perspective, Robby would have been unable to *conserve substance*. You would have seen Robby's inability to understand that if no clay was added and none was taken away, then the amount of clay must remain unchanged. You could have seen Robby being fooled by outward appearances of the piece of clay.

Moreover, you could have predicted all of these things just by knowing that because Robby was three, in all likelihood, he would be in Piaget's preoperational stage.

Questions and possible answers such as these are central to this text, and very often answers can be based on particular theoretical or conceptual frameworks.

However, we want to emphasize that this text is not a sourcebook for learning in great detail about such things as child development, early childhood education curricula and classroom practices, or procedures for intervening in the lives of children who present with particular problems. We focus instead on the processes of observing and recording behavior, processes or techniques that can be applied to virtually any situation or set of circumstances in which observation and recording skills are needed. Except for the practice exercises provided in this text, we leave it to you to find the occasions for such application and thereby also to find the specific content of your observation and recording activities.

The preceding discussion has much to do with the importance of observation. However, there is a broader aspect to the importance of observation. Observation is crucial because so many of the sciences—social and physical—must gather data that can be seen, heard, smelled, touched, or tasted. Such data are called **empirical** data, which are data that depend on experience or observation rather than abstract theory.

A psychologist must eventually leave abstract theories of human behavior and explore and measure the "real" behavior of "real" people. Exploring and measuring require observation. A psychologist interested in studying children's aggressive behavior must at some point stop thinking about aggression only in theoretical terms

empirical
Having to do with things that can be seen, heard, touched, smelled, and tasted; data obtained by direct observation and not through abstract thought processes or theory; tied to the "real" world.

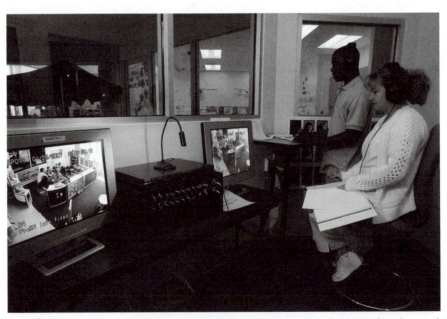

A psychologist must eventually leave abstract theories of human behavior and explore and measure the "real" behavior of "real" people.

and identify what he means by aggression in empirical terms. The psychologist must observe and record visible behaviors exhibited by children—behaviors that he believes indicate aggression. It is likely that he will accept as aggression behaviors such as hitting, pushing, name calling, or taking a toy away from another child. But regardless of its definition, the idea of aggression must ultimately be linked to something directly observable. Based on that observable behavior, the psychologist assumes the presence or existence of aggression.

YOU AND THE OBSERVATION PROCESS

In a very real sense, you will be acting as a scientist when you observe children. You will be doing what every scientist or researcher must do if she is to learn about the real world. Because of the purposes that are part of their occupations, scientists and researchers have to work with ideas that are abstract or removed from everyday life. But all of us deal with abstract ideas at some time. Examples can be found in our everyday language. We use words as symbols that stand for something else. The word *chair* stands for a piece of furniture that one sits on (usually). In ordinary conversation, most of us can agree on what is meant by *chair*. However, a problem arises when we move away from casual conversation and toward descriptions of abstract ideas such as truth or beauty.

The generally acknowledged goals of science are description, explanation, prediction, and control. Being able to explain something indicates that one understands it, knows how it operates, and knows why it operates in that manner. Explanation first requires description. The explainer must know what he is looking at; he must be able to show the phenomenon to others, if only through a verbal description or "picture." In some instances, the explainer may have to make it clear why he thinks he will see what he is looking for in the specific phenomenon chosen for observation. In your case, you will be looking at children, some of whom will be a phenomenon for you to describe, explain, maybe predict, and—consequently—understand.

You may decide to observe a three-year-old child for evidence of egocentrism. It will probably seem reasonable to do this because, according to Piaget, a child of this age is typically egocentric in some behavior and thinking. Recall our earlier discussion regarding recent findings that children are not as egocentric as Piaget thought. This new evidence might change your views of egocentrism and how and where to look for it. Nevertheless, if you decide to pursue egocentrism among three-year-olds, you will first have to define it so that you will recognize it when it occurs. You will describe those behaviors that fit your definition of egocentrism, or from which you infer its presence.

Participation as an observer is not just a matter of watching children play, for example, and then writing down what you have seen. What you have observed must make sense and must be given meaning. Even so, there is no guarantee that your meaning will be the only valid one or that you will even take notice of everything of

Can you actually see aggression or only behavior that you interpret as aggression?

significance in the situation. Validity (accuracy) and completeness depend on the perspective from which you observe and on your skill as an observer. Observation entails the noting and recording of "facts." We refine this meaning to include the idea of looking for something in a *controlled, structured* way. "Controlled" means that your observations are not random or haphazard. You know beforehand *what* you want to observe, *where* you want to observe, and essentially *how* you want to observe. All these factors contribute to the "structured" character of your observations. Your observations evidence structure when you use predetermined observation forms, whether those provided in this manual or others constructed by yourself or someone else.

Thus, what you do in the observation setting will be distinctively different from what the "average" person will do when casually watching children play, show emotion, and so on. However, facts are seldom if ever pure or self-evident. We must process them in some way. To process a fact means to think about it, give it a verbal label, or put it into some meaningful relationship with other facts. We seldom deal directly with the objects, events, and people in our world; rather, we deal with what is said about them. But saying something about an object already involves interpretation and a perspective. Finding the appropriate words indicates knowledge of language, knowledge of the object, and the ability to place the object in a relationship with other objects or with other relevant information. Here is an illustration.

Think for a moment of what is involved in "watching children play." At the very least, you must have some idea of what play is. How do you know it is play you are observing rather than some other kind of activity? If you believe that everything young children do is play, you will make no distinctions among the behaviors they exhibit. But if your perspectives (ideas, views) on play are more sophisticated, you are likely to classify play and nonplay activities according to criteria based, perhaps, on a theory. Or you may identify different types or characteristics of play, possibly using Craig and Kermis's (1995) six categories or forms of play, which are as follows (see Chapter 17 for a more complete discussion of these categories):

1. Sensory pleasure
2. Play with motion
3. Rough-and-tumble play
4. Play with language
5. Dramatic play and modeling
6. Games, rituals, and competitive play

Can you see how it is possible to view play (or anything else) in either a simple or a complex way? Let us look at one more illustration of this essential point.

Although the 1977 writings of early childhood educators Constance Kamii and Rheta DeVries may seem especially outdated eight years into a new millennium, what they have to say is still current and relevant. In their discussion of Piaget's ideas about the development of intelligence, they also deal with a necessary component of all observation—the processing of facts. They use the example of a child understanding the concept of "capital" (specifically, as represented in the statement "Washington, D.C., is the capital of the United States"). A sixth grader has some understanding of such a statement, but as Kamii and DeVries point out, with six more years of living, studying, and other maturing experiences, the statement will take on richer and more elaborate meanings. As a result, write the authors, free association to the word "Washington" might raise from the child such responses as "The White House, the Capitol, the Lincoln Memorial" (p. 372). The adult's range of responses to Washington would be even broader than the child's (perhaps including "taxes," "an area of land 10 miles square," or going to war in Iraq). Like the child's, the adult's response would be relevant to the particular word and its accepted set of meanings. They would not include a response such as "The price of eggs in China" or "Napoleon" (Kamii & DeVries, 1977, p. 373). The idea of putting one fact into a relationship with other facts (processing) is conveyed in the following passage:

> These free associations illustrate Piaget's view that since knowledge is organized in a coherent, whole structure, no concept can exist in isolation. Each concept is supported and colored by an entire network of other concepts. (Kamii & DeVries, 1977, p. 373)

This example from Kamii and DeVries has to do with you as an observer and with your obligation to process what you perceive as facts. Kamii and DeVries's thesis is simply that no one can make sense of, say, Fact 1 without being able to put it into some kind of relationship with Fact 2, or Fact 3, and so on. It is this organizing of concepts that makes up the processing of facts; again, it is guided by developmental or behavioral theories and personal perspectives.

It is clear by now that observing is not simply looking *at* something. Disciplined, scientific observation is looking *for* something in a particular way (or ways). These particular ways of observing children are discussed in Chapters 4 through 12.

There is a final aspect of observation worth noting. The phrase *observation process* has been used several times. That phrase has two meanings of interest to us. First, *process* refers to a series of related activities that require time to accomplish. Thus, to observe a child involves a number of activities and behaviors on the part of both the child and the observer. The child has to exhibit the behaviors of interest to the observer, and the observer has to do something with those behaviors. She must see them, and then record and interpret them. Process also involves structure of some sort. Structure may be inherent in the situation itself, to the extent that certain activities have to follow a particular sequence or time order. For example, you have to observe a behavior before you can record and interpret it. The observer can impose other kinds of structure on the situation, as in choosing a particular method of recording behaviors or a particular theoretical perspective from which to interpret and explain the behaviors.

In its second meaning, *process* can be used as a noun, where it refers to a sequence or series of actions or changes that bring about some kind of result or consequence. *The American Heritage Talking Dictionary* (1995) also includes in its definition of process "a series of operations performed in the making [or treatment] of a *product*" (italics added). We may not usually think of others or ourselves as "products," but we are indeed that. And, of course, change is always involved in the making of any product, including the product that is you—your skills, values, attitudes, and personality. Change is part of observation (and vice versa), for the child will not remain the same even in the short period of time required to do an observation exercise, let alone over a period of weeks and months. You too will change. You will learn about developmental theories, norms, and research studies. You will acquire knowledge of observation techniques and skill in performing them. Your knowledge of theory and your observation experiences will interact with each other and be enhanced or improved. Your attitudes concerning children—how they grow and develop, who they are, where they "fit" in the life cycle—may also change.

We wish you success on your journey.

SUMMARY

Observation is something we do continually, whether we are aware of it or not. We observe largely through our eyes and ears, taking in various kinds of sensory information. All observation, however, whether casual or scientifically rigorous, consists of more than the physical reception of stimuli. We truly observe or "see" when what we have received through our senses has meaning for us. We see when we can put our observations into a mental framework that has personal relevance. All of us have personal frameworks within which we describe and interpret what happens in our world. These frameworks can be called our personalities. It is also possible to have more formal frameworks to describe and interpret observed phenomena. These formal frameworks can be called theories.

Observation is critical for a number of reasons. The most basic reason is that ultimately we learn about reality by observing it, by having contact with it through one or more of our five physical senses. It logically follows, then, that if we are to understand children, we must watch them, listen to them, and touch them. Moreover, we must think about the information we have gotten in these ways and make some sense of it in order to act with and toward children in appropriate and meaningful ways.

STUDY QUESTIONS

1. What is the importance of seeing in a physical sense and seeing in an observational sense? How are these two kinds of seeing related?

2. Do you think observational skills are important or unimportant to being a good teacher or child care worker? Defend your position with specific reasons. Do the same regarding the importance or unimportance of observation to science and the individual. Are your three sets of reasons like or unlike one another? In other words, is observation for the teacher, scientist, and the ordinary person actually three different activities, or do they share some commonalities?

3. With respect to the last part of question 2, how might observation done by a scientist in an experimental setting differ from observation done, say, by a preschool teacher in a natural setting or context? If there are any differences, what form would they likely take?

4. This chapter argues that observation is affected or determined by our personalities (i.e., our knowledge, values, attitudes, and experience). How could you prove this argument to be true or false? The practical exercise that follows helps illustrate how our personalities, past experiences, values, and knowledge can affect our observations.

5. It's been said that it is impossible not to communicate. Is it also impossible not to observe? Take the broadest possible view of observation to answer this question.

PRACTICAL EXERCISE

What we would like you to get out of this first chapter is some sense of how much our personalities or our experiences influence the observation process when we engage in it, which is most of the time. Although completing this exercise will require you to do some work, we believe it will be well worth your time and effort.

The essential theme or purpose of this exercise is to ask several individuals to describe or explain some object, sound, or event and then to compare their responses in the context of their professions or occupations. Select two or three individuals whose professions or occupations are very different and to whom you could have access for discussion or interviewing. For instance, you could play a taped recording of a piece of music (classical, jazz, rock), or you could show each person a photograph of a building or some other object. The key to successfully performing this exercise is to match the task with the individuals' respective professions in such a way as to emphasize the differences in their responses.

For example, playing the opening bars of Beethoven's Fifth Symphony to a professional musician, an attorney, and an automobile mechanic would likely result in very different comments, explanations, or understandings. One would predict that the musician's responses would be quite detailed, informed, and sophisticated, whereas the responses of the other two individuals would be more general and less knowledgeable regarding the finer points of Beethoven's music. This would precisely point up how who we are determines how we see (hear) things and interpret their meaning or significance.

This same general procedure could be done using, say, a picture of a building. Again, one would expect an architect's responses to be very different from that of a land developer or a historian.

CHAPTER 2

An Introduction to Growth and Development

OBJECTIVES

After reading this chapter, you should be able to

- Define the concepts of growth and development.
- Describe various characteristics and principles of development.
- Discuss the different views that are held regarding certain characteristics of development.
- Discuss the relationship between one's views on development and what one sees when observing children.
- Discuss the models that influence developmental theories.

GROWTH AND DEVELOPMENT: SOME GENERAL CONSIDERATIONS

Your understanding of development is essential to observing children effectively. This is especially true if you deal with young children in any meaningful capacity for any appreciable length of time. Indeed, understanding how children change over time is one of the basic components of good child care, in whatever settings or situations you can find children. However, *Seeing Young Children: A Guide to Observing and Recording Behavior* is not a primary text in child development or developmental psychology. Even to include a chapter on development and its accompanying issues and concepts might make the text both longer and more complicated than it needs to be. Nonetheless, not all readers will bring with them knowledge of the principles of development, nor will all be students who can take courses in developmental psychology or child development, and therefore they will have no use for a chapter of this kind. If you are already knowledgeable about

KEY TERMS

prelinguistic
complexity
differentiation
hierarchical integration
directional
growth
quantitative changes
qualitative changes
emergent properties
mechanistic view
activity versus passivity
organismic view
constructivist theory
contextualism
stage theorists
cephalocaudal principle
proximodistal principle
id
ego
superego
psychosocial crisis
trust versus mistrust
classical conditioning
operant conditioning

child development, you may omit this chapter and do no harm to your observation efforts.

Guideposts for Exploring a Child's World

Papalia, Olds, and Feldman, authors of *A Child's World: Infancy Through Adolescence* (2006), present what in an earlier edition (1999) they then called "guideposts for exploring a child's world" but most recently refer to as "a broad consensus ... on several fundamental points" with respect to children's development (p. 9). We shall continue to refer to these fundamental points as guideposts. We offer these to you now as a general framework within which to discuss the concept of development.

First Guidepost

The first guidepost speaks to the interrelatedness of all the domains of development—that is, the areas of physical, emotional, social, intellectual, and psychological changes that occur throughout the life span. Developmental psychology textbooks necessarily divide the child into functional areas (domains) and essentially deal with one area or domain at a time, because it is virtually impossible to study the entire child all at one time. "Dividing" children in this way can give the impression that they are actually segmented in such a piecemeal fashion. The fact of the matter is that children are all of a piece, and although development does not occur at the same pace for each domain, each domain affects and is affected by the others. Thus, physical development will affect social or emotional development, for example, with a host of interactions taking place among other developmental areas.

Second Guidepost

The second guidepost states that a wide range of individual differences characterize normal development. A basic assumption of the behavioral sciences is that every individual is unique and distinct in certain ways from every other individual. There are physical differences, differences in temperament, intellectual potential, emotional responsiveness, and so on. As Papalia and colleagues (2006) put it, "Some of the influences on individual differences are inborn; others come from experience. Most often, both types of influences work together. Family characteristics, the effects of gender, social class, race, and ethnicity, and the presence or absence of physical, mental, or emotional disability all make a difference" (p. 9).

Third Guidepost

The third guidepost reflects the interactive nature of development. The statement "*Children help shape their own development and influence others' responses to them*" reflects such interaction (Papalia et al., 2006, p. 9, italics original). This guidepost also defines the developing child as active rather than passive, a conclusion that entails the theoretical issue of activity versus passivity. Perhaps of special significance to your own observations is the fact that a child's behavior, personality characteristics, temperament, and physical appearance, among other factors, help to determine how other people will treat or respond to the child. In turn, others' responses and characteristics help to determine the child's behavior. An aggressive child, for instance, might tend to evoke aggressive responses from another child or from an adult, whereas a warm, friendly, affectionate child might tend to evoke warm, friendly responses from others. Generally speaking, people tend to treat us the way we treat them.

Fourth Guidepost

The fourth guidepost refers to contextual influences on development. You will find this guidepost consistent with Vygotsky's sociocultural views on development. The basic meaning of this fourth guidepost is that development necessarily takes place within an environment of one kind or another. As Papalia and associates (1999) point out, "In studying children, we need to determine whether patterns of development are universal or specific to a given culture. And since what happens around children affects them in many ways, it is important to look at development in context" (p. 2). In their most recent publication (2006), these same authors expand on this idea of context: "Each child develops within a specific environment, bounded by time and place. A child born in the United States today is likely to have very different experiences from a child born in colonial America or from a child born in Greenland or Afghanistan" (p. 9). The authors' reference to "environment" bears on the issue of multiculturalism or cultural diversity, which is discussed elsewhere in this text. They cite a number of environmental influences that could be pertinent to your observations: New technologies, various medical advances, and rapid and sometimes profound social changes all contribute to changes in children's developmental contexts (p. 2).

Fifth Guidepost

Children's resiliency despite the important effects of early experience forms the fifth guidepost. The essential argument here is that ordinarily, although a single, isolated traumatic experience can have serious emotional consequences for a child, irreparable damage does not necessarily occur. These authors offer a rather optimistic outlook on children's resiliency: "A traumatic incident or a severely deprived childhood may well have grave emotional consequences, but the life histories of countless people show that the effects of painful experience, such as growing up in poverty or the death of a parent, can often be overcome" (Papalia et al., 2006, p. 10). Although a detailed discussion of brain development is beyond the scope of this text, suffice it to say that the findings of present-day brain research have profound implications for child development and social policy (see Papalia et al., 1999, p. 167). Even prior to present-day discoveries regarding the brain, there was ample evidence of the deleterious effects on children's development caused by impoverished, unstimulating environments. It has also been known for some time that a stimulating environment can enhance brain growth and functioning.

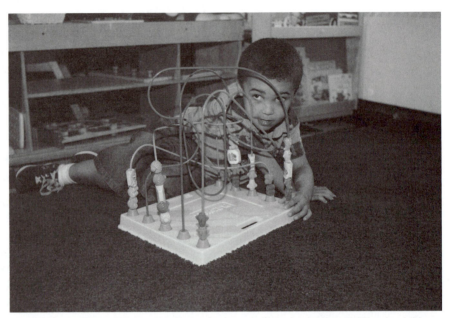

A stimulating environment can enhance brain growth and cognitive abilities in children.

Although it may be unlikely that the typical child care provider or early childhood educator will have much, if any, clinical concern with children's brain development, child care professionals will certainly be concerned with providing developmentally appropriate stimulation within the child care and early education settings. In this light, therefore, the effects of early experience on children's brain and behavioral development will assume great importance.

Sixth Guidepost

Papalia and colleagues' sixth and final guidepost essentially refers to the cumulative nature of development: "*Development in childhood is connected to development throughout the rest of the lifespan*" (2006, p. 10, italics original). Development does not end at some intermediate juncture in the life span. It continues for life or, as these authors put it, "As long as people live, they have the potential to change" (p. 10). *Cumulative* means that a child's developmental level is not separate or independent of all the changes that have occurred up to the present moment. A child's abilities, skills, knowledge, and experiences are all the consequences of everything that has occurred in his or her past history. The accumulated maturation and experiences form the foundation for all else that will follow in the child's future development. Perhaps a simple example will help.

Hector is a four-year-old who has a rather extensive speech vocabulary and expressive skills. He can say things like "Mommy, I want another glass of milk" or "I don't want to go to school today." But Hector's present language abilities did not come about on the spur of the moment. He did not go to bed on a Monday evening with no speech and wake up Tuesday morning being able to speak in complete and often grammatically correct sentences. He had to go through some preliminary stages of speech acquisition that included cooing, babbling, one-word phrases, two-word phrases, and so on. The language skills that Hector has at four years of age are the cumulative result of all the other **prelinguistic** skills he developed at an earlier time in his development.

In short, Hector's language skills at four years of age are the accumulation of all the skills he acquired up to the present time.

A Seventh Guidepost

We would add a seventh guidepost to this list. Development manifests the characteristics of **complexity**, **differentiation**, and **hierarchical integration**.

These are significant characteristics, and they should become evident to you if you observe children over any appreciable length of time. Development is thought to be directional, and it is out of this directionality that complexity, differentiation, and hierarchical integration arise. To say that development is directional means that developmental change contributes to the essentially forward direction of the developmental process.

The idea of a "forward direction" to development can apparently involve at least two ideas or approaches: One can ask whether development leads to some "ideal goal" or "most mature level of functioning" (Mussen, Conger, & Kagan, 1979, p. 34). Or one can more simply define **directional** as meaning that "development can always move toward greater complexity" (Sroufe & Cooper, 1988, p. 7), a concept we continue to discuss more fully.

Not all psychologists believe that development moves toward some ideal goal. As Mussen and colleagues (1979) point out, "Learning theorists do not assume that the child is necessarily traveling in any special direction, even though his behavior is changing every day." In this context, behavior and development lead to the ability to survive in an environment—to adapt to the demands of a particular physical and psychological environment. Piaget, on the other hand, thought of the individual as progressing toward a state of developmental maturity characterized by certain mental abilities such as the ability to reason and deduce logical conclusions. What is relevant to your observations is the question of how you will interpret differences among children of various ages, as well as differences that a given child will exhibit

prelinguistic
Vocalizations that occur prior to actual speech (cooing and babbling, for example).

complexity
Directional development that results in more sophisticated and refined behavior, emotion, ability, and language.

differentiation
A process in which behaviors that are initially expressed in a diffuse, nonspecific way eventually separate out and become more skilled, specific, and independent of one another. Also refers to learning a new skill and, during that process, having to practice only that skill, isolating it from other skills already mastered.

hierarchical integration
A process in which skills and behaviors that are initially separate and independent of one another are combined and can work together as a harmonious unit (e.g., the skill of grasping an object and the skill of moving the hand toward an object are combined to form the integrated skill of reaching and grasping).

directional
Development that moves toward a greater complexity or ideal goal.

Guideposts for Exploring a Child's World	
Guidepost	**Implications for Observation**
1. All the domains or areas of development are interrelated.	Each developmental area affects and is affected by one or more of the other developmental areas. This is important to keep in mind as you observe children. It may help you understand, for example, how Peter's small physical size can adversely affect his social interactions with his larger peers.
2. A wide range of individual differences characterize normal development.	Do not expect each child to be like every other child. Tammy will grow and develop at her own pace and in unique ways that differ from Samantha's. This principle of individual differences applies to every child.
3. Development is active and interactive.	Children are not merely passive recipients of environmental stimulation; rather, they actively seek experiences. Especially important is the interactive nature of development. A child's behavior, personality characteristics, temperament, and physical appearance, among other factors, help to determine how other people will treat or respond to the child. In turn, others' responses and characteristics help to determine the child's behavior.
4. Development necessarily takes place within an environment of one kind or another.	This guidepost refers to the contextual influences on development. Vygotsky's sociocultural views on development emphasize this guidepost. Of special importance to child care providers are the environmental influences provided by a child's family, peer group, society, and culture.
5. Children are resilient despite the important effects of early experience.	This guidepost distinguishes between the effects of relatively brief, infrequent experiences and the effects of experiences that are repeated and of relatively long duration. Resiliency means that the child can recover even from negative or adverse experiences if they do not persist for long periods of time.
6. Development is cumulative.	A child's developmental level is not separate or independent of all the changes that have occurred up to the present moment. This essentially means that one cannot ignore the effects of the child's past development on her present developmental level or the potential effect of her present level of development on her future development.
7. Development manifests the following characteristics:	
a. Complexity	This simply means that development leads to more complex, sophisticated behavior and abilities. The four-year-old's physical–motor actions, speech, thoughts, and emotions, for example, are more mature, sophisticated, and of a greater variety than the two-year-old's.
b. Differentiation	Differentiation means that behaviors that are initially expressed in a diffuse way eventually separate and become more skilled, more specific, and more independent of one another. Perhaps the most obvious example of this characteristic can be observed by comparing an infant's movements with those of a three-year-old. When a three-month-old lying in his crib reaches for an object suspended above him, he tends to involve his whole body, whereas a three-year-old's reaching and grasping involve only the arm and hand.

(continues)

Guideposts for Exploring a Child's World (continued)	
Guidepost	**Implications for Observation**
c. Hierarchical Integration	Hierarchical integration allows the child to combine various skills, behaviors, and movements so that they work together as a harmonious unit. Finger movements, for instance, not only become differentiated (separated) from larger arm movements, but each type of movement can serve a different purpose. The fingers and arm can work independently of each other or can work together as an integrated unit.

Adapted from Papalia, Olds, and Feldman (1999). The seventh guidepost is excerpted from the current chapter.

in his behavior. Will differences and changes be most meaningfully explained as quantitative or as qualitative? Will you see the child as progressing toward some optimum goal or end state of development in which all behaviors build onto one another and ultimately contribute to the child's reaching that optimum goal? Or will you see the child as changing because of the continual learning of responses, but responses that do not necessarily lead to any particular goal or developmental objective?

Complexity, Differentiation, and Hierarchical Integration

There is another characteristic of development that most psychologists would agree on regardless of their theoretical orientations: Development, as a reflection or manifestation of its directional aspect, results in increasing complexity in organization and functioning. As a child gets older and more mature, his behavior, emotions, motives, abilities, and language become more sophisticated and refined, not less so. This increase in complexity is partly the result of the child's learning how to do more things, but there is something else. The child's knowledge and abilities increasingly form a unified, integrated whole. Psychologists speak of differentiation and hierarchical integration when referring to this movement toward complexity. "Differentiation" means that those behaviors that are initially expressed in a diffuse way eventually separate out and become more skilled, more specific, and more independent of one another. "More specific" means that previously unspecialized body parts and responses become specialized (see Figure 2-1); they take on particular functions or play particular roles. For example, the very young infant exhibits seemingly random muscle movements; she moves almost her entire body when responding to even a specific, focused stimulus such as a pinprick to the foot. Later on, however, she is able to move just her foot, thus indicating that body movements and muscle groups have become differentiated and capable of responding more precisely to specific stimuli.

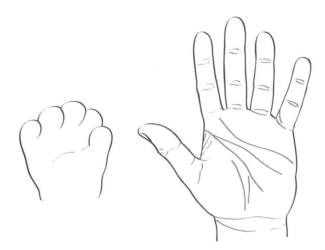

Figure 2-1 The change from this fetal hand to a fully formed hand is an example of differentiation.

Hierarchic integration takes place when the child can combine various skills, behaviors, or movements and have them work together as a harmonious unit. Thus, finger movements become differentiated from larger arm movements, and although each type of movement can serve a different purpose and be brought into play independently of the other, the arms and fingers can also work together as an integrated unit. This coordination permits the child to reach for and grasp an object. Reaching and grasping generally also involve visual functioning, which illustrates even greater integration. As another example, the child initially differentiates single words as she acquires a speaking and listening vocabulary; eventually, she combines those words into complex, grammatically correct sentences. With this integration, she can express increasingly more complex thoughts and ideas.

DEVELOPMENT: SOME BASIC MEANINGS AND CONCEPTS

In its most basic meaning, *development* refers to change over time—change in the structure, thought, or behavior of an individual that comes about from biological and environmental influences. Therefore, the scientific study of child development is the study of how children change over time as well as how they stay the same. However, developmental change is not just any kind of change. It is orderly, systematic, and to some degree predictable change that, for the most part, contributes to the individual's survival and ability to adapt to the demands imposed by the environment. Shaffer and Kipp (2007) define *development* as "systematic continuities and changes in the individual that occur between conception (when the father's sperm

Development, as a reflection or manifestation of its directional aspect, results in increasing complexity in organization and functioning.

penetrates the mother's ovum, creating a new organism) and death. By describing *changes* as 'systematic' we imply that they are orderly, patterned, and relatively enduring so that temporary mood swings and other transitory changes in our appearances, thoughts, and behaviors are therefore excluded" (p. 2, italics original).

Growth versus Development and Quantitative versus Qualitative Change

growth
Increase in size, function, or complexity to some point of optimal maturity; associated with quantitative change.

One place to start our discussion is to make a brief distinction between growth and development. **Growth** basically refers to changes in the amount of something. Getting taller and heavier, adding more words to one's vocabulary, and a family

quantitative changes
Growth; changes in the amount, number, or quantity of something (e.g., increases in height and weight).

qualitative changes
Change in psychological functions such as speech, emotions, and intelligence; involves change in the fundamental organization of behaviors and behavior patterns; change in the child's cognitive structure.

emergent properties
A term used in connection with qualitative change, emergent properties are traits or characteristics that are not present at an earlier stage of development but emerge as the individual moves from one developmental stage to another. For example, walking can be thought of as emerging out of the earlier behaviors of crawling and creeping.

having more children are reasonable examples of growth. Although physical growth as it actually occurs in the human body, for example, is quite complicated, we want to consider development as being conceptually more sophisticated or complicated than growth. Because we can define differences between growth and development, we can also define differences between quantitative and qualitative change.

Generally speaking, **quantitative changes** characterize growth, and **qualitative changes** characterize development. With qualitative changes, we see changes that result in a reorganization of the child's behaviors and behavior patterns. Qualitative change is not simply adding more of the same thing, as in physical growth, where more bone and flesh tissue are being acquired to make the child taller and heavier, or as in language development, when the child acquires more words in his vocabulary. Something different emerges (resulting in what are called **emergent properties**) from the developmental process. Some theorists argue that these differences are not predictable from earlier developmental stages, capacities, and skills. "Qualitative change," write Papalia and associates (2006), "is a change in kind, structure, or organization. It is marked by the emergence of new phenomena that cannot be anticipated easily on the basis of earlier functioning, such as the change from a nonverbal child to one who understands words and can communicate verbally" (p. 10).

Because this is an important concept, a simple example of emergent properties is in order. Water is composed of the two gases hydrogen and oxygen. Both of these gases are tasteless, colorless, odorless, and invisible. If we knew nothing about the composition of water, in all likelihood we would never predict that water would be the result of combining hydrogen and oxygen. Thus, we can say that "waterness" is an emergent property. Being transformed from two gases to water is therefore a qualitative change. In a similar fashion, if we assume that walking and running are not simply more crawling and creeping, then progressing developmentally from crawling and creeping to walking and running represents qualitative change and emergent properties.

There are other considerations that we need to take into account in order to understand development more fully. It is the obligation of child care providers to understand what is going on in the lives of the children in their care. Such understanding requires more than simply watching children change. The observer should have some understanding of the context of this change, of some possible explanations as to how change occurs, and of some of the issues that accompany the study of development. But how we see the world and how we conceptualize human nature influence such understanding. Theories and worldviews influence or determine how we see the world and how we conceptualize human nature, so we now turn to these topics.

Development: Some Basic Meanings and Concepts—A Summary	
Concepts	**Brief Description**
Growth and Change	Growth in this text refers primarily to changes in the amount or magnitude of something. A child grows physically taller (adds more inches to her height); her arms, legs, and trunk increase in circumference; and she becomes heavier. Thus, growth essentially involves adding on more of the same thing—more bone tissue, muscle tissue, and so on. This adding-on describes quantitative change, which is the kind of change that characterizes growth. We can also speak of quantitative changes in such things as vocabulary—the child acquires more words with which to communicate—or an increase in the number of facts or pieces of information that make up the child's body of knowledge. Note, however, that increases in vocabulary and knowledge contribute heavily to development and qualitative change.
Development, Qualitative Change, and Emergent Properties	Rather than a change in the amount of something, think of development as changes in the way a child is organized, with resulting changes in how the child behaves. Through development, a child is structured differently and functions differently from one developmental period or stage to another. This characterizes qualitative change. For example, progressing from crawling or creeping to walking is a qualitative change because walking is not simply more crawling or creeping. Walking is qualitatively different from crawling and creeping. As well, expressing oneself in complete sentences is not simply more of the cooing and babbling characteristic of vocal expressions during infancy. In a sense, therefore, Amanda at three years of age is a different person from who she was at one year of age. She can now walk, run, skip, climb, communicate fairly complex ideas and emotions, and engage in much more sophisticated thinking. These changes emerge from earlier skills and abilities (which points up the fact that development is cumulative) but are qualitatively different from those earlier skills and abilities. Thus, walking is an emergent property of crawling and creeping, talking is an emergent property of cooing and babbling, and so on for similar areas of development.

DEVELOPMENT: SOME THEORETICAL CONSIDERATIONS

Models of Development: A Brief Review of Some Worldviews of the Basic Nature of Humans

The discussion of theory very often puts people off because they "just want the facts." But theories are an indispensable tool for understanding those things we call facts. Indeed, a fact can never stand by itself; it needs to be put into some kind of relationship with other facts. We can acquire new knowledge precisely because of the knowledge we have already acquired. We can learn calculus only if we have learned algebra, and algebra only if we have learned some basic mathematics. In turn, we can learn mathematics or arithmetic only if we have some understanding of the concept of *number.* This is why it is so important for child care providers to accept children where they presently are and allow development to proceed from there. It is detrimental to developmental progress to ignore the learning that has or has not already occurred.

It is important for child care providers to accept children where they presently are and allow development to proceed from there.

Why Study Developmental Theories?

Why is it important to study developmental theories? Patricia Miller (1993), in her book *Theories of Developmental Psychology*, offers some insights regarding their importance: "A developmental theory organizes and gives meaning to facts of development. Facts do not speak for themselves.... 'Science is built up of facts, as a house is built of stones; but an accumulation of facts is no more a science than a heap of stones is a house'" (p. 9). She writes further: "A theory gives meaning to facts, provides a framework for facts, assigns more importance to some facts than others, and integrates existing facts" (p. 9).

Therefore, we need theories in order to understand children's development properly. However, there is no need in this text to go into a greatly detailed discussion of developmental theories. With this limitation in mind, we want to discuss briefly four basic questions that have been raised in connection with development. This author is indebted to Patricia Miller (1993) for her insightful discussion of these four questions, which she identifies as the main issues of developmental psychology.

Basic Issue One: What Is the Basic Nature of Humans?

As Miller (1993) argues, "[A] theorist's view of development is closely tied to his view of human nature" (p. 18). Put another way, one's view of development is affected by one's worldview. There are three basic worldviews that have a bearing on our conception of human nature. The first of these is referred to as the **mechanistic view**.

mechanistic view

A theoretical or philosophical perspective that conceptualizes human beings and other living creatures as being like machines in that they are essentially passive and act primarily as responders to environmental stimuli. (*See organismic view.*)

activity versus passivity
Two opposing points of view regarding the extent to which the child participates in his own development. The passive view holds that the child is primarily a *reactor to the environment and soaks up stimulation like a sponge; the active view sees the child as an actor who seeks stimulation rather than passively waits for it to occur.*

organismic view
A theoretical or philosophical perspective that conceptualizes human beings as active participants in their own development rather than as passive reactors to the world around them. (*See mechanistic view.*)

constructivist theory
A theory of human development that is organismic in its basic orientation. Constructionist theory assumes that the developing child participates in the developmental process and literally constructs his or her own reality. This reality undergoes a series of reconstructions that bring it more and more in line with the reality assumed by most adults in a given culture or society. This theory most appropriately falls within the broader organismic view. (*See organismic view.*)

contextualism
A concept most notably associated with the Russian psychologist Lev Vygotsky, who argued that a child's development cannot be studied, understood, or take place outside of some cultural context or other. In other words, all development change—as well as, for that

As the term implies, this perspective sees the world as a kind of machine that must wait for some external force to act on it in order to get it running. This notion is not unfamiliar to us because we must activate nearly all the machines that are part of our daily lives. An automobile will not start unless we turn on the ignition, and it will not move unless we put it into gear and press on the accelerator. We have to turn on our computers before they will operate, and we must have installed the appropriate software if they are to accomplish the tasks we set for them.

An important related issue is that of **activity versus passivity**.

The mechanistic view of human beings thinks of us as essentially passive because, after all, machines are essentially passive. This is not just to say that we literally sit in a corner somewhere merely waiting for environmental stimuli to come along so that we can respond to them. It is a matter of degree rather than an all-or-none affair. The central question is how much of a role does the individual play in his or her own development?

The second worldview is called the **organismic view**.

This view is in sharp contrast to the mechanistic view in that it sees humans as active participants in their own development. People do not sit idly by waiting for some environmental stimuli to which to respond. Human beings get themselves up and running and do not have to wait to be motivated by the outside world. As Miller (1993) writes, "[C]hildren 'construct' their knowledge by actively formulating and testing hypotheses about categories of objects and causes of events" (p. 19). Therefore, human beings are actively engaged in their own development. Piaget thought of the child as an active, stimulus-seeking organism, which is why his theory is often referred to as a **constructivist theory**.

The first two of these views might be more familiar to you than the third view. The third view is referred to as **contextualism**, which says that development and behavior can be understood only within some kind of social or cultural context. Consequently, we can understand children's development and behavior only by knowing their developmental history, which includes all of the things they have already experienced through the socialization that has occurred within their social and cultural environment.

Therefore, we can think of ourselves as being like a machine or like a living thing, but both of these perspectives allow us to understand ourselves without necessarily accounting for any particular social context. There are other issues that go along with these three worldviews, and developmental theories attach themselves to one or the other of these three views.

Basic Issue Two: Is Development Qualitative or Quantitative?

Although the distinction between qualitative and quantitative development and change has already been discussed, it warrants some further discussion here. Quantitative change is the easier concept to grasp, probably because it entails the matter, all current behavior—has to be seen as part of, or as taking place within, a larger social/cultural environment.

notion of changes in the amount of something. (Miller [1993] also includes changes in frequency or degree as constituting quantitative change.) In the earlier discussion of growth, the concept of quantitative change was relevant. Growth—let us say physical growth—consists of adding on more and more body and bone tissue, and the child consequently gets bigger and taller. However, it is important to recognize that many—perhaps most—quantitative changes result in or contribute to qualitative changes. Certainly the birth of a baby—which changes a family quantitatively—also alters a family qualitatively by changing its interaction patterns, communication styles, and so on.

Qualitative changes, on the other hand, are changes in kind or type. As Miller (1993) writes, "Qualitative changes typically involve changes in structure or organization" (p. 21). Recall the earlier discussion of emergent properties, a concept that describes a transformation from one state to another. In addition to the earlier example of how hydrogen and oxygen combine to form water, this transformation can also be illustrated by the various stages a butterfly goes through when it evolves through the phases of pupa, larva, caterpillar, and finally a full-fledged butterfly. It is generally believed that each succeeding stage or phase is essentially unpredictable from any of the earlier stages or phases. Of course, in actuality, we can and do predict such changes, but only because we have studied them and have learned what those changes are. The qualitative changes tend to be of special interest to developmental psychologists. But again, we cannot overlook growth because quantitative change is also an important characteristic of human development.

Basic Issue Three: How Do Nature and Nurture Contribute to Development?

This issue has to do with the underlying causes of development: How much of development depends upon one's genetic inheritance and how much upon one's experiences? This question has a long tradition in psychology, and numerous discussions have taken place regarding what percentage or proportion of a particular trait, ability, or characteristic is due to heredity and what proportion to environment.

Although there is still some dispute about the relative importance of nature and nurture, the more central question now is how do heredity and environment work together or *interact* with each other to bring about developmental change? As Miller (1993) puts it, "Nature and nurture are inextricably intertwined" (p. 23). This means that development absolutely depends upon the contributions of both heredity and environment. Indeed, without heredity there would be no human being, and without an environment there would be no being who is uniquely human.

Papalia and colleagues (1999) also speak to this issue:

> Today, advances in behavioral genetics are enabling scientists to measure more precisely the roles of heredity and environment in accounting for individual differences in specific traits, such as intelligence, and how the strength of those influences can shift throughout life…. When we look at a specific child, however, research with regard to almost all characteristics points to an intermingling or interaction of inheritance and experience. Thus, even though intelligence has a strong heredity component, parental stimulation, education, and other variables do make a difference. And while there is still considerable dispute about the relative impact of nature and nurture, many contemporary theorists and researchers … are less interested in arguing about which of these forces is more important than in finding ways to explain how they work together to influence development. (p. 20)

Basic Issue Four: What Is It That Develops?

In its simplest form, we can partly answer this question by listing the behavioral domains in which psychologists are interested. The domains of cognitive, social, emotional, physical, and language make up most of the content of human development. (Just as a point of reference, Papalia and associates [2006] reduce this list of domains to three: physical development, cognitive development, and psychosocial development [p. 10].) Of course, as an observer of children, you will be interested in all these areas, and your observation exercises will require you to delve into many of these aspects of children's behavior. If you are a professional child care provider and educator, you will most certainly be concerned with how children progress in each of these functional areas.

One more issue important to understanding development and to observing how children change over time is the question of whether development occurs in stages, a question that is answered "no" by the mechanistic model and "yes" by the organismic model. The mechanistic theorists follow a quantitative line of thinking regarding developmental change, whereas organismic theorists follow a qualitative line of thinking regarding developmental change. Mechanists argue that development is continuous, which means "always governed by the same processes, enabling prediction of later behaviors from earlier ones" (Papalia et al., 2006, p. 26). Organicists argue that development is discontinuous, or occurs in a stage-like fashion that results in a series of qualitative changes. Stages in development are frequently depicted as a set of stairs that the child must climb. In effect, as the child progresses from one step to the next, she progresses from a lower stage or level of development to the next higher stage or level. In contrast, the mechanistic view sees developmental progression as more like walking up a hill, where progress is at least perceived as more gradual or less abrupt than when climbing up a set of stairs.

Stage theorists see development as universal, whereby "every person in every culture goes through the same stages in the same order, though the precise timing may vary" (Papalia et al., 2006, p. 21). The **stage theory** also usually imposes the additional requirement that no stage may be permanently skipped or temporarily bypassed and returned to later. Thus, in Piaget's theory of cognitive development, children must progress through the sensorimotor, preoperational, concrete operational, and finally the formal operational stage. They cannot move from the sensorimotor to the concrete operational stage, for example, thereby omitting the preoperational stage. In stage theory, individuals can differ in the speed with which they progress through the stages and in the final stage reached (not everyone reaches Piaget's final stage of formal operational thinking, for instance). The various theories of development, broadly speaking, fall within the mechanistic, organismic, or the contextualist model of development. There is a historical pattern that characterizes to which of the models various theories have subscribed. Freud, Erickson, and Piaget favored the organismic model, and their theories are stage theories. Learning theories—such as Skinner's theory of operant conditioning—favor the mechanistic model and do not subscribe to the stage view of development.

One important feature of stage theories is that they allow us to recognize certain principles or laws by which change can be described, explained, and predicted. It is the orderliness and predictability of change—within certain limits—that help make possible the scientific study of children.

Perhaps the most evident sequences that take place in a child over time are those that describe physical–motor development. The sequences in which motor abilities emerge have been designated as principles, which means that they operate predictably in nearly all children in all cultures. The **cephalocaudal principle** (head-to-tail) of motor development says that the child first gains control over the movements of his head and neck (lifting the head up off the mattress, for example), whereas control over foot movements comes last. A second principle, the **proximodistal principle**, says that the child first gains control over those body parts closest to the body's midline—the shoulders, upper arms, and chest; then he gains control over the more distant parts such as the fingers (see Figure 2-2). These sequences also describe a pattern that progresses from gross (large) muscle control to fine (small) muscle control. This genetically preprogrammed sequence of motor skills can be observed as the child accomplishes the milestones in motor development depicted in Table 2-1.

Papalia and colleagues (2006) offer a very good synopsis of just where contemporary developmentalists stand with respect to the relative influence of the

stage theory
A theory that holds that development occurs in a step-like fashion, with each step or level qualitatively distinct from, and more complex than, previous levels.

cephalocaudal principle
The principle that describes motor development as progressing in a head-to-foot direction; the child first gains control over the head and neck and proceeds down the body to finally gain control over the legs and feet.

proximodistal principle
The principle that describes motor development as progressing from the midline of the body outward to the extremities; thus, chest, shoulders, and upper arms come under control before the hands and feet.

mechanistic and organismic models:

> Today the pendulum has swung back part way. Quasi-organismic approaches centered on the biological basis of behavior are on the rise; but instead of attempting to delineate broad stages, theorists seek to discover what specific kinds of behavior show continuity or lack of continuity and what processes are involved in each. There is wide agreement that influences on development are bidirectional: Children change their world even as it changes them. A baby born with a cheerful disposition is likely to get positive responses from adults, which strengthen her trust that her smiles will be rewarded and motivate her to smile more (p. 27).

Figure 2-2 Physical–motor development occurs along cephalocaudal (head-to-tail) and proximodistal (center-to-edge) principles.

Table 2-1 Selected Developmental Milestones			
Age	**Postural Control**	**Locomotion**	**Manual Control**
2–3 Months	Holds head steady when in an upright position. While in prone position, lifts head up far enough to see what is in front of her.		Starts to reach for objects, but efforts are poorly coordinated. Holds on to objects for short time.
4 Months	Holds chest up while in prone position. Head control more stable than before.	Rolls over from back to stomach and from stomach to back.	Shows better-coordinated visually directed reaching, but attention alternately shifts from hand to object (Faw & Belkin, 1989).

(continues)

	Table 2-1 Selected Developmental Milestones (continued)		
Age	**Postural Control**	**Locomotion**	**Manual Control**
5–8 Months	Gets into sitting position by himself; sits by himself unsupported. Most can stand while holding on to something.	Some can move in a side-stepping fashion while holding on to furniture. From 5 to 8 months, most learn to crawl with the body on the ground, or creep on hands and knees; some scoot in a sitting position.	Craig and Kermis (1995) point out visually directed reaching at 5 months. Up until that time, infant has the individual component skills but cannot put them together in a coordinated fashion. Eight-month-olds like to pass things from one hand to the other.
9–12 Months	By 12 months, about half of all infants can stand by themselves (Craig & Kermis, 1995).	By 9 months, most can pull themselves to a standing position; some can "cruise" while holding on to furniture. Most babies walk alone between 11 and 13 months (Craig & Kermis, 1995).	Most 12-month-olds can oppose the thumb and forefinger in a pincer grasp. They can open drawers, turn handles and knobs, and insert things into small openings (Craig & Kermis, 1995).
18 Months	Almost all children of this age have enough postural control to walk alone; however, they cannot kick a ball because of unsteadiness.	Nearly all children of this age walk alone. Some still have trouble climbing stairs; kicking a ball is hard for most, and pedaling a tricycle or jumping is virtually impossible (Craig & Kermis, 1995).	Most can stack blocks to build a small tower. Can scribble with a crayon or pencil. They are better at feeding themselves, and some may be able to partly undress themselves.
24 Months	Can balance briefly on one foot. Balance during locomotion is good.	Can walk and run, pedal a tricycle, jump with both feet, and climb up steps.	Can throw a ball; will put things into and take things out of containers; manipulate objects of all kinds.

Compiled largely from Craig and Kermis (1995).

DEVELOPMENTAL THEORIES: A GENERAL OVERVIEW

Rather than deal exclusively with specific theories, we briefly present the general frameworks or perspectives within which specific theories espouse their concepts and principles. Explicit discussion of such theorists as Piaget, Vygotsky, and Skinner is reserved for the particular observational contexts in which their theories can be applied.

Psychoanalytic Perspective

Sigmund Freud

The first framework or perspective is the psychoanalytic perspective, as originated and developed by Sigmund Freud. Here, Freud's theory is dealt with only briefly, mainly because, for the present author, such Freudian concepts as the unconscious and repression, among others, are more suitable in a clinical, therapeutic setting than in a more typical child care or early childhood education setting.

This is not to say that none of Freud's ideas or concepts is relevant to our present purposes. We can still talk meaningfully about the **id**, **ego**, and the **superego**, which are the structures that Freud hypothesized make up the personality.

The ego is the part of the personality that orients the individual toward reality. This is why Freud argued that the ego operates according to "the reality principle." It is the ego's responsibility to help the individual meet his or her needs, interact appropriately with other people, and accomplish tasks and meet goals and objectives. As the same time, however, the individual has to be aware of being part of a larger social community, the members of which also have their own needs, desires, and goals. In contrast, the id does not worry about other people's needs, wishes, or goals. Freud hypothesized that the id operates according to "the pleasure principle," which in essence abides by the motto "I want what I want when I want it."

The superego is the conscience, and as Papalia and associates (2006) put it, the superego "incorporates socially approved 'shoulds' and 'should nots' into the child's own value system" (p. 29). The ego essentially derives from the superego and is guided by it. (Within Freud's conceptual framework, the relationship between the ego and superego makes sense. It seems logical that in order for the ego to be reality oriented, it must possess some measure of social awareness and moral awareness, whatever way the individual's society defines morality.) Freud placed a heavy emphasis on biological factors, and he theorized that "personality is formed in childhood, as children deal with conflicts between these inborn urges and the requirements of civilized life" (Papalia et al., 2006, pp. 27–28).

Erik Erikson

Another prominent theorist whose work falls under the psychoanalytic perspective is Erik Erikson and his psychosocial theory of personality development. Erikson's theory comprises eight stages that cover the entire life span. Each stage involves a **psychosocial crisis** that individuals must adequately resolve if they are to develop in an optimal fashion. Erikson did not throw out Freud's ideas; he kept such concepts as the id, ego, and superego. He also subscribed to the notion of stages, believing that progression through the various stages is biologically or maturationally determined.

In this view, the child has no choice but to begin in the oral stage, then move to the anal stage, and so on. Maturation figuratively kicks the individual into each successive stage of development. However, what is not exclusively maturationally determined is the psychosocial crisis with which the child—and the adult—must deal,

id
That part of the personality in Sigmund Freud's theory that functions from the moment of birth. The id operates according to what Freud called the pleasure principle. In essence, the id is concerned with meeting the child's needs and desires, but perhaps most frequently the id can be thought of as contributing to the child's self-centeredness. The id's guiding theme is "I want what I want when I want it."

ego
That part of the personality in Sigmund Freud's theory that has the function of keeping the child in touch with reality and with the demands made on the child by the family and other individuals and groups in his larger social community. The ego is also that part of the personality that gives the individual a sense of identity.

superego
That part of the personality in Sigmund Freud's theory that develops out of the id and the ego and essentially acts as the individual's conscience. *See id and ego.*

psychosocial crisis
A concept in Erikson's theory of personality development; a crisis is a conflict, a turning point, or time of special sensitivity to particular social influences.

A Summary of Five Basic Issues in Developmental Psychology	
Basic Issues	**Discussion**
1. What is the basic nature of humans?	
a. The Mechanistic View:	This view asserts that people are like machines and must be "turned on" by some kind of stimulation from the outside world. Thus, people respond to external stimuli, and their future responses under similar circumstances depend upon the consequences of their previous behavior. If their responses are rewarded or reinforced, they are more likely to repeat that behavior. They are least likely to repeat behavior if it is punished or not reinforced. Consequently, the mechanistic view sees us as essentially passive with respect to our development.
b. The Organismic View:	This view is almost diametrically opposite the mechanistic view. The organismic view sees humans as active participants in their own development. Rather than waiting for some external stimuli to which to respond, humans are seen as active, stimulus-seeking organisms who, according to Piaget, for example, literally construct their reality through their interactions with the environment. Piaget's theory of cognitive development is sometimes referred to as an interactionist or constructivist theory.
c. The Contextualist View:	This is the view taken by Vygotsky, who essentially argued that development and behavior can be understood only within some kind of social or cultural context. Consequently, we can understand children's development and behavior only by knowing their developmental history, which includes all the things they have already experienced through the socialization that has occurred within their social and cultural environment.
2. Is development qualitative or quantitative?	Refer to "Development: Some Basic Meanings and Concepts" on page 26.
3. How do nature and nurture contribute to development?	This issue has to do with the underlying causes of development: How much of development depends upon one's genetic inheritance (nature) and how much upon one's experiences (nurture)? Despite this issue's long, controversial history, the consensus is that nature and nurture work together to guide and influence development. Neither heredity nor environment works alone in the developmental process. Rather, they function interactively, each one contributing its necessary share to the child's development.

(continues)

A Summary of Five Basic Issues in Developmental Psychology (continued)	
Basic Issues	**Discussion**
4. What is it that develops?	This question simply inquires about the content of human development. Typically, the domains of cognitive, social, emotional, physical, and language behavior make up most of the content of human development. Children's functioning in these areas will be the usual focus of your observations.
5. Is development continuous or discontinuous?	The mechanistic and organismic perspectives answer this question differently. The mechanistic view, such as that taken by behaviorists, argues that development is continuous, which means "always governed by the same processes, allowing prediction of earlier behaviors from later ones." This is the central characteristic of quantitative change. The organismic view, such as that taken by Piaget and other stage theorists, argues for discontinuity (or qualitative change) in development. The analogy of a hill and a set of stairs can be used to illustrate the differences between developmental continuity and discontinuity. Continuous or quantitative change is analogous to walking up a hill: The child progresses higher and higher up the hill, but nothing significantly new or different manifests itself in the child's functioning or behavior. The increased elevation is simply more of what she achieved at earlier, lower elevations. Climbing stairs, on the other hand, represents qualitative or discontinuous change because each step is different in some significant way from all the steps below it and all the steps above it. Step 3 is not merely more of steps 1 and 2, even though the principle of cumulative development dictates that step 3 builds upon steps 1 and 2.

trust versus mistrust
The first crisis in Erikson's theory; the infant's experiences with his environment and the people in it will determine whether he resolves the crisis or conflict by establishing a stronger sense of trust than of mistrust. A sense of trust will enable the infant to see his world as a predominantly safe, nurturing, and trustworthy place.

and that uniquely characterizes each stage. The first, or oral stage, emerges according to a maturational timetable, and the psychosocial crisis associated with the oral stage is that of **trust versus mistrust.**

With a "good," "positive," or "healthy" resolution of this crisis, the child will move forward into the next stage and its crisis possessing a general or basic sense of security and confidence in the environment and the people in it. Erikson postulated that successful resolution of each of the crises throughout the life cycle results in healthy ego development.

The significant advantage of Erikson's theory is that it takes into account the social and cultural environment in which children develop. In this regard, Erikson is closer to Vygotsky's view of development than are some of the other theorists.

The Learning Perspective

Papalia and colleagues (2006) define learning as "a long-lasting change in behavior based on experience, or adaptation to the environment" (p. 31). Learning theories fall under the mechanistic model of development. Learning theories tend to regard people, as well as other organisms that are capable of learning, as being like machines. Consequently, human beings are essentially passive rather than active, and development is gradual and continuous (as in climbing a long, gentle hill), as opposed to step-like and discontinuous (such as going up a set of stairs). Learning theorists fall toward the environment end of the heredity/environment continuum, which means that experience and learning are considered the primary sources of developmental change. Learning theories also focus on overt (visible) behavior as the source of their data; feelings and thoughts, although important from a practical point of view, have relatively little scientific importance because they cannot be observed directly but must be inferred from overt behavior.

Behaviorism and social-learning theory are two of the more important of the learning theories. Within the behaviorism framework there are two kinds of learning: classical conditioning and operant conditioning.

classical conditioning
A form of learning in which a neutral stimulus—one that evokes no response—becomes paired with a stimulus that does. Eventually, the neutral stimulus evokes the response; for example, a puff of air on the eye causes the individual to blink, a soft tone does not; if the tone and the puff of air are both administered very close together in time, eventually the tone by itself will cause the individual to blink.

operant conditioning
A form of learning in which the consequences of a response determine whether that response is likely to be repeated under the same or similar circumstances; for example, if a child's whining gets her the attention from the teacher that she desires, the child is likely to whine in future situations when she wants attention.

Classical Conditioning

Classical conditioning occurs when a neutral stimulus—a stimulus that initially does not arouse (elicit) a particular response—is paired with a stimulus that does elicit a particular response. Repeated pairing of these two stimuli results in the neutral stimulus acquiring the power to elicit the response. For example, if you were to have your eyes checked for glaucoma, the ophthalmologist would blow a puff of air against your eyeball, which ordinarily would cause you to blink. If for several times he were to sound a tone immediately before the puff of air, eventually just the tone would cause you to blink your eye before you even felt the air against your eyeball. It is important to note that classical conditioning is mainly concerned with involuntary responses—responses or behaviors over which we have little or no control.

Operant Conditioning

Operant conditioning is concerned with voluntary responses. The term *operant* means that the individual operates on the environment by responding to stimuli in a particular way. To operate on the environment is to respond to it, and the response influences or changes the environment and evokes some kind of response from it. The conditioning or learning of a response depends upon its consequences. If a behavior results in a satisfying or pleasant state of affairs, and if the individual repeats the behavior under the same or similar circumstances in order to bring about that pleasant state of affairs, then the behavior can be said to have been reinforced. Operant

reinforcement
A condition in which an individual's response to a stimulus has rewarding or satisfying consequences; those consequences provide reinforcement of the response, thus increasing the probability that, in the future, the individual will respond in similar fashion to a similar stimulus.

conditioning theory is often referred to as reinforcement theory. A **reinforcement** is any consequence of a behavior that in fact strengthens that behavior or increases the probability that the behavior will be repeated in the same or similar circumstances. It is clear that both of these theories place a great deal of importance on the environment and the experiences it provides.

Social-Learning Theory

Social-learning theory places a lot of emphasis on observational learning. Children learn a great deal by observing and imitating other people (models). The American psychologist Albert Bandura is credited with developing many of the ideas of modern social-learning theory. An important distinction between social-learning theory and operant conditioning is that the former recognizes the importance of thinking: "[C]hildren's cognitive responses to their perceptions, rather than reflexive responses to reinforcement or punishment, are seen as central to development" (Papalia et al., 2006, p. 29). The importance of adults modeling appropriate, desirable behavior that children can imitate plays a prominent role in social-learning theory. Interestingly, Piaget viewed the child's ability to delay imitation as a cognitive milestone. Observing a model's behavior, then later imitating that behavior when the model is no longer present, signifies that the child is capable of forming a mental schema for that behavior, retaining it in memory, and then performing the behavior at some suitable later time.

vicarious reinforcement
Reinforcement that an individual experiences indirectly through observing someone else being reinforced or rewarded for his behavior. The concept of vicarious reinforcement is usually associated with social learning theory. (*See vicarious punishment.*)

vicarious punishment
Similar to vicarious reinforcement, vicarious punishment is punishment a child experiences indirectly when he or she observes another child being punished and reacts as though he or she had been punished. (*See vicarious reinforcement.*)

Social-learning theorists believe that "people learn appropriate social behavior chiefly by observing and imitating models—that is, by watching other people. This process is called *modeling* or **observational learning** (Papalia et al., 2006, p. 32; italics and boldface original). There are several important concepts associated with social-learning theory, the more important of which for us are vicarious reinforcement and vicarious punishment. **Vicarious reinforcement** occurs when, for example, Victor sees Suzanne receive an award from an adult for helping put away the big blocks during cleanup time. If at the next cleanup time Victor helps put away the big blocks because he also wants to receive a reward, then it is likely that Victor's behavior has been vicariously reinforced by having seen Suzanne's similar behavior reinforced at an earlier time. **Vicarious punishment** works in the same way, only this time Victor may decide not to behave in a certain way because earlier he witnessed another child getting punished for the very behavior he was contemplating.

It should also be noted that according to social-learning theory, children actively choose the models they will imitate, frequently imitating models whom they perceive as powerful, capable of giving out rewards, or who are in some other way desirable or appealing. Put another way, "The specific behavior people [children] imitate depends on what they perceive as valued in their culture" (Papalia et al., 2006, p. 32). Children's natural tendency to imitate behavior makes it clear that adults should not say to a child "Don't do as I do; do as I say." This is especially true with young children

sensorimotor period
The first stage in Piaget's theory of cognitive development; in this stage, the infant learns about his environment by active manipulation of the objects in it; learning and intellectual development are accomplished by use of the physical senses and motor abilities.

preoperational period
The second stage in Piaget's theory of cognitive development. It is defined primarily by the child's ability to use language and otherwise engage in symbol manipulation (what Piaget called the "symbolic function"). Unlike the later stages, however, the preoperational child is not able to engage in true operational thinking.

concrete operational
The kind of intellectual ability possible to the child in Piaget's stage of concrete operations. Concrete operational thinking allows the child to adapt to various aspects of his environment through the use of systematic logic. Such thinking is characterized by the ability to (1) reverse mental actions, (2) move away from the appearance of things to their reality, (3) attend to several aspects of a situation at a time rather than just one, and (4) see others' points of view—that is, there is a decline in egocentrism.

formal operational
The name Piaget gave to his fourth and final stage of cognitive development. An individual who is in the formal operational stage is able to think abstractly, deal with hypothetical situations, and understand the concept of conservation of number, area, volume, length, and so on.

whose language and intellectual skills are not yet developed well enough to discern the wisdom—or lack thereof—of such advice.

The Cognitive Perspective

Cognition refers to various mental functions—thinking, processing of information, memory, as well as expressing thought by way of one's behavior. Piaget's theory of cognitive development perhaps is the best-known attempt to explain how children develop intellectually. The principles and concepts of Piaget's theory are described more fully in the background information provided in the observation exercises that are germane to cognitive behavior. Suffice it to say that Piaget proposed four stages in the child's cognitive development: the **sensorimotor period**, the **preoperational period**, the **concrete operational**, and the **formal operational** stages. Recall that Piaget's theory is sometimes referred to as a constructivist theory because he believed that children literally construct reality through their own cognitive processes. At first, children's reality is commensurate with their as yet immature perceptions and conceptualizations of the world. With increasing maturity, these perceptions and conceptualizations begin to match more closely those of the adults in their society and culture (or initially, at least, those of the adults in their families and other intimate social groups to which the children belong).

Children actively choose the models they will imitate, imitating models whom they perceive as desirable or appealing.

assimilation
A mental process in which the person attempts to make a stimulus or piece of information fit into what she already knows.

accommodation
A mental process in which the person changes his cognitive structure or sensorimotor scheme to deal successfully with a new situation; for example, a child accommodates when he comes to understand that not every four-legged animal is a doggie.

schema
Piaget's term for a concept or mental representation of events in the world.

behavioral schemes
Organized patterns of behavior.

cognitive schemes
Mental representations or concepts of the environment.

sociocultural theory (also sociohistoric theory)
The name given to Vygotsky's theory of mental development in which the emphasis is shifted away from the child in explaining development and to the influence of the individual's social or cultural environment.

The concepts of **assimilation** and **accommodation** can be very useful when observing and interpreting children's cognitive behavior and abilities. Piaget proposed the idea of cognitive or mental **schema**, which Shaffer and Kipp (2007) define as "an organized pattern of thought or action that is used to cope with or explain some aspect of experience" (p. 60). Piaget identified **behavioral schemes**, which are organized patterns of behavior, and **cognitive schemes**, which are mental representations or concepts of the environment.

As children mature, their schemes become more sophisticated and more capable of dealing effectively with the world. According to Piaget, when confronted with an object, person, or event (stimulus), children attempt to make it fit into their already acquired schemes. If they are successful because they are already familiar with that object, person, or event, then assimilation occurs and, in effect, no new learning will take place. If, on the other hand, the stimulus is unfamiliar or novel enough so that it cannot be assimilated—it will not fit into an existing scheme—then the unfamiliar stimulus must be accommodated. Children do this by changing or expanding their schemes, and this change or expansion results in learning. If the same stimulus is experienced again, assimilation can occur because the stimulus will now fit into the newly acquired scheme. Thus, whereas assimilation requires no cognitive reorganization, accommodation does, and it is precisely such a restructuring that characterizes and results in learning.

A brief example might be helpful. Imagine a child who has a cognitive scheme for cat because she has a pet cat, Tiger. She has never seen a dog, however, and when she sees one for the first time, she tries to assimilate this new animal into her scheme for cat. This is understandable because, despite their differences, cats and dogs do share some features in common—they have four legs, claws, fur, and sharp teeth. The child calls this dog "kitty," but her mother says, "No, that's not a kitty, that's a doggie." Now the child has to reconcile her mistake by discerning some significant differences between the two animals and forming a new scheme for "dog." Piaget hypothesized that cognitive development takes place through these ongoing and alternating processes of assimilation and accommodation.

Vygotsky's Sociocultural or Contextual Perspective

The last perspective we will discuss in this chapter is Vygotsky's **sociocultural theory** or sociohistorical perspective on cognitive development. Vygotsky's views are presented in some detail elsewhere in this text, and so we touch on his ideas only briefly here.

Vygotsky believed that one's development is a product of one's culture. In his theory, development "referred largely to mental development, such as thought, language, and reasoning processes. These abilities were assumed to develop through social interactions with others (especially parents) and thus represented the shared knowledge of the culture" (Vasta, Haith, & Miller, 1995, p. 23). In contrast with

Piaget's belief that all children's cognitive development progressed through similar stages, Vygotsky viewed intellectual abilities as being specific to the child's culture (Vasta et al., 1995, p. 23).

One very significant derivative of Vygotsky's theory is the emphasis on individual differences and the influence of context on such differences: "Individuals set goals within a particular context as they perceive it and then select new goals within the new context that they seek out or that then presents itself. Success depends on how appropriate a behavior is to its context" (Papalia et al., 1999, p. 36). Vygotsky's emphasis on context emphasizes that children's learning depends upon cooperation between the children in a particular cultural or social setting and those members of that cultural or social setting who are more experienced and cognitively advanced than the children are at their various levels of development. The concept of behavior being situation-specific, or context-specific, is very useful when interpreting the meaning of children's behavior.

EXPLANATION OR INTERPRETATION OF GROWTH AND DEVELOPMENT: THE PRACTICAL SIDE TO OBSERVING BEHAVIOR

The study of growth and development is not just the study of theories. Indeed, from the standpoint of teachers, parents, and child care providers, growth and development are eminently practical. One does not have to be knowledgeable about formal developmental theories to observe changes that take place in children over time. What could be more practical and useful than charting a child's progress in physical growth, vocabulary acquisition, social competence, or cognitive skills?

Not everyone needs to understand the latest theory of language development to observe meaningfully a child's progress from the earliest inability to understand and produce speech to the ability to speak in meaningful and grammatically correct sentences while expressing increasingly complex ideas. One need not be able to explain how mental development actually occurs before being able to know that such development is in fact occurring. This is not to downplay the importance of theories. We take the position that there should be an effective balance between the theoretical and the practical. Ultimately, it is important to know not only that changes are occurring, but also why and how they occur and what the changes can mean to parents, child care providers, early childhood educators, and students studying children's behavior.

The why and the how of development, as well as the relatively easy-to-observe aspects of growth and development, bring us to the issue of explanation or interpretation.

Explanation or Interpretation

The concept and study of development can be quite complex. This is especially true when one tries to explain (or interpret) development and answer questions such as "How does development occur?" Even though explanation is not always easy, it is an essential activity and one of the major goals of the empirical sciences. Explanation is part of observation. Even the simplest descriptions involve putting information into some kind of conceptual framework. Consequently, description, pure and simple, is virtually impossible. By merely describing a behavior, one has already begun the process of interpretation, of putting new facts into a relationship with other facts already known or understood. Because of the importance of this subject, we will devote time and space to some perspectives on interpretation and its relation to observing and understanding children.

Some Definitions and Conceptions of Explanation

To explain behavior, for instance, is to make it clear or understandable. Making behavior clear or understandable can, in turn, involve interpreting that behavior so as to go beyond the actions performed or the words spoken and give those actions or words meaning or significance for some purpose and within some context. In this case, *to explain* means "to offer reasons for or a cause of" [something] (*The American Heritage Talking Dictionary*, 1995).

In addition to the dictionary definition just offered, there is a conception of explanation that is especially relevant to the basic theme of this text. It is a conception proposed by Don Ihde (1977), who says that "explanation is any sort of theory, idea, concept ... that attempts to go *behind* phenomena, to give the reasons for it in terms other than what appears" (p. 34, italics original).

Although it may be a bit confusing at this point, Ihde's conception of explanation gets at the heart of what is involved in observing and explaining behavior and developmental change. How is this so, and what bearing does it have on your observations?

Observation is the cornerstone of the empirical sciences, which are those that rely on the physical senses to take in relevant data and measure that data in some way. Science also goes one step further. It tries to find a relationship among the data it acquires. It is not enough simply to gather information; one must try to see how the facts that science acquires fit into a broader theoretical framework. Indeed, Brandt (1972) notes that by themselves, observational data have very little meaning; such data essentially enable us to make inferences about people based on their behavior. More recently, Neuman (1994) confirms Brandt's point when he writes, "Displays of behavior do not give meaning; rather, meaning is inferred, or someone figures out meaning" (p. 334). Theories provide scientists with the means to make such

A Brief Summary of Three Developmental Theories	
1. Psychoanalytic Theories	
a. Sigmund Freud	Three of Freud's concepts are of particular interest to us: the id, the ego, and the superego. The ego orients the individual toward reality. It is the ego's responsibility to help the individual meet his needs, interact appropriately with other people, and accomplish tasks and meet goals and objectives. The ego also enables the individual to be part of a larger social community and to recognize that others also have needs, desires, and goals. The id is concerned with getting what it wants when it wants it. It is not concerned with other people's needs, wishes, or goals. The superego is essentially one's conscience, and as such, it guides the ego toward appropriate and socially acceptable behavior. The ego and superego are logically linked to each other because if the individual is to be reality oriented, she must have some measure of social and moral awareness, in whatever way the society defines morality.
b. Erik Erikson	Erikson's psychosocial theory defines eight stages of personality development that cover the entire life span. Each stage imposes what Erikson called a psychosocial crisis, which the individual must adequately resolve if she is to develop in an optimal fashion. One significant advantage of Erikson's theory is that it takes into account children's social and cultural environments, thus placing his theory closer to Vygotsky's views of development than do some of the other theories.
2. The Learning Perspective	
a. Classical Conditioning	Classical conditioning occurs when a neutral stimulus—a stimulus that initially does not arouse (elicit) a particular response—is paired with a stimulus that does elicit a particular response. For example, a puff of air against your eyeball would cause you to blink. If for several trials a tone were sounded just before the puff of air, the tone by itself eventually would cause you to blink. Classical conditioning is mainly concerned with responses over which we have little or no control (involuntary responses).
b. Operant Conditioning	Operant conditioning is concerned with voluntary responses. Operant means that the individual operates on the environment by responding to stimuli in a particular way. The consequences of an individual's responses influence or determine whether or not he or she will respond in the same way in the same or similar circumstances. If a response is strengthened by its consequence—that is, if the individual finds the response rewarding, pleasant, or desirable and repeats the response at some future time—the response is then said to have been reinforced. Operant conditioning is often referred to as reinforcement theory.

(continues)

c. Social-Learning Theory	Social-learning theory emphasizes observational learning. In large measure, children learn by observing and imitating other people (models). Unlike operant conditioning, social learning theory recognizes the importance of thinking. Thus, "children's cognitive responses to their perceptions, rather than reflexive responses to reinforcement or punishment, are seen as central to development" (Papalia et al., 2006, p. 29). Imitation is central to social learning theory. Two important concepts derive from the process of imitation: 1. **Vicarious reinforcement:** Samantha observes Belinda being praised (reinforced) by her teacher for helping to pick up the big blocks during cleanup time. Samantha then imitates Belinda's behavior because she, too, wants the teacher to praise her. The significance of vicarious reinforcement is that the teacher did not have to praise or reinforce Samantha's behavior directly. Samantha was vicariously or indirectly reinforced merely by watching Belinda being reinforced. 2. **Vicarious punishment:** Vicarious punishment operates on the same principle as vicarious reinforcement, except that the child observes another child being punished for a particular behavior. Punishment is intended to weaken or eliminate an undesirable behavior. If Gordon observes Timothy being punished for taking a toy away from Rebecca, Gordon will have been vicariously punished if he decides that it is a bad idea to repeat Timothy's behavior because he does not want to suffer the same punishment.
3. The Cognitive Perspective of Piaget and Vygotsky	
a. Piaget	Piaget proposed four stages or periods in the child's cognitive or intellectual development: the sensorimotor, the preoperational, the concrete operational, and the formal operational stages. In Piaget's theory, the child must go through every stage in the fixed order indicated here. Progress through each stage is accomplished by the two complementary processes of assimilation and accommodation. Assimilation occurs when the child experiences something with which she is already familiar and that therefore does not require her to make any changes in the way she thinks or processes information. When, however, the child is confronted with something with which she is not familiar, in order to understand this new experience, she must change the way she thinks—she must change or reorganize her cognitive structure. This change is accomplished through the process of accommodation.
b. Vygotsky	Vygotsky's perspective on cognitive development is a sociocultural or contextual one. He believed that a child's development is a product of his or her culture and that thought, language, and reasoning processes develop through social interactions with other people, especially parents. Piaget believed that all children's cognitive development progressed through similar stages, whereas Vygotsky saw intellectual abilities as being specific to the child's culture.

inferences. What a scientist (or parent or teacher) first requires are data, and data are frequently in the form of descriptions. Descriptions are a central part of your observation exercises. In addition to simply describing, you will try to interpret or explain—that is, give a meaning to what you have seen and described. How will you do that? One way is by looking at your descriptive data through a particular theoretical perspective, which will, in a sense, tell you what meaning could be put on what you have observed. But (and this is an important "but") that meaning, that explanation suggested by the theory, goes behind the phenomenon and is not itself experienced. You have supplied the meaning, but you have not experienced the meaning in the same way you have experienced the observed behavior, event, or object. In fact, your observed and objectively described data are connected to your explanation by an abstract conceptual framework, possibly a theory or your own personal beliefs.

Let us look at a simple example of how Ihde's notion of explanation might work. The example is given only to illustrate Ihde's concept of explanation; in a real situation, you would want a much larger and more representative sample of behavior before drawing any final conclusions. You are observing a group of four-year-olds playing outside on a playground, and the following is an example of your objective behavioral description:

Samuel walks over to Tommy, who is driving a truck around the sandbox on a road he's made by putting blocks of wood in the sand. "Can I play with you?" "OK," says Tommy, "but I'm the boss. This is my construction company, and you work for me!" Samuel nods affirmatively and asks, "Whad'ye want me to do, boss?"

You have seen Samuel approach Tommy at the sandbox; you have seen Tommy playing with a truck in the sand; you have heard their brief verbal exchanges. You could have described more than what is given in the example, but even this extremely small amount of information raises questions: What might this behavior signify? What meaning does it have beyond its mere occurrence? Now you are faced with that "something that is not itself experienced." You might offer one of several explanations or interpretations of the two boys' behavior and interaction. Suppose that you knew that Tommy's father owns a construction company. You could tentatively interpret Tommy's actions toward his play materials and toward Samuel as an indication of imitation or identification with his father. Tommy pretends to have some of his father's characteristics and behavior—he is the boss, he tells people what to do, and he behaves in an authoritative manner. In such an explanation, you would rely on a historical perspective—Tommy's family background—and would apply to it the psychological concepts of imitation and identification. You could also argue that Tommy is engaging in anticipatory socialization, which involves practicing some of the behaviors, values, and attitudes that are part of the adult role that Tommy imagines himself filling when he grows

Children need stimulation to grow intellectually and cognitively.

up. You could see Samuel as a follower or as emotionally dependent on Tommy in this particular interaction. There are other ways you could explain or interpret Tommy's and Samuel's behavior. Whatever they might be, however, they would not be visible, hearable, touchable, tasteable, or smellable.

That is what is meant by an explanation giving reasons for something in terms of other than what appears. What appears are the things you saw and heard take place between Tommy and Samuel. The "other than what appears" are the abstract ideas you used to explain what occurred—the ideas of identification, imitation, anticipatory socialization, and emotional dependency. However, you have not experienced identification. You have experienced some small portion of Tommy's behavior that, to you, indicated a particular psychological process. This general idea cannot be stressed too much. The sense we make of our world—at whatever level of sophistication—is formed through inferences that are founded on any number of factors or variables.

The very real possibility that observers will hold different perspectives justifies, if not demands, the gathering of different viewpoints before making judgments or decisions about a child. This will help to reduce the undesirable effects of bias, although bias itself cannot be eliminated.

Some biases and perspectives are personal, and none of us can completely escape or avoid them; for that reason, they are important. If you place a high value on neatness, for example, you should be alert to the presence and potential influence of this value when you observe children who do not fit your idea of how children should look when they come to school. There are other biases or perspectives that are directly related to the observation situation or are formalized as theories or philosophies.

The theory type of bias or perspective is of some concern in this text. Our intention is to have you ultimately bring together your knowledge of developmental theories and your observation skills so that you can look at, describe, and interpret various aspects of children's behavior in ways that suit your particular purposes. To accomplish this goal, you must be familiar with the concept of development, some of its general characteristics, and the differing ways that psychologists and theories view these characteristics.

Levels of Explanation

First Level of Explanation: Immediate Circumstances

Mussen and colleagues (1979) identify several levels of explanation. You can explain or interpret a child's behavior in terms of immediate circumstances. For example, Johnny leaves the big block area after his playmate Billy pushes him and says, "Go 'way, I don't wanna play with you anymore!" Johnny's leaving is a response to a present stimulus that immediately preceded his leaving the block area. This level of explanation is common because we all react to the demands that the environment makes on us at any given moment.

Second Level of Explanation: Historical Reasons

The second level of explanation goes behind the present situation to deal with historical reasons. Another child might have responded differently to Billy's command to "go 'way," perhaps telling Billy he should go away or even striking out at him. Johnny's reaction has an explanation that lies somewhere in his past experiences. His parents may have taught him that he should respond to aggression by walking away, or maybe in his past encounters with aggressive children, Johnny lost fights or arguments, so he avoids those situations. This level of explanation is perhaps relevant to Sroufe and Cooper's (1988) second factor required to explain developmental change, namely that present development is dependent on the development that has already occurred. In turn, future development is dependent on present development, and so on.

Third Level of Explanation: Adaptive Reasons

Mussen and his colleagues (1979) point out, however, that neither of these reasons explains the "purpose of the child's behavior." For purpose, we must look at the adaptive reason for the behavior: How does the behavior help the child to function within his physical–social setting or within the limits of his own personality and temperament? In the case of Johnny and Billy, there could be a number of adaptive reasons for Johnny's walking away. He might want to avoid the guilt he would feel if he violated his parents' or teacher's admonitions not to fight, he might want to avoid being punished by his parents or his teacher for fighting, or he might be afraid to fight because in the past he has been hurt by other children and wants to avoid being hurt again.

Fourth Level of Explanation: Evolutionary Reasons

The last level of explanation offers reasons on an evolutionary basis. Evolutionary reasons are concerned with how we have come to be what we are, as a species, and why we exhibit some of the behaviors that we do in particular circumstances. Mussen and associates (1979) give the informative, but perhaps somewhat distressing example, of a human baby crying when punished—distressing because, as some would argue, babies should not be punished—in contrast to young monkeys that tend to "cower and assume a submissive posture when punished by their parents." The critical point here, according to these authors, is that the two species, human and monkey, display different responses to punishment because of genetic forces that operated during our respective evolutionary histories. This is also significant in that each species is capable of certain kinds of behavior, abilities, and learning that are not necessarily possible for other species. A classic example is that of learning a true language, an ability that is possible only for human beings, even though other animals can communicate with one another through signs and signals.

We have just presented a brief overview of some developmental theories and perspectives that can be relevant to your observational goals and objectives. The chapter begins with a brief discussion of six issues on which there appears to be consensus among developmentalists; these issues are referred to as guideposts (see Papalia et al., 1999), and they are as follows:

1. Functional or behavioral domains are interrelated.
2. Development is characterized by individual differences.
3. Development is interactive.
4. Development is influenced by its context or environment.
5. Children are resilient and are not permanently shaped by single events or experiences.
6. Development is cumulative.

Some basic meanings and concepts of development are discussed. Development is defined essentially as orderly, predictable change over time. Such change is either quantitative or qualitative, and based on those two kinds of change, a distinction is made between growth and development. Growth is characterized by quantitative change, which is adding on more of the same thing, such as when a child gets taller by adding on more and more bone tissue. Qualitative change is the prominent feature of development, whereby change results from a reorganizing or repatterning of behavioral and cognitive structures. Thus, quantitative change is a difference in degree or amount, and qualitative change is a difference in kind.

Various models of development are discussed. Four basic issues or questions are discussed in connection with these models. The first question asks, "What is the basic nature of humans?" Three views or models fall under this question: the mechanistic model, the organismic model, and the contextualist model. The second question debates whether nature or nurture provides the primary impetus for development. The third issue concerns whether developmental change is quantitative or qualitative change. The fourth question deals with what it is that develops, or what the domains of development are. An additional issue regarding whether development does or does not proceed in stages is also discussed. The stage concept is related to the mechanistic and organismic models of development.

This chapter also presents an overview of several developmental theories. Adopting the easy-to-follow organization of Papalia and colleagues' (1999) discussion of various theories, we put these theories under the general rubric of perspective. The psychoanalytic perspective is discussed as represented by Sigmund Freud and Erik Erikson. Freud's concepts of id, ego, and superego are presented, as well as the role each of these personality structures plays in a child's personality development. Erikson's concept of the psychosocial crisis is also discussed.

The learning perspective includes operant conditioning, classical conditioning, and social-learning theory. The terms *operant* and *reinforcement* are briefly defined. Observational learning (imitation), vicarious reinforcement, and vicarious punishment are briefly explained in the discussion of social-learning theory.

The cognitive perspective includes the theories of Piaget and Vygotsky. Piaget's concepts of assimilation and accommodation are discussed at some length. The sociocultural framework of Vygotsky's theory is briefly discussed.

STUDY QUESTIONS

1. What is a major difference between growth and development? Do you think the difference is an important one with regard to observing and understanding children? Why or why not?

2. Mussen and his colleagues (1979) identified four levels of explanation: immediate, historical, adaptive, and evolutionary. Describe three imaginary observation situations in which the first three levels of explanation might be used to understand or explain a child's behavior.

3. Describe in your own words what is meant by the statement that explanation attempts to go behind a phenomenon. What does this statement have to do with observing and interpreting children's behavior?

4. One teacher believes that children are passive with respect to their development; another teacher believes they are active. What differences might you observe in the respective classrooms of these two teachers? What kinds of interactions might take place in the two contexts?

5. Of the two concepts, individual differences and universal patterns of development, which one do you think would be easier to base conclusions on after observing some children's behavior?

PRACTICAL EXERCISE

For some readers, Chapter 2 might be one of the more difficult chapters in this text, but we urge you to try to reach a reasonable understanding of at least the basic principles underlying growth and development, as well as an understanding of the models of development we have discussed.

To one degree or another, each of the observation exercises found in Chapters 14 through 18 requires the understanding and application of developmental principles, especially when interpreting the behaviors you have observed. Interpretation is also aided when put into the context of a theory because it is the purpose of a developmental theory to provide a basis for understanding and explaining behavior and how behavior changes (develops) over time. Because it would be difficult if not impossible to suggest an exercise that would capture or involve all the concepts discussed in Chapter 2, we have confined our focus to the three perspectives on development discussed on pages 36 to 44 of the text.

For this exercise, observe and record in as much detail as you can the behavior of a child between the ages of three and five years. You need not determine ahead of time the specific kinds of behaviors you are going to observe; rather, simply choose a child whose behavior seems interesting to you, and begin recording your observations in a narrative form. Observe and record for about five minutes or so. If necessary, read again the information regarding the psychoanalytic, learning, and cognitive perspectives on development as discussed in the text, and then try to explain or interpret your observations based on each of those three perspectives. Finally, try to answer the following questions:

1. Which, if any, of your interpretations seems to make the most sense?

2. Which perspective, if any, seems the most credible or useful in light of the observation data you have tried to interpret?

3. Can you explain or interpret your data without using any of the three perspectives? Justify your answer.

4. Are any of the other concepts discussed in Chapter 2 useful in interpreting your data? Justify your answer.

5. Can you explain the behavior you have observed without necessarily using any of the concepts or principles discussed in the chapter? Justify your answer.

6. After you have made the explanations called for in questions 3, 4, and 5, do they help you better understand the child's behavior?

General Guidelines for Observing Children

After reading this chapter, you should be able to

- Discuss the steps that must be taken to prepare to observe.
- Discuss the role of inconspicuousness in observing children.
- Analyze the role of professional ethics in observation.
- Identify factors that affect observation.
- Discuss the three categories of errors in observation.
- Discuss the three aspects that affect the accuracy and reliability of observation.
- Analyze the potential dangers of evaluating the worth of children's behavior.
- Distinguish several kinds of groups.
- Discuss several approaches to group observation.

OBSERVATION: SOME PRELIMINARY THOUGHTS

The following guidelines provide a framework within which you can formulate your own thinking and behavior for various observation situations.

PREPARATION FOR OBSERVING

Preparation involves several organizational steps that you must take before you enter the observation setting.

KEY TERMS

event

participant observation

What Are Your Purposes?

There are many reasons to observe young children. You should have yours clearly in mind as you approach your exercises. Identifying your objectives is a central task because everything else depends on it. Objectives must be defined precisely enough to bring the observational activity down to a manageable size. Brandt (1972) confirms the importance of this issue when he points out that behavior in naturalistic settings is so complex that one simply cannot observe or study all aspects of the situation at one time. He goes on to note that the task of the observer ("investigator") is not to take in all aspects of the situation at once but to select and study the most important elements of the total situation. Brandt's advice relates to the statement made in Chapter 1—scientific observation is not merely looking *at* something; it is looking *for* something.

Observational objectives are numerous. An objective might be to gain experience in observing children of various ages. Gaining experience in observing children, on the other hand, can ultimately serve further purposes that are more specific and sharply defined. Learning how children behave in particular situations, and why they behave as they do, is such a purpose. This information could be used to change the equipment and materials in a classroom or to change the arrangement of the equipment and materials. Modification of seating patterns during story time might be made because of a teacher's observation that certain children, when together, seem to foster arguments or inattentiveness to the teacher. Or a teacher and her staff may want to assess the effectiveness of their efforts to bring a shy four-year-old out of his shell, so to speak, and to encourage him to interact more with the other children.

Teachers observe for various reasons. What might this teacher's observational goals be?

Some observational objectives are not specifically identified beforehand. Nonetheless, as in the example of children's disruptive behavior during story time, certain behaviors and events are noticed because a teacher and staff are alert to the general objective of using observation to promote the well-being of the children in their care.

In relation to the exercises in this text, you must consider the following questions.

Why Are You in a Particular Observational Setting? What Are You Supposed to See There?

The success of your efforts to see what you are looking for depends only partly on your knowledge, values, experiences, and skill. Objectives have to be matched with resources, settings, and recording methods. For example, if an exercise calls for observing an infant's reflexes, it would be inappropriate to observe preschoolers. If you are to observe behaviors that occur infrequently, time sampling should not be the method you choose because time sampling is best used with behaviors that occur often (see Chapter 7).

Other questions must also be answered before you begin to observe.

What Developmental Area or Behaviors Are the Focus of the Observation?

Are you there to observe social behavior, language behavior, or physical/motor skills? The answer could depend on the age of the child or children you are observing. You could observe reflex behaviors in an infant, but this would not be your focus when observing a three-year-old. Similarly, you would not observe social behaviors in a four-month-old infant, but you would expect such behaviors in a three-year-old.

How Much Time Are You to Spend Observing the Behaviors You Have Selected?

Are you to observe for several minutes, an hour, or for as long as the behaviors occur? The answer depends on a number of factors. Also, a distinction must be made between the amount of time you will simply be in the observational setting and the amount of time you actually observe and record behavior. You may be required to spend several hours in the classroom, for example, but actually observe and record behavior for only 20 or 30 minutes. The recording techniques you use also determine time. If you use the time-sampling technique, in a class of 15 children you might observe each child for only 1 or 2 minutes. The narrative description, on the other hand, might require 5 or 10 minutes for any given child, depending on how long a particular behavior or sequence of behaviors lasts, your ability to write continuously for that length of time, and other considerations.

Whom Are You to Observe?

The answer might seem obvious, but the question must nonetheless be considered carefully. An answer partly lies in appropriately matching a child's developmental level with the behavior you want to observe. For example, you would not observe a group of two-year-olds for samples of cooperative play, or a two-month-old infant for samples of fine motor behavior such as stringing beads or picking up small objects between the thumb and forefinger. Also, are you to observe one child or a group of children? If one child, may it be any child, or must it be a particular child? If you are to observe a group of children, may it be any group, or must it be a particular group?

Of course, the subjects of your observations are determined by the actual population of children in any given child care center. For example, if you are in a facility that serves only two-year-olds, such recording formats as checklists, time samples, frequency counts, or event samples will have to be appropriate to the behavioral capacities and developmental levels that two-year-olds are likely to exhibit. The narrative description does not require such planning because anything and everything the children do is a matter of interest for your analysis. This brings us to the next question.

How Are You to Record Your Observations (Checklists, Duration Record, Narrative Description, Event Sampling, Time Sampling, etc.)?

This question was partially answered with the preceding question/answer, but there are considerations other than the children's ages and developmental levels. If you want to preserve the raw data, such recording formats as the narrative description, event sample, anecdotal record, or diary would be the appropriate ones to use. If you want to know only whether or not a particular behavior has occurred, or whether or not a child possesses a particular skill, and you are not interested in the details or context of the behavior or skill, then the time sample, checklist, or duration record would be an appropriate choice. There are also considerations of time, ease of use, and the amount of prior preparation each format requires. The narrative description and event sample, for instance, require some planning with regard to whom you are going to observe and when and where you are going to observe. But these factors require far less effort than does preparing a suitable checklist or time sampling instrument.

What Kind of Interpretations Are You to Make (Based on a Given Theory, on What Has Taken Place in the Setting)?

This text does not specifically instruct you on how to interpret the information you will acquire through your observations. This is because observational data can be so varied or open-ended that it would be impossible to anticipate the kind of information your

Observation can take place inside the classroom.

observations will yield. Moreover, accurate or valid interpretations really can be made only through repeated observations that take into account the children's environments, experiences, and developmental levels.

However, it is prudent to understand that there are at least two basic frameworks within which interpretations can be made: interpretations based on a particular theory and interpretations based on what has taken place in the setting, with no strong emphasis on theory, or some combination of the two. As we have stated elsewhere in this text, your observations can help you understand what you might be learning about child development theory, and your knowledge of theory can help you understand and interpret your observations. For this author, it is primarily a matter of which of these two aspects or frameworks you want or need to emphasize.

Some of these questions are directly related to the specific recording technique you use. Let us look at the question of how long to observe. On the one hand, a time sampling procedure requires observing and recording for intermittent but uniform and relatively short periods of several seconds or minutes. On the other hand, event sampling and the narrative description call for observation over longer periods of time. In event sampling, the length of the time you observe and record depends on how long the child exhibits the desired behavior, or what is called the **event**. In the narrative description, the length of time you observe depends mostly on such things as how much information you want or need and how long you are physically and mentally able to observe and record behavior. As you will learn later, the narrative description tries to capture as much information as possible, and the observer makes no prior

event
Behaviors that can be placed into particular categories; for example, hitting to get a toy away from another child is a behavior that can be put into the category "instrumental aggression."

judgments or decisions as to what is or what is not proper "grist for the mill," so to speak.

Where Are You Going to Observe?

The site of your observations is related to your objectives, and as they change, the site may have to change. If a limited number of facilities are available, the observations, or certain aspects of the observations, will also be limited. Under those conditions, your observations will have to fit the possibilities afforded by the setting. For example, if the only structured environment in which to observe children is one local center that provides child care to children from three through five years of age, then you will not be able to observe two-year-olds. Your observation exercises are limited to the children accessible to you and to the characteristics and abilities typical of those age groups. In other cases, you might have access to a number of facilities and opportunities, such as child care centers, nursery schools, kindergartens, elementary schools, and public playgrounds, which offer a wide range of ages and environments. Under those conditions, you will have more flexibility. You will need to match carefully observation exercises and purposes with specific settings.

What May You Do in the Setting?

Knowing why you are in the observation setting includes knowing what you may or may not do there. Some settings may give you considerable leeway to do what is

Some schools have observation rooms with one-way windows and countertop desks.

necessary to accomplish your objectives. Others may be more formal and not allow certain behaviors. For example, some center directors or teachers may not allow you to sit out of the way just observing and recording; instead, you may be asked to help the children during toilet time, snack time, or when they dress to go out. You may be required to step outside the classroom to take notes. In those cases, you will have to rely on your memory until you can get to your notebook and record your data. What you may do can be affected by the recording technique you choose. For example, a checklist would not prevent some participation on your part. A teacher might have fewer objections to in-classroom recording with a brief checklist than with a more elaborate narrative description. You need to learn what is allowed and expected of you as an observer before you take on that role. This is made doubly important by the fact that child care center directors, school directors, and classroom teachers differ widely in their expectations regarding acceptable behavior.

It is possible that you may experience difficulties in completing some observations because of limitations imposed by the setting. Therefore, if there are other options open to you, you may want to select a more compatible observation setting.

There is another important aspect to the issue of what you may do in the setting. In many child care centers and schools, anyone not officially associated with the facility has to have a signed permission slip before being allowed to enter the facility to observe or conduct any kind of business. This is a matter that you will have to determine ahead of time and plan accordingly.

Inconspicuous Observation

Why Be Inconspicuous?

Conventional wisdom says that observing a phenomenon changes it. Observing people can change their behavior, although we may not know how much their behavior changes. Their awareness of the observer's presence can distract them or motivate them to behave in ways they believe will please the observer. Behavioral changes brought about by the act of observing are of deep concern to researchers who want to study groups such as gangs, families, or nonindustrialized societies. Such researchers— anthropologists and sociologists, for example—sometimes attempt to minimize these unwanted effects by engaging in what is called **participant observation**. This means that the observer becomes part of the group and participates in as many of its activities as is appropriate for the circumstances. Teachers are participant observers as a matter of course, and there is little doubt that they are accepted by the children and can observe them without unduly influencing their behavior in ways that fall outside the planned goals and general intentions of the child care center. We recognize that, as one person communicated to us, education precisely involves changing behavior. But the term *unduly*, as just used, refers to what is akin to the unintended effects of socialization. The unfamiliar person in the center or classroom can affect children's

participant observation
When an observer becomes part of the group she is observing and participates in as many of its activities as is appropriate, with the objective of reducing the effects of observation on the group's behavior.

behavior, feelings, performance, and the like in ways that are not in the children's or the facility's best interests or within their stated objectives. It can be quite different in the case of an observer who is not perceived as part of the group or setting, particularly someone who comes and goes. Some believe that the observer will eventually blend into the group and be accepted, which reduces the impact of being watched by an outsider. One can argue that it is virtually impossible for an observer to mask her reasons for being in the group well enough for the group to forget those reasons. In short, the argument goes, those being watched will always perform for the person doing the watching.

There is one further consideration worth mentioning with regard to being inconspicuous. Every child care center or early childhood education classroom consists of two environments: a general environment and a developmental environment. Bentzen and Frost (2003) define these two environments as follows:

> The **general environment** is relatively fixed and constant. It's made up of the physical equipment and materials, together with their spatial arrangements and locations. It contains the cues or stimuli to which children and adults can respond. The general environment is the one that exists before anyone sets foot in the center or classroom and is an *objective environment*. (p. 7, italics and boldface original)

> The **developmental environment**, on the other hand, exists within the general environment and is an environment in action. Once established, the general environment does not depend on anyone for anything more (with such obvious exceptions as replacing broken or missing equipment and materials, adding new equipment, or rearranging equipment and materials). The developmental environment, however, is dynamic and constantly changing. For example, as part of the general environment, wooden blocks essentially remain constant, but as part of the developmental environment, blocks can assume as many meanings and uses as there are children who play with them. In an objective sense, wooden blocks are what they are; in a subjective sense, they are whatever children want them to be. The developmental environment is highly subjective. (p. 7)

There may be some exceptions to this influence. Thorndike and Hagan (1977) believe that, unlike older children and adults, young children have not yet acquired the ability to conceal themselves from public scrutiny, which allows us to learn more about them through observation than we can about older children and adults. Inconspicuous observation tries to prevent or minimize unwanted influence on behavior. The operative phrase here is *unwanted influence on behavior*. Unwanted influence is not as much of a problem with staff members, who, by definition and necessity, are participant observers whose objective is precisely to influence children's behavior in ways that are congruent with the planned goals and general intentions of the child care center. However, students or other individuals who are not consistently part of the setting are potentially part of the developmental environment with which children interact. It is the effects of these interactions between children and the occasional observer that can influence children's behavior in ways that are not consistent with the child care center's goals and objectives. Therefore, it is these undesirable influences—whether actual or potential—that require such observers to be as inconspicuous as possible. We must also point out that "inconspicuous" does not necessarily mean out of the children's sight or hearing, although things or people that can be seen or heard can definitely be part of the children's developmental environment and thereby influence their behavior. It remains a debatable point whether being observed continues to have an influence on behavior after the observer has become an accepted member of the group. Anecdotal reports on the issue do indicate that young children adapt well to the presence of unfamiliar persons. It might be prudent for you to determine empirically whether or not the children in a particular setting and under particular circumstances do in fact adjust to the presence of unfamiliar persons. This determination should guide or at least contribute to any further decisions regarding your observations.

Perhaps the most fruitful way to think about being inconspicuous is to consider whether your presence and behavior are influencing children's behavior in any way that contradicts the center's mission and goals or negatively affects the children's development and well-being.

The Difficulty of Remaining Inconspicuous

Being inconspicuous is not always easy. Any unfamiliar person in the classroom is likely to capture the attention of the children until the novelty has worn off. Sometimes observation booths are available, which allow you to observe without being seen (through the use of two-way mirrors). Their use is based on the assumption that the children do not know there is anyone behind those mirrors, or that if they do know, an unseen observer interferes less with normal behavior than one who is visible. The author's experience has been that children learn all too quickly about the existence of observation booths, as well as whether anyone is inside watching them. However, it is also likely that if they are engrossed in play, children will rather quickly forget that there is anyone in the observation booth watching them, or maybe even that there is an observation booth at all, although we do not want to put too fine a point on the issue.

It is also true that children can become very curious about someone writing in a notebook, perhaps especially so if they are not used to seeing other, familiar adults who also write in notebooks. The best advice we can give you if a child asks what you are

This observer is engaging in participant observation. By becoming part of the group, he has become inconspicuous as an observer.

doing is simply to reply "I am working" or some other such brief but true explanation. However, do not tell the child that you are watching him and writing down everything he does. This serves no legitimate purpose, but it might make the child nervous or self-conscious, or otherwise cause him unnecessary discomfort.

There are additional problems when observation objectives call for recording behaviors that cannot be observed from a distance. Language behavior, for instance, requires you to be close enough to a speaker to hear him. Naturally, getting that close, as well as having to be there with notebook (or, if permissible, tape recorder) in hand, brings with it the possibility of calling attention to yourself. Problems can also arise when there is uncertainty concerning whether you should intrude into a situation. The role of the participant observer comes into play here. Teachers, center directors and staff members, and other similar individuals are necessarily participant observers at some time or another. Nonetheless, being a participant brings with it a potential problem that the detached observer may not have to face—namely, how to carry out one's responsibilities with the children and, if it is necessary or desired, at the same time observe and record behavior. Krogh (1994), for example, stresses the importance of teachers observing children in the classroom, but she also points up one of the difficulties:

> Take advantage of every opportunity to observe each individual child. Observation can be formal: make notes on what you see and keep a record for future reference. *Much of the time, however, formal*

observation isn't possible because interaction with the class is necessary and desirable. (p. 89, emphasis added)

How and When to Be Inconspicuous

In spite of the difficulties mentioned here, reliable and inconspicuous observation is possible within the requirements and limitations of the given situation. In this writer's view, an extremely important part of being inconspicuous is remaining as detached as possible or necessary from the children and their activities. This does not mean you should be cold and aloof, but only that you not try to influence behavior beyond what is required by the observation objectives or beyond what you are permitted to do in the setting. This advice should be followed according to its intent and within its appropriate context. For example, naturalistic (or informal) observation depends on the subjects of study exhibiting behavior spontaneously, not at the prompting of the observer. But there are occasions when children are asked to behave in particular ways, such as in testing situations or formal research studies. In those contexts, the observer has to intrude into the children's environment in a way dictated by the purposes of the study or test. More generally, however, nearly every environment demands some particular behaviors from the individuals in it. Most environments, for example, require individuals to behave in a socially conforming manner. Even young children must learn to conform to the demands imposed by various environments or settings. Naturally, they are just learning about such things as what behavior is appropriate under what circumstances—when it is permissible to run and shout, where and when one may go to the bathroom, and so on. All of this notwithstanding, this writer would contend that at the earliest ages, children begin to acquire some understanding of what is and what is not acceptable behavior. The key, of course, is to match one's demands to the child's ability to meet them; adults' expectations should be developmentally appropriate.

Morrison (1995) speaks to this issue in the context of adults modeling appropriate behavior for children to imitate. He cites four specific techniques that the early childhood professional can use "to help children learn through modeling," and two of these techniques are of immediate interest here: modeling and supervision. Briefly, "modeling occurs when the professional practices the behavior expected of the children." "Supervision," in turn, "is a process of reviewing, insisting, maintaining standards, and following up" (p. 480). In any child care setting, therefore, adults hold certain expectations regarding children's behavior. It is important to keep in mind that those same adults will hold expectations regarding your behavior while you are in the setting doing your observations.

Other kinds of demands are made, too, depending on the purpose and characteristics of the setting. In other words, our actions are almost always structured in some way; they occur within some set of acceptable boundaries. Inconspicuousness can be achieved by not further structuring or affecting children's behavior beyond what is already part of the setting and situation. Consider a brief example.

Suppose that you want to observe a child's language behavior. This could require writing down word for word what the child says, to whom she speaks, and any other important circumstances surrounding her use of language. Language is a complex phenomenon, however. One can study just the language itself—that is, such things as vocabulary, sentence structure, and sentence length. One can also examine the conditions under which the child uses language and for what purposes—to ask for help, to give commands, to ask questions, to self-regulate behavior, or to persuade others. All these aspects are part of language development and usage.

If you are interested, for example, in seeing how Jenine uses speech under naturalistic or nontest conditions, you would have to allow her language to occur on its own. Thus, Jenine might speak very infrequently and not say very much when she does speak. If so, you may be unable to tell much about her language proficiency but a great deal more about the social and psychological aspects of her speech—the circumstances under which she tends to talk, to whom, to what ends, and so on. What do you do in such a case?

You could remain inconspicuous by accepting Jenine's speech behavior as it naturally occurs. But, if the circumstances warrant it, you could also test Jenine by engaging her in a conversation and trying to draw out of her more speech than she had demonstrated up to that point. In such an instance, you would be trying to determine her level of language ability, the level at which she is able to communicate with speech. Here a distinction is made between learning (ability, skill, proficiency) and performance. The distinction is important and useful, for it points out that a child may know how to do something but may not necessarily exhibit her ability. Most of us know how to hit, for example, but we do not go around hitting; we do not ordinarily demonstrate this skill.

If you test the child in any way, but your objectives do not justify testing, then you have unnecessarily sacrificed inconspicuousness. You have entered into the setting and changed what occurred there. Again, however, merely being present in an observation setting sacrifices some inconspicuousness. Of equal concern is how much freedom you will have to test or interfere in any way with what is going on. In a preschool, for instance, the teacher may not allow you to interact with the children; you may have to be a nonparticipant observer. The freedom issue is directly related to the process of prior preparation. Consequently, how much you are allowed to participate, or how much influence you are allowed to exert, should not take you by surprise. Participation is an aspect of observation that you should always discuss with the person in charge of the setting before you begin to observe.

In summary, think of inconspicuous observation as observation that imposes or introduces nothing into the observation setting, or on the persons and objects in the setting, beyond what is necessary to achieve legitimate objectives. Your objectives must never conflict with the objectives, philosophy, or procedures of the preschool, school, or any other location in which you are doing the observing. Nor must your objectives and procedures violate the rights or privileges of any individual or group. There will be some contexts where the restrictions are fewer than those in private facilities. Public places, such as government buildings, playgrounds, and parks, are governed by laws, regulations, and even philosophies. But these are different from the regulations and philosophies governing child care facilities, if only because the latter have the specific goals of caring for and fostering young children's growth, development, physical safety, and psychological security. Some of the concerns and issues raised here also apply to professional ethics and confidentiality.

Professional Ethics and Confidentiality

Professional ethics and confidentiality are concerns that are inseparable from all observation activities. When you go into a particular place, you are, in some cases, a guest (such as in a private preschool or a public elementary school). In all cases, you are a representative of your school or institution. This means that your behavior reflects not only on yourself but on your school and your department as well. If you are not a student, you still have obligations to those whom you are observing. You also have obligations to others who might have come before you and laid the groundwork and good will so necessary for observation and research activity. You also have an obligation to anyone who might come after you. One person's improper behavior can spoil it for everyone else.

The full scope of the ethical conduct issue, although an extremely important issue, cannot be covered in its entirety in this text. A copy of ethical guidelines can be obtained from NAEYC. It is a document to which you should refer whenever you are uncertain of how you may behave in any child care setting or, for that matter, in any other situation that involves children.

What we present next is an abbreviated treatment of professional ethics and confidentiality—enough information, we trust, to get you started on your observations. However, bear in mind that every child care facility will have its own set of principles by which you must conduct yourself, principles that are relevant to the unique circumstances that exist in that particular setting. It is hoped, of course, that if you are in a formal child care setting, the staff there will be familiar enough with the broader aspects of ethical conduct to direct you toward all the proper behavior.

The Need for Professional Ethics

Research using human subjects is open to intensive scrutiny today. Gone are the times when a researcher is at liberty to do almost anything he wants in the name of science. The rights, safety (physical and psychological), and privacy of the individual are now extremely important when conducting research. These restrictions sometimes make the study of human behavior difficult; nonetheless, the protection of rights and safety justifies that difficulty and must be preserved. Your observations are, strictly speaking, a form of research; they provide the methods and data for answering research questions. You are trying to learn about children, to understand their behaviors and how they change over time. In doing this, you will ask yourself questions; you will construct a written record of what certain children do in various situations; you will make interpretations and might even evaluate children's behaviors. In short, you are getting information about people, which must always be done with care and sensitivity. Care and sensitivity are often best served and achieved by being objective rather than subjective. An accurate description of behavior—that is, simply conveying what happened, what was said, and what actions were performed—is usually preferred over making judgments about the desirability or value of the behavior. It is imperative that you keep in mind that even so-called objective descriptions can sometimes reveal information that is potentially embarrassing or could be misused to characterize unfavorably an individual or group, which is a situation that is unacceptable under any circumstances. However, even positive or seemingly harmless information places children and their behavior at the focus of attention, and that can cause some parents and teachers discomfort or even alarm. This concern can be partly alleviated by not using the children's real names, thus assuring parents and teachers that your observation reports will not reveal the real identity of any child. This is an assurance that is required by the ethical concern for privacy and confidentiality.

There are other concerns that involve ethics. Parents may feel distressed at the possibility of an outside observer discovering any deficiencies in their child. Parents often compare their child with other children: "Does Aletha talk as well as her age mates?" her family might ask. Carl's father may ask whether Carl is as coordinated physically as the other children in the preschool—especially the other boys. Renee's mother may express concern about whether Renee is socially popular, a leader, or bright. Parents might be touchy about anyone other than the school staff observing and recording their child's behavior and developmental progress. This is especially true if the child has any characteristics that set him apart from others in a way that the parents view as unfavorable. Such sensitivity on the parents' part must be matched by your own equal, if not greater, sensitivity. You must protect the child's and the parents' privacy, and you must give careful consideration to their feelings.

There is one guiding principle that is worth mentioning, perhaps because it is so easily and so frequently violated, and because it seems to cover so many situations in which ethics play a part. The principle is this: Do not communicate (talk, write, use nonverbal gestures) about any child to anyone other than the person who gave you permission to observe. ("Anyone" here includes your roommate, your best friend, your parents....) Furthermore, if you do discuss a young child with some appropriate individual, be certain that the child in question, any of the other children, and any other adults do not overhear what you say. Remember, when it comes to young children, "Little pitchers have big ears."

This principle does not rule out discussing a child privately with an instructor or in a formal classroom setting, when the purpose is to aid your understanding of the child or the observation process, or to solve problems you may be encountering in doing the observations. Such discussions can still be carried on without violating the child's and the parents' rights to privacy and confidentiality.

Privacy, confidentiality, and rights also include the right of parents not to have their child be a subject of observation. Therefore, if any parents do not want their child observed and information about him recorded, you are obligated not to do so. It may be less obvious, but if a child does not want to be observed, the same ethical constraints apply as when parents refuse their child's participation. This leads to the issue of permission.

Permission extends beyond just the specific target of observation and study. You should not—indeed may not—walk unannounced and uninvited into a classroom to do your exercises. Prior permission is always necessary; at the very least, it is a sign of courtesy and respect for the teachers, staff, and children. In some instances, it can also be a matter of trespassing on private property. Gander and Gardner (1981) suggest that written permission be obtained when observing in schools. The district supervisor or principal and the teacher can grant such permission. Gander and Gardner also point out that school officials act *in loco parentis* ("in place of the parents"), and additional permission from the parents is therefore not necessary. Some schools have parents sign a form stating whether or not any outsiders may observe their child. This form is usually kept on file at the child care center or classroom.

In situations where adult roles are less clearly defined than they are in the schools (e.g., in clubs, Sunday schools, and similar organizations), Gander and Gardner recommend that permission (written and signed) be obtained from those in charge and from the parents. If you observe in a public place, such as a park, swimming pool, or playground, permission is not necessary. Nonetheless, even public settings require that you be unobtrusive; you are not permitted to disturb others, to try to get children to perform for you, or in any way to violate the rights of others in the setting. It is further suggested that, in a public place, if you are going to record the behaviors of children whose parents are present, you explain what you are doing and ask their permission (Gander & Gardner, 1981). Asking is a gesture of courtesy, and it may help avoid suspicion.

Professional Behavior

Professional ethics demand that you behave at all times in a professional manner. This is a significant and weighty obligation, for it requires that, when necessary, you set aside your own personal preferences and wishes. Always act in accordance with the legitimate requirements and expectations (1) of the observation setting; (2) of those individuals in that setting and, in the case of minors, of those persons responsible for them; (3) of the faculty and institution whom you represent; and (4) of the observation exercises themselves. This last item refers to being intellectually honest in the performance of your exercises. In other words, be faithful to the discipline and subject matter of which your observations are a part.

Factors That Affect Observation

Observation consists of seeing certain things and recording what you have seen in a way that can be used for a particular purpose. Making meaningful, useful observations is not an easy task. There are a number of factors that can affect your observations.

Sensitivity and Awareness

Earlier, we discussed how sensitivity to children changes with experience and training, which are long-term influences. However, there are more immediate influences that can limit your sensitivity and awareness and possibly bias your observational data and interpretations. At this very moment, you possess a particular understanding or, as Lay and Dopyera (1977) put it, a "set of understandings or discriminations that you are capable of making about any child you encounter" (p. 70). Whatever your level of skill or understanding, there will be times and conditions when you will not observe at the level of which you are capable. Certain things will interfere with how you see the subject of your observations.

Fatigue, Illness, and Discomfort

Fatigue is an obviously limiting condition, as are illness, physical discomfort, and psychological disturbances. These conditions can distract you and take your attention away from the task at hand. You can also be distracted by psychological disturbances such as personal problems, anxieties and fears, or trying to do too much at once. Sometimes disturbances will come from the external environment and can limit your perception—noise, temperature extremes, poor lighting, or crowded conditions. Many of these variables will be beyond your personal control, but your ability to recognize the effects they have on you can be invaluable. At the very least, you will be able to identify potential sources of distraction and other types of error and, if possible, offset them in some way.

One way to offset the effects of these conditions is to try to avoid them altogether. For instance, fatigue, illness, or discomfort might justify postponing your observation until those conditions are remedied. If that is not possible or feasible, you might try doing several observations at different times. In either case, the chances are that your observations and written reports will be more objective and accurate than they would otherwise be. Keep in mind that children also suffer from fatigue, illness, and discomfort. Although these conditions are part of being human, and they are certainly of concern to all early childhood educators and other professional child care workers, sometimes the bias they impose on children's behavior and general functioning will work against you meeting your observation purposes or goals. Again, taking the steps discussed here might alleviate the situation.

The Influence of Self or Personality

Perhaps one of the most difficult factors influencing observations is your own self or personality, a problem Lay and Dopyera (1977) refer to as "sorting out 'you' from what you view" (p. 72). Our individual experience, attitudes, needs, desires, and fears tend to act as filters through which we not only process what we observe, but that also affect what we notice in the first place. An observer may, for example, have a tendency to project his own feelings onto a child; he may believe that the child feels what he thinks he felt as a child or would feel in the present situation. Or a teacher may tend to dislike or like someone who has certain characteristics or exhibits certain kinds of behaviors. These biases can influence the teacher or observer to pay either too little or too much attention to certain aspects of the child's behavior or personality and obstruct perception of other equally important features. This seems to be especially true when the behaviors or characteristics are disliked or considered taboo by the observer. In such a case, there is an inclination to be turned off by a child who displays these traits. Such a negative reaction can be a powerful determinant of how you see and interpret that child's behavior. This becomes important again during the evaluation process.

Controlling our Biases

We all have biases, and although they cannot be completely eliminated, we can be conscious of them and take steps to control them. It is very important that the traits or characteristics that we like or dislike, easily accept or do not easily accept, do not cause us to lose our objectivity. It is particularly important not to pass judgment on children or make evaluative statements that reflect poorly on their character or worth.

To say, as an example, that a child is aggressive or dependent, meaning that he is to be thought of forever thereafter as having an aggressive or dependent personality, is not part of your observation exercises. However, you certainly may describe aggressive or dependent *behavior* when a child displays it. The focus on behavior can be illustrated by the now well-known advice to parents on how to respond to a child's misbehavior: Do not tell the child that she is a bad girl. Tell her that what she did is wrong. The behavior is the focus of criticism, not the basic worth and character of the individual. Positive self-esteem should always be reinforced in the child's mind, despite lapses into behavior that adults find undesirable.

Although it was stated previously that "we can be conscious of [our biases] and take steps to control them," we must also say that one of the problems with biases is that they do not necessarily jump up and bite us on the nose. They often operate outside of our conscious awareness, similar to the way we can be critical or sarcastic and express sincere surprise and disbelief when a friend (or enemy) tells us that we are, in fact, critical or sarcastic. It is not always possible (and certainly not easy) to identify our biases or the reasons we have them. But maybe there are occasions when it is more important to recognize other behaviors that might be founded on an unconscious bias and deal with those rather than with the bias itself.

For example, suppose that for whatever reason, you particularly dislike aggressive children, or aggressive behavior of any kind, no matter who displays it. (Or it might be dependent behavior that especially irks you. Or perhaps you dislike children who do not come to school looking as neat and clean as you think they should; select your own bias.) This means that you might have a tendency to overgeneralize from your observations of a child's aggressive behavior and label the child as aggressive (or dependent or dirty). In other words, you have gone from seeing an aggressive episode to judging a child's personality or character. Although you may not understand why you dislike aggressiveness, you can always search for and root out language that reflects an overgeneralization or hasty conclusion based on very limited evidence.

Influence of the Setting or Situation

Other factors that could influence your observations are those imposed on you by the setting and the individuals in it. These include such things as the size and arrangement of the physical space; the equipment and materials available to the children and, in some cases, to you; and the characteristics, skills, and personalities of the children. The size and arrangement of the space can limit your observations by making it difficult to stay close to a given child or to be inconspicuous. Equipment and materials have an influence by providing, or failing to provide, children the means of exercising their skills and pursuing their interests. Characteristics of the children affect what you can do in the setting because they help determine the kinds of behaviors that will be exhibited. Some children may be active physically, others passive and inactive; some may talk a lot, others little; some may interact a great deal with their peers, others hardly at all. The presence of various behaviors can provide you with examples of what you want to observe. Whether the absence of certain behaviors is to your disadvantage depends on your objectives. For example, if Tasha typically avoids her classmates, that avoidance might give you valuable information about her self-concept, her social skills, or her status among her peers. If, however, your aim is to observe normal or more extensive social behaviors and interactions, you may have to select another child.

Categories of Errors in Recording Observations

There are three categories of errors you can make in recording your observational data: (1) errors of omission, (2) errors of commission, and (3) errors of transmission (Richarz, 1980).

Errors of Omission

Errors of omission occur when you leave out information that is helpful or necessary to understanding a child's behavior. If your objectives call for it, you should include enough information to provide a complete picture of what happens during a behavioral episode. Such a picture helps you form broader and more generalized conceptions of a particular child than would otherwise be possible. Consider the following example.

Millard, a four-year-old preschooler, is playing by himself in the sandbox with a small dump truck. While he is playing, Kent comes over and, without saying a word, grabs the truck out of Millard's hand. You happen to look over toward the sandbox just as Millard hits Kent and grabs the truck. How might you describe and interpret this episode? You could decide that Millard had behaved aggressively toward Kent, and you might continue to observe the behaviors of the two children. The point here is that something important would be missing if you had accepted the incident as it appeared. Your interpretation of Millard's behavior as aggressive would be premature and not quite correct. You would have left out the critical incident of Kent initiating the aggressive action. Some would call Millard's response assertiveness. Missing part of a behavioral sequence or interaction may not make your objective description invalid; you could record very accurately the behaviors and events you did happen to observe. But remember that it is not just the descriptions that are important; they must acquire a meaning that will help you understand the child and his behavior. In the example of Millard, the meaning of his actions toward Kent would have been significantly altered, if not distorted, by leaving out the critical segment of behavior. You will describe for a purpose, and part of that purpose will be to understand the broader context of the behavior.

There are many reasons that errors of omission are made: various distractions, simply missing behaviors that have already occurred (as in the preceding example), or poor note-taking. Note-taking is heavily influenced by the passing of time. You may not be able to take many (or any) notes during the observation session and therefore may have to rely on memory. The longer you wait to record your observations, the more you are likely to forget. Naturally, this argues for writing up your notes as quickly as possible. A very important factor is the particular way you see what you are observing: what and how much you perceive; whether what you notice is meaningful to you and, in your opinion, worth writing down; and the relationship between what you see and the purpose of your observations at the time.

Errors of Commission

In contrast, errors of commission occur when you include more information than is actually present in the situation. This involves such things as reporting that behaviors, speech, or interactions took place when in fact they did not, or reporting that certain persons were in the setting/situation when they were not present at all. These errors are also made for a number of reasons, including inattention, relying on a faulty memory, and those factors that contribute to errors of omission. It is not always easy to catch these errors, particularly when they stem from your individual way of seeing. We all have gaps in our perception and understanding, or at least they may be thought of as gaps by someone who sees things differently from the way we do.

Errors of Transmission

The third category is called errors of transmission. In this case, the fault lies in recording the behaviors you observe in improper sequence. This can be a serious mistake, for it is frequently the order of events that gives them meaning: What happens at 9:20 A.M. can influence what happens at 9:35 A.M., and so on. The chances of making this type of error can be reduced if you record the time at which you observe a particular behavior. Under some circumstances, you can record the times at which a given behavior begins and ends, or the time at which you start and stop observing and recording a behavior. This can be done for each behavior, event, and interaction that you observe throughout the entire period. Besides reducing errors of transmission, timing behaviors gives you information about such aspects as the length of the child's attention span and the proportion of time the child spends on particular activities.

Three Aspects of the Observation Process

If you are careful to avoid these errors, accurate and reliable observation is possible. There are three aspects of the observation process that, if you keep them clearly in mind, will increase your accuracy and reliability: (1) objective description, (2) interpretation (inference or explanation), and (3) evaluation.

Objective Description

This is the foundation of observation because so much else depends on it. Objective description, sometimes referred to as reporting, consists of recording what you see as precisely and completely as possible. However, the term *completely* must be considered in relation to your specific purposes. There are occasions when you will want a great deal of information, which will therefore require a great deal of recording. On other occasions, your purpose may be satisfied by just recording whether a specific response has occurred, as in the case of recording how often children act "aggressively." The key word here is *objective,* which the *American Heritage Talking Dictionary* (1995) defines as "Having actual existence or reality.... Uninfluenced by emotions or personal prejudices: *an objective critic.*" Objective reporting leaves out your interpretations, evaluations, impressions, and speculations, and the descriptions of what you see and hear would be agreed to by anyone observing the same scene. For instance, the statement "Carlita climbed on a tricycle and rode across the room for about ten feet.

The trike tipped over; Carlita fell off and began to cry" is an objective description. Another observer would describe the events much the same way. It is important to remember that absolute objectivity is not possible. Each of us views the world from a bias or perspective that differs from someone else's. In the case of the Carlita example, just being able to describe Carlita as "riding a trike across the room" requires knowledge of tricycles and of what is meant by "riding." An acceptable level of objectivity is possible, however, in part because we in this culture share common language, values, norms, and experiences; therefore, most of us understand riding trikes.

When does objective description occur? Objective description occurs at the time you are actually recording behavior and are using the narrative description, event sample, anecdotal record, or diary description recording methods. These methods require you to describe in as much detail as possible only what you are seeing or hearing, without any embellishment or interpretation. Reasonable objectivity is achieved if several observers' descriptions are pretty much in agreement. In such recording methods as checklists, rating scales, frequency counts, or duration records, objectivity must be achieved at the time you construct the recording instrument. So, for example, the items in a checklist must describe or represent behaviors that are directly observable, rather than such things as moods, feelings, and intentions or motives, which are not directly observable and must be inferred from direct observations.

Interpretation/Explanation

Interpretation means going beyond your objective descriptions and trying to explain or give them some meaning. If, in the Carlita example, you were to add "because she was hurt," that would be an interpretation, especially if Carlita herself had not indicated that she was hurt. The "because she was hurt" is an interpretation (possibly an accurate one) because it goes further than simple description. You and your roommate, for example, might disagree about whether Carlita was hurt; your roommate could interpret her crying as resulting from fear or frustration rather than pain or injury.

Interpretation or explanation, then, involves attempts to identify the cause of some behavior or event; to assign motives to an individual; to determine the objectives of a behavior; in short, to provide any additional information that might make your objective descriptions more meaningful than they would otherwise be. Such additional information also includes or comes from one's knowledge of child development and developmental theory. The role of theory becomes rather obvious, for example, when, in the context of interpretation, one tries to offer some possible reasons or explanations for a child's behavior. The main point is that wherever the information comes from, it moves the observer from what has been observed to—it is hoped—some deeper understanding of the behavior's meaning or significance.

When does interpretation occur? Interpretation can occur at various times, depending upon the recording technique. In the narrative description, for instance, interpretation takes place only after behavior has been objectively recorded because in the narrative description, any and all behavior is a legitimate focus of your observations. It is after your data have been recorded that you might want or need to interpret the meaning of the behavior with respect to a child's developmental progress, adjustment to a particular setting, or for other appropriate reasons.

In the event sample, anecdotal record, and diary description, some interpretation is needed prior to actually recording any behavior. You must decide whether that behavior fits your definition of an event (event sample), is atypical or unusual enough to warrant anecdotal recording (anecdotal record), or is a new behavior that adds to your understanding of the developing child (diary description).

In the remaining recording techniques (checklists, rating scales, frequency counts, and duration records), interpretation is also needed at the time of recording. You must decide whether an observed behavior does or does not fit into any of the descriptive categories you have selected for inclusion in the recording instrument. Of course, further interpretation might be called for if you want to use your data to make decisions about children's overall developmental progress or simply to understand the possible meaning of a child's behavior in a particular situation.

Evaluation

This third aspect of observation is possibly the most dangerous part of the observation process, for it is at this point that you apply your values and attitudes to the child's behavior, characteristics, and personality. Evaluation refers to placing a value on, or judging the worth of, something. Unfortunately, it is all too easy to make hasty judgments or to form stereotypes about someone. Once we have the stereotype, there seems to be no need to learn more about the individual and possibly to modify our opinion of him based on further contacts and interactions.

The groundwork for evaluation is already laid during the observation and recording process, for it is there that such terms as *dependent, aggressive,* and *anxious* are used to describe and explain behavior. What is critical here is that terms such as these are often used in careless ways. They can be legitimate concepts, but they should always be strongly linked with observable behavior. Moreover, labeling a child as lazy, for example, does not explain the child or his behavior. "Lazy" is a convenient way of summarizing one's views or attitudes about a child. What has to be described are the behaviors that led to the decision to call him lazy. What has to be explained are the reasons for those behaviors.

Derogatory labels such as "lazy," "dull," and "unattractive" should not be in the observer's written vocabulary. Any conclusions concerning a child's general characteristics or traits should be based on frequent, representative, and objectively described samples of behavior. This advice applies to both positive and negative attributes.

When does evaluation occur? Evaluation almost always occurs after you have acquired your observation data because you need time to interpret that data to make decisions or draw conclusions. Evaluation should go well beyond forming impressions about such things as a child's personality or abilities and labeling him or her dependent, aggressive, or using other such descriptors. We need to recognize what appears to be a natural human tendency, which is to summarize our perceptions and impressions of other people through the use of convenient descriptive labels. Thus, we might refer to some people as charming and intelligent and to others as boring and stupid. When it comes to young children, however, it is absolutely critical not to apply labels to them, especially negative, derogatory labels. Moreover, labels can be like stereotypes, which frequently consist of hasty decisions about a person or group that are false or incomplete because at best they are based on anecdotal evidence. One undesirable consequence of a label or stereotype is that we have no incentive to learn more about the person or group or to seek evidence that contradicts our hasty, false, or incomplete impressions and perceptions. This is why repeated observations are essential to understanding children's personalities, abilities, and developmental progress.

Consequently, evaluation is most useful and appropriate for making program or curriculum decisions regarding the kinds of experiences and environments that will best promote children's optimal growth and development. In this light, you can see why evaluation must take place after you have the appropriate quantity and quality of observation information.

GROUP OR INDIVIDUAL OBSERVATION

The distinction between individual and group observation is an important one. It represents a distinction between data that are useful for one purpose and data that are useful for quite a different purpose.

Limitations of Group Observation

First, it is virtually impossible to observe a group and gain significant information about specific individuals. Meaningful observation of specific individuals is similar to having a meaningful conversation. You can listen to only one person at a time, and only one person can speak at a time; otherwise, the conversation becomes incomprehensible. If you wish to observe even as few as two children simultaneously, you must watch first one child, then the other, shifting your attention back and forth between them.

Observing more than one individual at a time makes sense when there is an interaction going on. When two individuals are influencing or responding to each other, the interaction and its context also become important. There is an inseparable relationship between behavior and the setting in which it occurs. Behavior is influenced and governed by the characteristics of the setting, which include the nature, purpose, and location of the interaction, and the specific persons involved. Your comments in a conversation are governed in part by the other person's comments, by where you are, and by the topic of conversation.

A peer group working together on a project.

Keep in mind that if you observe a group, you will be unable to obtain much information about individuals. You can study the behavior of groups as well as the behavior of individuals in groups, but it is necessary to consider the differences. Some of what we have just said can be qualified by considering the use of today's available technology. Videotaping, for instance, provides nearly unlimited repeated observation of a group's (or a child's) behavior and activities. The rewind mode of the VCR or DVD means that you can concentrate on the behaviors of every child in a given group, and you can do so at your leisure. The potential loss of information that results from having to shift your attention back and forth between children has been remedied by the videotape. Nonetheless, we would still point out that even with videotape viewing, each rewind and replay represents an actual shift in your attention from one child to another. The tape has simply greatly expanded the time you have to make the shift, thereby allowing observation for as long as is necessary to obtain the information you desire or need. Schickedanz, Schickedanz, Hansen, and Forsyth (1993), for example, corroborate this advantage of videotaping when, in discussing the specimen record (narrative description) technique of recording observations, they write, "This technique was extremely difficult before audio and video technology gave the researcher the tools with which to observe a moment in a child's life over and over again" (p. 26).

A word of caution, however: It is easy to become enthralled by technology, especially if it appears to make our jobs easier to perform or if it appears to give us data of a depth and scope that are not otherwise possible. It is our contention that a videotape can never take the place of a skilled observer, no matter how sophisticated the technology might eventually become. For one thing, the tape that has recorded young children's behavior in a child care setting is no better than the individual viewing that tape. It is not the video camera that does the seeing or the hearing. It is human eyes, ears, and brains that ultimately have to make sense out of what the camera has captured. Videotaping is extremely limited when compared to the freedom and flexibility an observer has to have when applying his or her skills "while on the move," so to speak. It is difficult, and in some cases impossible, to take a camera into all observation environments, nor would it always be desirable to do so. With a videotape, you have frozen in time a relatively small segment of the behavioral stream, but you cannot freeze the entire stream, any more than you can with more mundane observational techniques. However, this is not the purpose of observation. The best we can hope for is to find representative samples of children's behavior from which we can draw reasonable, meaningful conclusions that help us better understand the children in our care.

In the final analysis, you have to do the observing, not the camera. Whatever use videotaping has in the observation of young children, its use, in this writer's view, is at best secondary to the goal of acquiring and refining personal observational skills.

What Is a Group? Perspective One

A group is sometimes defined as a collection of individuals who are assembled in a particular place. This simplest of groups has no purpose around which it is formally structured; it merely consists of a number of persons who happen to be in the same place at the same time. However, you will recognize that they could gather together for common reasons, such as to shop or watch a sporting event. Of much greater interest is the true group, which is a collection of individuals who are organized around a common purpose and who have an identifiable social structure.

Some groups are formed by an outside authority or agency. A school system establishes kindergartens, elementary schools, and high schools; a community agency, church, or parents' group sets up a nursery school, and so on. Such groups can be referred to as institutional groups (Brandt, 1972). This kind of formal group can contain subgroups that are spontaneously formed by the members themselves. Membership is often determined by mutual interests and common characteristics. "Mutual interests and common characteristics" can include age and developmental level, two factors specified by Bukatko and Daehler (1995) when they define a peer as "a companion who is approximately the same age and developmental level" (p. 564). Their further comments on peers and peer groups are instructive:

> Peers, however, usually function as equals, and it is primarily among equals that children can forge such social skills as compromising, competing, and cooperation. Thus, experiences with peers afford the child unique opportunities to construct social understanding and to develop social skills. (p. 564)

This description suits those settings where the children tend to be homogeneous with respect to age and developmental level. But such homogeneity does not always prevail, thus limiting the usefulness and applicability of the concept of the peer group.

A preschool class, for example, could be an institutional group; a public kindergarten and elementary school class are clearly institutional groups because of their connection to the larger educational system. The third-grade classes of two city schools could comprise peer groups. But three children who play together in Mrs. Martin's preschool are also a peer group. This kind of group could be the focus of your observations.

The following discussion of the question "What is a group?" might require a background or an interest that some readers may not have. Therefore, Martin and O'Connor's (1989) systems approach to the study of groups can be omitted without doing harm to the reader's overall understanding of groups or to his or her ability to observe them. We offer the lengthier treatment of a group's characteristics for those who want to delve more deeply into the dynamics of group functioning.

What Is a Group? Perspective Two

There is another way of defining or looking at the concept of group that is worth a little bit of discussion. Patricia Yancey Martin and Gerald G. O'Connor (1989), who take a systems perspective on social phenomena, identify the characteristics of small groups based on what they define as a group's four components. These are of interest because they can provide a framework within which to put your observations of children's group behavior. We adapt these authors' broad and somewhat theoretical views on groups to fit the case of children.

GROUP COMPONENTS

Component One: Member Characteristics

"*Member characteristics* are the properties, or qualities, of individuals who belong to groups" (Martin & O'Connor, 1989, p. 165; italics original). The authors cite a number of individual characteristics that are of significance to observers of young children.

There are the demographic characteristics of age, gender, race, ethnic and cultural heritage, and religious commitment. They also cite the extremely important factors of "unique family and developmental biography and a distinctive psychological makeup and style" (p. 165). Also included in member characteristics are "feelings of self-concept or self-esteem" (p. 165). These feelings translate into differences in assertiveness, in how loudly or persistently a child will talk, and so on. The length of time a child has belonged to a specific group is also important and can have a bearing on how that child behaves in the group.

The premise here is that these member characteristics affect how a group will engage in various activities, as well as the outcomes of those processes. Think of this premise as essentially meaning that all stimuli to which the group responds, all behaviors displayed by the group, as a group, fundamentally depend upon the characteristics, abilities, personalities, and so on of its individual members. They are the filters through which all inputs come into the group and outputs leave the group. Think of it this way: There can be no track team if the persons who are to make up that team cannot run. A group of preschoolers cannot be a goal-striving group if the individual members do not have the wherewithal to accomplish the necessary tasks leading to the final goal.

Consider the following illustration: A group of four, four-year-olds wants to engage in some imaginary play in which one of the children is a doctor, another is a nurse, and the other two are patients. It may matter very little whether or not these children have accurate knowledge about what physicians and nurses actually do; it is, after all, *their* fantasy, and they have no obligation to conform precisely to reality. The "doctor" can do doctor things as he or she sees fit. But it may make a difference to the success of their play if they can agree on who will assume each of the required roles. If each child wants to be the doctor, or the nurse, or the patient, and if each is unyielding in his or her insistence on playing that specific role, the imaginary play will never happen. It is then that "all behaviors displayed by the group, as a group, fundamentally depend upon the characteristics, abilities, personalities, and so on of its individual members."

Component Two: Member Behaviors

Member behaviors are defined very simply by Martin and O'Connor (1989) as "the actions of individuals in a group," although they add "during group meetings" (p. 165). We can replace this last phrase by "during group activities" or "during group interactions." Martin and O'Connor emphasize that member behaviors will differ according to the basic purpose of the group—a task group, for instance, as opposed to a play group. It is essential to note that, according to the authors, "member behavior is necessary for group development" and that "without member behaviors, individuals remain isolated and a group never forms" (p. 165).

Member behaviors appear so basic a requirement that you might wonder why Martin and O'Connor even mention it. For our purposes, we would only ask you to keep in mind that not just any collection of individuals constitutes a group. There must be some consistent behaviors that "connect" members in some meaningful way. Furthermore, as we discuss later, an essential characteristic of a group is the relationships, or relationship patterns, that eventually form and distinguish not only one group from another, but also distinguish a group from a nongroup.

Component Three: Group Contextual Characteristics

"*Group contextual characteristics* are the properties of a group as a system that are relatively constant or enduring" (Martin & O'Connor, 1989, p. 167, italics original). These characteristics "include the social, relationship, and procedural phenomena that *emerge* through members' individual and interpersonal behaviors" (p. 167, italics original).

Group contextual characteristics depend upon the interactions among group members, which lead to the development of such things as "group goals, rules, procedures, a common identity, shared standards for assessing both each other's and the group's actions and progress, and so on" (p. 167). Martin and O'Connor (1989) identify three contextual characteristics of small groups: group norms, group climate, and "a group's normal round of procedures" (p. 167). These deserve some discussion.

Group norms are shared standards for appropriate behavior. As Martin and O'Connor put it, "norms have a *should* quality to them" (p. 167, italics original). It is important to point out that norms are often associated with roles, which are recurring patterns of behavior that are in turn associated with a position in a social group. (For example, the social position of teacher requires such role behaviors as giving instructions, handing out assignments, and giving grades.) Of potential interest to the observer of young children is Martin and O'Connor's claim that "certain aspects of the *role of group member* are normative, that is, they are required because of shared expectations for members' behavior, whereas others are not" (p. 167, italics original). For example, a preschool group may have the (adult-generated) expectation that there be no behaviors such as pushing or other forms of aggression, but there may be no particular expectation regarding the kinds of games or activities the group should engage in.

Group climate is very close if not identical in meaning to our concepts of setting, situation, and context. Martin and O'Connor (1989) define *group climate* as "the shared socioemotional atmosphere or mood of a group" (p. 168). You should recognize that a group's climate can remain relatively stable or it can change. Changes can be the result of things that happen within the group as such, or that affect the group in relation to its environment (Martin & O'Connor, 1989, p. 168). For example, an especially dominant child might leave a group, which could leave the group without an effective leader. The effects of that situation depend, of course, on a number of factors, but the broad effects could be a dramatic change in how the group behaves, the goals or tasks it undertakes, and even whether the group stays together at all.

Moving the group to another environment (climate) can also change the dynamics and relationship patterns for the better or for the worse. Different equipment and materials in the new setting, for instance, might change the group's behavior and possibly even its leadership. In a former setting, one child may have been the leader because of his or her skill with a particular piece of equipment. In a new setting, a different child may be especially competent with yet a different piece of equipment, thus gaining the group's deference with respect to its use and role in the group's functioning. The possibilities are great indeed.

A group's normal round of procedures is, according to Martin and O'Connor, "the agenda of typical or routine activities that a group follows to accomplish its goals" (p. 168). Preschool groups may establish such rounds of activities if they exist long enough for the members to reach this kind of agreement and settled routine. Of course, it is also possible that the simple addition of a new but dominant member might change the round for as long as that individual is present in the group. That is to say, a group's normal round of procedures depends on the group's purposes as well as on all of the components being discussed.

Component Four: Group Episodes

Group episodes, say Martin and O'Connor (1989), are "shared, system-level events, incidents, or happenings that occur in groups that are characterized by continuous activity" (p. 168). The authors present an informative analogy for thinking about group episodes: "Episodes are like scenes in a play; each has distinctive content and meaning but can be understood fully only in relation to the total 'drama' or group context" (p. 168). The concept of episode reflects the extreme importance of context in understanding behavior. Indeed, it can be said that an individual's behavior ultimately has meaning only in some social context or other. This is so because human beings can seldom, if ever, totally remove themselves from the social environment or from the already existing influences of such an environment.

It is assumed here that as "a series of shared events," episodes "are more than the discrete acts and behaviors of individual members" (Martin & O'Connor, 1989, p. 168). Essentially, this means that episodes depend for their meaning or significance on the relationships among the group members rather than on the actions of any particular person or persons in the group. Martin and O'Connor (1989) assign episodes the very important role of giving "meaning to members' behavior and help[ing] them interpret and make sense of what is said and done" (p. 168).

Your observation exercises will use the episode concept. According to the concept, children's behavior, as individuals, can make sense only when viewed from the perspective of the larger group and its influence on each individual member. Each member's behavior connects with someone else's behavior, which is how relationships are established. Ultimately, a network is constructed in which the behavior of a number of individuals combines or interacts to produce what we call a group. Sarah's behavior while in the group is affected by, say, Mark's behavior. Staying with Martin and O'Connor's analogy, Sarah and Mark are actors in a play. One does or says something as a result of what the other has done or said, like following the directions of a script. Most importantly, Sarah's behavior, as an individual, makes the most sense when it is considered in relation to Mark's behavior. This relationship is the group episode, or it forms part of a larger group episode. Relationships also make behavior social; their absence effectively leaves behavior asocial (or nonsocial).

SOME APPROACHES TO GROUP OBSERVATION

As Almy and Genishi (1979) point out, "Teachers have always known that every group of children has its own distinctive qualities. Like individuals, each group or class is unique." Each group also has distinctive influences on its members; therefore, the group is part of the setting. Here is an example:

Julie, Erica, and Floyd often form a small play group. Their activities are varied, ranging from dramatic play, where Floyd nearly always plays the daddy and Julie and Erica take turns being the mommy, to building with big blocks, where there is no set or consistent pattern of interaction among the three children. They seldom quarrel, and any disagreements tend to be short-lived. None of the three children seems to emerge as a leader.

From time to time, Erica also participates as a member of another group, this one consisting of herself, Roger, and Tanya. However, these three children seem more restricted in their activities. They seldom play house because arguments usually break out between Erica and Tanya over who will play the mother. Roger does not like to build with blocks, and the girls do not press for that activity. Tanya seems more of a leader than a follower, although Erica will occasionally challenge her attempts to lead. This second group does not play together for the relatively long periods of time that characterize the play of the first group.

How could you approach these two different situations?

One way would be to concentrate on the behaviors of each child as an individual. You would notice the different responses, play patterns, and peer relationships, but they would be put solely in the context of the individual. Thus, you could describe Erica's behavior in each of the two groups: what she said and how she said it, her gross and fine muscle activities, her social and emotional responses, and so on.

A second approach would be to observe individual behaviors, as before, but place them within the larger framework of the three-person groups in which they occurred. Now Erica's behavior is seen in light of its group context. You might notice, for instance, that her language usage differs, depending on which group she is in at the time. You might try to describe the relationship between her language and the characteristics of the group and its members. It would also be of interest to examine other interaction patterns and attempt to explain them, perhaps on the basis of the children's differing personalities or the different way the teacher treats the two groups.

A third approach would be to look primarily at the group itself, taking less account of the behaviors of each single member and more account of how the three children are acting as a single unit. You could describe the group as though it were an individual, even attributing to it characteristics or traits—a friendly group, a hostile group, or a hardworking group.

Children behave differently in different groups and situations.

Behavior can be significantly influenced by the larger group, although such influence is not always dramatic. Some children take very little part in the group life of their peers, seemingly preferring to focus their attention and energy on trying to please adults (e.g., see Almy & Genishi, 1979). Groups, in turn, react differently to different individuals. Some children are not readily accepted into a group, whereas others are not only accepted but quickly become leaders. As illustrated in the previous example, children behave differently in different groups and situations. We have all known someone who acted so differently from what we are accustomed to that we tried to explain the unusual behavior by saying it was her companions that caused the change in her personality.

Your Goals in Observing Groups

The preceding discussion emphasizes the need to observe children in context and to determine how their actions might change in various settings. All of us belong to a number of groups—a family, school, work organization, and social organizations—and our positions and behaviors vary from one group to another.

Your goals in observing groups will vary, depending on what you want to learn. A goal could be to determine how a child's behavior differs in various groups. In our opinion, leadership and follower patterns in various groups are especially worthy topics for observation. We believe this because in human groups a leader usually either naturally emerges or an individual is selected to lead the group. This being so, it stands to reason that leaders must have characteristics that set them apart from followers. A child may have "charisma," which the *American Heritage Talking Dictionary* (1995) defines as "a rare personal quality attributed to leaders who arouse fervent popular devotion and enthusiasm." In the case of children, such a definition may be an overstatement, but the basic meaning applies. A child might assume the role of leader because of his greater physical size and strength, because he has special expertise or skill, or because he has personality characteristics (friendliness, generosity, an outgoing nature) that make him popular with the other children. Strictly speaking, we suppose, it may be somewhat inaccurate to say that young children really possess the kinds of qualities that are possessed by adults who are considered leaders. On the other hand, leadership must be viewed in the context in which it occurs. It would therefore be equally inaccurate to assess children's leadership behaviors from the perspective of situations and characteristics that tend to define or characterize adult leadership. The same argument is valid for assessing patterns of follower behavior and the characteristics of children who are followers in specific situations.

All of this notwithstanding, you may want to look for answers to such questions as these: How do leaders emerge in different situations and groups? How does leadership change in a given group? How does a particular child express his or her leadership (e.g., through size and strength, skillfulness in social manipulation, and so on)? Is a particular child a leader in all situations or only in some? How do the other children respond to a child's attempts to be a leader? Can you identify specific behaviors or approaches taken by children who try to lead but fail? What seems to turn off the other children to the efforts of these would-be leaders? What behaviors or approaches appear to be successful when used by a particular child?

Sometimes group patterns of behavior might be of interest. These can be discerned through a frequency checklist that records how many children use a particular space or engage in a particular activity (e.g., see Appendix 5). A checklist will not tell you about the dynamics of group interaction, but it will tell you which classroom areas or activities are the most popular and draw the heaviest traffic. This information is important in planning future activities or arranging the physical environment. Very useful information can also be obtained by keeping a record of the particular areas and activities that are used by specific children. A teacher may notice, for instance, that Jonathan usually spends his free play time in the big block area. Repeated observations reveal that Jonathan's fine motor coordination is poor. This could mean that he feels uncomfortable in activities that require skilled hand–eye coordination. As a result, he plays with equipment and materials that involve large muscle groups. Here you have an example of a child matching his abilities with the opportunities provided by a given environment. This information would be relevant to a group observation if the teacher concluded prematurely that Jonathan plays in the big block area because of the other children who play there. In other words, Jonathan's play and social behavior might erroneously be interpreted in terms of group membership rather than in terms of his difficulty in performing fine motor tasks.

Groups and individual behaviors within groups are important aspects of understanding children. Your overall objectives for observing will determine where and how groups fit into your specific observation activity.

SUMMARY

There are a number of steps that must be taken before entering the observation setting. The most important step is determining the purpose of your observation; this will affect everything else you do. Selecting the site of the observation and knowing what you may do in the observation setting are also steps in the preparation process.

The chapter presents a series of questions that you are to ask and answer before you even enter the observation setting:

1. Which developmental area or behaviors are the focus of your observation (physical/motor, social, language, etc.)?

2. How much time are you to spend observing the selected behaviors (several minutes, an hour, for as long as they occur)?

3. Whom are you to observe (individual children, a group, a particular child, several particular children)?

4. How are you to record your observations (checklist, duration record, narrative description, time sampling, event sampling)?

5. What kind of interpretations are you to make (based on a given theory, on what has taken place in the setting)?

Being inconspicuous when observing is very important. Naturalistic observation requires as little interference with children's behavior as possible. There are times, though, when children are asked to behave in particular ways, such as in testing or formal research studies. Your overall observation objectives will determine whether you remain completely separated from the children's ongoing behavior or intervene in some way.

The need for professional ethics cannot be too heavily stressed. Ethics and confidentiality protect the rights and well-being of everyone associated with your observations. Professional ethics is discussed under the general notion of professional behavior.

Making meaningful, useful observations is not easy, and several factors that affect observation are discussed. Your sensitivity to children, fatigue, illness, and discomfort all contribute to what you see when you look at children. However, the most difficult factor influencing observations is your personality—your values, attitudes, experiences, knowledge, and so on. These attributes act as filters through which you process what you see and that affect what you notice in the first place.

The influence of the setting and situation is also discussed. Space size, equipment, materials, people in the space, and how they are arranged will all affect your observations.

Three categories of errors are covered in the chapter. There are errors of omission, commission, and transmission. These errors affect the accuracy and reliability of your observational data. In spite of the possibility of error, however, accuracy and reliability can be achieved, and three aspects of observation are discussed in this regard: objective description, interpretation, and evaluation. Evaluation is characterized as possibly the most dangerous part of the observation process. It is in evaluating a child that you attach a value to her behavior, her character, and even her worth as an individual. Extreme caution is advised, and even positive evaluations must be supported by frequent, representative, and objectively described samples of behavior. In any case, derogatory labels and descriptions must never be part of a child's observation record.

Distinctions are made between individual and group observations. The limitations of observing groups of children are presented, with a significant limitation being the loss of information about specific individuals. It is pointed out that one can study the behavior of groups and the behavior of individuals in groups, but the differences should be borne in mind. Several kinds of groups are defined, but peer groups are the most likely focus of your observations. Several approaches to observing groups are discussed. Some goals of group observation include issues such as documenting changes in children's behavior as they functioned in different groups, leadership and follower behavior patterns in various groups, and assessing the effect of a group on a particular child's behavior.

The concept of group is also discussed by way of viewing a group as characterized by four components: (1) member characteristics, (2) member behaviors, (3) group contextual characteristics, and (4) group episodes. Three specific contextual characteristics of small groups are also discussed: (1) group norms, (2) group climate, and (3) a group's normal round of procedures.

STUDY QUESTIONS

1. Your overall purpose for observing is a key element to success. Identify and discuss some of the problems an observer might encounter if she did not have her objective clearly in mind before entering the observation setting.

2. List some questions concerning professional behavior that you think should be answered before starting to observe in a preschool. How would you answer them?

3. How are interpretation and evaluation related? Which one has to be done first, and why?

4. Why is objective description important to the accuracy and reliability of observation?

5. Give some examples of when group observation is more valuable than individual observation. How would you actually do the observing?

ⓅⓇⒶⒸⓉⒾⒸⒶⓁ ⒺⓍⒺⓇⒸⒾⓈⒺ

This chapter contains a great deal of important information, but most of it is fairly easy to grasp. However, there is one topic that might cause some problems, and that is the topic of groups and how to observe the behavior that occurs in groups. Therefore, it may be useful for you to try out a practical assignment before you get to the more formal observation exercises later on in the text.

On page 84, we describe two groups of three children each. One group consists of Julie, Erica, and Floyd; the other consists of Erica, Roger, and Tanya. A key element here is the fact that Erica belongs to both groups, but the other children are members of only one of the groups. We discuss three approaches one could take to study these two groups and the different situations they present: (1) observe the behavior of each child as an individual, (2) observe individual behaviors but put them within the larger framework of the three-person groups, and (3) look primarily at the groups themselves and deemphasize the behaviors of the individual members.

For your practice exercise, try the following. Go into a setting where groups are likely to occur, and identify two groups of three to four children each. Be careful not to select too large a group, or the observation and recording tasks may become too difficult. It is critical that one of the children be a member of both groups so that in some manner he or she will move back and forth between them as the occasion requires or allows.

Having completed the groundwork, try each of the three approaches. Reread the more detailed description of these approaches found on pages 84 and 85 of the text so that you have a complete idea of what each approach entails and how each is accomplished. It may also be useful to have a discussion with others who are doing the same exercise and to compare your findings, the problems you may have encountered, and so on.

ALTERNATE PRACTICAL EXERCISE FOR CHAPTER THREE

The observation guidelines presented in this chapter define the general framework within which observing and recording behavior take place. This framework establishes such things as (1) the professional[sol]ethical standards to which everyone must adhere; (2) the conditions created by an observer that either work for or against the best interests of the children and the mission of the child care facility (e.g., the issue of conspicuousness); and (3) the factors that can affect the validity and reliability of your observation data (e.g., the observer's bias, personality, mood, physical condition, and various recording errors). Put another way, the observation exercises and recording techniques, by themselves, are only tools in search of the conditions essential for their proper use. These guidelines *are* those necessary conditions.

PART ONE

We suggest the following additional exercise for Chapter 3. Pick several of the guidelines discussed in the chapter, and think of as many possible consequences as you can of not following those guidelines. For instance, what are the possible consequences of trying to observe and record a child's behavior when you are fatigued or in a bad mood? Or what are some of the possible consequences of being more conspicuous in the classroom than is required by your observation assignment or allowed by the child care facility? That is, how might your conspicuousness adversely affect the children's behavior, your observation data, or the proper functioning of the child care center? Think of as many ways as you can of being inappropriately conspicuous. Include the circumstances under which your presence or behavior might be inappropriately conspicuous. Under what circumstances might your presence or behavior not violate this guideline?

INTRODUCTION AND PREPARATION

As a real, practical activity, observation is "all of a piece": It possesses its own integrity or unity, especially when it is done with skill. But like any process, observation consists of parts or elements, each of which must fit well with all the other parts if it is to be successful. The 10 chapters in Part Two discuss what we have chosen to call the elements of observation. The distinction between Part One and Part Two is somewhat arbitrary, for, in fact, developmental theories and the general guidelines for observing children (Chapters 2 and 3) are every bit as much the elements of observation as are the various methods of recording behavior. However, the term *elements* is particularly appropriate in this case because it describes those special components of observation that make possible the objective recording of behavior and the keeping of more or less permanent records. Without such elements, observation remains merely casual watching, similar to what one does while sitting on a park bench or in a restaurant. Unfortunately, this kind of observation is subject to all of the adverse effects of no predetermined observation plan and a fallible memory.

The intent of Part Two is to provide you with at least eight ways of recording behavior in almost any setting or situation. We must stress that none of the methods is of much use without careful prior preparation—preparation that ranges from knowing where you are going to observe, to having some understanding of how children develop, to familiarity with your method of choice and how to use it properly and effectively.

Given all this, we believe that if judiciously studied and reasonably mastered, these elements of observation will, with persistent application, help make you a skilled and astute observer of young children's behavior.

CHAPTER 4

Methods, Behavior, Plans, and Contexts

After reading this chapter, you should be able to

- Relate the concept of method to observation.
- Identify the role of behavior in observation.
- Interpret the relationship of a plan to observation.
- Analyze the relationship between observation and the context in which it occurs.

methods

behavior

setting

situation

context

status

role

HOW TO DO IT: SOME PRELIMINARY THOUGHTS AND CAUTIONS

This chapter discusses the concept of methods of observing and recording children's behavior. **Methods** are the "how-to-do-it" aspects of the observation process.

We go through our lives using methods of one kind or another to accomplish tasks. Any method is in some ways similar to observation—it depends for its success on an individual's skills, knowledge, experience, and other factors that go into making that person who he is. Just as there is more to observation than what meets the eye, there is more to a method than what one reads in a book or hears from a teacher.

A method is a way of doing something. The *American Heritage Talking Dictionary's* (1995) definition gets at some important features of *method:* "A means or manner of procedure, *especially a regular and systematic way of accomplishing something*" (italics added). The words *regular* and *systematic* exemplify the essential character of the observation methods discussed in this text. The term *methodology* is also useful in understanding the concept of method. The *American Heritage Talking Dictionary* (1995) defines *methodology* as "[the] orderly arrangement of parts or steps to accomplish

method

A set of instructions that specifies what one must do to accomplish some task; it may also describe how to do what needs to be done.

an end.... The procedures and techniques characteristic of a particular discipline or field of knowledge."

As defined, methodology can actually refer to the total observation process, which includes all the preparatory steps necessary for successfully observing and recording behavior. Method addresses the specific recording technique to be used. Given all this, then, a method specifies a procedure by which one can accomplish a goal. In this text, a method is considered a set of instructions with two major characteristics: (1) it must specify what one has to do to achieve some objective, and (2) it may also describe how to do what one needs to do to achieve the objective. "What" provides the objective of the instruction, and "how" describes the actions or steps that lead to the accomplishment of the objective. In short, methods are designed to give one the skill, understanding, and knowledge necessary to achieve some end.

Methods can be applied in almost any context and for any reason, as long as some goal or task has to be accomplished. Methods can range from the simple to the relatively complex. Spodeck and Saracho (1994) make the following claim: "Other ways to characterize a good teacher of young children include identifying what such teachers know *as well as what they should be able to do*" (p. 3, italics added). "Able to do," for this writer, specifies the need for some kind of method, or for what Spodeck and Saracho call "techniques." They identify four areas of knowledge that are critical to being a good teacher: "Knowledge of basic health and safety measures; techniques to present activities to children; classroom management techniques; and knowledge of the content of early childhood curriculum" (pp. 3, 5).

The methods associated with keeping children safe and healthy might be considered relatively simple to implement, even though the knowledge on which the method is based may be relatively complex or sophisticated. As Spodeck and Saracho state, "[Teachers] must understand the nature of disease and infection, proper handling of food and materials, and proper sanitary procedures, especially in relation to toileting" (p. 3). Being able to do what is necessary, for example, to keep food preparation areas aseptic involves a method, but a rather simple one.

As a more complicated, contrasting example, suppose that you were asked to intervene in a child care center situation. It is your first day on the job in a local center, and some of four-year-old Margaret's behavior is disruptive and possibly harmful to the other children. Suppose further that this particular center uses behavior modification principles and techniques to change children's undesirable behavior as well as to establish desirable behavior. The head teacher tells you first to determine a frequency baseline for Margaret's target behavior. Then she instructs you to weaken or eliminate the target behavior through the use of nonreinforcement. Finally, she tells you to establish a new behavior, initially on the basis of a continuous reinforcement schedule and gradually going to a variable ratio schedule of reinforcement. Could you do this? Again, it would depend on your understanding of such concepts as baseline frequency, nonreinforcement, and continuous and variable ratio schedules of reinforcement. It would depend further on your ability to implement or apply these principles, to translate them into actual practice.

Consequently, the directions on how to observe and record behavior will be useful only if, first, you understand what the directions mean and how to use them, and second, you know something about the subject to which the method is being applied. You must already have knowledge to acquire more knowledge and skill to acquire more skill. Descriptions of methods will not provide an unerring path to successful observation; none of the techniques is self-evident or self-explanatory, not even to observation experts. Instructions are potentially a means of developing the skill and knowledge needed to use a particular observation and recording method. If that use becomes a natural part of you, your reading about observation methods will have been successful.

Again, critical relationships exist between you and what you see, and between you and any how-to-do-it approach to an activity.

Behavior: A Central Element of Observation and Recording

behavior
Anything an individual does that can be directly observed by one or more of the five physical senses.

Behavior is the major object or focus of everything you will do in observing and recording. What is absolutely crucial to your understanding of the meaning of behavior is that with respect to observing it, you will be focusing on the actions of children as they respond to various stimuli. These stimuli come either from outside themselves or originate from within their own bodies or minds. Pillari (1998), a social worker, captures the essence of behavior—for our purposes—when she defines it as "everything that is potentially *observable* about a person or event" (p. 2, italics added). To put it most simply, behavior will be considered anything an individual does that can be directly seen, heard, smelled, tasted, or touched. The word *directly* means that the behavior you are observing is right there or immediate. Walking, running, eating, and speaking are examples of directly observable behaviors. They involve visible or muscular actions or audible responses. It is behavior, then, that one observes: a child walking around the room, talking to a friend, or painting at an easel.

Behavior Sampling and Observation Plans

Behavior has an important characteristic: It occurs continuously, without ceasing, for as long as one is alive. Even sleeping is a behavior, although it is not as exciting as a hockey game. If one is alive, one is behaving. Herbert F. Wright (1960) captured the continuous quality of behavior when he referred to it as a "stream": "The behavior of a person is a lifelong continuum. It is in the nature of a stream that it can never be seen in its entirety" (p. 73).

Wright's behavior-as-a-stream metaphor is a useful one. Observation can be thought of as entering that stream at some point and taking a sample of the behaviors that flow by. However, entering the stream and taking a sample is somewhat like going

The observation setting—a preschool in action.

shopping. You need a plan to do it successfully. Deciding what to buy and where to buy it is analogous to deciding what behaviors to observe in children (aggression, dependency, language) and where you might find those kinds of behaviors—in a preschool classroom or on a public playground. Deciding how much you are going to buy is like deciding how much of the behavior stream you are going to observe on a given occasion. Finally, you must decide how to get to the store and bring home your purchased goods. This is comparable to choosing an observation method, a way to enter the child's stream and take a sample of the behavior you want.

A question may arise as to what should drive or motivate one's observation objectives. Some might argue that children's needs determine what one observes or why one observes in any child care or early education setting. This is far too restrictive a criterion; it does not account for legitimate purposes for observing young children's behavior other than meeting their immediate needs. To be sure, child care staff are obligated to hold needs as their primary concern, and much of what they observe will be directed toward that end. However, there are students who must observe young children's behavior simply to learn how to observe and do it well. And on occasion, even professional early childhood educators and child care workers conceivably may want and need to observe and record young children's behavior only to refine and hone their observational skills and techniques. To expand on the shopping example, parents may shop for food and clothing specifically for their children, and those needs determine the shopping list. But it is equally true that these parents at some time must shop to meet their own needs as well.

The method you choose will determine some of the other details required by your plan, such as how much of the behavior stream you are going to observe, and the form that the observational data will take. A narrative description, for example, covers a large portion of the child's behavior stream, and the data are in narrative, or raw form. Time sampling deals with smaller portions of the behavior stream, and the final data can be just a check mark indicating whether a given behavior or category of behaviors has occurred.

Your overall plan must always come first. All other decisions follow from that plan.

Settings and Situations

setting
The physical environment in which an observation takes place; it includes such factors as physical space, objects in that space, and opportunities and resources that permit people to behave in certain ways.

situation
The social and psychological characteristics and conditions that exist in a particular setting—the nature of the children's play, events that occur that may change the character of the ongoing activities, and so on.

Setting and **situation** can have different meanings. Setting, for some (Wright, 1960), covers tangible factors such as physical space, the objects in that space, and opportunities and resources that permit individuals to behave in certain ways. An early childhood classroom is a setting because it has observable and measurable physical dimensions located in a specific place. A classroom setting contains equipment and materials that the children can use to behave in particular ways, such as blocks to build with, tricycles to ride, and books to read. For further reference, see NAEYC's *Developmentally Appropriate Practice* (Bredekamp & Copple, 1997).

In contrast to setting, situation is mainly concerned with the social and psychological conditions in the setting. What is the nature of the children's play—active and cooperative, or active and individualized? What kinds of activities are being encouraged by the teacher (or by the children themselves)? What unexpected event may temporarily capture the children's attention and thereby change the ongoing behavior stream?

Settings and situations are related to one another in a special way—situations occur within settings. Settings have physical and social-psychological characteristics. Physical spaces generate feelings in us. We do not respond the same way to every environment. Different people also create different atmospheres.

Wright (1960) made three assumptions concerning the relationship of setting to situation. First, he assumed that some settings are more conducive to certain situations than to others. Some settings, for example, promote certain social interactions better than others. Something as simple as seating arrangements can work for or against children talking to one another.

Second, he assumed that the relationship is not fixed. He noted that although the same setting can support different situations, identical situations can occur in different settings. As an example, two groups of children could use the same setting at different times, and both groups could be active, outgoing, and cooperative. Or, in contrast, one group could be subdued and withdrawn, showing little interaction with materials or among themselves.

The idea of identical situations occurring in different settings is illustrated by the following example. Think of two Head Start classrooms. Each is conducted in a different setting, yet many of the same activities can take place, and much the same warm, supportive atmosphere may characterize both situations.

Finally, Wright assumed that "the behavior of the child at a particular time does indeed depend more directly upon the situation than upon the setting in which it takes place" (p. 77). Wright's third assumption has the most implications for us as observers.

Context

context
A term that combines setting and situation to include all aspects of an environment—time, space, circumstances, other people, and physical and psychological conditions.

status
A position within a social group or organization; teacher, student, child, adult, president, and parent are examples of statuses.

role
Recurring behaviors and behavior patterns that are associated with specific statuses; teachers' role behaviors include teaching, grading, and counseling students, for example; parents' role behaviors include nurturing, protecting, and socializing the child.

The word **context** is more suitable than *setting* or *situation* because context includes setting and situation. Context involves place, time, circumstances, other people, and even psychological and physical conditions. Places, times, and people determine or influence how we behave and feel. Places allow some behaviors but not others. Compare what you may do on the beach with what you may do in an office. Physical space permits some activities yet excludes others. (Can you swim in a bowling alley, for example?) Personal interactions are also affected by context. Individuals occupy statuses within social groups, and those **statuses** require certain behaviors or **roles**. These statuses and roles regulate individuals' behavior toward one another. Think of the relationship between a teacher and a student. The status of teacher requires certain kinds of role behaviors, such as teaching, grading, and counseling students. Student is a different status, with different role behaviors, such as attending class and doing

A situation like story time may occupy some of your attention during observations.

homework. The nature of the student–teacher interaction is largely determined by these statuses and roles.

If you observe children in a preschool classroom, the classroom is the broad context for the children's behavior. But there are smaller settings and situations within the overall classroom context, and these smaller settings may occupy some of your attention during observations. Snack time, story time, free play time, nap time, and the block, art, and sandbox areas are examples of these smaller physical and social environments. These smaller contexts can determine what the children are allowed to do and the behaviors they exhibit.

ⓈⓊⓂⓂⒶⓇⓎ

This chapter discusses the idea of method, which is defined as a set of instructions that tell us what to do to accomplish some task or objective. It is pointed out that methods do not guarantee success. The effectiveness of any method depends on the skills and knowledge of the individual using it. Thus, to acquire knowledge and skill, one must already have knowledge and skill.

Behavior is the central element in all observation of children. Behavior is anything a person does that can be directly seen, heard, smelled, tasted, or touched. Behavior is also discussed in metaphorical terms as a stream that never stops as long as one is alive. Sampling involves entering the child's behavior stream and catching a portion of the behavior flowing by. Plans are the prearranged steps one takes to enter the stream and sample the desired behavior.

Setting and situation are also covered in the chapter. Setting is the physical aspects of the child's environment; situation is the social and psychological characteristics of the environment. Both of these terms are combined into the general term *context*, which includes all the factors that pertain to setting and situation.

ⓈⓉⓊⒹⓎ ⓆⓊⒺⓈⓉⒾⓄⓃⓈ

1. Describe a method you use in a common daily activity. What skills and knowledge are required to use this method? How is the method you have described similar to an observation method? Do they share any characteristics?

2. Why is visible behavior a central part of observation, rather than such things as thoughts or feelings?

3. What is the relationship between plans and methods? Are they similar or dissimilar? How?

4. Describe an imaginary context. How might the characteristics of that context affect the observation of behavior?

5. If you wanted to observe and record such things as thoughts or feelings, how would you have to go about it? What would you have to do to make such observation and recording possible?

PRACTICAL EXERCISES

We suggest the following several exercises to help you better understand the key concepts discussed in Chapter 4.

Think of a behavior or functional area—"functional area" here meaning such things as social, emotional, language, or motor functioning—and describe how that behavior might actually look. Do not observe a child to do this exercise, but simply imagine what you might see a child do or hear a child say that would, for example, illustrate social or emotional behavior. What characteristics might the setting and situation (context) have that would promote or be conducive to such behavior? In what context would you be less likely to see the behavior you have described? What characteristics would the behavior you have described have to have in order for you to be able to observe it directly? What could you not directly observe that still might be associated with social or emotional behavior or development?

Staying with that same behavior, what recording method could you use to give you the most useful information about the child you are observing? It would be best if you did not read the chapters describing the various recording methods or techniques before completing this part of the exercise. Instead, rely on your own ingenuity to devise a recording technique or method that would serve your purposes. If, however, you have already read these chapters, try to devise a method that is not specifically discussed in the text.

Finally, how would you plan your observations to make them most effective? What ingredients would you have to account for in your plan? Under what circumstances could you observe and record a child's behavior with out having a predetermined plan? What recording techniques do you think would be most useful or practical for this unplanned observation session? What recording techniques would be the least useful or practical in such an unplanned observation?

CHAPTER 5

An Introduction to Observation and Recording Methods

ⓄⒷⒿⒺⒸⓉⒾⓋⒺⓈ

After reading this chapter, you should be able to

- Discuss the differences between formal and informal methods of observation.
- Compare open versus closed methods of recording behavior.
- Describe the relationship between the degree of selectivity and the type of method used for recording behavior.
- Identify the role of inference or interpretation in the observation process.

ⓀⒺⓎ ⓉⒺⓇⓂⓈ

formal observation method

informal observation method

raw data

degree of selectivity

inference

METHODS OF OBSERVING AND RECORDING BEHAVIOR: SOME GENERAL CHARACTERISTICS

Eight methods for observing and recording behavior are covered in this text: (1) narrative description, (2) time sampling, (3) event sampling, (4) anecdotal records, (5) diary records, (6) frequency counts, (7) checklists, and (8) rating scales. Each of these procedures has its own characteristics, uses, advantages, and disadvantages; each is best used under certain conditions for certain objectives. Before learning about each method, it is useful to consider several general characteristics of these observation methods.

Goodwin and Driscoll (1980), among others, distinguish between the broad categories of **formal** and **informal observation methods**. These authors also describe several distinctions among formal methods: (1) open versus closed, (2) degree of selectivity, and (3) degree of observer inference required.

formal observation method

A method of observing and recording behavior that is highly structured and controlled; it typically involves a great deal of prior preparation, including the construction of elaborate data forms and training of observers. Formal methods are often used in research studies.

informal observation method

A method of observing and recording behavior that lacks the strict research format of formal methods; it is less structured than a formal method and is suitable for immediate use by teachers and others who can use the method for day-to-day program operation and interactions with children.

Because of their importance in understanding the different methods, we will discuss the general features of formal and informal methods and the distinctions among formal methods.

Formal and Informal Observation

Formal and informal methods of observation differ mainly in how strict the conditions are for using them. Formal methods are conducted in a highly structured manner, which is why they are usually chosen for research studies. Goodwin and Driscoll (1980) outline some of the factors involved in using formal observation methods within a research context. They note that research typically involves the careful definition of categories, developing sophisticated data forms, training observers and ensuring their interreliability, and developing sophisticated procedures for recording, analyzing, and interpreting research data.

The relationship between formal observation and research studies is conveyed by the term *controlled*, which is an alternative to the term *formal*. Research is a highly controlled activity, and when observation is used in research studies, it is also controlled.

Informal methods, in contrast, "are not as structured or as elaborate" an approach to observation (Goodwin & Driscoll, 1980). The strict research format is missing in informal observation; informal methods are therefore more suited to "the planning and daily operation of educational programs." They are also more suited than formal methods to an immediate, intuitive use. This does not mean that attributes such as accuracy and dependability may be sacrificed when using informal methods. But, compared to formal methods, informal ones may be easier and more appropriate to use under some circumstances. Informal observation is also called naturalistic observation, a name that captures the ideas of ease of use and lack of tight control.

Open versus Closed

raw data

Descriptions of behavior and events as they originally occurred.

Recording techniques can be classified according to whether they are open or closed (see Wright, 1960; Goodwin & Driscoll, 1980). Open and closed methods differ in whether they preserve the **raw data** for later analysis. A distinction is appropriate here. Raw data are descriptions of behavior and events as they originally occurred. Pillari (1998), citing Coombs (1964), describes raw data as "bits of information the investigator selects and constructs as empirical facts for further analysis" (p. 2). Data, on the other hand, are described as "the body of facts that have already undergone interpretation according to the investigator's chosen method" (Pillari, 1998, p. 2). So, for example, a narrative description of two children playing together in the big block area is raw data. But if that description is reduced to a check mark on an observation sheet, the raw data are lost, even though, by Pillari's definition, you have preserved data. In short, then, open methods preserve raw data; closed ones do not.

Please note the important connection among data, method, and interpretation. It should be clear that preservation of raw data can be significant, inasmuch as different interpretations can be made of the raw data, thereby yielding different sets of data. However, loss of raw data results in the loss of any data other than that provided by the investigator or observer through interpretation according to some method.

The contrast between open and closed methods can be illustrated by an analogy to two books. Imagine a book containing information about children. Imagine further that although you are permitted to look in this book to learn its contents, you have been given a limited time to do so. Consequently, the best you can do is summarize some of the information using a coding scheme. Furthermore, once you leave the book, it is closed and locked up; there is no going back to read more. Later, you look at your notes and you see that the book talked about aggressive behavior 13 times,

Raw data are descriptions of behavior and events as they originally occurred.

dependency behavior 8 times, and not at all about language behavior. Your summary record might mention children's names, but there is no description of how the aggressions were expressed. You cannot go back to the book and figure out how you came to the decision to note Melinda's hitting Johnny as an aggressive event. Indeed, you have no record of Melinda hitting Johnny at all; you have only a check mark to indicate that aggression occurred. There is no information on the circumstances surrounding the behavior. This is a description of a closed method. The raw data are still in the book, out of your reach.

Imagine a second book that, like the first, contains information about children. You are again permitted to use the book, but this time you are given longer to read. Rather than summarize, you record what you read in as much detail as you can. Now, instead of noting how many times one child behaved aggressively toward another, you describe those aggressive behaviors—who aggressed against whom, in what specific setting and situation, the consequences of the behavior, and so on.

When you leave this second book, it remains open to you. You brought with you so much of the second book that you can examine and reexamine your records and notes. You may come to conclusions about the children and their behaviors that would not have been possible from your summary of the first book. The second book is like an open method—the raw data are in your hands, to use as you wish.

Degree of Selectivity

degree of selectivity
A characteristic of observation and recording methods that determines how many behaviors are targeted for observing and recording. Methods vary from completely unselective (specimen record) to highly selective (such as the event sample).

Degree of selectivity, which is closely related to openness and closedness, determines how many behaviors are targeted for observation and recording. Some methods are very unselective; no specific behaviors are chosen ahead of time, and almost everything that occurs is acceptable for observing and recording. Other methods are the opposite because the observer records only specific behaviors that she has chosen before entering the observation setting. For example, only instances of dependency behavior or of interpersonal exchanges between a child and an adult might be recorded in a closed method. Instances of motor behavior would be disregarded.

Degree of selectivity is comparable to the size of the holes in a fishing net. If the holes are small, you can catch fish of all sizes and kinds. If the holes are large, only the bigger fish will be caught, and the smaller ones will escape through any hole larger than they are. Similarly, if an observation method's degree of selectivity is low, it is like fishing with a small-holed net. You will catch the small details of behavior, context, and sequence. If the degree of selectivity is high, of course, the holes in the observation net are large and will capture only certain behaviors.

This analogy also points up the close relationship between selectivity and the characteristics of openness and closedness. The number of details that can be recorded with a particular method is comparable to the number of fish that can be caught with a particular net. The bigger the holes in the net, the fewer the number of fish; the smaller the holes, the larger the number of fish, because the net is capable of catching big fish as well as small ones.

Degree of Observer Inference Required

inference

A conclusion that is based on directly observable data, premises, or evidence, but is not itself directly observable. The conclusion is reached through a mental process.

Inference means drawing a conclusion based on data, premises, or evidence. For our purposes, inference means the same thing as interpretation or setting out the meaning of something. Inferences or interpretations are essentially conclusions that are based on directly observable data, but are not themselves directly observable. The conclusion is reached through a mental process—a connection is made between information we can perceive directly through our physical senses and some other condition that we cannot learn of in that way.

You say "hello" to a friend, and she makes no response. You might infer—interpret her behavior to mean—that she is (1) angry with you, (2) angry with someone else, (3) preoccupied, (4) ill, or (5) teasing you, among a number of other possibilities. Whatever the case, your friend's anger, preoccupation, illness, or teasing is not what you observe. You can observe only the fact that she walked by without speaking to you. The rest is inference.

To put it into the context of children, think of all the times in the past when a child on some given day behaved in ways that were not typical of him or her. The child may have been sluggish or apathetic, or perhaps appeared to have been overstimulated and demonstrated an activity level that was much higher than usual. What did you do? What did you think? It is almost certain that at the very least, you attempted to make some sense out of the child's unusual behavior. You wanted to know the reasons for the behavior. Suppose that the child's apparent listlessness was caused by the fact that her parents had argued before she left for the child care center. What you will have seen, however, is not the parents' quarrel but the child's response to the quarrel. Learning about the incident may give you a basis for understanding the child's behavior, but it nonetheless may still remain an inference on your part until you learn firsthand from the child (or from someone else) why she is listless or overstimulated (or whatever mood the child may display).

Various methods require different degrees of inference. Methods also differ as to when in the observation process inferences must be made. Some methods require no initial inference because they involve no preselection of the behaviors to be recorded. Considerable inference may be involved if one wants to give meaning to the behaviors after they are recorded. In a case like this, inference takes place after the fact. It is not involved in decisions regarding behaviors to record, or categories a behavior should be in, at the time of the observation. Some methods do require inferences at the time of initial observing and recording. Making inferences during the recording phase of observation does not rule out making inferences later on. The inferences made during and after observing and recording serve different purposes.

If you do not care what kinds of fish you catch, you will use a net that will get you all kinds of fish, and there is no need to be choosy while you are fishing. Once you have hauled in your net, however, you might be interested in examining your catch. What kinds of fish are they? What does it mean to have caught them in these particular waters, under these particular conditions? Of what significance is it to have found this species of fish in the same area as this other species?

Suppose, though, that you do care what kind of fish you catch; you want a fish of one particular species. In this case, you have to know something about that fish; you have to be able to recognize it when you see it. Consequently, you throw out your net when that particular fish swims by and not at any other time. Can you see the similarity to observation methods and the degree of inference required? With an open, unselective method, you do not worry about what behaviors are being caught in your net; indeed, you trap or record as many of them as you can. If you wish, you can examine your raw data and make inferences after the fishing is done. But with a closed and selective method, you make an on-the-spot decision or inference as to whether Betsy's taking a toy away from Susan is an example of aggressive behavior. Is it the kind of "fish" you are looking for? If it is, then you record it; furthermore, once you have it and many others like it in your net, you can analyze and use the data. For example, the number of times various children exhibit aggression can form the basis for a behavior modification program in the classroom. Frequent aggression by a child, as documented by observation records (frequency counts, for example), can give the teacher a measurable basis for judging whether she has successfully eliminated the undesirable behavior.

Although you cannot eliminate inference entirely, you can maximize the accuracy of your inferences by carefully defining your target behavior. This is referred to as operationally defining a behavior. In the example of Betsy taking a toy away from Susan, for instance, the act of taking a toy away from another child could be part of your operational definition of aggressive behavior. You would define aggression or aggressiveness before you ever entered the observation setting. If, however, you go into the observation setting with little or no idea of what constitutes aggression, it will be much more difficult to decide whether or not Betsy displayed aggressive behavior when she took the toy away from Susan.

It is difficult if not impossible to avoid having to make inferences altogether. It is possible that several observers could witness Betsy's behavior and disagree on their interpretations of that behavior. One observer could argue that Betsy did not really take the toy away from Susan, but that Susan actually was ready to give the toy to Betsy, in which case Betsy's behavior was not aggressive. It is much like a father who watches his young son push another boy to the ground yet argues that his son was not aggressive but merely assertive.

Table 12-1 and Table 12-2 in Chapter 12, which are a sample checklist and a checklist with some developmental norms, respectively, might offer a useful illustration of differing degrees of inference involved in completing such checklists. For example, item number 1 of Table 12-1 says "Vigorous and energetic in his attack on a project." Clearly, "vigorous" and "energetic" are behavioral descriptions that require a considerable amount of inference on the part of the observer. It is not unlikely that several observers could disagree on whether a child's approach to a project was in fact vigorous and energetic. In sharp contrast, item number 1 of Table 12-2—"Puts together 3-piece puzzle"—requires relatively little inference. Either a child can do it or he cannot. It is unlikely that this item would leave as much room for disagreement as did the first item in our example.

The issue of when during the observation process inferences are made is covered in the discussion of the methods themselves.

SUMMARY

This chapter covers some important characteristics of methods of observing and recording behavior. Two types of methods are discussed: formal and informal. These types differ primarily in the strictness of the conditions that govern their use. Formal methods are characterized by careful prior preparation and strict control of all aspects and phases of the observation and recording process. Informal methods involve a less structured and less elaborate approach to observation, and for this reason they are often used by teachers in the classroom.

Formal methods can be described along the dimensions of openness versus closedness, degree of selectivity, and degree of inference required. Openness versus closedness refers to whether or not the method preserves the original (raw) observational data. An open method is compared to a book that one is allowed to read and take extensive notes on, which can then be used at a later time. The notes preserve much of the original book (the raw data). A closed method is compared to a book that one is given only limited time to read, thus requiring brief note-taking in the form of a code. These notes omit the details of the book's content and thus fail to preserve the raw data. Degree of selectivity refers to whether the observer may record anything that occurs during the observation session or is restricted to certain predesignated behaviors and events. Selectivity is presented as analogous to a fish net with holes of varying sizes: the larger the holes, the greater the degree of selectivity; the smaller the holes, the less selective a method is. Degree of inference required is discussed in terms of whether inferences are made at the time of initial observing and recording or at a later time. Some methods require immediate inference at the time of recording; others use inference when the observing and recording are completed.

STUDY QUESTIONS

1. What do the terms *formal* and *informal* mean with regard to observation? What do they mean with regard to a social gathering, for example? Are the meanings similar or different in the two situations? Explain.

2. To what, other than observation and recording methods, might the characteristics of openness and closedness be applied? Do the essential meanings of openness and closedness change or remain the same in the different applications? Explain.

3. How are openness and closedness related to degree of selectivity? Could they be independent of each other? That is, could a method be closed without also being selective, or open without also being unselective? If you answer yes, how could this be so?

4. What is the difference between observation and interpretation?

5. Why is the distinction between "raw data" and "data" an important one? What is the significance for you, an observer, of the difference between these two kinds of information? What role do the two kinds of data play in your own observation activities?

6. What is an operational definition, and what role does it play in inference or interpretation?

ℙℝ𝔸ℂ𝕋𝕀ℂ𝔸𝕃 𝔼𝕏𝔼ℝℂ𝕀𝕊𝔼

This exercise assumes that you have not yet read any of the chapters that deal specifically with the recording techniques. The purpose of this exercise is to determine whether or not the names of the various recording techniques, and the names alone, provide you with any insight concerning how they "work" or how they might be constructed and used. For example, does the name "time sample" or "narrative description" give you any feel or intuition regarding its purpose and how it would be used in an actual observations setting?

Choose one or more of the recording techniques—we suggest you choose at least two—and imagine that you are observing a group of three-year-olds in a child care center. Pick a particular behavior or activity (for example, play, aggression, or speech), and using the recording techniques you have selected, provide imaginary or hypothetical data in a form that you think your recording techniques would actually require. In other words, if you choose the narrative description and you wanted to observe play behavior among some of the three-year-olds, how do you think your observation data would look? What form would your data take in your final observation report?

We suggest you save these imaginary observation records and eventually compare them with a "real" observation report that you have completed in the appropriate observation exercises in Chapters 6 through 12 of this text.

CHAPTER 6

Narrative Descriptions

OBJECTIVES

After reading this chapter, you should be able to

- Define the role of narrative descriptions in the observation process.
- Identify the relationship between the recording technique and the selectivity of the narrative description.
- Determine the limitations of narrative descriptions.
- Explain the role of inference in narrative descriptions.
- Identify the advantages and disadvantages of narrative descriptions.

KEY TERMS

narrative description

specimen record

structure

control

INTRODUCTION

Before beginning our discussion of the narrative description, we want to make a general statement that applies to all the recording techniques covered in this text. Any information, regardless of how it is obtained, is potentially useful in helping parents better understand their children and helping child care staff plan a broad curriculum or, on a more limited scale, particular activities and experiences. For this writer, the observation-recording techniques discussed in this text have two major purposes. The first and most basic or elementary purpose is to practice and refine one's observation-recording skills. Under this rubric, observing and recording behavior are done for their own sake, and no broader purpose or objective is necessary. However, limiting oneself to this first purpose would not serve anyone well in the long term. The second major and more inclusive purpose of these observation-recording techniques is to gather information that is practical and useful to parents and child care staff.

The ultimate goals of observing children's behavior is to understand children, to chart their ongoing growth and development, and to use the information you have gathered to foster their growth and development and to help parents do the same. This means that in whatever capacity you work with children, your motive and objective for observing and recording their behavior are to meet children's needs as they are expressed and identified in the professional child care setting or in any setting where children can be found.

In this light, therefore, we propose a basic principle: *Observational data that are useful for planning curriculum are potentially useful for parents in understanding their children's growth and development. Conversely, any observational data that are useful for parents are potentially useful for child care staff in planning and implementing curriculum.*

GENERAL DESCRIPTION

The first formal method of observation to be discussed has a rather confusing history with respect to its name. We call it the **narrative description**, although it is also labeled **specimen record**, and, sometimes, if a distinction is not made, *running record*. Although the narrative description and the specimen record are for us the same thing, we use only the term *narrative description* in this text. We mention *specimen record* to prevent confusion should you come across that term in your other reading. These other names are not particularly relevant to our purposes, so we do not dwell on them. But we do need to point out that our term *narrative description* is a modification of Lay-Dopyera and Dopyera's (1982) term *descriptive narrative*, which apparently is their version of the specimen record. Our decision to make this change is based on our desire to emphasize as clearly as possible the essential characteristics of this method: It is first of all a *narrative* in its basic form, and it *describes* behavior.

The narrative description is a formal method of recording behavior because it requires what Irwin and Bushnell (1980) describe as "more rigorous detail and predetermined criteria" (p. 103). It is the rigorous detail and predetermined criteria that impose **structure** and **control** on the narrative description; these are among the characteristics of formality. The informal counterpart of the narrative description, which can be referred to as the running record, is described as a "classroom observational technique for teachers and it involves taking on-the-spot records of behavior as it is occurring" (cited in Irwin & Bushnell, 1980, p. 100). The narrative description also records behavior as it is occurring but, strictly speaking, not on the spot. Consequently, the difference between the narrative description and the running record seems rather subtle and in actual practice may be difficult or even unnecessary to preserve. Even though we do not use the term *running record* in this text to mean redundant the same thing as *narrative description*, for our purposes the primary

narrative description
A formal method of observation and recording in which you continuously record in as much detail as possible what the child does and says, by herself and in interaction with other persons or objects. *See also specimen record.*

specimen record
A formal method of observation and recording in which you continuously record in as much detail as possible what the child does and says, by herself and in interaction with other persons or objects. *See also narrative description.*

structure
In the context of observation, structure refers to observing and recording behavior in a systematic, patterned way such that the observer knows why he or she is in the observation setting and by what method the behaviors of interest will be recorded.

control
Related to structure, control also refers to observing young children's behavior in a patterned, systematic way. The observer controls the observation by knowing her purpose and being able, for the most part, to accomplish her objectives.

The narrative description is a formal method of recording behavior.

difference between the narrative description and the running record is one of formality. By definition, the narrative description requires knowing ahead of time when, where, whom, how, and why you are going to observe. The running record is more spontaneous and directed more by the perceived requirements of the moment than by planning. These technical differences notwithstanding, the running record shares with the narrative description the same characteristics of rich, detailed, and continuous recording of behavior over some period of time. In short, think of the running record as the informal application of the narrative description, or as a "spontaneous" narrative description.

This text stands by Irwin and Bushnell's (1980) assertion that narrative descriptions are usually based on predetermined criteria such as the time of day, the person, and the setting. The observation exercises—particularly when they are used by students learning to observe and record behavior within an academic setting—impose criteria such as these, and it is therefore technically more correct to speak of the narrative description than of the running record. For professional child care providers, however, there is little or no need to adhere to this distinction between the narrative description and the running record. Indeed, this writer assumes that under most circumstances, the running record—as defined—probably will be used more frequently than the narrative description.

As Schickedanz, Schickedanz, Hansen, and Forsyth (1993) write, "The specimen record [narrative description] is used mainly to get a detailed picture of some aspect of a child's everyday behavior" (p. 26). This text's use of the narrative description includes getting a detailed picture of children's behavior and permits one to go beyond "everyday behavior" to include atypical or unusual behavior, if the circumstances warrant it and call for detailed descriptions.

The predetermined criteria just mentioned refer to such things as when, where, whom, how, and why you are going to observe. (You should resolve all of these issues during the planning process discussed in Chapter 3.) As you now know from our previous discussion, an informal approach to, or application of, the narrative description (again, the running record) would not rely on knowing all these things ahead of time. Once again, a professional child care provider or early childhood educator directly participating in the facility's ongoing activities and responsible for the children's welfare may discover whom she wants to observe only after she notes a particular child's—or group of children's—behavior that she decides merits further attention.

In any case, in the narrative description technique, you continuously record in as much detail as possible what the child does and says, by herself and in interaction with other persons or objects. The chief goal of narrative recording is to obtain a detailed, objective account of behavior without inferences, interpretations, or evaluations. It is an important feature of the narrative description in that it details not only behaviors, but also the context (setting and situation) of the behaviors and the sequence in which they occur. It is also essential that the behaviors be described and not simply referred to in broad terms. A good description should enable the reader to close his eyes and get a mental picture of the scene. To say "John played with the big blocks for 20 minutes" tells very little about John, the big blocks, the meaning of *played*, or where all of these events took place. The potential completeness and inclusiveness of the narrative description are captured in Goodwin and Driscoll's (1980) assertions that videotapes, audio tapes, or movies can be used by themselves or in combination with written notes to record a permanent account of children's behavior. Although the written narrative description is not as capable as movies and videotapes of "mirroring" the original raw data of the observation, it is capable of yielding rich, detailed information. Narrative descriptions can provide permanent behavioral records that are complete, objective, and descriptive (Goodwin & Driscoll, 1980). (See Table 6-1.)

Table 6-1 An Illustrative Narrative Description

Observer's Name Alice Thompson (Teacher)

Child/Children Observed Melissa L.

Child's/Children's Age(s) 4 years, 3 months **Child's/Children's Sex** Female

Observation Context (home, child care center, preschool, school) Children's Delight Preschool

Date of Observation February 25, 2008 **Time Begun** 9:20 A.M. **Time Ended** 9:30 A.M.

Brief Description of Physical and Social Characteristics of Observation Setting
Children are busily engaged in various free play activities. The overall mood seems upbeat. Of the usual 15 children who are enrolled, only 12 are here today—3 are ill, according to the parents' telephone communications with the director this morning. Although the children's moods seem good, they are more quiet than usual—not as much loud talking as sometimes takes place.

Objective Behavioral Descriptions (OBDs) and Interpretations:
Narrative Description

OBD 1: [Time Begun 9:20 A.M. Time Ended 9:22 A.M.]

Melissa (M) arrives about 35 minutes after the other children have arrived and started their activities. She puts her coat in her cubby and then stands in the doorway of the main classroom and looks around; she remains motionless for about two minutes, moving only her eyes as she glances at other children and their activities.

Interpretation 1:

Melissa seems shy, almost withdrawn. From moment of arrival, she seemed reluctant to enter into things. May be because she didn't want to come in the first place; her reluctance was mentioned by her mother several days ago. No specific reason was offered.

OBD 2: [Time Begun 9:22 A.M. Time Ended 9:24 A.M.]

M. walks toward reading area on far side of the room from the cubbies. As she walks, she scrapes the toe of her right foot at each step, doing this for about 5 feet. She passes by the puzzle table where 2 children are seated; no communication is exchanged. She walks to a table with some books lying on it. Tina, José, and Miguel are seated at the table; José and Miguel are sharing a book; Tina (T) is watching them "read." Melissa says nothing to the three children as she sits down.

Interpretation 2:

Melissa still seems uncertain; even her motor behaviors seem restricted; she walks slowly, shuffling, as though unsure of herself and of her relationship with the other children or her environment. Seems to have trouble deciding what to do. Not at all communicative; makes no overtures to any of the children who were "available" for such.

(continues)

Table 6-1 An Illustrative Narrative Description (continued)

OBD 3: [Time Begun 9:24 A.M. Time Ended 9:29 A.M.]

José and Miguel do not look up or acknowledge Melissa in any way. Tina says, "Hi, Melissa, wanna read a book with me?" M. cocks her head to one side and says, "I don't know how to read." T. replies, "We can look at the pictures." M. looks over toward the big block area and without looking at T. says, "OK." Tina smiles and goes to a shelf containing a number of books. M. picks up one of the books already on the table and flips through the pages. T. returns with a book and says, "I like this one; let's look at this one." M. merely nods; T. sits down close to M., but M. moves slightly, keeping a distance of about 6 to 8 inches between her and Tina.

Interpretation 3:

Tina seems outgoing and friendly as Melissa approaches; M. is still uncommunicative; still seems shy and uncertain; speaks softly as though afraid of being heard. Tina persists in spite of M.'s apparent lack of enthusiasm. M. also seems distractible or inattentive. She shies away from T.'s efforts to get close physically. Tina moves at a quick pace—much more energetic than M.

OBD 4: [Time Begun 9:29 A.M. Time Ended 9:30 A.M.]

José looks up and says, "Hey, you two, wha'cha doin'?" Tina tilts her head upward, thrusts out her chin slightly and says, "Never mind, we're busy." Melissa says nothing, but gets up from the table and walks toward big block area. Miguel still reads.

Interpretation 4:

Tina is much more outgoing and sure of herself than M. T. didn't interact too much w/ José and Miguel; may have felt left out of their activity. T. definitely seemed pleased to see M.; displayed no unfavorable response to M.'s "unsocial" behavior. T.'s response to José was quite assertive, but in a friendly way; almost like she claimed Melissa as her playmate, maybe in retaliation for the two boys ignoring her earlier. M. still seems uninterested, even uncertain of what to do.

Open versus Closed

The narrative description is the most open of all the observation methods. Its openness is a result of its unselectiveness and the amount of information it enables you to gather. The record preserves descriptions of behaviors, chronological sequences, and contexts. Consequently, those data are available in their original, unprocessed form for further examination and analysis.

Degree of Selectivity

The narrative description is not selective at all. Everything that occurs within an observation period is fair game for the recorder's pen. One observes and records with a small-holed net, being perfectly willing to haul in any kind of behavior that happens by.

We should emphasize that, strictly speaking, selectivity is inherent in all recording methods. This is because an observer cannot see everything and must decide from among any number of persons and events exactly whom and what to watch. Consequently, degree of selectivity is relative and depends upon the specific recording method you are using. When we say that the narrative description is not selective at all, we mean only that selectivity operates minimally compared with other methods.

Degree of Inference Required

At the time you are observing and recording, little inference is required because everything that takes place is targeted for recording. When observing with the narrative description, therefore, you do not have to consider whether the behavior or the context is the right one, just as when fishing with a small-holed net, there is no concern about whether you have trapped a carp or a minnow. One is as good as the other. Again, however, interpretations may be attempted after the fact. Inference becomes necessary whenever you want to give to the original data any meaning that goes beyond that provided solely by objective description. In other words, you may want to examine your fish once you have brought them into the boat. You may wonder why carp and minnows got trapped in the net at the same time. Or you may want to examine your descriptions and try to determine why Beth Ann is friendly toward Juan, whereas in the same context she is hostile toward Hakim. In this case, your "recording net" has "trapped" two different kinds of behavior on the part of Beth Ann: friendliness and hostility. Seeking a possible reason for these two different behaviors ("fish") might lend insight into some or all of the children involved.

Advantages

Before we discuss some of the specific advantages of the narrative description, we want to offer an overarching characterization of this recording method that, for this writer at least, justifies calling the narrative description the "Queen" of the recording techniques.

The more mundane, albeit practical, attribute of the narrative description is that it can be used in combination with any other recording method (or, conversely, any other recording method can be used in combination with the narrative description). We will delve into this feature in more detail in the following pages. The more fundamental and pervasive attribute of this recording method is that in a very real sense, none of the other methods could exist without the narrative description. We are speaking metaphorically here because behavior (or what we call the "behavior stream") does not appear as marks on a checklist or a time sample. Behavior flows continuously, and this ongoing continuity, along with behavior's contexts, persists even if our actual observations are ever so brief or even nonexistent.

Thus it is that a simple check mark on a checklist signifying the presence or absence of a particular skill has to derive from behavior that existed both before and after the check mark was recorded. Therefore, in some fashion or other, as we observe and record behavior, we are working off a mental narrative description that provides what is needed to record the behavior in the first place. This is why we choose to call the narrative description the "Queen" of the recording methods.

Some Specific Advantages of the Narrative Description

Some of the advantages of the narrative description stem precisely from its openness and lack of selectivity. Because of these characteristics, the method can provide a complete account of what has occurred during the time you were in a child's behavior stream. Furthermore, the narrative description has the important advantage of capturing context (setting and situation) along with behavior. Wright (1960) placed considerable importance on this combination: "Everyone knows, at least intuitively, that the meaning and significance of an action and even its occurrence depend directly … upon the coexisting situation" (p. 87). Information concerning what and where can be especially useful when trying to understand individual children and how they behave in various contexts. As is well known, every child has his own unique style, attitudes, fears, and abilities. The narrative description, like a fishing net with small holes, catches these differences, these nuances in children's behavior, and permanently preserves them. Furthermore, it catches all these behaviors, contexts, and styles under naturalistic conditions, without the artificial influences of experiments in a laboratory.

The Narrative Description's Versatility

The narrative description has the distinct advantage of being very versatile, and this versatility can be considered in a number of ways. As you will eventually learn, leaving aside the narrative description itself, of the six remaining recording methods discussed herein, some form of narrative description is found in three of them: event sampling, diary description, and anecdotal records. However, it is just as significant that the narrative description—or running record—can be used in combination with time sampling (Chapter 7), frequency counts or duration records (Chapter 11), and checklists and rating scales (Chapter 12). In short, the narrative description can find a "home" almost anywhere.

The narrative description also reveals its versatility in the kind of information you potentially can extract from your objective behavioral descriptions and interpretations. For instance, suppose that you use the narrative description as a formal method and decide that you want to observe behavior during several sessions of free play over the course of several days. Your Objective Behavioral Descriptions (OBDs) could, with proper analysis, yield some of the same information that a time sample, checklist, rating scale, frequency count, or duration record would give you about a particular behavior or pattern of behaviors. Your OBDs and interpretations could provide information concerning, say, social behavior (or any other behavior of interest to you). You could record how often social interactions occurred (frequency count), how long they lasted in each behavioral episode (duration record), who initiated these interactions and with whom (information similar to that obtained by a checklist), and so on. Additionally, you would have detailed descriptions of social behaviors and their contexts that these other methods, used by themselves, would not give you. Let us illustrate how narrative descriptive data could inform the completion of a checklist and a time sample.

Using one of the sample checklists found in Chapter 12, we will depict how checklist data might look after an analysis of the first two OBDs depicted in Table 6-2. Bear in mind that the time span during which these hypothetical data "were recorded" is from 9:05 to 9:17, a total of 12 minutes. Had all the OBDs been considered (an omission that we will ask you to correct), the entries in the checklist would be different. Also, for the sake of preserving space in Table 6-3, multiple entries appear in the "Observed" columns. Note also that the numbers are circled to identify to which child the checklist entries pertain.

Table 6-2 Narrative Description (During Free Play)

Observer's Name Estelle Gibbons (Center Staff)

Child/Children Observed Cassandra, Carla, Michelle

Child's/Children's Age(s) 4 years, 8 months; 4 yrs, 9 mos.; 4 yrs, 6 mos.

Child's/Children's Sex F, F, F

Observation Context (home, child care center, preschool, school) Humpty Dumpty Child Care Center

Date of Observation April 24, 2008 **Time Begun** 9:05 A.M. **Time Ended** 9:55 A.M.

Brief Description of Characteristics of Physical and Social Environment
The children appear to be in a good mood today, and the teachers and aides seem to share their mood. It is raining, and knowing that they will not be able to go outside, the children seem doubly intent on focusing their physical energy on the activity areas, which are already in a bit of disorder. The general demeanor is in somewhat sharp contrast with yesterday's emotional climate.

Objective Behavioral Descriptions (OBDs) and Interpretations:
Narrative Description

OBD 1: [Time Begun 9:05 A.M. Time Ended 9:07 A.M.]

Cassandra arrives early today. She hangs her coat in her cubby and immediately goes to the big block area, where I happen to be standing. She says "Hi" and then begins to stack 3 wooden blocks on top of each other. At that moment, Carla and Michelle come into the room. Seeing them, Cassandra leaves the big block area and walks over to them.

(continues)

Table 6-2 Narrative Description (During Free Play) (continued)

Interpretation 1:

Cassandra seems especially animated today, despite the rather gloomy weather outside. Her walk is brisk, and her greeting to me is cheerful. She seems to have a purpose already in mind as she begins stacking the wooden blocks, but she apparently finds her two closest friends more appealing than playing by herself in the big block area.

OBD 2: [Time Begun 9:08 A.M. Time Ended 9:17 A.M.]

Cassandra greets Carla and Michelle. After talking briefly, the three of them walk over to the puzzle area. Cassandra takes down a puzzle from the shelf, and the three girls sit down at the table. Cassandra pours the puzzle pieces onto the table, and the three of them begin putting the puzzle together. The puzzle contains about 50 pieces that eventually will form the picture of a bear sitting under a tree. They speak to each other in moderately low tones as they ask each other to pass a piece of the puzzle or to put a particular piece into a particular spot. At one point, for example, Cassandra says to Michelle, "Michelle, put that piece over here; it looks like part of the bear's head." Michelle replies, "Yeah, you're right. I'll put it right there." Some of the puzzle pieces are quite small, but the children handle them using pincer movements of the thumb and forefinger.

Interpretation 2:

The three girls are very amicable and cooperative as they interact with one another in their joint task. Cassandra seems to have especially good shape perception, and she more frequently than Carla or Michelle sees where a particular puzzle piece fits. Cassandra also seems to direct the general flow of activity, although she does so quite subtly and without any hint of bossiness or coercion. This is an untested assumption, but I would not be surprised if Cassandra suggested the puzzle activity in the first place. Cassandra's fine finger movements as she handles the various pieces of the puzzle are precise and well coordinated.

OBD 3: [Time Begun 9:18 A.M. Time Ended 9:30 A.M.]

Cassandra leaves the puzzle table and walks up to Mrs. Parsons (a staff member). "Mrs. Parsons, can Carla, Michelle, and me finger paint?" Mrs. Parsons answers affirmatively. Cassandra returns to the puzzle table, speaks briefly to Carla and Michelle, and the three girls then walk over to the finger painting area. Cassandra sets up an easel while telling the others to do the same. Cassandra then hands a smock to each girl, takes one for herself, and puts it on. "I'm going to paint a picture of the ocean," says Cassandra. "What are you going to paint?" She doesn't wait for an answer, but grabs some paint off the shelf and moves to her easel.

Interpretation 3:

Cassandra definitely takes a leadership role in this episode, and she does so almost matter-of-factly. Carla and Michelle show no signs that this bothers them. Cassandra's behavior also appears quite focused, as if she knows exactly what she wants to do and how she wants to do it. I also get the impression that Cassandra derives some sort of energy from her two companions.

OBD 4: [Time Begun 9:32 A.M. Time Ended 9:40 A.M.]

Cassandra dips her right hand into the pool of paint and sweeps her hand from left to right across the paper on the easel. Her movements nearly cover the paper's entire width. The paints are a mixture of colors, and she comments on the final effect of the blend: "This is a special ocean that looks like a rainbow." She looks over at Carla's and Michelle's paintings, frowns, and asks, "What is that?" Carla replies, "It's a bird. Do you like it?" "Yeah, it's kind of nice," says Cassandra. Michelle does not respond, but continues spreading paint on her paper.

(continues)

Table 6-2 Narrative Description (During Free Play) (continued)

Interpretation 4:

Cassandra's arm–hand movements are smooth and well coordinated. Using precise finger movements, she adds small dabs of paint at various parts of her picture. Carla and Michelle also show good arm–hand coordination. Carla does not exhibit the finer finger movements that Cassandra does, but I don't think it's because she can't. Michelle uses much the same gross and finer muscle movements as Cassandra.

Table 6-3 Checklist to Assess Social Behaviors in Humpty Dumpty Child Care Center			
Social Behavior	**Observed**		
	Yes	**No**	**Sometimes**
Is friendly and outgoing	①		
Plays with the majority of other children in most of the activity areas		①, ②, ③	
Plays only with certain children in certain activity areas	①, ②, ③		
Seeks adult approval			
Seeks peer approval			
Is willing to take turns			
Makes transitions easily from one activity to another	①, ②, ③		
Adjusts easily, quickly to new, unfamiliar activities			
Is independent	①		
Shows distinct mood changes			
Is appropriately assertive	①		
Shows skillful use of language in his/her social interactions	① ②		

Children Observed

1. Cassandra 2. Michelle 3. Carla

Note: As an exercise, we recommend that you complete Table 6-3. Analyze the remaining OBDs and interpretations in Table 6-2, and enter additional checklist data relevant to Cassandra's, Carla's, and Michelle's social behavior.

Now let us see how a time sample might look using the same data from Table 6-2, which we duplicate and label as Table 6-4.

Table 6-4 Narrative Description (During Free Play)

Observer's Name Estelle Gibbons (Center Staff)

Child/Children Observed Cassandra, Carla, Michelle

Child's/Children's Age(s) 4 years, 8 months; 4 yrs, 9 mos.; 4 yrs, 6 mos.

Child's/Children's Sex F, F, F

Observation Context (home, child care center, preschool, school) Humpty Dumpty Child Care Center

Date of Observation April 24, 2008 **Time Begun** 9:05 A.M. **Time Ended** 9:55 A.M.

Brief Description of Characteristics of Physical and Social Environment
The children appear to be in a good mood today, and the teachers and aides seem to share their mood. It is raining, and knowing that they will not be able to go outside, the children seem doubly intent on focusing their physical energy on the activity areas, which are already in a bit of disorder. The general demeanor is in somewhat sharp contrast with yesterday's emotional climate.

Objective Behavioral Descriptions (OBDs) and Interpretations:
Narrative Description

OBD 1: [Time Begun 9:05 A.M. Time Ended 9:07 A.M.]

Cassandra arrives early today. She hangs her coat in her cubby and immediately goes to the big block area, where I happen to be standing. She says "Hi" and then begins to stack 3 wooden blocks on top of each other. At that moment, Carla and Michelle come into the room. Seeing them, Cassandra leaves the big block area and walks over to them.

Interpretation 1:

Cassandra seems especially animated today, despite the rather gloomy weather outside. Her walk is brisk, and her greeting to me is cheerful. She seems to have a purpose already in mind as she begins stacking the wooden blocks, but she apparently finds her two closest friends more appealing than playing by herself in the big block area.

OBD 2: [Time Begun 9:08 A.M. Time Ended 9:17 A.M.]

Cassandra greets Carla and Michelle. After talking briefly, the three of them walk over to the puzzle area. Cassandra takes down a puzzle from the shelf, and the three girls sit down at the table. Cassandra pours the puzzle pieces onto the table, and the three of them begin putting the puzzle together. The puzzle contains about 50 pieces that eventually will form the picture of a bear sitting under a tree. They speak to each other in moderately low tones as they ask each other to pass a piece of the puzzle or to put a particular piece into a particular spot. At one point, for example, Cassandra says to Michelle, "Michelle, put that piece over here; it looks like part of the bear's head." Michelle replies, "Yeah, you're right. I'll put it right there." Some of the puzzle pieces are quite small, but the children handle them using pincer movements of the thumb and forefinger.

(continues)

Table 6-4 Narrative Description (During Free Play) (continued)

Interpretation 2:

The three girls are very amicable and cooperative as they interact with one another in their joint task. Cassandra seems to have especially good shape perception, and she more frequently than Carla or Michelle sees where a particular puzzle piece fits. Cassandra also seems to direct the general flow of activity, although she does so quite subtly and without any hint of bossiness or coercion. This is an untested assumption, but I would not be surprised if Cassandra suggested the puzzle activity in the first place. Cassandra's fine finger movements as she handles the various pieces of the puzzle are precise and well coordinated.

OBD 3: [Time Begun 9:18 A.M. Time Ended 9:30 A.M.]

Cassandra leaves the puzzle table and walks up to Mrs. Parsons (a staff member). "Mrs. Parsons, can Carla, Michelle, and me finger paint?" Mrs. Parsons answers affirmatively. Cassandra returns to the puzzle table, speaks briefly to Carla and Michelle, and the three girls then walk over to the finger painting area. Cassandra sets up an easel while telling the others to do the same. Cassandra then hands a smock to each girl, takes one for herself, and puts it on. "I'm going to paint a picture of the ocean," says Cassandra. "What are you going to paint?" She doesn't wait for an answer, but grabs some paint off the shelf and moves to her easel.

Interpretation 3:

Cassandra definitely takes a leadership role in this episode, and she does so almost matter-of-factly. Carla and Michelle show no signs that this bothers them. Cassandra's behavior also appears quite focused, as if she knows exactly what she wants to do and how she wants to do it. I also get the impression that Cassandra derives some sort of energy from her two companions.

OBD 4: [Time Begun 9:32 A.M. Time Ended 9:40 A.M.]

Cassandra dips her right hand into the pool of paint and sweeps her hand from left to right across the paper on the easel. Her movements nearly cover the paper's entire width. The paints are a mixture of colors, and she comments on the final effect of the blend: "This is a special ocean that looks like a rainbow." She looks over at Carla's and Michelle's paintings, frowns, and asks, "What is that?" Carla replies, "It's a bird. Do you like it?" "Yeah, it's kind of nice," says Cassandra. Michelle does not respond, but continues spreading paint on her paper.

Interpretation 4:

Cassandra's arm–hand movements are smooth and well coordinated. Using precise finger movements, she adds small dabs of paint at various parts of her picture. Carla and Michelle also show good arm–hand coordination. Carla does not exhibit the finer finger movements that Cassandra does, but I don't think it's because she can't. Michelle uses much the same gross and finer muscle movements as Cassandra.

The following—Table 6-5—reflects the narrative description information contained in Table 6-4. Note how much simpler, but sketchy, time sample data are compared to narrative description data.

Table 6-5 Hypothetical Time Sample Depicting Social Interactions of Three Children								
Behavior Categories	Time Intervals							
	1	2	3	4	5	6	7	8
General Response to Setting 1. Enters setting willingly (specify which areas involved—big block area [BBA], reading area [RA], etc.)	①	②	③	①				
2. Enters setting reluctantly	1	1	1	1				
3. Refuses to enter setting								
General Response to Environment 4. Uses equipment/materials freely	①	②	③	①				
5. Limited or sporadic use of equipment/ materials	4	4	4	4				
6. No use of equipment/materials								
General Response to Others 7. Seeks or is in contact with peer(s)	①	②	③	①				
8. Seeks or is in contact with adult	7	7	7	8				
9. Avoids or breaks contact with peer(s)								
10. Avoids or breaks contact with adult								
11. Reluctant contact with peer(s); contact lacks motivation or concentration on part of child								
12. Reluctant contact with adult; contact lacks motivation or concentration on part of child								

Children Observed
1. Cassandra
2. Carla
3. Michelle

KEY
BBA—Big Block Area
PA—Puzzle Area
FP—Finger Painting Area

The Random Aspects of the Narrative Description

Another advantage of the narrative description is that its use is not necessarily constrained by predetermined conditions or circumstances. In other words, its use borders on randomness. We say this in spite of Irwin and Bushnell's (1980) assertion that the narrative description is a formal recording method, which strongly suggests that the narrative description is anything but random. Nevertheless, for most practical purposes, the narrative description does have a strong element of randomness. You are entering a child's or several children's behavior stream to record as much of this behavior as possible [begin italics] *without special regard for what the behavior or the situation might be.* [End italics] (In contrast, in Chapter 8 you will discover that the event sample is not at all random; it directs your entry into the behavior only when you observe a particular preselected behavior or behavioral event.) This random aspect, as well as a broad variety of behaviors and contexts it records, offers a distinct advantage: You can capture behavioral snapshots at any time of the day or in any conceivable situation. Consequently, with a sufficient number of narrative descriptions you will get a reasonably representative sample of a child's behavior across a number of different situations. However, keep in mind that it is only by entering the behavior at a number of different points that you will gain an adequate understanding of the children in your care. This same representativeness will also give parents and child care staff a more complete picture of how their children are developing and functioning.

In short, the narrative description is usable under many circumstances and conditions. It is what we can call a "generic or pervasive" recording technique. It requires no prepared observation sheets or coding schemes, nor any special language or jargon. The richness and subtlety of plain language are major strengths of the narrative description, although they are strengths that depend on the observer's language skills.

The Advantage of Permanence

The permanence of the narrative description is also an advantage. Such records get more valuable as they get older. It is useful to compare earlier narrative descriptions with more recent records. This comparison helps us learn about changes in children's behavior and development across time and place (see Wright, 1960; Gaver & Richards, 1979).

The narrative description allows considerable variations in the amount of time spent in the behavior stream. Narratives may describe behaviors ranging from several seconds to 12 hours or more (see, e.g., Barker & Wright, 1951). The extended record usually involves several observers taking turns recording.

Disadvantages

Energy and Time Considerations

The narrative description can cost a great deal in staff energy and time. The method can be inefficient for obtaining representative samples of behavior quickly. Part of the inefficiency comes from the failure to quantify behavioral data ahead of time through a predetermined coding scheme. For example, you cannot record the frequency of a behavior at the time you observe it. Narrative descriptions can be analyzed for such things as frequency counts, time sample, and duration data, but these analyses would have to be done after the observation session. They could also be time-consuming.

Skill and effort are needed to notice and get down on paper the numerous details that are the goal of narrative description. Lay-Dopyera and Dopyera (1982) comment that observations may have to be limited to relatively brief periods of time because the writing is so intense, which suggests the method of time sampling.

A Brief Introduction to the Uses of the Narrative Description

We cannot detail all the possible uses of the narrative description, but we believe there are many. As one example, we tried to demonstrate briefly how narrative descriptions could be used to provide information for a checklist. Admittedly, converting narrative descriptive data to checklist data—or to any of the other coded recording methods—is not as efficient as simply using a checklist at the outset. This relative inefficiency notwithstanding, we strongly urge you not to reject the narrative description solely or primarily because it is more time-consuming than some of the other methods. Instead, try to strike a balance between the amount of effort and time the narrative description requires and the richness and completeness of the data it provides. Put another way, let the objectives of your observations determine whether and when you will use the narrative description.

Jalongo and Isenberg (2000) write that the narrative description, what they call the specimen record, is "often used to discover causes and effects of behavior by studying what precedes and follows an event" (p. 292). Beaty (2002) echoes Jalongo and Isenberg by stating that this method can be used "to discover cause and effects of behavior," but she also includes the additional purpose of "child development research" (p. 34).

It is easy to see how the narrative description can reveal cause-and-effect relationships. This ability is the natural product of (1) being unhindered by any constraints imposed by time, context, or behavior; and (2) the emphasis on capturing the full details regarding the natural flow and continuity of the child's behavior stream.

Using the Narrative Description? A First Visit with Florence

At this juncture we want to introduce a fictitious, but plausible, character whom we shall name Florence. For our purposes, Florence is a student learning how to observe and record young children's behavior. In that respect, she is like all the readers of this text who are also students. But Florence can stand in for anyone who has a professional or otherwise significant relationship with children. Florence is going to be with us throughout our discussion of the various recording methods—Chapters 6 through 12.

Child Care as Drama

We introduce Florence by establishing a context or background within which she will carry out her role as observer. A child care center or early education classroom can be thought of as a play (drama) that is continuously in progress whenever children are in the child care space and for however long they are in that space. The professional staff produce the play; they provide all the resources necessary for the play to occur. These resources include the physical space/location, the equipment and materials, and the curriculum that determines or influences how that space and equipment will be used. The children, in turn, are the script writers and the actors. The scripts are largely spontaneous: They potentially can change from one moment to the next, and they include everything the children say and how they say it, and everything they do and how they do it. The children create the acts and the scenes within the acts.

For example, at 9:05—5 minutes after the children first arrive at the child care center—George and José go to the sandbox and begin playing together with the trucks, pretending that the long wooden blocks laid down on the sand are the roads. At 9:08 they suddenly stop playing and walk over to the finger painting area, where they put on plastic aprons and start applying different colored paints to the large pad of paper setting on an easel. They stay with this activity from 9:09 to 9:12. We could say that Act I in our child care drama is free play, and the first scene in this act stars George and José playing in the sandbox. Scene 2 finds our same two characters acting out their script in the finger painting area. For as long as free play (Act I) lasts, whenever the children you are observing change the location of their play or significantly change their behavior in that location, you could designate that as a scene change. When free play ends and, say, snack time begins, that could be the beginning of Act II in our child care drama. This shifting of acts and scenes would continue for as long as the children are in the child care setting.

You, the observer, are in the audience watching the play and trying to observe and record these changes in acts and scenes, as well as the actions and the dialogue that the children/actors have spontaneously written into the script. However, you are not in the audience as a drama critic. Your goal is not to decide whether the play is a good one or a bad one, or to pass *critical judgment* on how well the actors say their lines or portray their characters. You are there to learn how children change over time and how and why they do what they do. From that foundation a number of secondary, though very important, reasons emerge. If you are a parent, you want to learn as much as you can about how your child functions in the child care setting. Does Lucinda get along well with her peers? Is Roberto less shy than he used to be? Are Gretchen's motor skills improving, and is she more willing to do things that involve the small muscles, such as stringing beads or playing with small puzzle pieces? How is Willard's speech? Does he use more complete sentences? If you are one of the staff, the things that concern the parents would also concern you. In addition, of course, you would have concerns that are more narrowly limited to the daily operation and functioning of the child care center or early education classroom.

In our script, Florence is a student learning how to observe and record young children's behavior. We are going to "reveal" Florence's thought processes as she tries to decide which of the recording methods she wants to use and why. We must impose a modest but diminishing restriction: Florence's knowledge consists only of the information contained in the chapter in which she appears and, where applicable, all the information contained in the previous chapters. This means that with each succeeding chapter, Florence will be able to make increasingly better informed decisions about which recording method to use in her particular circumstances. In the present chapter, she will have access only to the information about the narrative description. In the next chapter, she will be able use what she knows about the narrative description and the time sample, and so on through all the chapters dealing with the recording methods.

We will use Florence's mental deliberations to identify some of the uses for each of the recording methods. Bear in mind that although she will always choose the method that is the subject of that chapter, she will, with the exception of this present chapter, make some comparisons and contrasts among the various methods and then tell herself, who is really you, the reader, the basis of her final decision. Now, let us take a peek at what Florence is thinking.

FLORENCE AND THE NARRATIVE DESCRIPTION

Florence is given the assignment of observing and recording the behavior of a group of three-year-olds. She has studied the chapter on the narrative description, and thus far this is the only recording method about which she has any knowledge. She is faced with the initial task of finding out what kinds of information the narrative description can give her. A related question is this: What can she do with this information once she gets it? This is how Florence might reason with herself. (Please note that we have taken some artistic license in the way we present Florence's thoughts. It is doubtful that anyone actually thinks in the complete, grammatically correct sentences we attribute to Florence. But we are more interested in giving you what we hope will be useful information than in duplicating precisely how a person actually thinks.)

I have to observe fifteen three-year-olds, and the only recording technique I know about so far in my child development course is the narrative description. The author of my observation text calls the narrative description the Queen of all the recording techniques, so that tells me that I can gather all kinds of information about children's behavior using this method. I think what's important is that the narrative description is supposed to capture as many details as possible, and it's also supposed to include information about the setting and the situation. Let's see, the setting and situation are the context of the behavior, so for me that means that the context provides the background for the children's behavior. The narrative description requires a lot of writing if I'm going to get as many of the details of the children's behavior as I can. Well, obviously in that case I'm going to be able to observe only a few children at a time, which means that if I eventually want to observe all the children, I'll have to do a series of narrative descriptions over a period of time. But that's good, because the more narrative descriptive data I can record, the more accurate and useful the picture of the child will be for parents and child care staff. Parents and child care providers are always interested in how well their children are growing and developing and what new skills and abilities they're acquiring. It just occurred to me, the narrative description might be especially effective in gathering information where the child is involved in activities and interactions that parents might not be able to observe at home. If my descriptions are sufficiently detailed and complete, and if my interpretations are reasonable and insightful, then parents and staff will have a series of "snapshots" of the children that can give them a better understanding of how they're functioning in a variety of conditions and situations. Now, if my instructor or someone in the child care center where I'm observing asks me how she could use my narrative descriptions, how can I answer? I guess one of the most obvious uses is for staff conferences and parent–staff conferences. Since Jalongo and Isenberg, and Beaty, say that the narrative description is good for getting information about cause-and-effect relationships, I can imagine a situation where there is concern about a child's occasional aggressive behavior. The narrative description could help to identify the circumstances or interactions that lead up to (and possibly be the cause of) his aggressiveness and those that seem to stop that behavior. That information could be very useful in planning the child's activities or play partners. I guess I better stop thinking and start observing.

SUMMARY

The narrative description is a formal method of observation. In this technique you record in as much detail as you can everything that occurs in the way of behavior and its context. The record is objective, without any evaluations or interpretations in the narrative description itself. The narrative description is the most open of all the observation methods. It is not at all selective, and it involves no inferences at the time of initial recording.

There are a number of advantages to the narrative description. It provides a rich, detailed account of a child's behavior and the circumstances in which it occurred. The record is permanent and can be used for a later comparison with more recent records. However, the method is costly in time and effort, and it is not very efficient for quickly gathering representative samples of behavior. The technique also requires skill because of the many details that are the targets of narrative description.

STUDY QUESTIONS

1. What is a distinguishing characteristic of the narrative description? What are some advantages and disadvantages of this characteristic?

2. How does the narrative description's degree of selectivity affect the way that one specifically records observational data?

3. Under what conditions would you probably not want to use the narrative description? Under what conditions would you probably want to use the method?

4. What is the role of interpretation in the narrative description? When is interpretation most likely to be used or needed?

5. When would what you intended to be a narrative description actually turn out to be a running record? Would the data differ significantly between the two reports? Explain.

PRACTICAL EXERCISE

This exercise asks you to observe and record the behaviors of two individuals—a child whom you do not know and an adult—preferably someone your own age—whom you know very well (a roommate, close friend, family member) and with whom you spend a fair amount of time. The exercise is intended to illustrate some of the dynamics involved in interpreting someone's behavior.

An assumption underlying this exercise is that interpreting the behavior of a child whom you do not know and the behavior of an adult whom you know quite well can be quite different experiences. A further assumption is that because you are also an adult, you will have an easier time getting some meaning from another adult's behavior than you will getting some meaning from a child's behavior, especially a child you have never before met or observed. In other words, you will be testing this author's hypothesis that understanding or meaningfully interpreting children's behavior really depends on getting to know the children and observing their behavior over time and in many different contexts. Becoming familiar with children helps you enter into their mindset, so to speak, and be more in tune with how they think and possibly why they do what they do. Of course, such familiarity depends to some degree to how much you know about how children in general grow and develop—that is, how much knowledge you have about child development.

To complete this exercise, observe and record an adult's behavior for about 10 or 15 minutes, or some other period of time that is possible and comfortable for you. What interpretations can you offer for this individual's actions? That is to say, can you come up with any explanations for this individual's behaviors? Can you attribute to him or her any motives, intentions, emotions, and the like? Immediately after you have completed your observation of the adult, ask him or her about the motives, intentions, or feelings that you believe were associated with the behaviors you observed and recorded. How accurate were your interpretations?

Follow the same procedure with a child. We suggest you choose someone who is somewhere between three and five years of age. To help you complete this exercise properly, observe a child in a structured child care setting, and ask one of the staff members to observe the child with you. When you have acquired a reasonable amount of data, share your interpretations with the staff member who observed with you. How do your interpretations compare with those of the staff member?

Time Sampling

OBJECTIVES

After reading this chapter, you should be able to

- Relate the importance of the representativeness of behavior to the time sampling method.
- Determine the most appropriate coding system to use in a particular time sampling observation.
- Identify the characteristics of time sampling in relation to the dimensions of open versus closed, degree of selectivity, and degree of inference required.
- Analyze the advantages and disadvantages of the time sampling method of observation.

GENERAL DESCRIPTION

If you select one piece of candy from a box containing 50 pieces of candy, you have sampled that candy. One of the purposes of such sampling might be to help you decide whether or not you will like the candy that you have not tasted (sampled). Sampling spares you the necessity of eating the whole box while at the same time allowing you to judge the overall quality of the whole box based on the quality of the piece you have eaten. Consequently, sampling requires less time and effort than methods that do not sample.

These same principles apply to **time sampling**: Out of the total amount of time a child is in the observation setting, the observer selects or samples a relatively small amount of that total time and observes the child during that time period. It is essential to understand, however, that you are also sampling behavior and not just time, because you are observing to see whether a particular behavior occurs. What must happen is that the two samples of time and behavior must coincide, which is to say that a particular

time sampling

A formal method of observation and recording in which you record selected behaviors during preset uniform time periods and at regularly recurring or randomly selected intervals.

behavior is recorded as having occurred only if it is observed during the preselected period of time. If the behavior takes place outside of the selected time frame, it is disregarded. So, for example, you might decide to observe each of 15 children for one minute and record—by a check mark—all instances of aggressive behavior. If, during Sarah's minute, she displays aggressive actions, you would so indicate on your time sampling observation form. If while observing Karl, however, you happen to see Sarah display aggression, you would not record it, because your focus is on Karl and not on Sarah, and because her aggressive behavior did not occur within the preselected time period that you had set aside to observe her.

Although somewhat dated but still relevant, Irwin and Bushnell's (1980) discussion of time sampling still offers some valuable insights into the technique. First of all, these authors make an interesting statement that adds to the meaning of time sampling: "[u]sing observation to *sample, rather than to describe behavior*" (p. 148, emphasis added). This distinction is vital because one must understand the difference between (1) merely recording a mark on a form every time a particular behavior occurs and (2) actually describing that behavior in considerable detail (as in the narrative description). Irwin and Bushnell complete the partial sentence previously quoted with "made it necessary to place some restrictions on what would be observed" (p. 148). One of these restrictions is that "the behavior occur frequently enough that the observer could be reasonably sure of being able to see it" (p. 148). Citing another, much earlier source, they write that "if the behavior to be observed occurs less than once in fifteen minutes on the average, time sampling should not be used" (pp. 148–149). This writer sees no reason to depart from that prescription. All this, by the way, has to do with the notion of **representativeness**.

representativeness

A desirable feature of behavior samples; representative samples are those that exemplify or reflect the typical characteristics of the larger population or class of behaviors of which the sample is a part.

Representativeness of the time sample is extremely important: "The length, spacing, and number of intervals are intended to secure representative *time samples* of the target phenomena" (Wright, 1960, p. 93, italics original). Brandt (1972) makes the same point when he notes that smaller behavior samples are chosen so as to reflect the characteristics of the larger population from which they are taken. However, Brandt points out that representativeness is possible only for those behaviors that occur frequently.

Representativeness is not only important to the time sampling technique; it also bears on almost every aspect of child care professionals' dealings with young children. Small, isolated examples of children's behavior might be interesting, but they might not reveal much if anything about the children's typical behavior. If you ordered steak in a restaurant, and it was either very good or very bad, that good or bad steak would be a representative meal if you could legitimately draw conclusions about all the other items on the menu that you had not ordered and tasted.

With respect to recording behavior, you want your recording techniques to capture behaviors that are representative of other behaviors that you were not able to observe and record. If you accomplish this, then you may draw conclusions concerning those other behaviors. To put it another way, you could predict what those other behaviors would likely have been had you observed them instead of the ones you actually did observe.

The probable frequency of various behaviors is not too difficult to estimate or predict, and, again, Irwin and Bushnell are very helpful. They identify as infrequent such behaviors as grief, hysteria, and tree climbing, which, on reflection, make sense. More frequent behaviors include such actions as talking, eating, smiling, and playing (Irwin & Bushnell, 1980, p. 149). They also note that if uncertain about the relative frequency of various behaviors, the observer may have to do some preliminary observations in order to determine which ones can reasonably be recorded with a time sampling technique.

Frequent child behaviors include such actions as talking, eating, smiling, and playing.

A time sampling session might be structured in the following manner. The observer spends three minutes on each of 15 children in a preschool classroom. She observes the first child for three minutes. Using a previously coded observation sheet, she records each instance of dependency or cooperative behavior exhibited during that period. The observer then moves on to the second child and repeats the process, until she has observed and recorded the dependency and cooperative behaviors of all 15 children.

There are numerous variations of the time sample. Variations are possible not only in the length and distribution of time intervals, but also in recording techniques. For instance, an observer might decide to spend six minutes on each child, but follow an on–off, observe–record procedure. This is especially appropriate when using a combination of coding scheme and narrative description. Here, he could observe the child for one minute, indicating only whether the target behavior(s) occurred. The second minute could be used to write a brief narrative description of the behavior and its context. The remaining one-minute intervals would be used in the same on–off fashion until the six minutes of observation were completed. The time periods could be divided in some other way—for example, observe for 10 seconds and record for 50 seconds. The variations possible are revealed by Goodwin and Driscoll's (1980) report of studies in which observation and recording took place as frequently as every 3 or 6 seconds.

Certain behaviors are always preselected as targets for observation—for example, the children's dependency, speech utterances, or attentiveness to assigned tasks might be chosen. Coding schemes are often used with the time sampling method. These schemes require making an appropriate mark on an observation sheet whenever the child displays the behavior of interest. There are two kinds of coding systems: category and sign systems (Irwin & Bushnell, 1980; Goodwin & Driscoll, 1980, p. 154). A sign system, say Irwin and Bushnell, "requires that the categories of behavior be mutually exclusive" (p. 154). This means that no given behavior can be placed in more than one category because each chosen category excludes all others. The category system also requires "mutually exclusive categories of behavior but, in addition, the categories must be *exhaustive*. They must include the total range of behaviors so that anything the child does can be tallied" (Irwin & Bushnell, 1980, p. 155, emphasis original). Exclusiveness, for instance, would be violated if a respondent to a survey questionnaire were asked to indicate his or her religious preference using the following format:

Christian	☐	Muslim	☐
Baptist	☐	Jewish	☐
Catholic	☐	Other	☐

As you can see, Baptists and Catholics are also Christians, which leaves open the opportunity for the respondent to place a check mark in at least two places (if he or she is also either a Baptist or a Catholic). The criterion of exhaustiveness would be violated if all the possibilities were not accounted for in the behavior recording form. So, for instance, the form in the previous example would be both exclusive and exhaustive if it read as follows:

Christian ☐   Jewish ☐
Muslim ☐   Other ☐

Here, provision is made for any respondent to indicate his or her religious preference—or no preference at all—because the category Other takes into account those individuals who are Hindu, Sufi, atheist, agnostic, or what have you. It is generally easier to construct an exclusive set of categories than an exhaustive one. Let us look quickly at a coding scheme that uses a sign system.

Examine Table 7-1. In this example, several facets of a child's behavior are defined for notice and recording. The categories are Task Orientation, Cognitive, Motility, and Interpersonal Behavior. These broad categories are further divided into specific behavioral characteristics. Thus, if you observe what you interpret as interpersonal behavior (broad category 4), you would then determine the direction or pattern of the behavior—Child to Teacher, Child to Other Child, or Other Child to Child. From there you would have to make yet another decision about the nature of the interpersonal behavior using the descriptions provided in the checklist: Complies, Ignores, Resists, and so on. Table 7-1 gives you enough space to record the behaviors of eight children, or of one child over eight time intervals, whichever best suits your purpose. Space is provided at the end of the table for doing either one or both of the following: (1) briefly describing the context of the recorded behaviors and/or (2) recording the names of the children observed and using the line numbers as codes to quickly identify the child being observed at any particular time. (If John's name is recorded on line 1, then the numeral "1" thereafter refers to John. This eliminates the need to repeatedly write "John." We also recommend that you circle the children's identification numbers. This will avoid confusion when, for example, numbers are also used to indicate such things as behaviors or categories of behaviors. (See Table 7-5 for an example of when a distinction would be important.)

This format is easy to use. You must first specify the time intervals you will use. Your choices are almost unlimited, but they must be tempered by the purpose of your observation and the practicality of any given interval. For instance, it would not make much sense to observe for 1 minute and then wait 10 minutes before observing and recording again. This scheme would waste precious time. It would also be difficult to observe for 1 second and record for 1 second. The time intervals are far too short to be manageable and adhered to with any accuracy, and 1 second is not nearly long enough to fully comprehend what a child is actually doing.

Bear in mind that the sign-system time-sampling format illustrated in Table 7-1 is just one of many possible formats. (It is included here because it was an actual instrument used by students in the early childhood education program at Pennsylvania State University.) Table 7-1 might seem a little less daunting if you understand that

Table 7-1 One Example of a Time Sampling Format: Sign System								
Behavioral Signs	Time Intervals							
	1	**2**	**3**	**4**	**5**	**6**	**7**	**8**
1. Task Orientation: A. Attentive to teacher; B. Intent on individual work; C. Disinterest; D. Attentive to other children; E. Social work; F. Intent on nonteacher-prescribed work; G. Aimless wandering; H. Verbally disruptive; I. Physically disruptive								
2. Cognitive: A. Seeking information; B. Offering information; C. Curiosity and experimentation; D. None								
3. Motility: A. Expansive; B. Average; C. Constricted								
4. Interpersonal Behavior								
4.1 Child to Teacher: A. Absent; B. Present								
4.1a Response to Teacher Initiation: A. Complies; B. Ignores; C. Resists; D. None								
4.1b Seeks Help, Support, Approval: A. Absent; B. Present								
4.1c Verbalization to Teacher: A. Confident; B. Hesitant; C. Whine; D. None								
4.2a Child to Other Child: A. Absent; B. Present								
4.2a Type: A. Active interchange; B. Approaches tentatively; C. Passive watching; D. Imitates; E. Avoids								
4.2b Tone: A. Friendly; B. Neutral; C. Hostile								
4.2c Control: A. Dominates; B. Neutral; C. Passive								
	1	2	3	4	5	6	7	8

Children Observed

1. __Aliya _____   4. _____   7. _____

2. __Corrine _____   5. _____   8. _____

3. __Carlita _____   6. _____

Modified from a time sampling form originated by Donald S. Peters, Ph.D. (Pennsylvania State University).

PART TWO

many time sampling formats are a type of checklist. The particular one illustrated here required a little more preparation and planning than, say, the checklist in Table 12-1 (page 200). Nonetheless, in both cases, the observer had to determine ahead of time what kinds of behaviors were of interest to her and the language she was going to use to define or describe those behaviors.

Although Table 7-1 looks complicated, with a little study and some practice, you will find it relatively easy to use. Each child you are observing is given an identification number by writing the child's name on one of the numbered spaces listed under the heading "Children Observed." Let us look briefly at some data pertaining to three hypothetical children illustrated in Table 7-2. We have arbitrarily listed Aliya as the first child, and her identifying number is 1. (We suggest that you circle each child's identifying number, as we did, to distinguish it from the other numbers you will use to identify the various behaviors and their descriptions.)

Because you have to be aware of 11 behavioral categories in this particular recording instrument, it would be appropriate to give yourself enough time both to observe the child and determine into which of the behavioral categories his or her behavior fits, and to record the numbers that apply to those categories. Thus, giving yourself 20 seconds to observe, 20 seconds to record, and 20 seconds before observing the next child will keep your total time per child to one minute. This

Table 7-2 Example of a Partially Completed Time Sample for Three Hypothetical Children: Sign System

Behavioral Signs	Time Intervals							
	1	2	3	4	5	6	7	8
1. Task Orientation: A. Attentive to teacher; B. Intent on individual work; C. Disinterest; D. Attentive to other children; E. Social work; F. Intent on nonteacher-prescribed work; G. Aimless wandering; H. Verbally disruptive; I. Physically disruptive	① D	② A	③ G					
2. Cognitive: A. Seeking information; B. Offering information; C. Curiosity and experimentation; D. None	① A, B	② A	③ D					
3. Motility: A. Expansive; B. Average; C. Constricted	① B	② B	③ B					
4. Interpersonal Behavior								
4.1 Child to Teacher: A. Absent; B. Present	① A	② B	③ A					
4.1a Response to Teacher Initiation: A. Complies; B. Ignores; C. Resists; D. None		② A						

(continues)

Table 7-2 Example of a Partially Completed Time Sample for Three Hypothetical Children: Sign System (continued)

Behavioral Signs	Time Intervals							
	1	2	3	4	5	6	7	8
4.1b Seeks Help, Support, Approval: A. Absent; B. Present		② B						
4.1c Verbalization to Teacher: A. Confident; B. Hesitant; C. Whine; D. None		② A						
4.2 Child to Other Child: A. Absent; B. Present	① B	② A	③ A					
4.2a Type: A. Active interchange; B. Approaches tentatively; C. Passive watching; D. Imitates; E. Avoids	① B							
4.2b Tone: A. Friendly; B. Neutral; C. Hostile	① A							
4.2c Control: A. Dominates; B. Neutral; C. Passive	① B							
	1	2	3	4	5	6	7	8

Children Observed

1. __Aliya _____   4. _____   7. _____

2. __Corrine _____   5. _____   8. _____

3. __Carlita _____   6. _____

Modified from a time sampling form originated by Donald S. Peters, Ph.D. (Pennsylvania State University).

would seem to be a very manageable time frame, and, at least in principle, you could observe and record the behavior of 15 children in 15 minutes using this format. Of course, the time intervals you use with this and any other time sampling instrument depend on you and your particular circumstances. Let us see how a brief time sample of Aliya, Corinne, and Carlita's behaviors might actually look using Table 7-2. Please note that these samples could, but do not, reflect observational data acquired through another recording technique such as the narrative description or event sample, what we choose to call "parallel recording." In the case of our three hypothetical children, we simply provide an illustrative time sampling record so that you can see how such a record would look. We also provide a brief explanation of the recorded data.

According to the recordings indicated in Table 7-2, Aliya was Attentive to Other Children (as indicated by the letter "D" under the Task Orientation category). In the Cognitive category, she was both Seeking and Offering Information. Her Motility was average. Under the general category of Interpersonal Behavior, no Child-to-Teacher interaction was observed; therefore, category 4.1 (Child to Teacher) was marked Absent. Consequently, categories 4.1a through 4.1c were left blank because there was nothing to report regarding Child-to-Teacher interactions.

Corinne (child number 2) was observed as Attentive to the Teacher, and in the Cognitive category, she was Seeking Information. Corinne's Motility was average. In category 4.1, Child-to-Teacher interaction was observed, which required responses to categories 4.1a through 4.1c. In Corinne's case, her Response to Teacher Initiation was compliant; she sought Help, Support, or Approval; and her Verbalization to Teacher was confident. You should be able to figure out the data for Carlita on your own.

A POSSIBLE PRACTICAL EXERCISE

At this juncture, let us introduce a practical exercise. Look at Parten's six classifications of play or social interaction, found in Table 7-3a. Parten's classification is an example of a category system, which, again, means that her scheme is both exhaustive and mutually exclusive. Construct a time sampling format that allows you to record the occurrence of Parten's play behaviors. This can be done by building a table consisting of "cells" that accommodate each of the six play categories and each of the children that you will observe. When completed, the form might look something like Table 7-3b.

Choose a time sampling interval (such as 10 seconds for observing, 10 seconds for recording, and 40 seconds of waiting before moving on to the next child). If you observe Eiswari engaging in any one of Parten's six play categories, put a check mark in the cell (box) under Eiswari's name and to the right of the category that applies to it. Then move on to Michael, and repeat the same process until you have observed all the children listed on the form. Of course, you may enlarge the form to include more children, or reduce it to include fewer children than are allotted space in the example. You can also draw vertical lines down the columns to make spaces for repeated observations of the same children. Thus, if you divide each cell into, say, four equal parts, you can observe each child four different times without having to construct more forms.

As they stand, the entries in Table 7-3b are straightforward enough not to require any explanation. If, however, these entries were accompanied by a brief description, which would be entirely appropriate, it might have been noted that Michael and Sun Lee were "partners" in the parallel play and that Beth and Miguel were engaged in cooperative play with each other. Without a narrative description, one might be tempted to infer the Michael/Sun Lee partnership, in as much as they were observed during adjoining time intervals. It also might seem reasonable to infer that Beth and Miguel were partners in cooperative play because their behavior was separated by only a one-minute interval. However, without the narrative description's

Table 7-3a Parten's Six Classifications of Play or Social Interaction

1. Unoccupied Behavior

Here the child is not engaging in any obvious play activity or social interaction. Rather, she watches anything that is of interest at the moment. When there is nothing of interest to watch, the child will play with her own body, move around from place to place, follow the teacher, or stay in one spot looking around the room.

2. Onlooker Behavior

Here the child spends most of her time watching other children play. The child may talk to the playing children, may ask questions, or give suggestions, but does not enter into play. The child remains within speaking distance so that what goes on can be seen and heard; this indicates a definite interest in a group(s) of children, unlike the unoccupied child, who shows no interest in any particular group of children but only a shifting interest in what happens to be exciting at the moment.

3. Solitary Play

This is play activity that is conducted independently of what anyone else is doing. The child plays with toys that differ from those used by other children in the immediate area—within speaking distance—and he makes no effort to get closer to them or to speak to them. The child is focused entirely on his own activity and is not influenced by what others are doing.

4. Parallel Play

Here the child is playing close to other children but is still independent of them. The child uses toys that are like the toys being used by the others, but he uses them as he sees fit and neither is influenced by nor tries to influence the others. The child thus plays *beside* rather than with the other children.

(continues)

Table 7-3a Parten's Six Classifications of Play or Social Interaction (continued)

| **5. Associative Play**  | Here the child plays with the other children. There is a sharing of material and equipment; the children may follow each other around; there may be attempts to control who may or who may not play in a group, although such control efforts are not strongly asserted. The children engage in similar but not necessarily identical activity, and there is no division of labor or organization of activity, or of individuals. Each child does what he or she essentially wants to do, without putting the interests of the group first. |
| **6. Cooperative or Organized Supplementary Play**  | The key word in this category is "organized." The child plays in a group that is established for a particular purpose—making some material product, gaining some competitive goal, playing some formal games. There is a sense of "we-ness," whereby one definitely belongs or does not belong to the group. There is also some leadership present—one or two members who direct the activity of the others. This therefore requires some division of labor, a taking of different roles by the group members and the support of one child's efforts by those of the others. |

raw data and only the coded data of the time sample, such inferences would have to be considered unsubstantiated and therefore unjustifiable.

Yet another procedure can use the numbering technique to identify the children—as described earlier—and this modified form might look like Table 7-3c.

In this format you follow the same time sampling procedure as described earlier (or one devised by you), but in this case, if Eiswari displays parallel play, you simply write the numeral "1" in the box or cell to the right of the cell that contains the parallel play category. Again, you proceed in this fashion until you have observed all the children listed below the time sampling form. Because there are 22 columns in this example form, you could repeat this process 22 times for each of the 10 children, or you could observe and record the behavior of as many as 22 children. There are a number of possible combinations, although not all are equally desirable and practical. The time intervals used for Table 7-3b would be perfectly appropriate for Table 7-3c: 10 seconds observing, 10 seconds recording, and wait 40 seconds before moving on to the next child.

Parten's Play Categories	Eiswari	Michael	Sun Lee	Jethro	Beth	Ibraham	Miguel
Unoccupied Behavior	X						
Onlooker Behavior				X			
Solitary Play						X	
Parallel Play		X	X				
Associative Play							
Cooperative Play					X		X

Table 7-3b Time Sample Form for Recording Play

Possible Time Intervals: 10 seconds observing and 10 seconds recording; wait 40 seconds before moving to the next child

Table 7-3c Modified Sample Form for Recording Play

Parten's Play Category										
Unoccupied Behavior	2									
Onlooker Behavior			6	7						
Solitary Play		5								
Parallel Play	1		4							
Associative Play		3								
Cooperative Play				8	9	10				

Children Observed

1. Eiswari
2. Michael
3. Sun Lee
4. Jethro
5. Beth
6. Ibraham
7. Miguel
8. Ronald
9. Melissa
10. Juan

Much simpler coding schemes are available. Gander and Gardner (1981), for instance, note a procedure where each minute is divided into 15-second intervals that are represented in some kind of graphic form. During each 15 seconds of observation, if the selected behavior occurs, an "X" is placed in the appropriate spot on the form; if the behavior does not occur, an "O" is recorded. Over a period of three minutes the record could look something like the following, where each marks off a 15-second interval and each | marks the end of one minute (adapted from Gander & Gardner, 1981):

The form could be made more elaborate if prepared and printed ahead of time. It could look like the following:

The shaded portions mark off each 15-second interval—they replace the diagonal lines in the other example. They are clearly discernible and make for easy recording because the blank spaces in which the Xs and Os are to be put are also clearly delineated. This could be repeated any number of times for any number of children. The issue here is not how elaborate or fancy a form one can construct, but rather how clear and easy the form is to use.

It may be helpful if you can think of time sampling in relation to the concept of a behavior stream. A person's life consists of a continuous stream of behavior that flows through time. The time sampling method looks for samples of certain kinds of behavior in a child's behavior stream, but it looks for those behaviors only in specific parts of the stream identified by intervals of time. So, an observer using the time sampling method might reason along the following lines:

I am going to look for aggressive behavior in this group of children, but I want to observe all the children, and I'm interested in how often aggression is displayed among the group. Therefore, between the hours of 9:00 A.M. and 10:30 A.M., a one and one-half hour segment of these children's behavior streams will flow by. I want to enter into that one and one-half hour part of their lives and see what is happening. To do this, I am going to divide up the total 90 minutes among all 15 children, which gives me 6 minutes for each child. To get a reasonably representative sample of behavior, however, I will probably repeat this entire process several times over the course of a week so that I will end up with, say, three 6-minute recorded samples of behavior for each child. I will also need to observe the children during different times of the day and during different activities, which will contribute further to the representativeness of my sample.

Open versus Closed

Both Wright (1960) and Goodwin and Driscoll (1980) classify time sampling as a closed method. They consider it closed because of its use of coding schemes "at the point of initial data collection" (Goodwin & Driscoll, 1980). A coding scheme applied at the time of observation loses raw data; it is that loss that defines a closed method.

Time sampling methods are not always closed, nor need they be completely closed. We have considered the possibility of combining a closed coding scheme and an open narrative description or event sample. But even the use of only narrative descriptions is acceptable. Lay-Dopyera and Dopyera (1982), for example, describe the on–off sequence we discussed earlier as "observation, note-taking, and note expansion." Although time sampling often uses a coding scheme to record behaviors, the terms *note-taking* and *note expansion* indicate that a form of narrative record can also be used. The principal feature of time sampling is the use of precisely and uniformly defined time intervals, not the specific recording technique used. Consequently, we consider time sampling an open method to the extent that it preserves the raw data.

Degree of Selectivity

The time sampling method is very selective; it "fishes" with a large-holed net, and the net is cast only when the preselected behavior appears in the child's behavior stream. It is not like the narrative description, which, you recall, fishes with a small-holed net that stays in the stream throughout the observation period.

Degree of Inference Required

Time sampling does require initial inferences or interpretations. This is because the method requires you to make an immediate decision concerning whether to record a behavior. That decision is based on whether you see the behavior as falling under a particular descriptive category as an example of aggression, cooperative play, or what have you.

As with the narrative description or any of the other methods to be discussed, time sampling can require inferences at other times in the observation process. Once you have collected your data, you may want to use them to draw conclusions about such things as the relationship between the observed behaviors and certain characteristics of their context. For example, you may discover that Billy seems to behave aggressively when he is in the big block area during free play. However, drawing conclusions about such relationships requires information on context and behaviors that is not ordinarily obtained with coding schemes. Therefore, you may have to include some narrative description as part of your recording technique. In any case, such inferences would be made after the observations are completed; they are not an inherent part of the method but part of the use made of the recorded data.

Advantages

Time sampling has many advantages. There are no restrictions on the kinds of behaviors that can be studied with this method. Wright (1960) cites the range of behaviors that have been time sampled as early as the 1930s. He refers to behaviors ranging from "imaginative behavior" to "friendships and quarrels" to "tics or 'nervous habits'" (p. 93). The method has a long history, which attests to its reliability and usefulness.

The method is economical in terms of required time and energy. Time sampling is efficient because it regulates precisely the content of the observation and the amount of time one observes (Wright, 1960; Irwin & Bushnell, 1980). Efficiency is also achieved by using preestablished coding schemes, which reduces variability in an observer's judgments and inferences. This potential elimination of differing judgments contributes to an agreement among several observers, thereby increasing **inter-observer reliability**.

Time sampling also provides representative and reliable data if one gathers a large number of observations related to a particular research problem or developmental/educational purpose. Large numbers of recordings are possible because of the method's efficiency and the ease with which data can be recorded using coding schemes. Early childhood educators and other professional child care workers may never need to gather data for formal research projects, thus limiting for some readers the usefulness of learning about time sampling in a research context. Nonetheless, one can still be informed about the varied purposes for which this technique can be used, thereby conceivably resulting in other creative uses of the time sampling format.

Yet another advantage of the time sampling method is its ability to combine several different techniques for recording—coding and narrative description, for example. This allows the observer to use two different nets; one net catches limited kinds of data (whether the behavior has occurred at all), and the other net catches the details of context and behavior. One can also use event sampling or some other form of narrative description by itself.

inter-observer reliability

The degree to which two or more observers agree with one another as to what occurred during an observation session. High inter-observer reliability indicates minimal disagreement and relatively few differences in observers' judgments and inferences.

Disadvantages

This last advantage is an important one, for it also points up a significant disadvantage of a time sampling format that uses only coding schemes. Coding schemes do not capture the details of context, what the behaviors look like, how the behavior sequence turns out, how the behaviors change over time, or how the behaviors are related to one another (Wright, 1960; Irwin & Bushnell, 1980). Brandt (1972) points out these same weaknesses when he notes that time samples lack the continuity of event samples and also fail to record the full details of the behavioral context that are captured by event samples. From this perspective, then, time sampling is chiefly used to measure the frequency of behaviors.

Frequency of occurrence of a given behavior is a limiting factor, however. Behaviors are not displayed equally often, nor do all behaviors occur with great frequency. It makes no sense to record every 15 seconds whether a particular behavior took place when that behavior occurs every 28 minutes on the average. Gander and Gardner (1981) address this problem when they relate behavior frequency with decisions concerning the length of the observation periods and the length of the recording intervals. If a behavior can be expected to occur fairly often, it may make sense to set aside several segments of time for observing and recording and to specify recording intervals that are relatively frequent and short. Gander and Gardner use the example of a child's social interaction and suggest that "you might decide to observe for three five-minute sessions at five-minute intervals, and note whether your target behavior is occurring every fifteen seconds" (p. 452). This procedure assumes that social interactions take place frequently enough to justify dividing your recording intervals into such small segments. It therefore follows that longer recording intervals should be adopted when the behavior of interest occurs less frequently. But, as Gander and Gardner point out, these decisions take "a little experience." These decisions may also depend on the observer doing some preliminary observations to determine the frequency of the behaviors. Again, Irwin and Bushnell (1980) indicate that for time sampling to be an effective method, a behavior should occur at least once every 15 minutes on the average.

Time sampling does not treat behavior as it naturally occurs. When using predefined and restricted units of time, it is inevitable that the natural length of the behaviors will not correspond exactly to the somewhat arbitrary length of the observing and recording intervals. It is as though you throw your net into an entire school of fish, but you haul in only a very small number of them. From that very small number you will be able to tell almost nothing about the ones that got away. This has been referred to as "the observation of action fragments" (Wright, 1960, p. 100). A problem arises if these fragments do not accurately represent what is going on in the larger behavior stream. Here is an illustration.

You are observing a classroom, and you watch each child for five-second intervals and record on a precoded sheet any occurrences of aggressive behavior. After each interval, you move on to another child, repeating this procedure until every child has been observed. The process is then repeated until you have obtained some predetermined total number of observations. Suppose that while you are giving your five seconds of attention to Jean, she screams at Harold, "Get out of here, you bad boy!" You decide this is an example of verbal aggression, and you appropriately mark it as such on your recording sheet. You then shift your attention to the next child. What you may have missed from this sequence were the preceding dramatic play behaviors in which Jean was the "mommy" and Harold was her "son." "Mommy" was simply scolding her "son" for misbehaving, symbolically speaking. You may also have missed Harold's response: "I'm sorry, Mommy; please don't spank me." In this illustration,

Jean's remarks, taken out of context, misrepresented the larger sequence of which they were a part. This example argues for gathering a number of time samples to ensure the representativeness and validity of your data. One could also argue that sampling for longer time periods would increase the accuracy and representativeness of your data. But if your intervals are too long, you might as well use event sampling, because you are sacrificing the time sample's economy and efficiency. To observe for, say, five-minute periods to ensure the accuracy of your interpretation, but only to record the behavior with a check mark, would indeed be rather wasteful of your time. However, our goal here is to inform you of the advantages and disadvantages of time sampling, not to prescribe precisely when you should or should not use the technique and for what precise time intervals. As with many human endeavors, some judgment is required—and sometimes some experimentation.

Irwin and Bushnell (1980) also report that the use of predetermined categories might bias what the observer sees. As they put it, "[Y]ou look for things to fit the categories rather than describe what is occurring, and use of predetermined categories can cause you to overlook behaviors that might be important in helping understand the behavior or pattern under study" (p. 159). This weakness of time sampling is found in any method that is highly selective and closed.

A final comment on time sampling may have to do with either advantages or disadvantages, depending on your point of view. Coding schemes impose certain problems and obligations on the observer. Look again at Table 7-1. The categories (actually signs) in Table 7-1 may appear straightforward, but their simplicity is deceptive. Before you could use Table 7-1 as a time sampling technique, every one of those signs would have to be defined. How would you recognize "curiosity and experimentation" if you saw them? How would you know whether a child's verbalizations to her teacher were confident, hesitant, or whining? These decisions require inferences; moreover, they require consistent inferences. It is improper to accept a set of behaviors as verbally disruptive at one time, then a few minutes later put similar behaviors into a different category. Defining such descriptive categories as precisely as you can is a strength of the time sampling method, but at the same time, such definition requires a lot of prior preparation.

Some Uses and Applications of the Time Sample

As with our presentation of all the recording methods, the respective uses for these methods can usually be gleaned from the explanatory text. In this present section, we simply single out some of these uses as a way of emphasizing them for your convenience and clarification. Let us begin with Table 7-4, which is one illustration of how a completed time sample might look; it also suggests several uses for time sample data that we will briefly explore.

Perhaps two of the best clues to help you decide when to use the time sample are its eminent suitability for *efficiently gathering representative data* about

Table 7-4 Example of a Hypothetical Time Sampling Recording of Social and Play Behavior

Behavior	1	2	3	4	5	6	7	8
				Time Intervals				
Cooperates well with other children	①			④				
Does not cooperate with other children			③					
Displays outgoing, friendly behavior		②		④				
Displays aggressive behavior			③					
Shows independent behavior		②						
Shows dependent behavior				④				
Initiates play activity with other children—takes a leadership role	①							
Takes a follower role				④				
Appears to be liked by many of the other children—is popular	①	②		④				
Does not appear to be well-liked or popular			③					
	1	2	3	4	5	6	7	8

Children Observed

1. Margaret   2. Philip   3. Courtney   4. Patricia

Note: Selected time intervals are 30 seconds to observe, 15 seconds to record, and a 15-second wait before observing the next child.

children—the two clues are "efficiently" and "representative." Table 7-4 very nicely illustrates this method's efficiency and, implicitly at least, the representative character of the information it records. You can expect social and play behavior to occur frequently in a child care center, which is a necessary condition for using the time sample. Table 7-4 limits to eight the number of one-minute recording intervals, but this is an artificial limitation that need not be followed in a real-life observation session. If there were 15 children in this center, simply by increasing the size of the recording sheet by seven time intervals (columns), you could observe all of the children in about 15 minutes. If you repeated these sessions a reasonable number of times, you could be confident that the social and play behaviors you sampled would be representative of the social and play behaviors that you did not sample.

When might these kinds of data find useful application for staff and parents? Two such applications come to mind: (1) to determine which of the categories of behavior—aggressiveness, cooperativeness, friendliness, etc.—the children display the least or the most often; or (2) to determine which children are popular (social stars) or unpopular (social isolates), dependent or independent, leaders or followers, and so on for any behaviors or categories of behavior that interest you and that you include in your time sample form. Of course, what you eventually do with this information depends on your particular circumstances and needs, but it seems apparent that such information could help staff do such things as plan specific activities for the children or more general curriculum changes, or implement intervention strategies to change the character or frequency of certain behaviors. Such changes could consist of decreasing the frequency of aggressive behavior or increasing the frequency of cooperative behavior. The latter use would be in keeping with Beaty's (2002) assertion that a major purpose of time sampling is to gather "behavior modification baseline data" (p. 34).

Table 7-5 Time Sampling—Hypothetical Example Depicting Interactions of Three Children

Observer's Name Estelle Gibbons (Center Staff)

Child/Children Observed Cassandra, Carla, Michelle

Child's/Children's Age(s) 4 years, 8 months; 4 yrs, 9 mos; 4 yrs, 6 mos

Child's/Children's Sex F, F, F

Observation Context (home, child care center, preschool, school) Humpty Dumpty Child Care Center

Date of Observation April 24, 2008 **Time Begun** 9:05 A.M. **Time Ended** 9:55 A.M.

Brief Description of Characteristics of Physical and Social Environment
The children appear to be in a good mood today, and the teachers and aides seem to share the children's mood. It is raining. Knowing that they will not be able to go outside, the children seem doubly intent on focusing their physical energy on the activity areas, which are already in a bit of disorder. The general demeanor is in somewhat sharp contrast with yesterday's emotional climate.

Behavior Categories	Time Intervals							
	1	2	3	4	5	6	7	8
General Response to Setting 1. Enters setting willingly (specify which areas involved— big block area [BBA], reading area [RA], etc.)	①	②	③	①				
2. Enters setting reluctantly	1	1	1	1				
3. Refuses to enter setting	BBA	BBA	BBA	FP				

(continues)

Table 7-5 Time Sampling—Hypothetical Example Depicting Interactions of Three Children (continued)									
	Time Intervals								
Behavior Categories	**1**	**2**	**3**	**4**	**5**	**6**	**7**	**8**	
General Response to Environment	①	②	③	①					
4. Uses equipment/materials freely	4	4	4	4					
5. Limited or sporadic use of equipment/materials									
6. No use of equipment/materials									
General Response to Others	①	②	③	①					
7. Seeks or is in contact with peer(s)	7	7	7	8					
8. Seeks or is in contact with adult									
9. Avoids or breaks contact with peer(s)									
10. Avoids or breaks contact with adult									
11. Reluctant contact with peer(s); contact lacks motivation or concentration on part of child									
12. Reluctant contact with adult; contact lacks motivation or concentration on part of child									

Children Observed

1. Cassandra
2. Carla
3. Michelle

KEY

BBA—Big Block Area

PA—Puzzle Area

FP—Finger Painting Area

Let us look at Table 7-5 for one more potential application of time sample data. You will notice that this recording format indicates where in the child care classroom behavior is taking place. As it turns out, this can be very valuable information.

As we will stress more than once throughout this text, the context in which behavior occurs is extremely important. All behavior takes place within a physical environment of some kind or description, and child care professionals are usually very concerned about how they set up (configure) the various areas in the classroom and what equipment and materials these areas will contain. Table 7-5 takes into account three areas in our hypothetical child care center: the big block area, the puzzle area, and the finger painting area. Even though the above example is far from complete—it samples the behavior of only three children during only four time intervals—it nonetheless yields some potentially useful information.

For instance, we know that Cassandra, Carla, and Michelle enter the big block area willingly, they use the equipment and materials in the big block area freely, and they seek or are in contact with peers. Cassandra also enters the finger painting area willingly, but there she seeks or is in contact with an adult. The record ends there, so we have no way of knowing what might have transpired if the recording went to the eighth time interval or beyond. Nonetheless, it seems apparent that tracking changes in children's behavior as they move from one location to another is a reasonable application of the kind of information illustrated in Table 7-5. And, of course, the time sample's efficiency would permit such tracking of behavior for any number of children without having to expend the time and energy required by the narrative description.

Having said that, however, we ask you to recall from your reading of Chapter 6 that the narrative description can be used in combination with all of the recording methods discussed in this text. This means that you could supplement the time sample's coded data, as represented in Tables 7-4 and 7-5, with the narrative description's raw data, which would give you a more complete picture of what actually occurred. In other words, you would use two different nets: One net catches limited kinds of data (whether the behavior has occurred at all), and the other net catches the details of context and behavior (raw data). Any decision, of course, would, among other factors, depend on such things as what you want to do with the data or how many children you want to observe in the amount of time you have available.

FLORENCE AND THE TIME SAMPLE

As we follow our hypothetical student named Florence and "tune in" on her thought processes, this time she has more information and knowledge at her disposal than she did in Chapter 6: She has some understanding of the narrative description. This means that she can compare the narrative description with the time sample to determine which of the two methods will better accomplish the purpose of her observations. Florence's instructor gave her the assignment of observing a group of 15 four-year-olds to see which of two behaviors occurred more frequently during free play time—cooperation or aggression. It did not take long for Florence to realize that her decision would be a "no-brainer." Here is a brief sample of her reasoning:

Let's see, I have to observe 15 children and look for only two behaviors—cooperation and aggression. Well, to use the narrative description would not be very appropriate in this case because it requires a lot of writing and it's intended to record everything that happens during the observation session. My assignment doesn't require me to record everything that the children do during free play, only whether they are behaving cooperatively or aggressively.

Besides, to gather narrative descriptions on 15 children would take a lot of unnecessary time and effort. So it seems to me that the time sample is the recording technique to use for this assignment. Now, how shall I set this up?

Well, first of all, I have to make sure I know what cooperation and aggression will look like when I see them. That means I'll have to define them in some way. That shouldn't be too hard to do. So, if I see two or more children helping each other accomplish a common goal, such as building a block tower, that seems a reasonable example of cooperation. Or if one child helps another child find a toy, for example, or helps another child put on his coat, that also seems a reasonable example of cooperation. Aggression shouldn't be too hard to define. Of course, there's physical aggression and verbal aggression—pushing or hitting another child would be physical aggression, and hollering at or insulting another child would be verbal aggression. I have to keep in mind that the time sample will not tell me anything about the cooperative or aggressive behavior, but only that a particular child behaved in one of those two ways. Well, my instructor didn't tell me that I had to get any information other than whether or not the children exhibited either of these two behaviors. Then again, if I wanted to, I could write a brief description of those behaviors, and that would be a combination of the time sample and a modified form of the narrative description.

Now how do I record the information I need? I think I'll just rework Table 7–4 from *Seeing Young Children.* I'll keep the behavior categories that are relevant and perhaps add a few more. I'll need 15 columns in the time sample form so that I can accommodate all 15 children in the classroom. I'll give each child a number, and if the child I'm observing at a given time exhibits either cooperative or aggressive behavior, I'll enter his or her number in the appropriate box and circle it so that I know the number identifies the child observed. Wait a minute—what if the child I'm observing doesn't show either cooperative or aggressive behavior? I know—I'll add a category I'll call "Other," and I'll enter that child's number in that third category. From what I've read in the text, observing for 10 seconds, recording for 10 seconds, and waiting 40 seconds before moving on to the next child seems like a good way to go. Well, I guess I'm all set.

SUMMARY

The time sampling method has two distinguishing features. It observes and records selected samples of a child's behavior, and it does so only during predetermined intervals of time. Time sampling aims at representative samples of behavior. To achieve this requires you to observe over a large enough number of intervals to capture the typical quality of the behavior stream from which the sample is taken.

The variations on the time sampling method are numerous. Although coding schemes are usually used with time sampling, narrative description can be combined with such schemes. There are two general types of coding schemes: category and sign systems. A sign system of coding requires mutually exclusive categories of behavior. No given behavior can be included in more than one category. A category system requires mutually exclusive categories and exhaustive categories. The categories must include the total range of behaviors.

Time sampling varies on the dimension of open versus closedness. If only coding schemes are used, the method is closed; if combined with narrative description, it is open to that degree. The method is very selective and records only specific behaviors. Time sampling requires inferences at the time of initial recording; a decision must be made regarding whether to record a particular behavior. Inferences may also be needed after the data are collected, depending on your purposes.

Time sampling is economical of time and effort. It regulates precisely the content of the observation and the amount of time you observe. An important disadvantage of time sampling is that it does not capture the details of behavior and context. It is also not a useful method for recording infrequent behaviors. The amount of preparation needed to define the behavioral categories used in the coding scheme can be an advantage or a disadvantage, depending on your point of view and how skillful you are at defining these behavioral categories.

Tables 7-4 offers another example of how a completed time sample might look, as well as illustrating the basic concept of the time sample. Each child is arbitrarily given a number that identifies him or her as the subject of observation during any particular time period. These numbers are circled to make it clear that their only purpose is to identify each child. Again, we recommend this as standard practice in the event that you use a time sample format in which numbers are also used for identifying behaviors, abilities, and the like.

In Tables 7-4, 30 seconds are allotted to observing. This length of time should give you ample opportunity to judge (interpret) whether a given behavior fits into any of the descriptions used in your time sampling instrument. It is also possible or even likely that a child's behavior will fall into more than one descriptive category during an observation time interval, thus also requiring additional time to make note of the other categories.

STUDY QUESTIONS

1. What does it mean to say that a sample of behavior is representative? Why is representativeness a potential problem in time sampling? How can this problem be solved or at least minimized?

2. What is a coding system? When is a coding system necessary in time sampling?

3. Describe an example of a coding system. What are its characteristics?

4. What makes time sampling a closed and highly selective method? When might time sampling not be closed?

5. Why is inference necessary in time sampling? When does it occur?

6. Describe the two applications of time sample data that are discussed in the text.

PRACTICAL EXERCISE

This exercise is relatively straightforward. We will ask you simply to duplicate Florence's assignment and construct a time sample sheet that would be suitable for recording instances of cooperative and aggressive behavior among a group of four-year-old children and subsequently determining which of those two behaviors occurred more frequently. You can either follow Florence's idea of modifying Tables 7-4, or you can construct an entirely different time sample format.

Event Sampling

KEY TERMS

event sampling

event

OBJECTIVES

After reading this chapter, you should be able to

- Examine the differences and similarities between time sampling and event sampling.
- Identify behaviors that could constitute an event.
- Identify procedures to record an event.
- Identify the characteristics of event sampling in relation to the dimensions of open versus closed, degree of selectivity, and degree of inference required.
- Analyze the advantages and disadvantages of event sampling.

GENERAL DESCRIPTION

Event sampling is the last formal method of observation to be discussed. Just as the word *time* is central to time sampling, the word **event** is central to event sampling. Although both methods use the word *sampling*, their procedures and results are usually quite different.

The notion of an event is not difficult to understand, nor is the notion of event sampling. Life is a continuous stream of events; an event of some kind or other is taking place every second of every day. At least, that is how events may be conceptualized. Put differently, an event is essentially anything that occurs somewhere in the real world. Some events can be observed in a particular way, whereas other events either go unnoticed or cannot be noticed or observed in the normal course of things—for example, various kinds of electromagnetic radiations (X-rays, gamma rays), sound waves that are not within hearing, and so on.

As a formal recording technique, event sampling simply takes advantage of the pervasive occurrence of events by defining which specific

event sampling

 A formal method that observes and records specific kinds of behaviors (events) whenever they occur. It is a sampling technique because it takes out of the behavior stream only preselected behaviors or categories of behaviors.

event

 Behaviors that can be placed into particular categories; for example, hitting to get a toy away from another child is a behavior that can be put into the category "instrumental aggression."

events are of interest and waiting until they occur in the observation setting. In the context of observing children, events are behaviors that can be placed into particular categories. For instance, a quarrel is an event that is made up of specific observable behaviors such as loud speech, certain kinds of facial expressions, or arguing over such things as the possession of a toy. You observe two children exhibiting certain behaviors, and you must decide whether those behaviors belong to the category labeled "quarrels." Put another way, do those behaviors represent the event called quarreling?

Recall that in time sampling, preselected behaviors are the targets of observation and recording. However, whether you come away with any recorded instances of these behaviors depends not only on whether they occur, but also on whether they occur within specified intervals of time. So you can see that time sampling methods take two different samples out of the child's behavior stream: (1) specifically defined segments of time and (2) specifically defined behaviors. The limiting condition here is that these two samples must occur at the same time. The designated behavior must be displayed sometime during the designated time interval; otherwise, the behavior either escapes notice or it is not recorded because it did not occur at the proper time.

Event sampling differs from time sampling in that it takes only one sample from the child's behavior stream, namely specifically defined behaviors or events. Events are behaviors that can be placed into particular categories. For example, quarrels, as stated previously, can be an event. You observe two children exhibiting certain behaviors, and you must decide whether these behaviors belong in the category labeled "quarrels." The event must have certain characteristics if it is to be labeled a quarrel.

Event sampling seems simple. You select an event for observing, whether it be quarrels, social interactions, or dependency behavior. Again, you define the event in terms of the behaviors you will accept as examples of that event. You position yourself in the observation setting where the children can be seen, and you wait for the event to occur. (See Table 8-1.) When it does, you can do one of three things. Goodwin and Driscoll (1980) summarize the recording technique used with event sampling as immediate coding of the occurrence of certain events. However, Lay-Dopyera and Dopyera (1982) and Gander and Gardner (1981) write of describing the event in detail. As Gander and Gardner say, "[Y]ou should record the entire sequence of behavior from beginning to end in as much detail as possible to provide a rich body of information to use in drawing inferences" (p. 453). Therefore, you can choose (1) a coding scheme, (2) a narrative description, or (3) a combination of these two. The previous discussion of coding schemes in time sampling also applies to event sampling. When using narrative description, you will observe and record for as long as the event lasts. (Note how this differs from time sampling, where observing and recording are limited to predetermined periods of time.) Table 8-1 is an illustration of how an event sample might look.

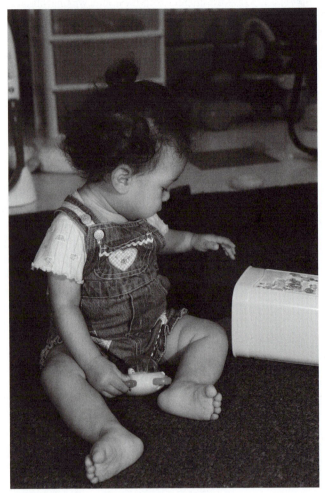

Event sampling differs from time sampling in that it takes only one sample from the child's behavior stream: specifically defined behaviors or events.

Just as a point of information, event sampling is similar in some respects to time sampling. Refer to Chapter 7, Table 7-1, for example. Each of the behavioral categories represents an event, and you record whether the event has occurred. You already know the two conditions that have to be present for time sampling to work. However, it is also characteristic of time sampling that very often no descriptions of the behavior are recorded, only whether the child has exhibited the behavior of interest. At the risk of confusing you, can you see how a time sample is in some instances very much like a checklist? Note, however, that checklists are usually concerned only with whether a behavior has occurred, not with when it occurred.

Event sampling, on the other hand, is very much like the narrative description, except that the event sample disregards any behavior that does not fit into the

Table 8-1 Event Sampling: Two Hypothetical Children's Social Behavior During Free Play

Observer's Name Susan Carroll

Child/Children Observed Francesca, Harold

Child's/Children's Age(s) 4 years; 4 years, 2 months **Child's/Children's Sex** Female, Male

Observation Context (home, child care center, preschool, school) Children's Delight Child Care Center

Date of Observation October 13, 2008 **Time Begun** 9:20 A.M. **Time Ended** 9:30 A.M.

Brief Description of Physical and Social Environment
Everyone seems especially active; the children's moods are upbeat. It's raining, and the children were told there will be no time spent outdoors today, but no one seems to mind having to stay inside. There is a lot of interaction among the children, which makes this a good time to observe their social behaviors.

Objective Behavioral Descriptions (OBDs) and Interpretations: Event Sampling

OBD 1: [Time Begun 9:20 A.M. Time Ended 9:24 A.M.]

Francesca and Harold pair off and walk over to the sand table. They are busily engaged in a conversation. Harold says, "Let's play construction company, and I'm the boss." Francesca replies, "OK, but I wanna drive the truck, 'cause my mommy says girls can drive trucks just as good as boys." Harold frowns briefly, then replies, "That's OK if you drive the little truck and I drive the big one. You gotta be strong to drive a big truck, and boys are stronger than girls." Francesca makes no response as she picks up the little truck and "drives" it over some pieces of wood that apparently serve as a road on the sand. Harold picks up his big truck and also starts to drive, when he suddenly drops his truck and says to Francesca, "Let's go finger paint." Francesca nods and follows him to the finger painting area.

Interpretation 1:

Both children's language skills are quite well-developed. Their sentences are complete, well-formed, and clearly express their thoughts. Harold quickly takes a leadership role when he suggests they play "construction company." Although Francesca agrees, she is not afraid to voice her opinion about girls driving trucks. Harold makes no objection to Francesca wanting to drive, but he again appears to assert his leadership role, first by insisting that she drive the little truck because she would not be strong enough to drive the big one, and second by suggesting a change in activity. Francesca seems very agreeable to Harold's directions, although not unduly acquiescent. Perhaps her positive attitude and response are a result of Harold's nonaggressive, amicable tone of voice and demeanor—he doesn't seem to come across as bossy.

OBD 2: [Time Begun 9:26 A.M. Time Ended 9:30 A.M.]

Francesca runs ahead of Harold to the finger painting area. She takes a plastic apron from a hook and hands it to Harold. Harold says, "Thanks," and puts it on. Francesca takes down an apron, puts it on, then says, "Let's paint a picture together. We'll paint a lake with some boats on it. OK?" Harold doesn't respond to her suggestion; instead, he cocks his head to one side and says, "You look funny in that apron." She laughs and says, "So do you." They both laugh, then walk over to an easel with large blank paper on it. Before they can begin painting, Harold says, "I have to go to the bathroom. I'll be right back." Francesca waits for about 30 seconds, then takes off her apron and walks over to the big block area where several children are playing.

(continues)

Table 8-1 Event Sampling: Two Hypothetical Children's Social Behavior During Free Play (continued)
Interpretation 2:
I find it interesting that this time Francesca seems to initiate taking a leadership role by getting to the finger painting area ahead of Harold and by suggesting a theme for their painting. Again, however, I wonder if Harold tries to diminish her leadership efforts by not responding to her suggestion, but instead commenting on how "funny" she looks in her apron. For her part, Francesca responds positively to Harold's remark and comes back with her own comment that he also looks funny in his apron. Harold responds positively to Francesca's retort. The fact that she doesn't wait for Harold to return from the bathroom possibly could be interpreted as a sign of independence.

definition of the particular event. The narrative description records everything, without considering into which specific category the behavior can be put. It bears repeating that unlike time sampling, event sampling cares nothing about when a behavior occurs; it is not limited by having to record only behaviors that take place during predetermined time intervals.

Open versus Closed

Both Wright (1960) and Goodwin and Driscoll (1980) classify event sampling as a closed method. For our purposes, though, it can be open or closed. If you include a detailed narrative description, you would preserve the raw data, thus fulfilling the requirements of openness. If only coding schemes are used, the method is closed.

Degree of Selectivity

There is a high degree of selectivity because only specific events chosen beforehand are observed and recorded.

Degree of Inference Required

The degree of initial inference is high, just as in the time sampling method. Recall that an inference is any decision as to whether a behavior or set of behaviors belongs to a particular category. Does Ralph's clinging to the teacher's hand belong in the category "emotional dependency"? Also remember that even the simplest of these inferences is not self-evident. One must recognize clinging behavior and must know or decide whether clinging is an accurate or appropriate element of emotional dependency.

Advantages

Event sampling shares some of the advantages of both the narrative description and time sampling. The potential for rich, detailed descriptions of behavior and its context is an advantage, just as it is in the narrative description. Event sampling can also be very practical; it is a very suitable method to use with behaviors that occur frequently. Of course, the infrequent observer may particularly find this an advantage; the odds are in favor of frequent behaviors occurring at the same time as infrequent periods of observation. Thus, teachers or others who are in the observation setting often and for relatively long periods of time would likely find event sampling a useful method.

Wright (1960) points out that event sampling "structures the field of observation into natural units of behavior and situation" (p. 107). These "natural units" allow you to study the relationships between behavior and its context. The narrative description does the same thing, but it captures everything in the behavior stream. Therefore, specific behavior episodes—the natural units of behavior—have to be acquired from the larger body of information. Even though event sampling deals with natural behavior units, it is limited because it breaks up the continuity of behavior. As a result, the inability of event sampling to preserve large segments of the behavior stream may be regarded as a disadvantage.

A final advantage of event sampling is that it can combine narrative description and coding schemes, thus gaining the efficiency of immediate coding and the completeness of the narrative description. Because events are predefined patterns of behaviors, you can use a coding scheme such as a checklist to record features of the context that are predictably related to the event. For example, in a preschool setting, various locations within the room (e.g., big block area, dramatic play area), kinds of equipment and materials (paints, crayons, puzzles, trikes, and so on), official activity at the time the event occurs, and the children and adults present at the time can be listed for easy checking and coding. The narrative description can be structured around questions that relate directly to the particular event. Positive social interchanges, for instance, have certain behaviors associated with them. Therefore, you can be prepared to record information concerning what the children said during the social episode; what physical actions the child performed (hugging, smiling, giving a toy); what immediately preceded the social behavior; or the outcome of the event (adapted from Wright, 1960).

Disadvantages

Some of the disadvantages of event sampling have already been mentioned. The most notable disadvantage is its unsuitability for studying infrequently occurring behaviors. However, this limitation also applies to time sampling. Also, if full details of behavior and context are desirable or necessary, event sampling may not be the appropriate method. The operative word here is *full*. Keep in mind an essential difference between the event sample and the narrative description: The event sample disregards the behaviors and contexts that both precede and follow the preselected event. (Recall that this is also true of the time sample.) If this requirement is strictly adhered to, it is possible that you might misinterpret a behavioral episode/event because you would not have recorded some critical behaviors that came before or after the event. For instance, if you want to observe and record aggressive events, the fact that you see four-year-old Billy push Hector could be the outcome of their mutual decision to pretend to be professional wrestlers and not a true example of aggressive behavior.

SOME APPLICATIONS OF THE EVENT SAMPLE

First, Some General Guidelines

Let us first begin with some guidelines to inform your decisions as to when to use the event sample or, for that matter, any other recording method: First, consider the ways in which the event sample is similar to, or especially compatible with, other recording methods. Second, based on your observation objectives, decide which recording method will best meet those objectives, considering such things as time, effort, and completeness of data, among possible other variables. For instance, leaving aside the highly structured time frame that the time sample requires, the event sample primarily differs from the time sample with respect to the amount of raw data you can obtain with the former but not with the latter. If detailed descriptions of behavior and context are important to your purpose, then the event sample would be the most productive method to use. Otherwise, you might want to consider the time sample or even the checklist as viable alternatives.

A Second Kind of Event: The "Space/Equipment" Event

At this—we hope not inopportune—juncture, we want to introduce another definition of *event* that is actually contained within the standard definition discussed earlier. This second definition will give you an additional advantageous use of the event sample. A physical environment of one kind or another is part and parcel of any early childhood curriculum; it is an inescapable context for any and all behavior. How space and equipment are used—how they affect children's behavior—is a continuing concern to a child care professional. Two basic factors operate here: (1) space and materials (equipment) would be largely irrelevant apart from children who occupy that space and use those materials, and (2) as already stated, space and various kinds of equipment and materials are the necessary context within which all behavior takes place.

Given the importance of physical space and materials, and given that no behavior can take place outside of, or independent of, a physical environment of some kind and description, it makes sense to define specific areas of an early childhood classroom or child care center as an event and to record the behaviors that occur "inside" that event. For example, under this definition the big block area is an event, and you could record all the behaviors that children exhibit there. This means that you would not be limited to selecting just one behavioral event such as language or motor behavior, which essentially you would have to do to be faithful to our original definition. With our alternative event, it is *where* the behaviors occur that establishes the boundaries of your observation, not solely the behaviors themselves.

Several things could be accomplished by adopting this strategy. The event sample could tell you *how frequently*, say, the big block area was used in the course of a given period of time. You could gain valuable information concerning *how children used* this area of the classroom. For instance, you might observe that when Betsy and Samantha come into the big block area, they typically just talk and seldom actually play with the blocks. In contrast, you might discover that Bruce and Chester hardly ever talk in this area but immediately busy themselves by stacking blocks, building an imaginary road for their trucks to drive on, and so on. Finally, you might learn *which children* use the big block area the most or the least often.

It is not difficult to see how you could use this kind of information. For example, if some of the children seldom go to areas of the classroom that require vigorous physical activity, but instead select activities that are more sedentary, you might decide to devise ways to encourage the less active children to play more vigorously in places like the big block area. Or, if in your observations of a particular space/equipment event, you discover that hardly anyone ever uses that area, that might be an incentive either to "eliminate that event" and replace it with one that will get more use or, as we mention just below, try to motivate the children to use that space more often.

The Relationship Between Our Two Kinds of Events

We do not want to leave this discussion of a second kind or definition of event without helping you see that they are inextricably related. As we have already stated, every observation and recording of a child's behavior has to take place within a space/equipment event—our physical environment is inescapable. Consequently, if you select children's speech behavior as the event of interest, where Rebecca utters her speech is of no consequence in the traditional event sample format; she has to be in one place or another whenever she talks. However, if you *are* interested in where Rebecca talks the most, then observing and recording Rebecca's speech at various places throughout the classroom will give you that information. Of course, we assume that you would have a valid reason for wanting that kind of information, which is a decision only you can make. Also keep in mind that *a physical space and its equipment and materials become an event only if and when behavior is occurring there.* This makes sense, of course, because it would be pointless to observe an area of the classroom or child care center when that area had no one in it.

A Few Suggested Applications of the Event Sample

Jalongo and Isenberg (2000) are quite general and rather limited in the uses they suggest for the event sample: "often used to get baseline data, information on how frequently a particular behavior occurs prior to an intervention strategy (e.g., a toddler crying when brought to child care)" (p. 292). Beaty (2002) is not any more liberal in her recommendations. She cites two basic purposes of the event sample: "for behavior modification baseline data; for child development research" (p. 34). We are not refuting these authors' recommendations for event sample use, but we respectfully refute the implication that the event sample is suitable only, or primarily, for gathering baseline data. Nonetheless, let us deal with the event sample and baseline data.

Baseline Data

Baseline data are typically used to develop strategies to change behavior in some way—increase or decrease a behavior's frequency, for example. Using either the original or the alternative meaning of *event*, or both, depending on the circumstances, you could gather baseline data for such purposes as lowering the frequency of a particular child's aggressive behavior, increasing the frequency of a child's social interactions, or motivating children to use a particular area of the classroom and get involved in that area's typical activities.

Let us turn to our earlier example of Betsy and Samantha in the big block area, where they mostly converse rather than play with the big blocks. A series of behavior samples of these two children in this area (defining a space/equipment event) could give you baseline information concerning exactly how frequently they use the big block area for its intended purpose. If they hardly ever actually play with the blocks, and if you think it is desirable that they do so, you might try to motivate them, perhaps by getting some other children to join them, or stimulating their curiosity by asking them what kinds of things they could build with the blocks. You probably would then want to do another series of event samples to determine whether your intervention strategy had in fact increased their block-playing behavior.

FLORENCE AND THE EVENT SAMPLE

We are back with our hypothetical student named Florence, who, in this current assignment, now has information and knowledge about three different recording techniques: the narrative description, the time sample, and the event sample. Her instructor wants her to observe some five-year-olds and gather information about how they communicate with one another during cooperative play—that is, how they use language in this situation. She must decide which of the three recording techniques would be most helpful in completing this assignment. Let us look in on how she might think in making her decision:

> I have to observe the language of five-year-olds during cooperative play. Well, I guess by definition, cooperative play requires quite a bit of communication if the children are to achieve a particular goal during their play. I think I can rule out time sampling as my technique of choice because that would give me no information about the quality or characteristics of their language. The narrative description would certainly give me the details that I will need to complete the assignment, but, as I recall, strictly speaking the narrative description is not concerned with what the children are doing at the time I am observing and recording their behavior. It's intended to take in information regardless of what the particular behavior happens to be. I guess I could say that in this case, the narrative description is not selective enough for me to focus in on language behavior during cooperative play. Of course, if by chance I just happen to be observing children who are engaged in cooperative play and I record their behavior using the narrative description, then I would be able to complete the assignment. But wait a minute—the event sample gives me as much detailed information as the narrative description, and I won't have to take the time and effort to record behavior that isn't relevant to my assignment. Of course, if I wait until I see cooperative play and then record the language behavior of the children involved, I'll actually be using the event sample and not the narrative description. So, it seems obvious that the event sample should be the recording technique I choose.

SUMMARY

Event sampling differs from time sampling in that it takes specifically defined behaviors or events from the child's behavior stream but is not concerned with when the behaviors occur or with the length of the recording period. Two kinds of events are discussed in this chapter. The more conventional kind of event is defined as behaviors that can be placed into certain categories; for example, loud speech and certain facial expressions could possibly be put into the category of "quarrels," which constitutes an event. The event must be carefully defined before beginning the observation. The second kind of event actually derives from, or is implicit in, the first and is given the name "space/equipment event." This simply means that the specific areas in the classroom where the behaviors you are observing take place constitute an event. Unlike the traditional event sampling, you observe and record any behaviors that occur in that location. It is the physical space and the equipment and materials that it contains that establish the boundaries and the identity of the behavioral event.

("Specific locations" are such places as the big block area, the puzzle area, the free play area, and the finger painting area.)

Event sampling is discussed as being either open or closed, depending on whether you use narrative description or coding schemes. A combination of both is also possible. This method is highly selective, and the degree of initial inference is high.

Event sampling shares some of the advantages of both the narrative description and time sampling. There is the potential for detailed behavioral descriptions and the use of efficient coding schemes. Infrequently occurring behaviors can be suitable targets for event sampling if you are in the setting often or for relatively long periods of time. There is the disadvantage that although event sampling records details of behavior and context, it still breaks up the overall continuity that characterizes all behavior.

STUDY QUESTIONS

1. How are time sampling and event sampling similar? What are some important differences?

2. What is an event? Give two examples of events, and identify some of the behaviors that make up each event.

3. Describe how you might prepare for and carry out an observation session using the event sampling method.

4. Compare the narrative description and the event sampling methods. How are they alike, and how do they differ?

5. Under what circumstances would you want to use event sampling rather than another method?

PRACTICAL EXERCISE

As you know by now, the event sample is really quite similar to the narrative description. The primary difference is that the event sample focuses exclusively on a particular behavior or pattern of behavior—an event—and is not concerned with what comes before or after that event. Put another way, the event sample is more selective than the narrative description, even though the information it gathers is as rich and detailed as the narrative description.

The purpose of this exercise is to illustrate the advantage of using the event sample (or, conversely, the disadvantage of using the narrative description) to record only specific behaviors or behavior patterns (events) that are of interest to you. This exercise will also support our earlier claim that we can justifiably call the narrative description the "Queen" of the recording techniques. This support will take form in the fact that specific events are embedded in almost any narrative description. The "trick" is to pull out these events from among other observation data that might be extraneous to that specific event.

Using the narrative description format, observe and record the behavior of several children for about 15 minutes. Make your notes as detailed and descriptive as you possibly can. Remember, record everything that you see, and make no effort to be selective regarding what you will or will not include. When you are finished, choose a particular event such as language, a particular kind of play behavior, or cooperation or aggression. Go through your notes and record verbatim on a separate sheet of paper all the descriptions that apply to the event that you have selected. (When you have done that, cross out those descriptions so that what you have left is two separate observation records.) Then compare the descriptions that tell you something about your specific event with the descriptions that at least seem to have no direct bearing on, or connection to, the event. Then answer two questions. First, how easy or difficult was it to pull out specific event information from a body of general and more or less unrelated information? Second, which of the two descriptive records that you have created has more information—the event sample record, or what remains after you have removed the event sample data from the general narrative description?

Do the results of this exercise tell you anything about the most appropriate uses for the event sample and the narrative description?

CHAPTER 9

Diary Description

KEY TERMS

diary description

OBJECTIVES

After reading this chapter, you should be able to

- Describe the characteristics of the diary description method of observation.
- Discuss the characteristics of the diary description in relation to the dimensions of open versus closed, degree of selectivity, and degree of inference required.
- Describe the advantages and disadvantages of the diary description.

GENERAL DESCRIPTION

Diary description is an informal method of observation, and it is considered the oldest method in child development (Wright, 1960). Traditionally, it is used over extended periods of a child's life (longitudinally). In this technique, daily records are made of selected aspects of the child's growth and development. It is not as inclusive as the narrative description because continuous contacts with the child over a period of weeks, months, or years prohibit the intense writing load required by the narrative description.

The diary record's objective is to "record … in sequence *new* behavioral events in the behavior continuum of one subject, usually an infant or a child of preschool age" (Wright, p. 80, 1960, italics original). Goodwin and Driscoll (1980) confirm this use of the diary, stressing a focus on the new behaviors that a child exhibits. These new behaviors are often part of a particular developmental area such as intellectual functioning, language behavior, and social-emotional behavior. This type of diary description has been referred to as a topical diary (Wright, 1960). Piaget's records of his own children's cognitive development are a classic example of a topical diary. A broader focus is maintained by what Wright called a comprehensive diary, which "records in order as much of everything new as it can" (p. 80). The general intent of the diary description is to chart a child's step-by-step progress over a period of time.

diary description
An informal observation method in which records are made daily of selected aspects of a child's growth and development. The topical diary restricts itself to new behaviors exhibited by the child in a particular developmental area, such as language or social and emotional behavior; The comprehensive diary records in order as much of everything new as it can.

The traditional diary description demands a close and almost continuous contact between the child and the observer. Such closeness is rarely achieved except by a parent or guardian.

Open versus Closed

Diary description is classified as an open method because it captures the details of the child's behaviors, behavioral changes, and their context. It preserves those details as raw data that can be examined, analyzed, or compared later with other records.

Degree of Selectivity

Although the comprehensive diary as described by Wright appears to be unselective, it does limit itself to new behaviors that add to the recorder's understanding of the developing child. Consequently, it is not as undiscriminating as the narrative description. The topical diary is even more selective than the comprehensive diary; it limits itself to new behaviors that occur only within specific areas of growth and development.

The general intent of the diary description is to chart a child's step-by-step progress over a period of time.

Degree of Inference Required

The level of inference required by the diary record is much like that required by the time sampling and event sampling methods. At the least, the observer must make judgments on whether a particular behavior is indeed new and whether it legitimately belongs in the topical area that is the focus of study. For example, is the smile displayed by two-month-old Rebecca a true indication of social behavior, or is it merely the result of gas pains? Any later use of the completed record can require further inference.

Advantages

The diary description shares with the narrative description richness of detail, breadth of coverage, and the permanency of the written record (Wright, 1960). The breadth of its coverage includes the context of the behaviors as they occur at a given time, and their sequence. Thus, rather than isolated incidents, behaviors become connected to one another within an unfolding developmental framework. This connectedness is part of the longitudinal character of the diary description. It should also be noted that longitudinal techniques—that is, the observation and recording of behavior over relatively long periods of time—yield more reliable data than do observations over relatively short periods of time. This is partly because the observations become more representative of the individual's "true" or typical behaviors and behavior patterns.

Permanency of the record allows future comparisons with other forms of observational data, including developmental norms.

Disadvantages

From the conventional perspective, the obvious disadvantage of the diary description is its limited usefulness to most observers. The need for continuous and close contact with the child rules out almost everyone but parents or other members of the child's family. Even teachers seldom have such an extensive relationship with a particular child (Goodwin & Driscoll, 1980). However, we discuss below another perspective on the diary description that possibly gets around this apparent disadvantage.

THE DIARY DESCRIPTION AND THE CASE STUDY— A BRIEF COMPARISON

As we have already mentioned, a disadvantage of the traditional diary description is that it requires continuous and close contact with the child over a relatively long period of time, a condition nearly impossible to achieve in a child care or early education setting. We have nonetheless included the diary description because historically, (for example, see Wright [1960]) it has been considered a legitimate method of recording and preserving observation data. Because *Seeing Young Children* is intended to serve the needs of anyone for whom observing and recording children's behavior is a useful or critical skill, we would be remiss if we did not include the diary as a legitimate recording method.

This author considers the diary description to be very similar in some respects to the case study, which is a technique frequently used by therapists to gather essential information about their patients. However, Charlesworth (2008) gives the case study an important role in gathering information about children in a child care or early education setting. For the sake of completeness, and to provide you with a specific alternative format that, for all practical purposes, can serve the objectives of a diary description, we offer you Figure 9-1, which we have adopted verbatim from Charlesworth (2008).

Table 9-1 illustrates how a diary description might look using a case study format.

Table 9-1 Sample Diary Description: Case Study Use
Imran, male, age 3 years, 4 months.
December 6, 2008.
Area of Observation: Social Development

Today, Imran initiated play in the big block area with Isela, a three-year-old girl. This is very unusual for Imran; in the three months (since September 2008) he's been attending the preschool, he has typically been shy and rather aloof. He is smaller than most of the other boys in the class, and the staff suspects that he is intimidated by their greater physical size. We have not, however, witnessed any bullying by the other boys.
 	
    Imran has an older, bigger brother, who may be contributing at home to Imran's apparent fearfulness or shyness in the company of the larger, stronger children. This is a possibility we should check out in our next parent conference.
 	
    Mrs. Owens (teacher) also witnessed Imran's behavior with Isela. She showed her pleasure with his actions by commenting on how nicely the two of them played together. Imran reacted positively to her remarks; he smiled and appeared to increase his efforts to interact with both Isela and the blocks. They played together for about 7 minutes, when Adrian, one of the bigger boys in the class, tried to join them. Imran almost immediately left the big block area and sat down with a book at one of the reading tables. No further interactions between Imran and any of the other children occurred for the remainder of the morning.

December 13
A real breakthrough seems to be taking place in Imran's social behavior. Since the observation of Dec. 6, the staff and I have been seeing what we think are glimmerings of a desire on Imran's part to be with at least a few of the other children. Today, at about 10:00 A.M., Imran "timidly" asked Michael K., who is not much bigger than Imran, if he would play in the sandbox with him. Michael agreed. The two boys played amicably with two trucks, driving them on "roads" they constructed with wooden blocks. Play lasted for about 9 minutes; it ended when time came for snacks.   It must be noted that during their play, Imran was not assertive. Michael pretty much dictated or directed what was to happen, who was to "drive" which truck, and where the "roads" were to be placed in the sand. Nonetheless, Imran did not appear especially anxious or intimidated by Michael's leadership role. He must be observed again to see whether he attempts to be more forceful in expressing his own desires or goals.

CASE STUDY REPORT

Your Name: _____ Inclusive dates of study: _____

Child's Name: _____ Location of study: _____

Child's Age/Date of birth: _____

I. Reason for choosing this child. Describe how you happened to select this child (e.g., physical appearance, convenience).

II. A brief description of the child's outstanding characteristics.

III. History and background. Include any information you cannot obtain about the child's family, ethnic/racial background, health history, birth and pre-natal periods, and so on.

IV. Physical and motor growth and development.

V. Cognitive growth and development.

VI. Affective growth and development.

VII. Summary and interpretation.

    A. In what ways has the child changed since you began your study?

    B. In which aspects of development is the child most advanced for his or her age? In which areas does the child show the slowest development? In which areas is development most typical?

    C. If you were assigned to work with this child as a teacher, what kinds of experiences would you plan to facilitate his or her development?

    D. How well do you feel the child's school program and family is meeting his or her needs?

    E. Include any other conclusions or recommendations.

    In writing your case study summary report, use *it seems, the evidence indicates, it may be,* and other qualifiers freely. Remember, you have only studied a small time period in the child's lifespan.

(Reprinted with permission from Thomson Delmar Learning, Clifton Park, New York. Charlesworth, R. [2008, seventh edition]. *Understanding child development: For adults who work with young children* [pp. 37–38].)

Figure 9-1 A Sample Format for the Case Study/"Case Study Report"

MORE ABOUT THE DIARY DESCRIPTION

The Diary Description, the Running Record, the Event Sample, and the Anecdotal Record

Although we stated earlier that typically the diary description is not a very suitable recording method for the child care provider or early childhood educator, its similarity to the event sample, the running record, and the anecdotal record, as well as a different view of what constitutes new behavior, warrants some brief comment.

This author's position is that the diary description can be thought of either as an informal narrative description (running record), a modified event sample, or an anecdotal record, although you must keep their respective differences in mind. Look again at the definition of the diary description:

> An informal observation method in which records are made daily of selected aspects of a child's growth and development. The topical diary restricts itself to new behaviors exhibited by the child in a particular developmental area, such as language, social and emotional behavior, and so on; the comprehensive diary records in order as much of everything new as it can…. The diary description shares with the narrative description a richness of detail, breadth of coverage, and the permanency of the written record (Wright, 1960). The breadth of its coverage includes the context of the behaviors as they occur at a given time, and their sequence. Thus, rather than isolated incidents, behaviors become connected to one another within an unfolding developmental framework. This connectedness is part of the longitudinal character of the diary description. (pages 000\-000 above)

The topical diary and the comprehensive diary are essentially concerned with new behaviors a child exhibits. (Depending on the circumstances, we shall assume that *new* can mean "infrequent" as well as "occurring for the very first time.") In contrast, the event sample is considered unsuited for observing and recording infrequently occurring behaviors, which seemingly prevents the event sample from doing the work of the diary record. The running record, which we have referred to as a spontaneous narrative description, and the anecdotal record, on the other hand, are ideally suited to capture a child's new or unusual behaviors. What is the significance of this for you, the observer? Let us look at an alternative perspective on how to gather information that is very similar to the information you would get from a diary description.

An Alternative Perspective

We suggest an alternative perspective on the diary description. In our initial discussion of the diary description, which presented the historical view of the diary, we wrote that proper use of the diary requires an intense, prolonged relationship with the child. The assumption is that this kind of relationship usually can be accomplished only by parents or a guardian. This restriction notwithstanding, we believe it is unrealistic to suppose that only parents or guardians are in a position to observe a child's new behaviors. It is also not unreasonable to assume that some of the behaviors a child exhibits during any given day at a child care facility can be characterized as new, at least insofar as none of the staff has seen them before. Furthermore, we would expand the meaning of *new* to include not just behaviors that a child exhibits for the very first time anywhere, but also behaviors that a child has never before exhibited in the child care center or early education classroom. This expanded meaning of *new* makes sense when put into the context of the space/equipment event discussed in Chapter 8 (the event sample). You will recall that all behavior takes place in, and is potentially influenced by, a physical environment. Shall we say that Francine's behavior is not new if, for example, she cooperates with Shelley in putting together a puzzle, when in the past she was never seen either going into the puzzle area or playing with Shelley? What is new here is Francine behaving within a new space/equipment event (the puzzle area) and participating in a new social interaction (playing with Shelley). Playing with Shelley might be especially significant if Francine's past interactions with Shelley had been indifferent or unfriendly. Or suppose that Alvin is a very shy four-year-old who was never observed initiating play with any of the other children. One day Alvin walks up to Amelio and asks him to play with him in the sand table. To the staff as well as his parents, Alvin's new social initiative could be an exciting development, one that could have been recorded in a conventional topical diary description.

A Brief Conclusion

What can we conclude about this potential mixture of the diary description, the event sample, the running record, and the anecdotal record? We introduce this "mixture" to point out how similar in some respects these recording methods really are and how the purpose of the diary description can, in the right circumstances, be achieved by at least three other recording methods. This is not to say that all of these methods are actually the same thing but are simply given different names. Let us briefly compare and contrast these four methods.

Some Similarities

Perhaps the most obvious similarity among the diary description, event sample, running record, and anecdotal record is that they all provide relatively rich, detailed descriptions of the behavior. Additionally, they should provide information about the context (the setting and situation) and the sequence of the observed behaviors. Let us look briefly at each of the three alternative recording methods.

The Event Sample

Even though, strictly speaking, the event sample is not the method of choice for recording instances of unusual or new behavior, if social behavior had been the preselected event, an observer could have recorded the "new" social behaviors of Francine and Alvin. What would have been missing, however, is everything that took place immediately before and immediately after that event. This omission violates an essential characteristic of the diary description, namely, that it must record as faithfully as possible the continuous flow of the child's behavior stream. In this hypothetical instance, the event sample would have captured what was essentially new in these two children's behavioral repertoire. Despite this "capture," we do not advise using the event sample primarily to record new behaviors, even though from time to time chance might favor you with just such behavior.

The Running Record

The running record, or on-the-spot narrative description, seems well suited to obtaining the kinds of behaviors traditionally reserved for the diary description. According to Jalongo and Isenberg (2000), the running record is concerned with "anecdotal information gathered during a specified time (e.g., during outdoor play) or over a period of time.... Often used to discover causes and effects of behavior by studying what precedes and follows an event" (p. 292). The phrases "during a specified time, "or over a period of time," and "by studying what precedes and follows an event" at least partly incorporate the conditions required by the diary description. Could we consider the running record to be essentially the same as the diary description? Strictly speaking, the answer is no, because the diary description is specifically earmarked for gathering longitudinal data about a child's development and behavior. This is not the purpose of the running record. We make this comparison between the diary description and the running record to point out that new behaviors, broadly defined, are not solely within the purview of the diary description. In other words, the running record can accomplish some of the same objectives as the diary description without having to contend with the diary's restrictions.

The Anecdotal Record

If we take new behaviors out of the total context within which they occur, what we possibly have left are anecdotes. Let us look again at the definition of the anecdotal record: "An informal observation method often used by teachers as an aid to understanding the child's personality or behavior. It provides a running account of behavior that *is either typical or unusual* for the child being observed" (see Glossary; italics added). The key word here is *unusual*, which is one of the definitive characteristics of the kinds of behavior the diary description is meant to record.

What Is the Upshot of All of This?

We provide you with these comparisons in the hope that you will not dismiss out of hand the possibility of gaining at least some of the valuable information that is the focus of the diary description, namely new behavior. One of the deterrents to using the diary description is that it involves extended periods of a child's life (longitudinal data). This requires that daily records be made of selected aspects of the child's growth and development. In short, a true diary description requires that one live with the child in order to observe a significant number of new behaviors that he or she might exhibit. Despite such strict conditions, it is important to know that if you cannot use the diary as it is traditionally intended, you can still obtain some of the same kinds of information as the diary with the modified event sample, the running record, or the anecdotal record.

FLORENCE AND THE DIARY DESCRIPTION

Our hypothetical student, Florence—who could actually be you, the reader—now has a considerable amount of knowledge and information about four recording techniques. Her instructor has given her the assignment of using what she has learned thus far to come up with a way to get the information that a diary would provide without requiring a prolonged, intense relationship that is characteristic of the traditional form of the diary description. The following is how Florence possibly might reason:

> This assignment seems easy enough. All I have to do is observe one child and record new or atypical behaviors, which, according to *Seeing Young Children*, is the usual purpose of the topical or comprehensive diary. To complete my assignment I have to choose from among four alternatives—the event sample, the anecdotal record, the running record (which I have to remember is an informal version of the narrative description), and the diary description, as it is traditionally defined. Well, I can immediately rule out the diary description because there is no way I can have prolonged and intense contacts with the child I'm going to observe. Let's see, I don't think even the modified event sample would be a good choice, because according to my text, this technique is not suitable for recording unusual or atypical behaviors. In addition, strictly speaking, unlike the running record or narrative description, the event sample does not record the behaviors that immediately precede and follow the event. Of course, if I decided to use the event sample and I just happened to come upon an unusual behavior, then this technique would give me the information I want. But it wouldn't be appropriate for me to depend on chance encounters with a child's unusual behavior, so that rules out the event sample. That leaves the anecdotal record and the running

record. I think I'll use the running record. It will allow me to record unusual behavior on the spot, and I can get rich, detailed descriptions of the behavior and its total context. Of course, that means I'll really have to be alert and ready to record any unusual behavior as soon as it occurs.

SUMMARY

The diary description is an informal method of observing and recording. It is considered the oldest method in child development. Historically, the diary description has been used over relatively long periods of a child's life to record selected aspects of her growth and development. Two types of diary descriptions are discussed in this chapter: the topical diary and the comprehensive diary. The first type emphasizes new behaviors demonstrated by the child; these new behaviors are often part of a developmental area such as intellectual functioning or language behavior. The comprehensive diary is broader in scope than the topical diary, and it records "as much of everything new as it can" (Wright, 1960).

The diary description is considered an open method; it preserves the details of the child's behaviors and their context. The diary is limited to new behaviors that add to the observer's understanding of some aspects of the developing child, so it is somewhat selective. The diary description requires inferences regarding whether a given behavior is new and belongs in the topical area being studied.

The diary shares with the narrative description the advantage of providing rich, detailed descriptions of behavior, breadth of coverage, and the permanency of the written record. Its major disadvantage, as traditionally depicted, is that not everyone can use it because it requires close, continuous contact with the child, such as that achieved by a parent or a guardian.

The diary description is briefly compared and contrasted with the event sample, the running record, and the anecdotal record, with the intent to show that if you want to record examples of new or unusual behavior, you need not be deterred by the strict conditions imposed on the diary's use, primarily conditions of close, prolonged contact with the child on a daily basis.

STUDY QUESTIONS

1. When are diary descriptions typically used?

2. How does the selectivity of the diary description compare with that of the narrative description and event sampling methods? To which of the latter two methods is the diary description most similar? Why?

3. How is inference involved in the diary description? In which other method or methods is inference involved in the same way as in the diary description?

4. Why is the diary description not a likely method for most observers?

5. The immediately preceding example of a diary description most appropriately illustrates the diary's use as a case study (see Irwin & Bushnell, 1980, p. 85). First, find out about some of the purposes for which a case study is used. How do the purposes of the case study conform to the characteristics of the diary description? What specific criterion of the diary description method is met in the example?

6. What characteristics of the modified event sample, running record, and anecdotal record make these three recording techniques reasonably suitable substitutes for the diary description?

7. Why can the modified event sample, running record, and anecdotal record not totally take the place of the diary description?

ⓅⓇⒶⒸⓉⒾⒸⒶⓁ ⒺⓍⒺⓇⒸⒾⓈⒺ

In this exercise you will be asked to use your imagination and construct a hypothetical diary description for an imaginary child whom we recommend be one to three years of age. We ask you to assume that you have a close relationship with this child and are thus able to observe him or her over relatively long periods of time and in many different situations. If you wish, imagine that you are the child's parent or an older sibling. Using what information you already know or can access about your child's likely present developmental level and future progress (based on his or her age), construct a (traditional) topical diary that deals with a particular area of development that is of interest to you. You could choose language, social development, physical and motor development, or any other functional area that you think could be directly observed fairly easily in an actual context.

There are two basic goals to this exercise. The first is to familiarize yourself with how a young child might, for example, speak, interact socially, or use his or her physical/motor skills. The second goal is to "predict" or identify the new or unusual behaviors that your child might exhibit as he or she grows and develops within the functional area that you have chosen. Keep the "as he or she grows and develops" within a reasonable time frame. In other words, do not project the changes that will occur in the behavior of a one-year-old when he or she is three or four years old. Instead, if you decide you want your imaginary child to be 18 months of age, what new or unusual behaviors might you expect when the child is 20 or 22 months of age?

To conclude this exercise, try to come to some idea about what it would actually be like to use the traditional diary description in a real-life situation. Would it be difficult or relatively easy?

CHAPTER 10

Anecdotal Records

OBJECTIVES

After reading this chapter, you should be able to

- Discuss the characteristics of the anecdotal record method of observation.
- Discuss the characteristics of the anecdotal record in relation to the dimensions of open versus closed, degree of selectivity, and degree of inference required.
- Describe the advantages and disadvantages of the anecdotal record.

KEY TERMS

anecdotal record

GENERAL DESCRIPTION

Introduction

Before getting into a general description of the anecdotal record, we want to alert you to what we consider to be two slightly different perspectives on the anecdotal record and its uses. The first of these perspectives we choose to call historical, mainly because of the dates of the references from which we draw our information about this recording technique. The second of these perspectives we will call contemporary, again because the cited literature is relatively current. By no means should you assume that the earlier references are out of date and no longer valid. None of the recording methods discussed in *Seeing Young Children* enjoys quantum leaps in technological advancement. Each recording method is and will likely remain as we describe it, and if the anecdotal record, for example, were defined and implemented totally differently than it currently is, it would have to be called something else. It is also likely that its new purpose would also be very different from its original one.

A More Historical Perspective of the Anecdotal Record

anecdotal record

An informal observation method often used by teachers as an aid to understanding the child's personality or behavior. It provides a running account of behavior that is either typical or unusual for the child being observed.

The **anecdotal record** is another informal method of observation. It is a method often used by teachers, and the record may follow a child from grade to grade and teacher to teacher. It is a record that teachers make for future reference and as an aid to understanding some aspect of the child's personality or behavior.

Goodwin and Driscoll (1980) list five characteristics of the anecdotal record. First, the record is the result of direct observation of a child. This is important, for it legitimately rules out records based on rumors. Second, the record is a prompt, accurate, and specific descriptive account of a particular event. This confirms the necessity of direct observation. Third, the anecdotal record supplies the context of the child's behavior; it identifies setting and situation so that the behavior is not separated from the events that influenced or caused it. This context includes accurate accounts of what is said by the child or other appropriate participants. Fourth, if any inferences or interpretations are made by the observer, they are kept separate from the objective description and are clearly identified as inferences or interpretations. Finally, the anecdotal record concerns itself with behavior that is either typical or unusual for the child being observed, which pretty much encompasses most of the behaviors a child is likely to exhibit. If the behavior is unusual, it should be so indicated. However, Irwin and Bushnell (1980) note that anecdotal records "are not limited to highlighting new behaviors" and that such records "report whatever seems noteworthy to the observer, whenever that behavior occurs" (p. 97).

Goodwin and Driscoll (1980) argue for recording only events or behaviors that reflect such things as a child's personality characteristics, rather than focusing on achievement, intelligence, and the like. The reason for this selectivity is that there are other, more effective ways of documenting behaviors such as achievement. However, these authors go on to recommend that even cognitive areas should be documented in the case of very young children.

Irwin and Bushnell point out the dual use of the anecdotal approach to record either usual or unusual behavior, uses with which Nilsen (2004) agrees. She writes that the anecdotal record can be used to "exemplify a child's typical behavior" or "record the details of an incident that is totally foreign to the child's typical behavior" (p. 48). Nilsen also mentions the use of the anecdotal record to "portray an incident that indicates a child's development in a specific area" (p. 48), a use for which the event sample is also suitable.

In our opinion, the anecdotal record is best suited to recording atypical rather than typical behavior. This use more closely conforms to the connotations of an anecdote or anecdotal evidence. Most simply put, and with regard to observing children's behavior, anecdotal evidence is evidence obtained from a source or under circumstances that are not representative of the child or the situation.

For example, if you observed two-year-old Mark and concluded that all two-year-olds are just like Mark, you would be basing your conclusion on anecdotal evidence. The behaviors and characteristics of one two-year-old do not necessarily reflect the behaviors and characteristics of all or even the majority of two-year-olds. In like fashion, behavior that is not typical for a particular child may not represent how that child behaves under most circumstances. Typically, two-year-old Mark might not be aggressive in his interactions with other children or with adults, but he may behave somewhat aggressively if he is frustrated by a game or a toy that he does not understand. One instance of aggressive behavior toward other people would be unusual and perhaps deserve to be noted in an anecdotal account, whereas aggressiveness toward some object may be more or less usual. Of course, the context or circumstances surrounding that unusual behavior should be recorded to help explain why Mark behaved as he did.

A More Contemporary View?

We believe it is important that you know that some authors appear to disagree in part with this author that the anecdotal record is best suited for recording unusual or atypical behavior. Ahola and Kovacik (2007), for instance, write the following about the anecdotal record:

> An **anecdotal record** is used to develop an understanding of the child's behavior, perhaps for the purpose of understanding a developmental concern, or to communicate aspects of a child's behavior to a parent. Observations recorded as anecdotal records can guide a teacher's capacity to learn how a child acts, reacts, and interacts, casting light on the mysterious workings of the child. (p. 17, boldface original)

They further define the anecdotal record this way:

> A brief, factual, objective narrative, written after an event. When viewed sequentially, anecdotal records should reveal insights into a child's developmental progress. (p. 17)

Ahola and Kovacik's use of the anecdotal record includes observing and recording any behavior that helps child care providers, teachers, and parents understand a child's developmental progress. This author does not disagree with this use of the anecdotal record, although the narrative description (or its "spontaneous cousin," the running record) and the event sample can also give you the same kind of information. In defense of recording atypical behavior, however, true developmental progress must inevitably entail new (atypical) behaviors and skills, especially during the child's earliest years, when new skills and behaviors are rapidly being acquired. All of this notwithstanding, we leave it up to you to decide whether the anecdotal record best serves your needs and interests. The critical issue here is whether you are able to obtain information that is useful in understanding children and fostering their growth and development.

A Brief Comparison of Three Recording Methods

There are similarities between the anecdotal record and both the narrative description and the event sample. As already mentioned, information in the anecdotal record is recorded in narrative form and includes the context of the child's behavior, which is also true of the narrative description and the event sample. In the narrative description, however, there is no effort to record only unusual behavior: Any and all behavior is recorded simply as it occurs. The anecdotal record might appear to be nearly identical to the event sample because both of these techniques do take notice of specific behaviors or categories of behaviors. However, the anecdotal record does not anticipate unusual behavior; it simply observes and records it when it occurs.

The event sample, on the other hand, differs from the anecdotal record in two important respects: First, the event sample is not suitable for unusual or atypical behaviors, and second, the observer identifies ahead of time behaviors or categories of behavior that he or she wants and expects to occur. This rules out unusual or uncharacteristic behavior because, by definition, it occurs too infrequently. It might be helpful to think of the anecdotal record as the technique to use when a child's behavior takes you by surprise and you consider it worthy of recording.

The hypothetical example of an anecdotal record shown in Table 10-1 might not seem any different than a narrative description, perhaps particularly because of its length. However, note in the "Comments" section that on several occasions the record indicates that Melissa's behavior is unusual for her and that this should be brought up at the next staff meeting. From these comments you could legitimately infer that this is a reasonable example of an anecdotal record. Additionally, the length of any anecdotal record should not be arbitrary or left merely to whim. Because the context of any behavior is so important to understanding that behavior, the amount of contextual information should be sufficient to help you understand and give meaning to the behavior observed.

One last comment is in order. The hypothetical example given in Table 10-1 would reasonably meet the requirements of an event sample if Mrs. Thompson had been looking for any example of social behavior and by chance happened to observe Melissa on that particular day, time, and circumstance. The event sample, as a recording technique, does not rule out recording unusual or atypical behaviors as such. What is ruled out, however, is using the event sample specifically to record unusual or atypical behaviors. Therefore, the anecdotal record is the method of choice when behaviors occur that are not anticipated or predicted—again, a characteristic that makes them atypical.

Table 10-1 A Hypothetical Anecdotal Record

Observer Mrs. Thompson **Child Observed** Melissa

Observation Setting Preschool classroom, during free play

Date 11/23/2004

Melissa came to school late today. She stood in the doorway to the main classroom and just looked around for about half a minute at the other children involved in various activities. She then walked across the room toward the reading table, scraping the toe of her right foot for about 6 steps or so. She picked up her pace a bit and, on reaching the table, sat down. Tina, José, and Miguel were already seated at the table. Tina had been watching the two boys "read" a book together; she greeted Melissa with a bright, "Hi, Melissa, wanna read a book with me?" The boys neither looked up nor said anything. Melissa told Tina that she (Melissa) could not read, but Tina replied that they could look at the pictures. Melissa agreed with a softly spoken "OK"; she made no eye contact with Tina—in fact, she looked over toward the block area as she spoke her consent. As Tina went to get a book from the shelf, Melissa began idly flipping through some pages of a book that was lying on the table. Tina returned with a book, saying, "I like this one; let's look at this one." She tried to sit close to Melissa, but Melissa moved away slightly, putting 6 to 8 inches distance between them. José asked, "Hey, you two, wha'cha doin'?" Tina responded with "Never mind, we're busy." As she said this, she tilted her head upward and stuck out her chin slightly. Melissa made no response; she got up from the table and walked slowly toward the big block area. Mrs. Johnson announced cleanup time, but Melissa again did not make any relevant response; she did not participate in cleanup.

Comments

This is the second time in three days Melissa has been late for school. As I recall, on the other occasion she also seemed different from her "usual self."

Melissa stood in the doorway as though reluctant to leave her position there. I sensed that, momentarily at least, she would have rather been somewhere else.

M's response to Tina's suggestion to look at pictures uncharacteristically lacked enthusiasm. She usually likes to look at books.

I cannot understand M's reaction to Tina's trying to sit close to her. It's almost as though M. is rejecting Tina. The contrast between Melissa's and Tina's behavior seems especially marked.

Note: I'll have to do some follow-up observations of Melissa. Her seemingly apathetic, unsocial behavior needs to be checked—it may just be a bad day for her. Must check with some of my staff; they may have noticed she's become somewhat withdrawn over the past several days. Bring this up at next staff meeting.

Open versus Closed

The anecdotal record is an open method, assuming that it preserves the raw data provided by detailed description.

Degree of Selectivity

The anecdotal record can be highly selective, especially if the observer records only, as Goodwin and Driscoll (1980) phrase it, "strikingly unusual behavior." If one follows other criteria for the anecdotal record, however, selectivity decreases, and whatever is of interest can be the target for observation and recording.

Degree of Inference Required

Inferences or interpretations can be made in an effort to explain an event or behavior, especially if the behavior is not typical for the child. Again, determining whether a behavior is ordinary or unusual requires a decision that goes beyond immediate sensory information.

Advantages

An important advantage of the anecdotal record is that it gives the teacher a running account that helps him understand a child's behavior in particular situations and settings. It also allows continuing comparisons of a child's behavior, which then provides a way of documenting changes—for example, changes in the way a child handles stressful conditions, or in his social interaction patterns with children or adults. Irwin and Bushnell (1980) say that the anecdotal record is the easiest to do of the recording methods because it needs no special setting, codes or categories, or time frame. This claim has also been made for the narrative description.

The advantages of the anecdotal record can be drawn from a more recent source, even though these advantages do not differ from those discussed immediately above. But perhaps slightly different language will make the information clearer. Ahola and Kovacik (2007), for instance, give the following as advantages of the anecdotal record. First, it "*allows us to view the child's behavior within the context in which it is happening.*" Second, "*The anecdotal record allows us to view what are the most important and significant events without any preconceived ideas about what we 'should' be seeing.*" Third, "*The anecdotal record allows us to view actual development of the child, and in the case of children with special needs this is especially helpful*" (pp. 18–19, italics original). As a prelude to what is to come, can you see how the advantages discussed so far strongly suggest the uses to which the anecdotal record can be put?

Disadvantages

Despite their common use, anecdotal records are not necessarily easy to write. They have been criticized because of the relative ease with which bias can affect the selection of events to be recorded (bias that could creep in because the observer likes or does not like certain characteristics); the vulnerability of the record to improper wording, thereby leading to misinterpretation or negative value judgments about the child by the reader; and the obligation to use the record productively, which is not always easy.

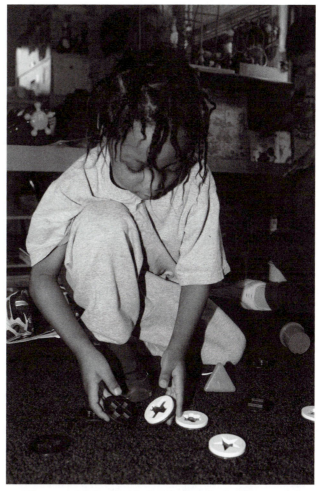

An advantage of the anecdotal record is that it gives the teacher a running account that helps to understand a child's behavior in particular situations and settings.

Yet another disadvantage of this recording method has to do with how it is sometimes used. The anecdotal record is a controversial technique in some quarters, partly because it is so easy to record negative biases or judgments about a child, a disadvantage just discussed. However, the consequences of such biases do not stop with the record per se. A child's anecdotal record sometimes follows her from grade to grade and from teacher to teacher, as part of her permanent, cumulative records. As each subsequent teacher inherits the child's records, the opportunity is created for the self-fulfilling prophecy (or for the Pygmalion effect) to operate. That is to say, there is sometimes a tendency on the part of teachers—and anyone else, for that matter—to perceive and treat a child in accordance with what has been said (written) about him. Sadly, if these perceptions and treatments are negative or derogatory, the child can also behave in ways that confirm others' expectations regarding his behavior, ability, self-worth, and so on. It should go without saying that this is a totally unacceptable use and consequence of the anecdotal record, and this note of caution must not be taken lightly.

Timing of the Recording: A Potential Disadvantage

We want to mention one final potential disadvantage of the anecdotal record that should not be overlooked. There is evidence of consensus among some contemporary authors that the anecdotal approach records behavior after it has occurred. Beaty (2002), for example, defines the anecdotal record as "a narrative of descriptive paragraphs, recorded *after behavior occurs*" (p. 34, italics original). Jalongo and Isenberg (2000) write that the anecdotal record is "a narrative (storylike), factual account recorded after behavior occurs" (p. 292). Ahola and Kovacik (2007), in turn, define the anecdotal record as "a brief, factual, objective narrative, written after an event" (p. 17).

We all know how fallible the memory can be, which potentially makes "post-observation" recording a threat to capturing richly detailed descriptions of behavior. Considering the proposed purposes of the anecdotal record, memory lapses resulting in the omission of important details would give those purposes short shrift. We therefore take the contrary position that it is far better to record the behavior while it is occurring rather than after it has occurred. We recognize, of course, that memory of details diminishes as time passes; it could therefore be argued that most details could be retained if the recording takes place very soon after the behavior has occurred. Nonetheless, it seems evident that records made on the spot will almost always be better than those made after the fact. We must offer one qualification to our objection, however. If you use the anecdotal method only to record new, atypical behavior, recording such behavior as it occurs would require that you always be prepared to do so. Such preparation might involve carrying a pencil and notepad so that your ability to record is "at the ready." Or, in this instance, using a small tape recorder to dictate what you are observing can be very helpful, assuming that you would be allowed to do so.

MORE ABOUT THE ANECDOTAL RECORD

Using the Anecdotal Record: Our Fifth Visit with Florence

The reasons for using the anecdotal record seem clear from the preceding discussion. It gives the observer—child care provider, early childhood educator, parent—an ongoing record to help him or her understand a child's behavior in particular situations and settings. It also allows ongoing comparisons of behaviors, which provide a way to document changes in the child's behavior. It is a record that one can make for future reference and as an aid to understanding some aspect of the child's personality or behavior.

One major difference separating the anecdotal record, narrative description, and event sample is simply the observer's intentions. However, intention is in this instance an all-inclusive concept. Let us illustrate by "listening in" again on Florence's thoughts as she deliberates about what recording method would best achieve her objectives:

> Let's see, Anthony is two years old, and he seems to be on the verge of showing some new social behaviors with other children in the classroom. I'd like to record as many of the details of these new behaviors as I can if and when they occur. I'll also eventually be able to make ongoing comparisons between his earlier and later social interactions. Not only would the staff be interested in Anthony's progress in this area, but his parents would also want to know how he is getting along with his peers. This knowledge would help the staff plan activities and experiences that might further encourage additional and ongoing interpersonal relationships. However, I have to decide which recording method will best help me meet my goals and the goals the staff might set for Anthony. Strictly speaking, the event sample doesn't seem to be the appropriate method because it's intended to record behavioral events that occur reasonably often. I learned that new behaviors and skills don't occur frequently enough or predictably enough to warrant using the event sample. Similarly, the narrative description also doesn't seem to be well suited because it involves some formal criteria that don't fit in with my objectives. I don't think the time sample or diary description will work very well in this case, either. The time sample won't give me any good raw data about Anthony's social interactions, and I could miss some very important behaviors that will help me keep track of and understand Anthony's social progress. As for the diary, I don't think my relationship with Anthony is nearly intense or prolonged enough to justify using it. I guess I will use the anecdotal record, but I won't be using it for recording typical behavior, although, according to the text, I could do so. I'll try to record Anthony's new or unusual social behaviors right at the time I see them. I'll have to figure out how I can be prepared to do this no matter when or where these behaviors occur. Maybe a tape recorder will work real well here. I'll ask the director if it's all right to use a tape recorder. I guess at the very least I'll have to carry a notepad and pen with me at all times.

SUMMARY

The anecdotal record is often used by teachers to help them understand some aspect of a child's personality, behavior, or overall developmental progress. Five characteristics of the anecdotal record are (1) it is the result of direct observation; (2) it is a prompt, accurate, and specific description of a particular event; (3) it gives the context of the child's behavior; (4) inferences and interpretations are kept separate from the objective description; and (5) it records behavior that is either typical or unusual for the child being observed. This last characteristic notwithstanding, some writers maintain that anecdotal records may report anything of interest to the observer.

The anecdotal record is an open method. Its selectivity varies somewhat, depending on whether you record everything of interest or only unusual behaviors. Inferences are required if you try to explain the meaning of a particular behavior or event. The method's important advantage is that it gives the teacher an ongoing record to help him understand a child's behavior in particular situations and settings. It also allows ongoing comparisons of behaviors, which provide a way of documenting changes in the child's behavior. An important disadvantage is that anecdotal records are not easy to write, and some critics argue that it is easy for bias to enter into the selection of events and behaviors to be recorded.

STUDY QUESTIONS

1. Why is the anecdotal record popular with teachers? How are such records used by teachers?

2. If the anecdotal record is used to record unusual behavior, how might records of such behavior be useful to a teacher? How might records of typical behavior be useful to a teacher?

3. On what does the degree of selectivity depend in the anecdotal record?

4. What makes the anecdotal record easy to use? Another method also claims to be easy to use for the same reasons. What method makes the same claim as the anecdotal record, and at the same time, how are these two methods different?

PRACTICAL EXERCISE

You should find this exercise fairly easy to complete and not too time-consuming. It is intended to emphasize the fundamental meaning or character of the anecdote and how that meaning figures into your possible use of the anecdotal record as a recording technique.

We will define an anecdote as a piece of evidence or information that initially applies only to the person or persons directly involved in that anecdote and that cannot be generalized to other similar persons or circumstances. Put another way, anecdotal evidence has limited application or relevance to individuals and events outside the anecdote's immediate context. For example, if you hear a precocious four-year-old using vocabulary and sentences that are more typical of a child several years older, you would be using anecdotal evidence inappropriately if you drew conclusions about the language ability of other four-year-olds whom you have not heard speak. In other words, anecdotal evidence is evidence gotten from a sample that is too small to permit making valid judgments about a larger population that you have not observed or studied.

For the first part of this exercise, we want you to write an anecdote depicting some usual or unusual behavior (your choice) exhibited by a hypothetical child between two and five years of age. If necessary, consult a child development text to inform yourself about the kinds of behaviors or abilities that you might see in a child of the age you have chosen. For the second part, actually observe a child and record his or her behavior using the anecdote as your recording technique. How close can your hypothetical anecdotal record come to your actual anecdotal record?

Frequency Counts or Duration Records

KEY TERMS

frequency count

duration record

OBJECTIVES

After reading this chapter, you should be able to

● Determine the relationship between frequency records and duration records.

● Examine the uses of frequency counts and duration records.

● Identify the relationships between frequency counts or duration records and event or time sampling.

● Determine the method of observation, degree of selectivity, and degree of inference required in using frequency counts or duration records.

● Explore the advantages and disadvantages of frequency counts and duration records.

GENERAL DESCRIPTION

The term *frequency* immediately identifies this method's primary characteristic. The observer simply makes a mark on an observation sheet every time a particular behavior occurs. A variation of the **frequency count** is the **duration record**. As Goodwin and Driscoll (1980) indicate, there are occasions when it is more useful to know how long a behavior lasts than just how often it occurs.

One use of frequency counts is to establish baselines in behavior modification. Baselines are simply frequency counts of a behavior that the teacher, experimenter, or therapist wants to modify. The effectiveness of the particular modification procedure is measured by whether the frequency of the behavior after the procedure is less than or greater than the

frequency count
An informal observation method in which the observer simply makes a mark or tally on an observation sheet every time a particular behavior occurs.

duration record
A variation of the frequency count in which the observer times how long a particular behavior lasts.

baseline frequency (less than or greater than, depending on whether an undesirable behavior is to be reduced or eliminated, or a desirable behavior is to be increased).

Both frequency counts and duration records require you to define, in advance, the behaviors you want to observe and record. The specific behaviors of interest are often dealt with as categories—for example, cooperative behavior, dependency behavior, aggression, or perhaps the various play classifications (parallel play, associative play, and so on). Frequency counts and duration records are similar to event sampling because the behavior or category must occur before it can be recorded. However, as verified by Goodwin and Driscoll's account, the frequency count can also follow a time sampling procedure, where one or more observers watch a child for designated periods and lengths of time. This affords the most economical use of time as well as an opportunity to gather a representative sample of a given behavior. Of course, when you use a time or event sampling format, you also take on the advantages and disadvantages of those methods.

Open versus Closed

Frequency counts and duration records are decidedly closed. Neither preserves any raw data.

Both frequency counts and duration records require you to define, in advance, the behaviors you want to observe and record.

Degree of Selectivity

Both methods are highly selective. If you are going to count something, you first have to specify what that something is. The same is true for measuring how long something lasts. Nevertheless, it is conceivable that frequency counts and duration records can be incorporated into some of the other methods already discussed. It can be very useful to time the duration of behaviors when using event sampling, for example. As discussed in Chapter 3, this can help prevent errors of transmission and give you relevant information about the child's attention span, level of interest in an activity, and so forth. Narrative descriptions can also make use of frequency counts, although it is likely that they would be made after the recording was completed.

Degree of Inference Required

Inferences and definitions are required in these methods because you must define ahead of time what specific behaviors are included in the category you want to observe and record. Such definitions are a form of inference: You are interpreting specific behaviors as indicating a category (cooperation, social interaction, and so on). Further inference is required as you observe a child doing various things. Do you see specific actions and responses as cooperation, dependency, or aggression, or do you see something quite different? Furthermore, it happens that even with the most carefully defined categories, children will display behaviors that do not exactly fit a category, or the behavior happens too quickly to be seen in its entirety. These conditions will call for a judgment from the observer.

Advantages

The most obvious advantage of the frequency count or duration record is its simplicity. Nothing seems easier than making a tally mark every time a particular behavior or event occurs. The recording technique itself is simple to use and entails very little effort from the observer. The duration record is more complicated than the frequency count because it involves using a watch to time the behavior. This is not in itself difficult, but it is an extra step that requires you to watch the behavior carefully to know when it begins and ends. This careful notice is also necessary in event sampling, but unlike event sampling, duration records do not involve the writing of narrative descriptions.

We want to emphasize here that "ease of use" refers primarily to the amount of effort one has to expend to record the observation data, as well as the amount of time and effort needed to construct a form on which to record the frequency or duration of various behaviors. If, however, one figures in the skill required to recognize the behaviors at issue and to make judgments concerning whether or not to mark a behavior as having occurred, the frequency count and duration record are no easier to use than any of the other recording techniques. It is not the techniques or the particular form on which you record your data that enable you to observe with skill and discernment. Rather, it is your skill, discernment, and understanding of the various techniques that enable you to properly use those techniques. Moreover, in this writer's view at least, the neatness and formality of the forms on which you record observations mostly concern either personal preference or what a particular recording format contributes to orderly record keeping.

Frequency counts have the advantage of giving almost immediate quantifiable data, which can in turn be used or represented in a number of ways. Goodwin and Driscoll (1980) mention representing the frequency of the behavior by bar graphs and using the data to calculate rates of behavior per some unit of time (such as the number of instances of aggression per minute), or to calculate the percentage of time a child spent in a particular behavior. For example, you could determine that of the total time observed, a child spent 30 percent of her time in cooperative play and 20 percent in solitary activity. Although a much more elaborate picture than most observers would construct, Figure 11-1 illustrates how these (hypothetical) percentages of time spent in cooperative and solitary play derived from duration record data could be depicted by a bar graph. Of course, other types of graphic representation can be used.

Frequency counts and duration records are also useful in noting changes in behavior over time. Duration records are appropriately used when the extent of the child's involvement is most important. The fact that a child exhibits a behavior may be less significant than how long she exhibits it. Social participation, for example, might

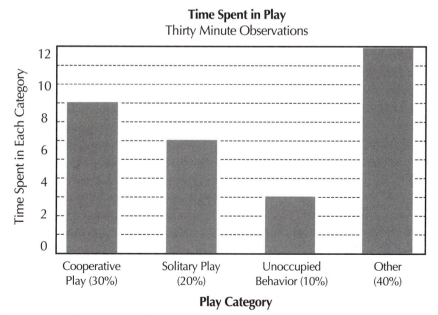

Figure 11-1 Time Spent in Play

be better evaluated in terms of the length of the interactions a child has than in terms of how often she has them. Frequent but very short social contacts might indicate an inability to sustain social behaviors. In this case, a simple frequency count could mislead the observer to the conclusion that the child is highly social.

Disadvantages

The primary disadvantages of frequency counts and duration records lie in their closedness. They reveal nothing about the details of the behavior or its context. Again, one might be recording action fragments that are not descriptive or indicative of the larger behavior stream.

Some Uses of the Frequency Count and Duration Record

There are situations when it might be important to know how often a child exhibits a particular behavior, perhaps especially when that behavior is an undesirable one such as aggression or unnecessary (inappropriate or unwarranted emotional) dependency. This is why frequency counts are used to acquire baseline data for possible use in behavior modification strategies. How often a child behaves aggressively against another child prior to intervention is compared with the frequency of aggression after intervention. If the behavior's frequency is reduced, then the intervention can be considered successful. We must add a qualification, however. Behaviors frequently are context-specific, which is to say they are influenced by where the child is (snack area, free play area, outdoor playground, etc.), who is there with him (his best friend or someone he dislikes), and the equipment and materials that are available to him (are there enough toys for everyone, or does having to share scarce toys possibly contribute to arguments or even physical fights?). So, for instance, if three-year-old Gregory's aggressive behavior appears to be largely restricted to those areas or activities that involve large muscle movements and a child named Bobby, whom Gregory does not like, any frequency data should take those contextual factors into account.

Of course, not all behavioral changes come about because of direct adult intervention; behavior changes in the natural course of growth and development. As we stated earlier, frequency counts and duration records are useful in noting these more "natural" changes in behavior over time.

As we also have already discussed, the frequency of behavior sometimes can be less important than how long the behavior lasts. Consequently, when the extent of the child's involvement is most important, the duration record can be the method of choice:

> The fact that a child exhibits a behavior may be less significant than how long she exhibits it. Social participation, for example, might be better evaluated in terms of the length of the interactions a child has than in terms of how often

she has them. Frequent but very short social contacts might indicate an inability to sustain social behaviors. In this case, a simple frequency count could mislead the observer to the conclusion that the child is highly social.

There are a number of ways you can structure the format (appearance) and the implementation of a frequency count or duration record. One such format is depicted in Table 11-1. This is a highly structured format where the recording form is carefully laid out ahead of time. Even though there is no mention of the time interval in this frequency count table, you would follow a time sampling procedure, and you would have to strictly adhere to a recording interval if you want your frequency counts to be valid and representative.

As you can see, Table 11-1 allows you to record the behavior frequencies of six children within four categories of behavior during five time intervals within each category. All of these dimensions and categories could be expanded, of course, to include more children, more categories of behavior, and more time intervals within each category. However, such expansion is not limitless and must be kept within reasonable, manageable bounds; otherwise, the form becomes too cumbersome to use effectively.

There might be occasions, though, when you want to record the frequency of particular behaviors of one child rather than a number of children. This was briefly discussed as one of the advantages of the frequency count, and we refer you again to Figure 11-1, which depicts the percentage of time a child spent in four categories of activity: Solitary Play, Cooperative Play, Unoccupied Behavior, and a fourth category designated as Other. This use of the frequency count would not necessarily require either a time sampling procedure or a carefully prepared recording form. But you would have to observe the child's behavior over a specific period of time, and you

Table 11-1 A Sample Frequency Count Format for Four Categories of Behavior																				
Name	**Aggression**					**Cooperation**					**Dependency**					**Autonomy**				
Barbara																				
Jason																				
Brian																				
Alice																				
Darius																				
Melinda																				
	1	2	3	4	5	1	2	3	4	5	1	2	3	4	5	1	2	3	4	5

would have to record carefully the amount of time he or she spent in each of the two types of play.

This sample frequency count format Table 11-1 is only one of many possible formats. You will see that you could record only five instances of each of the four behaviors designated for study. Five might be sufficient, however, if you were observing and recording for brief periods of time. It would probably be unlikely, for instance, that Brian would exhibit more than five aggressive behaviors within the span of one minute.

But the form is merely a concept, and it can be as flexible as you need it to be. Indeed, you can record frequencies on a blank sheet of paper. The spaces simply give you a visual reference to guide your recording of how often a specific behavior occurs. You simply make a mark (X) whenever the child exhibits the behavior of interest. Perhaps the most difficult task is to keep accurate track of the time periods within which you want to record the behavior. For example, if you are watching Barbara for one minute between 9:00 and 9:01 A.M., and you want to move on to Jason for the minute between 9:02 and 9:03, you must make certain that you do observe for precisely that period of time. If, in fact, you devote a minute and a half to Barbara and only 45 seconds to Jason, any differences in behavior frequency between the two children could be attributed to the differences in the amount of time you observed each child.

This sample also limits you to five "slots" to record the occurrence of a behavior. But if you wanted to record behavior frequencies over a long period of time (an hour or a morning, for instance) in order to establish a baseline on a particular child, an open-ended form would be appropriate. You would simply make a mark every time the behavior occurred. If, after you have completed the observation-recording session, you find that the frequency of the behavior was greater or less than desired, you could take steps to modify the behavior's frequency upward or downward.

FLORENCE AND THE FREQUENCY COUNT AND DURATION RECORD

Our student Florence is becoming confident about observing and recording young children's behavior. She has acquired quite a bit of knowledge concerning the various recording techniques, and she is feeling a sense of accomplishment as she nears the end of this part of her journey.

Her instructor has asked her to imagine that she is in a child care center that contains a fairly equal mixture of three-year-olds and five-year-olds. The director of the center is a little worried that more often than seems reasonable, the five-year-olds are behaving too aggressively toward the three-year-olds. She is also worried that these aggressive episodes are not fleeting and short lived, but persist long enough that they could result in serious injury to the younger children. However, the director is very aware of the potential unreliability of anecdotal evidence, and she wants to systematically gather information about the children's aggressiveness that can form a valid basis for taking steps to decrease or eliminate this undesirable behavior. Florence is given the task of constructing a frequency count/duration record that could be used to solve this director's potential problem. Here is how Florence possibly might approach her assignment:

> This assignment sounds interesting—I almost wish it were a real case and not a hypothetical one. Let's see, I seem to remember an example of a frequency count format in Chapter 11 of *Seeing Young Children*. Yes, here it is, Table 11-1, but it deals with four categories of behavior and not just aggression, and it doesn't involve any recording of how long a behavior lasts. Well, that shouldn't be too hard to fix. I should be able to modify Table 11-1 so that I can record if a child behaves aggressively toward another child, against whom the aggression is directed, and how long the aggressive episode lasts. I can even put in a place to record where in the child care center the aggressive behavior occurred. That should get me all the information my hypothetical center director needs.
>
> The first thing I need to do is construct a table that lists the names of all the five-year-olds in the leftmost column, give each three-year-old an identifying number, and build in two more spaces—one to record how long the aggressive behavior lasts and another to indicate where in the child care center the aggression took place. I can use a code to identify these areas, such as BBA for big block area, FP for finger painting area, PA for puzzle area, and so on. So if, for example, five-year-old Nathan behaves aggressively toward three-year-old Marie, I'll record Marie's identifying number to the right of Nathan's name, I'll check my watch to see how long the aggression lasted, and I'll write in the code that indicates where Nathan's aggression took place.
>
> I'll have to use pretty much the same technique as I would in the time sample. I'll have to decide on how long to observe each child, how long to record whether the behavior occurred, and how long to wait before I move on to the next child. I would guess 30 seconds to observe the behavior, 20 seconds to record all the information I need, and 10 seconds before I move on to the next child. I would also have to observe all of the children several times, probably over the space of two or three days in order to get fairly reliable representative data. Now all I have to do is make up the recording sheet.

ⓈⓊⓂⓂⒶⓇⓎ

The frequency count tallies the occurrences of a particular behavior. The duration record, a variation of the frequency count, measures the length of a behavior. The duration record is used when the extent of a child's behavior is more important than just its frequency.

Frequency counts and duration records are closed and highly selective; if you are going to count something, you have to know what that something is. Inferences are required in these methods because you must define beforehand what behaviors will fit the category you want to observe and record—for example, cooperation, social exchanges, and so on. Frequency counts have such advantages as simplicity of use, provision of immediate quantifiable data, and usefulness in noting changes in behavior over repeated observations. The chief disadvantage lies in their closedness; they reveal virtually nothing about the details of behavior and its context.

A duration record is really quite simple. It has the qualities of a frequency count but also records the length of time the behavior lasts. The sample form given here can easily be modified into a duration record by providing spaces for recording time spans. In fact, you may eliminate the spaces for frequency checks, because every time record also indicates the occurrence of the target behavior.

STUDY QUESTIONS

1. When might a duration record give more important information than a frequency count? Will a duration record lose information about frequency?

2. For what purpose might a frequency count be the most useful method of recording? For what purpose might it be the least useful method?

3. What do time sampling and frequency counts have in common?

4. What advantages and disadvantages does the frequency count share with time sampling?

PRACTICAL EXERCISE

We can state this exercise very quickly and easily. Construct the same frequency count/duration record recording sheet that Florence describes just above. If you are able, actually observe and record whether the child behaves aggressively, against whom, for how long, and in what area of the child care center.

Checklists and Rating Scales

After reading this chapter, you should be able to

- Determine appropriate uses of checklists and rating scales.
- Examine the characteristics of checklists and rating scales.
- Discuss the characteristics of checklists and rating scales in relation to the dimensions of open versus closedness, degree of selectivity, and degree of inference required.
- Discuss the advantages and disadvantages of checklists and rating scales.

checklist

static descriptors

actions

intra-observer reliability

inter-observer reliability

validity

GENERAL DESCRIPTION

A **checklist** is any record that denotes the presence or absence of something. A shopping list and a class attendance sheet are simple checklists. Checklists have many uses and are very simple to use. When observing children, checklists are used to record the occurrence of specific behaviors in a given context. Key terms here are *specific behaviors* and *given context*. The first term simply indicates that the checklist has to be made up ahead of time before you begin observing. This being so, it stands to reason that you cannot construct a checklist of any kind until you know what you want to include on that list. Think of it again in terms of a grocery shopping list, which, as we have pointed out, is really a type of checklist. As you put each item on the list into your cart, you check it off, thereby keeping track both of what items you have in your cart and what items you still have to find in the store. But you cannot do that if you have not prepared the list before you enter the store (or while in the store but before actually beginning to shop). *Given context* means that at least some of the behaviors on the list will likely occur in particular settings and situations. So, for instance, if your checklist concerns physical/motor behaviors, ideally you would want to observe for those behaviors in a setting where they are most likely to occur—the big block area, during outside play, and so on. This would increase the efficiency and productivity of your efforts. However, it must be emphasized that the checklist can be used almost anywhere—physical/motor actions at the snack table are just as legitimate as those displayed while climbing a jungle gym, even though they might differ in certain respects (e.g., fine versus gross motor activities).

Brandt (1972) notes two types of this recording method. One important class of items recordable by a checklist is what he calls **static descriptors**. Static descriptors refer to relatively unchanging characteristics of settings or children (people) that can easily be noted and recorded in a checklist. Such descriptors provide consistency in recording data. Age, sex, race, socioeconomic status, characteristics of the physical environment, and time of day are examples of common static descriptors.

static descriptor

A descriptive item that pertains to a highly stable characteristic of research subjects or settings (Brandt, 1972); age, sex, race, and socioeconomic status are examples of static descriptors. These descriptors are often recorded by a checklist.

The checklist can be used almost anywhere—physical/motor actions at the snack table are just as legitimate as those displayed while climbing a jungle gym.

actions

Behaviors; actions form a class or set of items that are recorded by checklists, what Brandt (1972) called action checklists.

A second class of items for checklist recording is **actions** (action checklists, Brandt, 1972). Actions are behaviors and are therefore of prime concern to observers of children. A typical action checklist records occurrences of specific behaviors during an observation period. A list of behaviors is made up for each child, and the observer marks the behaviors that the child exhibits anytime during the observation period. A checklist can also be used to record whether the child can demonstrate certain behaviors on request. In this case, the checklist becomes a form of assessment.

Examine Table 12-1 and Table 12-2. These particular examples are checklists that had been used in a local Head Start program known to the author (courtesy of

Table 12-1 Sample Checklist

Name _____	School or Agency _____
Age _____ Group_____	Sex _____ Time of Day _____
Date of Birth _____	Observer _____

Directions: Check only those statements which you feel are really true of the child.

Do not guess (if you are not certain) or make a premature judgment call.

1. ( ) Vigorous and energetic in his attack on a project
2. ( ) Overcautious, not venturesome, afraid to attempt the untried
3. ( ) Nearly always accomplishes tasks in spite of difficulties
4. ( ) Voice animated, alive
5. ( ) Does not become fatigued easily
6. ( ) Poor concentration (begins and ends activities quickly or abruptly)
7. ( ) Merely copies other children's reactions, not original
8. ( ) Concentrates well at his task
9. ( ) Original and inventive reactions
10. ( ) Curious and questioning
11. ( ) Expresses himself well for his age
12. ( ) Resourceful in dealing with difficult situations
13. ( ) Poor use of language for his age
14. ( ) Patient
15. ( ) Absorbed; self-sufficient in his activity
16. ( ) Restless; a certain dissatisfaction with his own activity
17. ( ) Retiring; wishes to be in the background
18. ( ) Even-tempered
19. ( ) Frequently disturbed; easily upset by the disagreeable or the exciting
20. ( ) Seldom disturbed; sudden changes in mood infrequent
21. ( ) Slow to adjust to a novel experience
22. ( ) Original in play
23. ( ) Is easily distracted from task at hand
24. ( ) Gives up easily; lacks persistence

(continues)

Table 12-1 Sample Checklist (Continued)
25. ( ) Submits to any child who takes the initiative
26. ( ) Dominates children of his own age (either sex)
27. ( ) Will submit to a specific child only
28. ( ) Submits to a leader only after a struggle to dominate
29. ( ) Is a follower to one specific group only
30. ( ) Occasionally dominates a group
31. ( ) Usually leads a small group
32. ( ) Decides who shall participate in the group activities
33. ( ) Can organize the activities of a group to carry out a definite purpose
34. ( ) Leads or follows as the occasion demands
35. ( ) Neither leads nor follows; plays alone

Note: Checklists are from actual centers and are intended as examples; they are not necessarily ideal for all ages.

Helen Chauvin, Director). As you can see from Table 12-1, behaviors can be checked off at any time, but the checker needs to observe the child actually performing the behaviors, or be certain that the characteristics in question are true of the child. What is important and useful about this checklist is that the teacher or observer is not bound by time or context. He can record the information at any time. (This list, incidentally, is only partial; the original contains 166 items.) Table 12-2 combines a straightforward list of motor and self-help skills with normative data that indicate the age at which children typically acquire various skills. For example, the part of the Inventory called the "Blueprint" indicates that by three to four years of age on the average, children acquire the large motor skills described by items 24 through 32.

The checklist in Table 12-1 might appear to be too subjective and require too much interpretation to be very useful. Some might also argue that the items in this checklist are not specific enough. We offer two responses to these criticisms. First, learning about children is almost always accomplished through repeated observations over a reasonable period of time. This is true no matter what recording technique you use. Consequently, after watching four-year-old Jeremy at the puzzle table, you might check item number 23 ("Is easily distracted from task at hand") because at the time you observed him, Jeremy appeared distractible. However, this one incident would not justify the conclusion that Jeremy is always, or typically, distracted from the task at hand, only that he was so at the moment you observed him. On subsequent occasions, he may be very focused on his task, in which case you would check item number 8 ("Concentrates well at his task"). Each observational record is only a snapshot that

Table 12-2 Physical Development Checklist Together with Some Developmental Norms

Child's Name _____   Date of Birth _____

Date _____ Teacher's Name _____

Directions: Check only those statements which you feel are really true of the child.

Do not guess if you are not certain.

1. Puts together 3-piece puzzle_____Yes _____ No
2. Snips with scissors_____Yes _____ No
3. Picks up pins or buttons with each eye separately covered_____Yes _____ No
4. Paints strokes, dots, or circular shapes on easel_____Yes _____ No
5. Can roll, pound, squeeze, and pull clay_____Yes _____ No
6. Holds crayons with fingers, not with fist_____Yes _____ No
7. Puts together 8-piece (or more) puzzle_____Yes _____ No
8. Makes clay shapes with 2 or 3 parts_____Yes _____ No
9. Using scissors, cuts on curve_____Yes _____ No
10. Screws together a threaded object_____Yes _____ No
11. Cuts out and pastes simple shapes_____Yes _____ No
12. Draws a simple house_____Yes _____ No
13. Imitates folding and creasing paper 3 times_____Yes _____ No
14. Prints a few capital letters_____Yes _____ No
15. Copies a square_____Yes _____ No
16. Draws a simple recognizable picture (e.g., house, dog, tree)_____Yes _____ No
17. Can lace shoes_____Yes _____ No
18. Prints capital letters (large, single, anywhere on paper)_____Yes _____ No
19. Can copy small letters_____Yes _____ No
20. Cuts pictures from magazines without being more than one-half inch from edge of pictures_____Yes _____ No
21. Uses a pencil sharpener_____Yes _____ No
22. Folds paper square 2 times on diagonal, in imitation_____Yes _____ No
23. Prints name on paper_____Yes _____ No
24. Kicks large ball when rolled to him_____Yes _____ No

(continues)

PART TWO

Table 12-2 Physical Development Checklist Together with Some Developmental Norms (Continued)

25. Runs 10 steps with coordinated, alternating arm movement_____Yes _____ No

26. Pedals tricycle 5 feet_____Yes _____ No

27. Swings on swing when set in motion_____Yes _____ No

28. Climbs up and slides down 4–6 foot slide_____Yes _____ No

29. Somersaults forward_____Yes _____ No

30. Walks upstairs, alternating feet _____Yes _____ No

31. Catches ball with 2 hands when thrown from 5 feet_____Yes _____ No

32. Jumps from bottom step_____Yes _____ No

33. Climbs ladder_____Yes _____ No

34. Skips on alternate feet_____Yes _____ No

35. Walks balance beam forward without falling_____Yes _____ No

36. Runs, changing direction_____Yes _____ No

37. Jumps forward 10 times without falling_____Yes _____ No

38. Jumps backward 6 times without falling_____Yes _____ No

39. Bounces and catches large ball_____Yes _____ No

Blueprint for Motor and Self-Help Skill Inventory

Developmental Levels	Large Motor				Fine Motor				Self-Help
3–4 Years	24	25	26		1	2	3		
	27	28	29		4	5	6		
	30	31	32						
4–5 Years	33	34	35		7	8	9		
	36	37	38		10	11	12		
	39				13	14	15		
5–6 Years									

captures a relatively brief behavioral episode from an ongoing, constantly moving stream of behavior. Therefore, conclusions should be based on the accumulation of a number of checklist records taken over time and in a variety of settings and situations.

Second, although it is sometimes undesirable to do so, we tend to speak of children's behaviors and abilities in general terms. Sometimes our general descriptions are based on repeated observations; at other times we may make snap judgments based on limited information. After seeing Anthony take a toy away from another child, we might remark, "Anthony is an aggressive boy, isn't he?" when, in fact, Anthony might hardly ever display aggressive behavior. Child care professionals should not draw premature overall conclusions regarding children's behaviors and abilities. Nevertheless, at the moment a child exhibits a particular behavior or ability, one checklist recording may legitimately be considered an accurate account of what was observed. Additionally, however, one checklist recording could very well be a premature conclusion if it were allowed to stand alone and unsupported by further observations. For the professional child care provider and early childhood educator, therefore, no single observational record acquired by any recording technique should be the basis of decisions concerning children's behaviors and abilities.

A shopping list is a reasonable analogy to this discussion. A shopping list is a checklist we use to make sure we buy all the items we need. If, for example, we cannot find the particular breakfast cereal we have listed on our checklist, we should not conclude that the store never carries it, but only that at the time we are shopping, the store is out of that particular cereal. If, however, after repeated trips to the store, we still cannot find Tootie Fruities, it might be appropriate to conclude that the store no longer carries it. In like manner, during one moment of observation, Miguel is easily distracted, and you indicate that on your checklist. But repeated checklist records might indicate that Miguel focuses very well on the task at hand. Again, it is the accumulated observational records that most accurately describe any given child.

There are so many kinds of checklists that they may not be easily recognized as such. Consider the following example. The Denver Developmental Screening Test, although called a test, is also a checklist. The Denver Test provides norms for various behaviors within four developmental areas. It also provides the examiner with a series of questions, directions, and actions to elicit particular verbal, cognitive, or motor responses from the child. The examiner checks whether the child can answer the questions and demonstrate the desired behaviors. The child's performance is also matched against the norms for his age. Similarly, a preschool teacher might want to determine what specific skills the children in her class have: Who can hop on one foot, bounce a ball at least 5 times, count to 10? Such a checklist can be used to measure a child's skills when she first enters the preschool program, and again at a later time (see Table 12-3). Brandt (1972) says that checklists are best used in situations where there are not a lot of different behaviors to be observed, the behaviors are easily placed into only one specific, mutually exclusive category, and the behaviors of interest are easy to observe.

Table 12-3 Possible Checklist to Chart Developmental Progress

Child Observed _____

Child's Age _____

Observation Setting _____

Date _____

Time _____

1. Imitates a 3-cube bridge_____Yes _____ No

2. Uses both hands to steady a cube tower_____Yes _____ No

3. Uses scissors to snip inaccurately_____Yes _____ No

4. Copies a circle_____Yes _____ No

5. Imitates a horizontal line and a cross_____Yes _____ No

6. Feeds self independently with a spoon_____Yes _____ No

7. Dresses/undresses with assistance for front, back, snaps, laces_____Yes _____ No

8. Jumps in place_____Yes _____ No

9. Pedals tricycle_____Yes _____ No

10. Washes/dries hands_____Yes _____ No

11. Bounces ball at least 3 times_____Yes _____ No

12. Holds crayon between thumb and first 2 to 3 fingers_____Yes _____ No

Checklists require a great deal of structuring; the items to be noticed in a behavioral situation are clearly established beforehand (Brandt, 1972). This criterion should be familiar to you because the idea of structuring and defining "items to be noticed" applies to many of the methods already discussed. Structuring and defining are also part of the characteristics of openness/closedness and degree of selectivity. It is important to recognize that any recording scheme that marks a category, item, or answer on an observation sheet is a form of checklist; therefore, its categories must be carefully defined.

If validity and reliability are of concern when using a checklist, carefully defined categories will potentially enhance both of these characteristics. There are two kinds of reliability that are relevant here: intra-observer and inter-observer reliability. If a checklist has **intra-observer reliability**, repeated use of the checklist by the same individual will yield the same results. So, for example, if the checklist categories have been carefully defined and prove to be reliable, every time an observer sees

intra-observer reliability

Repeated use of a checklist by the same individual will yield the same results if the checklist categories have been carefully defined and the observer knows the definition and recognizes the behavior as such.

cooperation, she will indicate on the checklist form that cooperation has occurred. Of course, the observer has to know how cooperation has been defined for the purposes of the observation, and she must be able to recognize cooperation when she sees it. But the checklist also has to contain the proper descriptions of cooperative behavior so that its occurrence can be noted. If there are no items on the checklist that pertain to cooperation, or if the items are not sufficiently descriptive, then reliability (and perhaps validity as well) will be reduced or sacrificed altogether.

It is the accumulated observational records that most accurately describe any given child.

inter-observer reliability
The degree to which two or more observers agree with one another as to what occurred during an observation session. High inter-observer reliability indicates minimal disagreement and relatively few differences in observers' judgments and inferences.

Inter-observer reliability deals with the stability or consistency of recordings made by more than one observer using the same checklist and observing the same child. That is, two or more observers have to make the same decisions regarding whether or not a particular behavior has occurred, and they must mark the same item on the checklist that indicates the occurrence of the behavior.

validity
Pertaining to the accuracy and soundness of an observation or interpretation; the degree to which something measures what it claims to.

Validity is a bit more difficult to achieve. Validity means that the checklist is indeed measuring or capturing the behaviors, skills, or characteristics that you say it is. In other words, if a checklist claims to allow an observer to record instances of children's motor functioning, it is valid if it does just that. But if the items on the checklist really have nothing meaningful to do with motor functioning, then the checklist is invalid and is of no use for its stated or intended purpose. Achieving validity in some behavioral areas is perhaps easier than in others. It would appear to be easier to make valid recordings of motor functioning, for instance, than it would be for cases of certain areas or aspects of intellectual functioning. It is beyond the scope of this text to get into the technical aspects of validity and reliability, but it is this writer's belief that for most normal uses of the checklist in child care situations and settings, the issues of validity and reliability will resolve themselves, especially if repeated observations and recordings are made over some period of time by several individuals. And, of course, such repetition is itself part of the process of improving validity and reliability.

Open versus Closed

Checklists are closed because they reduce raw data to a tally that indicates the presence or absence of a specific behavior.

Degree of Selectivity

The degree of selectivity is high because the behavioral items to be recorded are identified and defined before beginning the observation.

Degree of Inference Required

The inferences required in using checklists by themselves are similar to those required when checklists are incorporated into other methods (for example, time sampling, event sampling, and frequency counts). You must define in advance the behaviors or events that properly belong in your observational categories. However, there will be times when you will see a behavior that is ambiguous and does not clearly fit the categories. In that case, you will have to decide then and there whether the behavior fits your definition.

Table 12-4 is an example of a checklist that would be appropriate for an infant one to four months of age. To construct the checklist, we first had to identify a range of behaviors and abilities that normally apply to a child this age. In a real observation situation, we would also have to decide what abilities, behaviors, and characteristics are important or relevant to our purposes. Obviously, it would make no sense to include in our list an item such as "Can walk five steps or more." The actual appearance of the checklist is less important than its overall clarity and ease of use. Finally, of course, anyone using the list has to understand what he or she is looking for and has to recognize it when it occurs. In this example, we do not use the format typically used throughout this text. We are emphasizing only the kinds of checklist items that would be appropriate for an infant one to four months of age; furthermore, the list is very short and for the purpose of illustration only. Naturally, you may add to it and use it as an observation exercise or for other legitimate reasons.

Table 12-4 Sample Checklist for Infant One to Four Months of Age			
Behavior, Characteristic, Ability	**Yes**	**No**	**Comments**
Legs are slightly bowed in appearance			
Tears flow when crying			
Shows start of binocular vision (eyes move together)			
Displays well-developed rooting and sucking reflexes			
Grasps objects with whole hand in a palmar grasp			
Supports head and upper body on arms when in a prone (face-down) position			
Can follow a moving object held 12 inches away			
Imitates gestures that are displayed by another			
Can locate the source of a sound			
Smiling at or speaking to infant evokes babbling and cooing			
Friendly face or voice evokes smile from infant			

Advantages

Checklists have the advantage of being usable in many different situations and methods. They are efficient and easy to use. The checklist is efficient because it reduces complex descriptive information to a single tally or notation, thus providing easily quantifiable data. The notation often signifies a category such as social exchanges, quarrels, or task-oriented activity. These categories are defined by a group of behaviors that share certain characteristics. The checklist eliminates the need to record all the details of behavior. It can also be an advantage that a checklist used in any format or method requires careful prior preparation. The checklist also has the advantage of providing what is called baseline information, which can then be compared with similar checklist records made during subsequent observations. The data can reveal the developmental gains or behavioral changes that have occurred from one time to the next. One final advantage we shall mention is that the checklist can also serve to identify behaviors, skills, and so forth that one might want to observe and record in greater detail later on. This use of the checklist can save you a lot of time otherwise spent in waiting for a behavior to occur in order to record it using, say, a narrative description or event sampling technique. The checklist will tell you that the child can and does perform a particular behavior and that the behavior has become available for further, more intense observation.

Disadvantages

As with any method that does not preserve raw data, the checklist loses the details of the observed behavior and its context. This means that the observation record will consist mainly of action fragments or isolated impressions of the children observed. This makes it important to match carefully any recording method with your observation objectives.

Tips on Constructing Checklists

As we have already mentioned, the checklist is based on a very simple concept: It essentially lists a series of items or actions, the presence or absence of which is important to the individual using the checklist. We have already discussed the shopping list as one of the simplest examples. Airplane pilots use checklists to guide them through a series of steps that indicate the readiness of the airplane to fly safely. Although constructing a checklist requires some thought, ordinarily it can be a relatively easy process. If you want to construct your own checklists rather than using any of this text's examples, one way to begin is to use any set of developmental norms, milestones, or profiles as the content for your checklist. This author used this method to construct Table 12-4, for example. We want to emphasize that the goal of constructing any checklist is not to test your own creativity, but rather to come up with a practical, usable instrument that helps you understand children's behavior and assess their developmental progress. Consequently, use whatever resources will help you achieve that end.

    The checklists in Table 12-1, Table 12-2, and Table 12-3 display the basic principles that characterize almost any checklist. Perhaps the most basic characteristic of a usable checklist is that its content must represent directly observable behaviors. Decisions regarding whether any item in the checklist describes the behavior you have observed do involve interpretation. Following that, however, any further interpretation has to do with such things as determining the significance or relationship of the behavior observed to the child's other behaviors or to his or her overall developmental progress. How does the behavior you have observed fit into the general context of the child's development and experiences?

    We offer one more example of a checklist (see Table 12-5) that we constructed out of a hypothetical situation in which the objective is to determine how well four-year-old Dominic is adjusting socially to his early childhood program experiences. The primary task of this checklist is to identify the social behaviors and relationships Dominic does or does not exhibit in a variety of classroom situations. The information gathered in this way can then be used as a basis for further, more detailed observation, with the possible additional goal of planning and implementing activities and experiences that will benefit Dominic's social development. However, please note that this example by no means exhausts all the possible social behaviors that Dominic might display in a child care setting. Also, any checklist you devise or use should be appropriate to your particular circumstances, those of the children, and the overall observation context. Consequently, you would not adopt Table 12-5, either whole or

Social Behavior	Observed		
	Yes	No	Sometimes
Is friendly and outgoing			
Plays with the majority of other children in most of the activity areas			
Plays only with certain children in certain activity areas			
Seeks adult approval			
Seeks peer approval			
Is willing to take turns			
Makes transitions easily from one activity to another			
Adjusts easily, quickly to new, unfamiliar activities			
Is independent			
Shows distinct mood changes			
Is appropriately assertive			
Shows skillful use of language in his social interactions			

Table 12-5 Checklist to Assess Four-Year Old Dominic's Social Behaviors in a Hypothetical Child Care Setting

in part, if it did not suit your specific purposes. Nevertheless, the behaviors represented in Table 12-5 should adequately illustrate the checklist concept.

RATING SCALES: GENERAL DESCRIPTION

We have included a discussion of rating scales in the same chapter as checklists because they share some essential characteristics. However, pay careful attention to the differences between checklists and rating scales; otherwise, you may lose the advantages of one or the other, or unnecessarily suffer the disadvantages of one or the other of these two recording techniques.

Each of the names given to the recording techniques discussed in this text indicates the basic nature or characteristics of the technique. *Narrative description*, for example, indicates a description of behavior that takes the form of a narrative. *Event sampling* indicates that your observations will sample behaviors that you have defined as an event, and so on for each of the remaining techniques. The name *rating scales* follows this same pattern.

To rate something basically means to assign it a value or quality. Judges in a beauty contest rate the contestants according to their relative degree of attractiveness or talent. *Consumer Reports* rates consumer products such as refrigerators, stoves, and automobiles according to each product's quality, durability, reliability, value for dollar spent, and so on. An item that rates highly is an item that possesses these desirable characteristics to a large degree.

The term *scale* is a little more difficult to define in very simple terms. For our purposes, a scale is simply an instrument with which to measure or record the relative degree to which children possess certain skills, abilities, behaviors, personality characteristics, and so on. In everyday terms, we hear, use, and understand the word *scale* in many different situations. A bathroom scale measures how much one weighs, and typically the scale can measure a weight from 0 to 300 pounds. As is the case with most kinds of scales, what is measured falls along what is called a *continuum*, because what is being measured can be assigned a number (often a very large number, at least theoretically) of different values or quantities. For example, you might want to construct a rating scale to measure children's sociability, or ability to get along well with others. Sociability can be thought of as occurring in varying "amounts." You might decide to judge sociability according to three different degrees or relative amounts of this trait: Very Sociable, Moderately Sociable, Not at All Sociable. The most difficult task would be to distinguish among these three amounts or degrees of sociability as you actually observe a child during social interactions. How do you decide whether a child is "very" sociable or only "moderately" sociable?

Rating scales are similar to checklists, but they differ with respect to their essential purpose. Checklists basically indicate the presence or absence of something, and they need not make any other determinations. In the case of rating scales, determinations can be made with respect to such things as the quality of an individual's performance in some area. Appendix 1 contains examples of what this author has labeled developmental checklists. In point of fact, however, these checklists could appropriately be thought of as a simple form of rating scale. For example, the first checklist asks whether, by three years of age, the child runs well in a forward direction. Three options are available for a response to this question: "Yes," "No," and "Sometimes." These response options essentially assess a child's ability to perform a particular motor activity. The "Yes," "No," and "Sometimes" categories rate the child's ability in this area. Of course, the list of functions or behaviors in the appendix is more extensive than indicated in the example, and additional checklists or scales also deal with children of different ages. Note, however, that the categories of "Yes," "No," and "Sometimes" provide only a rather crude rating of the child's ability "to run well in a forward direction." The word *well* in the question attempts to account for the quality of the child's running ability. A rating scale with finer, more sophisticated distinctions would attempt to measure quality of performance within the scale itself.

As the preceding sentence indicates, rating scales are a little more complicated than simple checklists. Again, the simplest checklist merely indicates whether something is or is not present. For instance, can a child walk unassisted or not walk unassisted? (The "something" here that is present or absent is the ability to walk unassisted.) However, a rating scale could try to assess not only whether a child can walk unassisted, but also how well or how skillfully he or she walks. As you can see, such a determination of skill level requires greater observational skills than does making a check mark to indicate merely that the child walks. In short, in a simple checklist, the degree of competence in a given functional area is not an issue.

Another difficulty associated with the construction of rating scales is choosing the criteria or standards by which to judge children's competence or skill in a particular function or behavior. A rating scale requires some number of categories, each of which represents a different level of skill. Difficulty can be increased if you attempt a fine distinction among skill levels. At the extreme, you can attempt to make distinctions that are so small that it becomes nearly impossible to notice them. On the other hand, if the distinctions are too loose or too undiscriminating, the rating scale will not effectively or accurately record important differences in a child's abilities in a given functional area. As with the checklist, therefore, rating scales require considerable structuring. The behaviors or skills to be observed and evaluated by a checklist must be clearly established beforehand. Rating scales demand additional structuring. Not only must you define the behavioral categories to be observed, but you must also clearly define the characteristics by which you will judge different levels or degrees of performance skill.

Because rating scales share many of the characteristics of checklists, we recommend that you review the earlier discussion of checklists in this chapter to complete your understanding of rating scales and how they should be used.

Table 12-6 illustrates a simple rating scale. Once you understand the general concept of a rating scale, you should be able to construct as simple or sophisticated a rating scale instrument as your particular situation requires.

The five rating categories in the example are simple enough to think of, but some difficulty arises when it comes time to distinguish between excellent and very good, or very good and good, and so on. In practice, therefore, an observer would have to specify beforehand what, for instance, constitutes excellent versus very good ability to stack objects or to creep on hands and knees. Indeed, how finely one's rating categories try to distinguish degrees of skill will depend upon such things as the observer's skill, the behavior or function being rated, and the purpose of the rating scale in the first place. Other considerations may also apply.

Open versus Closed

Rating scales are essentially closed because they reduce raw data to a tally or mark that represents the presence of a particular skill or behavior and how well the child has performed that skill or behavior, or how much of a trait or characteristic the child possesses. However, one can base ratings on more extensive observational data such as data

Table 12-6 An Abbreviated Example of a Rating Scale (Motor Development: 8–12 Months)					
Motor Function	**Excellent**	**Very Good**	**Good**	**Fair**	**Poor**
Reaches with one hand, grasps an object when offered					
Transfers objects from one hand to another; capable of manipulating objects					
Can stack objects or place one object inside another					
Uses pincer grasp to pick up small objects, food					
Deliberately drops or throws objects but cannot intentionally put an object down					
Shows beginning ability to pull self to a standing position					
Begins to stand alone; leans on furniture for support; "cruises" around obstacles with side-stepping movements					
Creeps on hands and knees; crawls up and down stairs					

acquired through narrative descriptions or event samplings. Indeed, when using only the rating scale, you are in effect choosing a particular rating based on what might be called a "mental narrative description (or event sample)." You have to observe some behavior for some required length of time and then decide how to rate or judge its quality. In the latter instance, you are spared having to take extensive notes before marking the scale.

Degree of Selectivity

The degree of selectivity is high because the behavioral items to be recorded are identified and defined before beginning the observation. In this regard, the rating scale is very much like event sampling. Recall that in event sampling, you wait for a particular behavior or "event" to occur, and then you describe it. The rating scale requires the same procedure: You wait for a particular behavior to occur, and then you rate it according to the rating categories you have established.

Degree of Inference Required

The degree of inference required when using a rating scale is quite high. The checklist also requires a rather high degree of inference, inasmuch as the observer has to decide whether or not a particular behavior has occurred before making a mark on the checklist. At the very least, this same level of inference is required in the rating scale: Has the child performed a particular behavior, or does the child process a particular characteristic or skill? However, additional inference is required in the rating scale because the observer must make an immediate decision regarding the quality of the child's behavior or the extent of the characteristic being rated. Such a decision is actually an interpretation.

Advantages

One advantage of the rating scale is that, aside from the degree of inference required, the scale is relatively simple to use. It certainly is economical with respect to the time and effort needed to record behavior. In this regard, therefore, it is similar to the checklist. Brewer (1998) writes that rating scales "can also provide useful information for teachers as they plan learning experiences. It is most appropriate to use rating scales to compare a child's current behavior to his previous behavior" (pp. 471–472).

Disadvantages

There are several potential disadvantages to the rating scale, depending upon one's purposes. The rating scale requires a considerable amount of structuring. You need to give careful thought to the various aspects of the behavior you want to rate, and the rating categories probably require even more thought. Again, if you try to make discriminations that are too small or fine, it will be very difficult to notice the distinctions represented by your categories. If, on the other hand, your categories are not fine enough, then your observations will not reveal any significant differences in the child's behavior or skill.

Another potential disadvantage of the rating scale lies in the loss of data. The rating scale is a closed technique, unless you accompany it with other data such as those provided by a narrative description or event sample. You observe a particular behavior, and you must quickly decide at least two things: (1) whether or not that behavior meets the purpose of your scale, and (2) the degree or extent to which that behavior has been exhibited. Those information-rich decisions are reflected in a simple check mark or tally. Consequently, you will have no information on the actual behaviors on which you have based your ratings. You will not be able later on to refer to your objective behavioral descriptions to check the accuracy of your ratings. If you do not need such information, you will have spared yourself the time and effort of recording narrative descriptions or event samples. Recall that you can perform ratings based on narrative descriptive or event sampling data, thereby preserving a rich, complete source of information. See Table 12-7 for a summary of recording techniques.

			Table 12-7 Summary of Recording Techniques		
Method	**Open vs. Closed**	**Degree of Selectivity**	**Degree of Inference**	**Advantages**	**Disadvantages**
Narrative Description (Formal)	Open	Low degree of selectivity	Low at the time of observation; rises during interpretation	• Provides a complete account • Captures context (setting and situation) • It is a permanent record • Usable under many circumstances	• It is time- and energy-consuming • Can be inefficient regarding representativeness of behavior sample • Requires skill and effort to record all details of behavior
Time Sampling (Formal)	Open to extent it preserves raw data	High degree of selectivity	High initially, then it varies with subsequent use of data	• Suitable for all kinds of behavior • Economical of time and energy—very efficient • Yields representative data • Can combine different recording techniques	• Use limited by frequency of behavior • Does not treat behavior as it naturally occurs—"action fragments" are recorded • Predetermined categories may cause bias • Coding schemes may cause difficulty—requires precise, reliable use of categories
Event Sampling (Formal)	Open or closed, depending on use of coding schemes or narrative description	High degree of selectivity	High initially	• Can preserve raw data • Suitable for infrequently occurring behaviors • Records natural units of behavior • Can combine narrative description with coding schemes	• Not very useful for the infrequent observer—need to be in the setting often enough to see behavior when it occurs

(continues)

Table 12-7 Summary of Recording Techniques (Continued)					
Method	**Open vs. Closed**	**Degree of Selectivity**	**Degree of Inference**	**Advantages**	**Disadvantages**
Diary Description (Informal)	Open	Rather high, especially the topical diary	As high as time and event sampling	• Preserves raw data • Useful over longer periods of time—provides connection among behavioral events	• Of limited use to most observers; must spend a lot of time with the child
Anecdotal Record (Informal)	Open	High if only unusual behavior is recorded	High, especially if an explanation of the behavior is required	• Provides a running account of child's behavior in particular contexts • Allows continuing comparisons of behavior that permit documentation of change • Very easy to use—needs no special coding schemes, settings, or categories	• Open to observer bias via improper wording, dislike of the child, etc. • Controversial technique because of its susceptibility to bias
Frequency Counts or Duration Records (Informal)	Closed; preserves no raw data	Highly selective	High degree of inference	• Frequency count is very simple to construct and use • Duration a bit more complicated because it requires keeping track of time spent in a behavioral event • Frequency counts yield immediately quantifiable data • Useful in noting changes in behavior over time, especially duration record that indicates amount of time spent in given activities	Greatest disadvantage is their closedness; they reveal nothing about context or behavioral details

(continues)

	Table 12-7 Summary of Recording Techniques (Continued)				
Method	**Open vs. Closed**	**Degree of Selectivity**	**Degree of Inference**	**Advantages**	**Disadvantages**
Checklists (Informal)	Closed; raw data reduced to a tally mark; if used with narrative description or event sampling techniques, raw data can be preserved	Highly selective	High degree of inference	• Usable in many different situations and methods • It is efficient • Can provide "baseline" information to reveal developmental gains or behavioral changes • Can identify behaviors and skills that one might want to observe in more detail later on	Does not preserve raw data, so details are lost and only action fragments remain in the observation record
Rating Scales	Closed; the same conditions apply to rating scales as apply to checklists	Highly selective	High degree of inference	• Except for the degree of inference required, rating scale is simple to use • Economical of recording time and effort • Useful for planning experiences and for ongoing comparisons of a child's behavior (Also see advantages of checklists.)	• Requires a great deal of structuring • Loss of raw data • Requires a high level of inference (Also see disadvantages of checklists.)

Tips on Constructing Rating Scales

It is highly unlikely that in the typical child care setting you will need to rate children's behaviors, skills, or other indicators of developmental progress with the same precision required in a rigorous scientific study. Consequently, keep your rating categories simple, yet at the same time make them descriptive enough to make meaningful distinctions between levels or degrees of skill. However, bear in mind that one rating scale record is not sufficient for drawing conclusions or making decisions about a given child. This means that if you have constructed a reasonably useful rating scale, repeated ratings of a particular child will likely become more precise as you become accustomed to the instrument and more skilled in noticing the behavioral details by which to distinguish among various rating categories or levels of ability.

One of the distinct advantages of all the recording techniques discussed in this text is that any one of them conceivably can be used in combination with any other, if their combination makes sense and lends itself to practical use. For example, although the checklist typically does not retain raw data but merely indicates the presence or absence of something, observation data in the form of a brief narrative description could be entered into a checklist format. The final record would then be a series of short narratives, each depicting the various behaviors defined by the items in the checklist.

The rating scale could be approached in the same way. We offer Table 12-8 as an abbreviated example of how a rating scale/event sample combination might look. You will recognize that the same kinds of judgments required in the conventional rating

Table 12-8 A Completed Hypothetical Rating Scale Using Brief Narrative Description as a Method of Recording Observation Data

Child: Brandon (age three years)

Developmental Area: Speech and Language

Date: April 7, 2008

Observer: Dorothy Mitchell, Head Teacher

Duration of Observation: 9:20 A.M. to 9:45 A.M.

Behavior	Excellent	Good	Fair	Poor	Unable to Assess
Gives appropriate answers to simple questions	Responded well to my question "What are you doing, Brandon?"				
Provides additional information in a conversation (for example, "And I played with it, too.")			In a brief conversation with Samantha, his contribution to the conversation was minimal.		

(continues)

Behavior	Excellent	Good	Fair	Poor	Unable to Assess
Table 12-8 A Completed Hypothetical Rating Scale Using Brief Narrative Description as a Method of Recording Observation Data (Continued)					
Helps keep a conversation going "using a number of speech forms"	Following my question regarding what he was doing, he asked me, "Can you do this?"				
Speech is understandable		Had difficulty pronouncing a few words.			
Has a vocabulary of 300 to 1,000 words		A tentative conclusion at this time is that Brandon has a rather extensive vocabulary.			
Encourages others' behavior ("Let's play with the blocks. What shall we build?")					Did not observe this at this time.
Comments on the actions of others					Did not observe at this time.

scale will also have to be made using this modified format. Bear in mind that as with any observation record, the information in Table 12-8 has been recorded during one relatively brief occasion. Additional samples of Brandon's speech and language behavior would have to be obtained in order to make a reasonable assessment of his abilities in this functional area. Also note that Table 12-8 could be completed in the conventional way using a simple check mark or "X."

VIDEOTAPING AND AUDIOTAPING AS OBSERVATION TOOLS?

Videotaping

In this age of advanced technology, one would be hard pressed to ignore the use of video cameras in the observation of children. In the past this writer downplayed the use of video cameras, in large part because of the distinction made in Chapter 1 between seeing in a physiological sense and seeing in a psychological sense. Recall that, like the eye, the camera only captures an image, but it cannot do anything further with that image—it cannot infer any meaning from it. Meaning depends upon the interpretive capacity of the brain. And so it is that using a video camera will not provide you with any information about what you have taped other than the raw images of the children's behavior. You need those images, of course, but without your intelligence applied to them, they are useless for any purposes of observation.

It must nonetheless be conceded that videotapes of behavior can be especially useful for training or instructional purposes. Recording children's behavior on videotape "freezes" action patterns and sequences and allows you to view them again and again without losing any of the raw data contained in that behavior. This ability to watch behavior any number of times potentially enables you to see things that you might otherwise miss. For the relatively untrained observer, the usefulness of the videotapes is greatest when they are viewed with someone who is already skilled in observing and recording behavior in the traditional way. A skillful observer can direct your looking and your perceptual mindset toward significant actions and interactions along with their contexts. One significant advantage of using videotapes for training or instructional purposes lies in the fact that everyone is looking at exactly the same thing, which offers a consistent, reliable set of behavioral data upon which an instructor can base his or her teaching. Probably many teachers' personal experiences in reading students' observation reports will attest to the difficulty in evaluating the accuracy of those reports. A teacher who was not in the observation setting with the students has to accept their objective behavioral descriptions more or less at face value. Under those conditions, it is impossible to know what students actually did or did not see—or, for that matter, what was there to be seen.

But we cannot overemphasize the fact that the camera, in and of itself, cannot guarantee that you have recorded anything significant or useful to your purposes for observing in the first place. Nor, for that matter, is there any guarantee that what you observe without a video camera will be significant or useful to your purposes. Both circumstances require skill on the part of the observer. We are not suggesting that using a video camera will necessarily result in inadequate data or indiscriminant use of the camera. Nevertheless, we believe that under most circumstances in the professional lives of child care providers and early childhood educators, persistent and extensive use of a video camera would be unfeasible. Child care professionals simply cannot have undue restraints imposed upon them, and we view the video camera as an unnecessary restraint in many situations. However, we recognize that some of you will want to use the video camera regardless of its potential disadvantages, real or imagined. In that event, we can recommend only that you use it judiciously and in combination with sound, basic observational and recording skills.

Disadvantages

Let us examine some of the potential disadvantages of the video camera. It is nearly impossible to observe and record everything that goes on in the observation setting (any more than you can observe and record everything with the unaided eye). Even to attempt to record everything would require excessive amounts of tape and inordinate attention to the sheer act of managing the camera. For ordinary or typical observations, the video camera may actually restrict your ability to "see as you go" those events and behaviors that are useful to you in the longer run. It certainly limits your ability to participate in, or be sensitive to, the important things that are occurring in the child care setting. You are not making a documentary film; you are observing children for specific reasons, and a camera can be an encumbrance that restricts your ability to move freely and act quickly. Effective observation demands reasonable freedom of movement and reasonable freedom to make decisions concerning what is important and what will enhance your understanding of the children in the observation setting.

There is another potential limitation to the use of video camera, a limitation that has to do with what Gonzalez-Mena (1997) calls "soft eyes." Soft eyes involves a kind of seeing that enables one to look at a particular child while at the same time taking in what is happening in the entire classroom. This is an observational skill that Gonzalez-Mena believes is extremely important to providing children quality care. Focusing on a particular child demonstrates concern for and interest in that child, which is a feeling all children should have in interactions with their care providers. On the other hand, it is very important that the teacher or child care provider also be aware of what is happening with other children in other parts of the room. Soft eyes is a technique that allows efficient monitoring and supervision of young children. Gonzalez-Mena puts it this way: "The term 'soft eyes' refers to the skill that allows an early childhood educator to talk to another staff member or a parent while still being aware of what is going on in the rest of the room or play yard" (p. 155). Of course, soft eyes is more than just seeing: "[I]t also includes hearing and sensing what else is going on" (p. 155). It is doubtful—at least in this writer's view—that the soft eyes technique can be applied with optimal effectiveness when using a video camera.

If you decide to use a video camera for whatever reason, there are several things that you should, and in some cases must, consider before videotaping children in a child care setting. Permission from the children's parents is essential if you are on the child care facility staff. If you are an outsider and are there merely to observe, then permission all the way around is definitely required. Some parents might object even to still photographs of their children. Photographs and videotapes have a permanent, all-revealing quality to them that makes some people uneasy. It stands to reason that if permission is mandatory when observing and recording behavior using your normal, unaided senses and paper-and-pencil recording techniques, then the use of video cameras most decidedly requires permission.

If a child does not want to be videotaped, you must honor his or her wishes and not do so. However, it must be conceded that an initial reluctance on a child's part to be videotaped might be overcome if, for example, the child is permitted to become familiar with the video camera. But the main issue here is not how to enlist children's willingness to be taped, but whether a video camera is the best observational tool at your disposal. You should also be aware that the presence of a camera could influence the children's behavior. This might not always be undesirable under certain circumstances, but because this text deals primarily with observation that is as naturalistic as possible, children hamming it up for the camera or changing their behavior because of camera-induced anxiety falls outside of the purview of naturalistic as this author defines it.

Audiotaping

Audiotape recorders have even more limited value for the overall observation process than video cameras. Recording the sounds that are common to a child care setting might be valuable in certain instances, perhaps to capture such things as the general emotional "tone" of the situation at some given time. Audiotapes can also be particularly useful in recording children's speech for later interpretation and evaluation. But language skills consist of more than just words—facial expressions, body movements, and gestures are also very important in communication. If you want only to observe a child's verbal utterances, then taping can be useful, especially if you need verbatim records of a child's speech. If you want to observe the child's full range of communication skills, using only a tape recording will omit those additional facets of language that will provide you with other critical information. The best advice we can give regarding the use of video camera and audiotape recorders is to use them judiciously for purposes that legitimately serve the best interests of the children and your observation goals. It would be very easy to jump on the technology bandwagon and use these devices simply because they are available and seemingly glamorize your observation efforts.

SOME USES OR APPLICATIONS OF THE CHECKLIST AND RATING SCALE

Of all the recording methods discussed in this text, the uses for the checklist and rating scale are perhaps the most straightforward. Child care providers and parents always want to know what children can and cannot do and how well they can do it. Look again at Table 12-3, which we have partially duplicated on p. 222. We need to point out that this checklist pertains to physical–motor abilities, which in some respects are easier to interpret than more open-ended kinds of behaviors such as the social behaviors illustrated in Table 12-5. Consequently, what we have to say about Table 12-3 will not be completely pertinent to the checklist in Table 12-5 and its applications.

What could be simpler than watching a child pedal a tricycle and answering yes to the checklist item "Pedals tricycle _Yes No"? A rating scale would provide more information than the checklist alone, and, of course, a reasonably detailed description

Partial Duplication of Table 12-3 Possible Checklist to Chart Developmental Progress in Physical–Motor Functioning
1. Imitates a 3-cube bridge Yes_____ No
2. Uses both hands to steady a cube tower_____Yes_____ No
3. Uses scissors to snip inaccurately_____Yes_____ No
4. Copies a circle_____ Yes_____ No
5. Imitates a horizontal line and a cross_____Yes _____ No
6. Feeds self independently with a spoon_____Yes_____ No
7. Dresses/undresses with assistance for front, back, snaps, laces_____Yes_____ No
8. Jumps in place_____ Yes_____ No
9. Pedals tricycle _____Yes_____ No
10. Washes/dries hands_____Yes_____ No
11. Bounces ball at least 3 times_____Yes_____ No
12. Holds crayon between thumb and first 2 to 3 fingers_____Yes_____ No

of the child pedaling a tricycle would provide even more information than the rating scale. But, relative to the checklist, each of these additional responses—rating scale and narrative description—makes recording the child's behavior more difficult and time-consuming. Whether the added difficulty is warranted depends on your objectives. For now, let us look just at the checklist in Table 12-3.

Uses for the Checklist: A Brief Comparison of Two Checklists

As we have already mentioned, the most basic purpose of the checklist is to record whether or not a child has exhibited particular, predetermined behaviors. In other words, checklists essentially record the presence or absence of something. We used the shopping list as a common example of this kind of checklist. As you put each item on your list into the shopping cart, you cross it off to indicate that you no longer need to look for that item. The items that have not been crossed off are the ones you have yet to find. However, the potential problem with such a simple checklist is that if you leave the store with items that have not been crossed off, the checklist itself will not tell you whether the store did not have that item or whether you simply could not find it. This is a potential problem with the checklist illustrated in Table 12-3.

For example, one of the difficulties when trying to evaluate young children's motor abilities is that you cannot be certain that a child does not possess a particular ability simply because you have not observed it. This has to do with the difference between learning and performance. If a child performs a particular behavior, especially if she does so repeatedly, you can be certain that she has learned it. However, if you do not see her perform that behavior, it does not necessarily mean that she cannot perform it. Consequently, it may be premature to check "No" to the item "Jumps in place" in Table 12-3 if you do so only because you have not yet seen the child jumping in place. However, if you do witness Willard *unsuccessfully* trying to jump in place, then checking "No" would be appropriate at that particular time for that particular observation. The upshot of all this is that the most appropriate application or use of a checklist similar to that depicted in Table 12-3 is when the probability is relatively high that a child will be able to perform the behaviors on your checklist. Perhaps we can think of this use of the checklist as being similar to making a list of all your material possessions; you know you have a computer and a television set because you are looking at them as you put them on your list. You know Margaret can bounce a ball three times because you are watching her do it. This means that you must gear your checklist items to the ages and developmental levels of the children you are going to observe.

Of what practical value is such a checklist? What comes immediately to mind is that it can serve as a convenient and efficient way to compile an inventory of children's skills and abilities and to chart their change over time. This kind of inventory provides a basis for comparing children's earlier abilities with later ones, but only in what we shall call a "not-now-but-later" fashion. If on Monday, Willard unsuccessfully tried to jump in place, and eight days later you see him succeed at this task, your checklist, separated by an eight-day interval, provides a comparative record of Willard's developmental progress. Of course, this does not necessarily mean that Willard actually needed eight days to learn how to jump in place; he could have succeeded just two days later, on Wednesday, but you were not there to observe him. If, however, someone else was there and recorded his success on Wednesday, then you could update your records on Willard's progress.

A more "subtle" checklist is illustrated in Table 12-5, which we have duplicated p. 224. You will notice that the format and the requirements of Table 12-5 are different from the format and requirements of Table 12-3. Table 12-5 has added a third occasion for interpretation labeled "Sometimes." Additionally, marking a "Yes" or a "No" to "Is appropriately assertive," for example, may not be as clear-cut a decision as marking "Yes" to the item "Imitates a 3-cube bridge." The first item's subtlety lies in the descriptive word *appropriately*, and even *assertive* can under some circumstances be difficult to distinguish from *aggressive*. The potential difficulties in checking at least some of the items in Table 12-5 can come close to those you would encounter in the rating scale. Furthermore, we must bear in mind that the items selected for Table 12-5 are for illustration only, and by no means do they exhaust the total pool of possible items, nor are they as subtle as they could possibly be.

Your reasons for using the type of checklist in Table 12-5 would not differ fundamentally from your reasons for using the type of checklist in Table 12-3. In both cases you record whether or not something has occurred. Table 12-5 is more

Duplication of Table 12-5 Checklist to Assess Four-Year-Old Dominic's Social Behaviors in a Hypothetical Child-Care Setting			
Social Behavior	**Observed**		
	Yes	**No**	**Sometimes**
Is friendly and outgoing			
Plays with the majority of other children in most of the activity areas			
Plays only with certain children in certain activity areas			
Seeks adult approval			
Seeks peer approval			
Is willing to take turns			
Makes transitions easily from one activity to another			
Adjusts easily, quickly to new, unfamiliar activities			
Is independent			
Shows distinct mood changes			
Is appropriately assertive			
Shows skillful use of language in his social interactions			

sophisticated than Table 12-3, in part because your interpretations are more sophisticated or difficult in Table 12-5, as we have already tried to explain. In partial conclusion, then, you would be justified in using a checklist of almost any description if your primary objective is to determine what behaviors, skills, abilities, characteristics, and so forth that a child is able to exhibit, and you have no need for raw data that describe the details and contexts of those behaviors.

We cannot emphasize strongly enough the importance of getting a series of checklist records over a reasonable period of time. That will give you a relatively complete account of the child's abilities and of his or her progress from "ability absent" to "ability present."

A Brief Return to the "No" Response on the Checklist

There is a way to handle those situations when you do not observe a child performing particular behaviors, and for this we are indebted to Beaty (2002) for her example of a checklist (Figure 12-1) that we reproduce verbatim immediately below. An additional advantage to this checklist is that it allots space for what Beaty calls "evidence," which is really a brief narrative description. In the directions, Beaty writes, "Put *N* for items where there is no opportunity to observe." But also notice that Beaty would want you to record instances of a child's behavior only if it has occurred regularly. In this regard we differ from Beaty and do not put that restriction on the use of the checklist. Indeed, we encourage you to use the checklist to record behaviors that you either see the child perform for the first time or, if you can be certain, that she actually performs for the first time ever. The regularity of behavior that Beaty calls for can be assessed by completing a number of observations over time.

CHILD SKILLS CHECKLIST

Name _____   Observer _____
Program _____   Dates _____

Directions: Put a • for items you see the child perform regularly. Put an **N** for items where there is no opportunity to observe. Leave all other items blank.

Item	Evidence	Date
1. Self-Identity Separates from parents without difficulty		
Does not cling to classroom staff excessively		
Makes eye contact with adults		
Makes activity choices without teacher's help		
Seeks other children to play with		
Plays roles confidently in dramatic play		
Stands up for own rights		
Displays enthusiasm about doing things for self		
2. Emotional Development Allows self to be comforted during stressful time		
Eats, sleeps, toilets without fuss away from home		
Handles sudden changes/startling situations with control		
Can express anger in words rather than actions		

Figure 12-1 Child Skills Checklist (Used with permission from Merrill Prentice Hall: Columbus, Ohio. From Beaty, J. J., 2002, (*Observing Development of the Young Child*)

Uses of the Rating Scale

We see no need to spend a lot of time discussing the uses of the rating scale, inasmuch as they so closely resemble the uses of the checklist, with one important exception: The rating scale records the proficiency or quality of the child's performance of various actions. For your convenience, we have duplicated Table 12-6 to illustrate the idea of rating the proficiency or quality of function.

It is readily apparent that, like the checklist, the rating scale also records whether the child can perform particular behaviors. The potential difficulty consists in deciding on how competently or skillfully the child performs the behaviors. Such difficulty notwithstanding, the checklist depicted in Table 12-6, or any other similar to it, would be very useful in tracking the child's progress from the early to the later stages of skill acquisition. Depending upon when you began observing the child, such a record could proceed from no evidence of any ability to perform a particular action, on through the

Table 12-6 Duplication of An Abbreviated Example of a Rating Scale (Motor Development: 8–12 Months)					
Motor Function	**Excellent**	**Very Good**	**Good**	**Fair**	**Poor**
Reaches with one hand, grasps an object when offered					
Transfers objects from one hand to another; capable of manipulating objects					
Can stack objects or place one object inside another					
Uses pincer grasp to pick up small objects, food					
Deliberately drops or throws objects but cannot intentionally put an object down					
Shows beginning ability to pull self to a standing position					
Begins to stand alone; leans on furniture for support; "cruises" around obstacles with side-stepping movements					
Creeps on hands and knees; crawls up and down stairs					

entire continuum from poor to excellent. The record's usefulness would be enhanced further if the information acquired were compared to developmental norms.

FLORENCE AND THE CHECKLIST

Florence is given the assignment of deciding whether the event sample or the checklist is the more appropriate technique for recording the physical–motor skills and progress of a group of five two-year-olds in a child care center. She is also asked either to construct an appropriate checklist or to find one that would serve her purpose. The following is how she possibly might think through this assignment:

> Let's see, the event sample or the checklist? Well, motor skills—how a child uses her body, how she walks and runs and balances—these are things that are easy enough to observe. The question is, which of the two recording techniques would be more efficient in getting this information? The event sample would certainly get me some of the information I want. I simply have to define the physical–motor events that I am interested in, wait until they occur, and then write down a fairly detailed description of how the child performed those behaviors. But wait a minute—I need to get information about five children and how they are developing physically and motorically. If I used the event sample, I could spend a lot of time just waiting for a particular behavior to occur before I could record anything. Also, I would have to record the behavior by writing down a lot of words, and I would have to do that for each of the five children. With the checklist, however, I could describe ahead of time the characteristics of the motor behavior I was looking for, and it wouldn't be inconvenient to have a separate checklist for each child, or simply to write the child's initials in the appropriate space when he or she displayed the particular behavior on my checklist. Now that makes a lot more sense than the event sample.

SUMMARY

The checklist is a method with many uses, and it is very simple to use. A checklist is any record that denotes the presence or absence of something. Two types of this method are discussed in this chapter. One type of checklist records static descriptors, which are defined as "a set of descriptive items" that pertain to "highly stable characteristics of research subjects or settings." Age, sex, race, and socioeconomic status are examples of static descriptors. The second type of checklist records actions, which are simply behaviors. An action checklist records the occurrence of a behavior during the period of observation. Several examples of checklists are discussed.

The number of checklists is so great that it might be difficult to recognize some of them as checklists. The Denver Developmental Screening Test is offered as an example of a test that is also a form of checklist but may not be easily recognized as such.

Checklists are closed and highly selective: They do not preserve raw data, and behaviors to be recorded are identified and defined before the observation begins. Inferences are required with this method, because prior decisions must be made concerning what behaviors or events fit the categories chosen for observation and recording. Further, as with other methods that involve inferences, behaviors will at times be ambiguous and not clearly fit the predetermined categories. An interpretation will therefore be necessary before recording or not recording the behavior.

Checklists have the advantage of being usable in many different situations and methods. They are efficient and require little effort. A chief disadvantage is their closedness; the checklist will provide a record that will be composed of action fragments and isolated impressions of behavior and context.

Rating scales are also discussed as a variation of the checklist. A rating scale essentially assigns a value or quality to a particular behavior or skill; a rating scale also indicates the presence or absence of something. It is the act of assessing the quality of a behavior that makes a rating scale a bit more sophisticated than a simple checklist—the degree of inference or interpretation is much greater with the rating scale than with the checklist. The advantage of the rating scale, aside from the amount of structuring it requires, is that it is relatively simple to use. A significant disadvantage is that, like the checklist, you lose a lot of data.

The use of videotaping and audiotaping is also discussed in this chapter. Perhaps the biggest advantage of using a video camera is that you can capture behavioral details that can be viewed over and over again, essentially at your leisure. If this is done under the direction of a skilled observer, students can benefit greatly from being able to see behavioral episodes in detail and with sufficient frequency and consistency so as to profit from guided instruction.

However, it is important to remember that it is you, the observer, and not the camera that interprets the data the camera records. It is the brain and not the eye that sees in any meaningful sense. Thus, with respect to understanding children's behavior, a video camera is no better than the person using it. Excessive use of a video camera would also be impractical, because it would limit your mobility in the child care facility and your ability to observe "on the run."

STUDY QUESTIONS

1. What characteristics do checklists share with frequency counts and time sampling? How are they different?

2. Describe or list five examples of checklists (different from any discussed in this manual). What does your list suggest about the possible uses and kinds of checklists?

3. Construct a brief checklist, and then describe how you went about making it up, what use you had in mind, what factors you had to consider, and so on.

4. How might a multiple choice examination be considered a form of checklist? Could an essay examination also have any features of a checklist?

5. What are the essential differences between a checklist and a rating scale?

6. What does it mean to say that a rating scale requires more structure than a checklist?

PRACTICAL EXERCISE

As a practical exercise, design and construct a checklist based on some key developmental aspects of the one-year-old. Use it in a real observation. Have several individuals use it at the same time while observing the same child. You may want to repeat this process with several children. Compare your results. Did you achieve inter-observer reliability? How could your checklist be improved?

CHAPTER 13

Interpretation of Observations, Implementation of Findings, and Ongoing Evaluation

bias

ⓄⒷⒿⒺⒸⓉⒾⓋⒺⓈ

After reading this chapter, you should be able to

- Discuss the relationship among the activities of observation, interpretation, implementation of findings, and ongoing evaluation.
- Discuss the two roles or types of interpretation.
- Analyze the concept of bias in interpretation.
- Discuss the several meanings of implementation of findings.
- Analyze the components of implementation.
- Describe the process of ongoing evaluation.

OBSERVATION: SOME PRELIMINARY THOUGHTS

This chapter addresses the topics of interpretation, implementation, and evaluation. These topics are discussed to point out the importance of each one in its own right, as well as each one's relationship to the others.

INTERPRETATION OF OBSERVATIONS

Considerable space has already been given to the subject of interpretation, yet part of another chapter is devoted to this topic. This is done for two important reasons.

The more fundamental reason is to reemphasize the broad, inevitable role that interpretation plays in our lives. Our entire beings are involved in our views of the world, in the way we see people, objects, and events. There are no self-evident facts, but we do become so accustomed to certain facts in our world that they seem self-evident and require no further interpretation or processing. Once we understand what a dog is, we do not attach an interpretation to our every observation of a dog. We simply see a dog.

In this broad sense of interpretation, our knowledge, values, attitudes, and experiences act as filters through which what we observe must pass. Naturally, not everything that exists out there in the real world gets through our filters. Some things do not even get noticed; we sometimes fail to get a conscious sense impression of an object, person, or event. The incompleteness of our observations is partly the result of our interest at the time, our level of concentration, our bodily states such as fatigue or illness, what aspects of the situation we think are important, and the amount of time we have to observe. So we may not see Jerry sharing a toy with Jacob, or Tanya tripping over the corner of the rug, although we may be looking directly at the situation. We are not cameras and cannot merely point our eyes in some direction and register everything that occurs. This is a liberal use of interpretation, and the term *personality* can summarize the influence of who we are on what we see and on the meaning we derive from what we see.

A stricter use of interpretation involves an additional step. In this use, we interpret something when we consciously try to make it clear and give it a meaning that goes beyond our empirical data. If you will recall, *explanation* was defined earlier as "making clear or understandable ... to give or show the meaning or reason for." A major point here is that to explain, to make clear or understandable, often involves moving from something that is directly observable to something that is not directly observable or observed. For example, you repeatedly hear four-year-old Margo asking Mrs. Bergman for approval—something observable—and you conclude that Margo is an emotionally dependent child whose parents probably reinforce that kind of behavior at home—something not observed.

bias

A particular perspective or point of view; biases can be personal or based on a theory or philosophy.

When one interprets, one is really imposing a **bias** on some fact. The word *bias* is not meant in a negative sense. It refers to the inevitable absence of total objectivity and the inevitable presence of the observer's own unique filters. Because no two individuals are exactly alike, no two individuals see the same phenomenon in entirely the same way or to the same extent. Even a mother and father do not see their children in exactly the same way, nor does any child see his parents in the same way as his siblings see them. Indeed, it has been said that "there are as many families as there are family members." Simply translated, even though each family member shares a number of objective similarities with other members, probably none will describe or evaluate in identical ways his or her experiences while growing up. Each of us is a unique individual, and each of us imposes a unique perspective on our experiences. We have referred to personal biases and perspectives, which again are made up of our experiences, abilities, attitudes, and knowledge. There is another kind of bias that is more the product of formal learning and purposeful adoption than of forces and influences over which we often have no control. This is the bias (filter) provided and shaped by a theory, hypothesis, conceptual framework, or philosophy.

Theoretical biases may seem more important than personal ones. They are merely different, however, though related and interdependent. Learning a theory and using it to interpret behavior are most assuredly dependent on some of your personal characteristics—intelligence, aptitude, and potential to become a competent observer. Moreover, your values and general views about children can affect which theoretical position you feel most comfortable with emotionally and intellectually. If you believe that children learn on their own if opportunities are provided them, you are not likely to enjoy an educational approach that rigidly structures the classroom and its activities.

Biases formed from theories also have another effect on what you see. They direct your attention to only certain parts of a situation, event, or behavior. Mussen, Conger, Kagan, and Huston (1984) describe this state of affairs metaphorically, noting that every researcher possesses a set of biases or preconceptions concerning what qualities of an infant are important, and then he or she observes the infant through those biases and describes those qualities accordingly. It is not only theoretical biases that create this limited attention; our everyday biases do it, too. Can you imagine a father watching his four-year-old son Billy playing with some children in a schoolyard? Suddenly, while the father is looking right at them, Billy pushes a playmate; a fight breaks out between them and the other child hits Billy on the arm. It is not inconceivable that the father might blame the other child, that he might not "see" Billy as the instigator of the conflict. Indeed, all the father might see is the other boy hitting his son. This is called selective perception, meaning that people often see only what they want to see, or place importance only on what they think is important, and ignore everything else. The result of this is that just as we assign different degrees of importance to different events in our daily affairs, different theories assign different degrees of importance to various phenomena. Piaget, for example, focused his attention on cognitive or intellectual development, but Freud was interested in personality development. It therefore follows that if Piaget and Freud were able to observe a child together, each would concentrate on different facets of the child's behavior, and each would make different interpretations.

In summary, then, even the most simple, straightforward, and informal observations and encounters with the environment involve some form of interpretation. We must put what we see and experience into a relationship with what we already know. We often can do this without much conscious deliberation. More formal interpretations, on the other hand, require us to look at a phenomenon and make sense of it within a particular perspective or conceptual framework—a theory, for example. And this might require conscious thought.

The second reason for discussing interpretation again is that it is the foundation of implementation of findings and ongoing evaluation. Your interpretations will determine the nature of your findings, what you think is significant, or even whether you find anything at all. This is also the case with ongoing evaluation. Evaluation

Evaluation and implementation require you to make sense of your observations before you can put them to use.

involves making judgments about the value, effectiveness, or appropriateness of something. It stands to reason that such judgments involve some interpretations, and quite possibly both formal and informal interpretations, as previously discussed. In short, implementation and evaluation require you to make sense of your observations before you can put them to some relevant use. Uses and purposes vary, of course, and can range from merely wanting to understand some facet of a child's development and behavior, to wanting to assess whether an existing program is doing what it claims to be doing, to wanting to initiate a new program.

However, it bears mentioning that a series of observations, interpretations, and evaluations can still lead to inaccurate or inappropriate conclusions and decisions. The point, though, is that several observations are less likely than just one observation to result in wrong decisions or conclusions. This probably would also be especially true if more than one observer were involved and if, as a result, inter-observer reliability were established. Of course, much depends upon the skill and experience of the observer(s).

DEALING WITH OBSERVATION AND INTERPRETATION IN A MULTICULTURAL SETTING

Given that interpretation goes beyond what is directly observable, you have to look for something that will provide a basis for making inferences about a child's behavior that will help you understand it and, if necessary, respond to it in some way. This, after all, is what interpretation is all about.

Sometimes asking the right questions goes a long way in assisting the interpretation process. We are deeply indebted to Janet Gonzalez-Mena (2005) for her excellent treatment of this important facet of interpretation. Gonzalez-Mena identifies six questions that one could (should) ask when attempting to interpret children's behavior. Even a cursory examination of these questions will reveal their significance and their commonsense character:

1. *Are the children's basic needs met?* This question rests on the basic assumption that human behavior is purposive and not random or entirely unpredictable. Like the rest of us, children need to have their basic needs met. Hunger must be satisfied; fatigue must be eliminated through rest; fear or anxiety must be assuaged by the security and comfort provided by an adult; and children must be allowed freedom of movement—these are some of the requirements that need to be addressed.

A child's mid-morning fussiness could be the result of not having eaten for several hours. Or children's rambunctious behavior might stem from their not having had an opportunity to engage in large muscle activity for some appreciable period of time. As an interpreter of children's behavior, your objective is to understand that behavior, to make sense of it in order to be an effective child care provider, early childhood educator, and parent.

2. *Does the environment fit the child?* This question can fit into Piaget's concepts of assimilation and accommodation. The question is also relevant to J. McV. Hunt's (1961) concept of "the match." The issue of developmental appropriateness also comes into play here. Developmentally appropriate practice (DAP) requires that child care and early education environments appropriately meet children's needs and fit their unique, individual characteristics. Gonzalez-Mena's second question essentially asks whether the young child can respond to his or her environment in ways that foster cognitive growth, that permit optimal freedom of movement and appropriate interaction—in short, does the child gain the greatest benefit by being in that environment?

Gonzalez-Mena points out that when in an inappropriate environment, children need much more guidance or direction, and they are much more likely to misbehave than they would if they were in an environment that was more ideally suited to their age, developmental levels, and temperaments. Although preparing suitable environments for a number of children of different ages and developmental levels can be a daunting task, one is not absolved of the responsibility to try to provide such suitable environments.

3. *Is the child's behavior a cry for attention?* Arguably, human beings are basically attention seekers; all of us from time to time need and desire others to give us heed and acknowledge who we are and what we are trying to do. But as Rudolph Dreikers (1964) points out, a child's misbehavior can be based on the

mistaken goal of seeking attention in order to be at the center of things. Attention seeking can result in positive or negative behaviors. Gonzalez-Mena (2005) says that a child's need for attention should not be discounted and adults should respond to it: "Make a clear plan to lavish attention on children who need it when they are *not* misbehaving ..." (p. 128, italics original).

If you do not know the child very well, interpreting a given behavior as a cry for attention should rely on some knowledge of the child's history or on observing how the child responds when receiving the attention you believe he or she might be demanding. It is probably a safe assumption that if the behavior continues even after getting an adult's attention, attention was not the primary motivation for the behavior. This conclusion can be based on some principles of behavior modification, which argue that behaviors are strengthened when they result in desirable consequences.

4. *Is the child's behavior a response to feeling powerless?* Gonzalez-Mena (2005) states that "Children who feel powerless need to get in touch with their own power" (p. 129). Children need to feel that they have some control over their environments. This might be an instance of what some psychologists call a need for mastery. Again, however, coming to this interpretation will require more than just a passing acquaintance with the child you are observing. Assigning powerlessness as a motive for a child's behavior requires more than just casual or infrequent observation. It might also require you to observe the child in a number of situations over some reasonable length of time.

5. *Did the child learn this behavior by being rewarded for it in the past?* Gonzalez-Mena (2005) links this question to question 3, "Is the child's behavior a cry for attention?" She offers an informative example of how past rewards might come into play: "When asked to come inside for lunch, Taylor screams no and runs in the other direction. The teacher pays a lot of attention to Taylor, talking, scolding, and threatening until, finally, she manages to get him inside by promising that he can sit next to her at lunch" (p. 129). Although the issue of changing such behavior is not within the purview of this text, suffice it to say, as Gonzalez-Mena confirms, "the way to change the pattern is to remove the reward," which in this case is the teacher's attention (p. 129). The change process would be complete when the child learns to substitute a desirable behavior for the undesirable one.

6. *Does the child clearly understand why her behavior is inappropriate?* This may be thought of as a case of ignorance on the child's part. As Gonzalez-Mena so aptly points out, "Children have to learn about how their actions affect other people" (2005, p. 131). Some of the earlier questions appear to look for children's motivations as a basis for interpreting their behavior. This sixth question offers an important source of information upon which to base your interpretation. When looking to misunderstanding as a reason for a child's misbehavior, one may

Children need to feel they have some control over their environments.

reasonably assume that children will behave appropriately if they understand that their behavior is not acceptable in a given situation and are taught an appropriate behavior.

There are other questions that one can ask as a guide to understanding and interpreting children's behavior. Whatever other questions might come to mind, they should emphasize the critical importance of making sense out of the things that children do. As has been stated elsewhere, merely observing behavior without understanding it is essentially a pointless, fruitless endeavor.

Culture and Interpretation

Under present-day circumstances, the effects of culture cannot be ignored or over-emphasized. The concept of developmentally appropriate practice (DAP) also offers a cogent rationale for addressing the issue of culture and its effect on the overall observational process.

Children's different cultural backgrounds can affect your interpretations in at least two ways that are two sides of the same coin. One effect is to provide you with a context or framework within which to make sense out of children's behavior. If you observe that four-year-old Soo Lin, an Asian American, does not look adults in the eye, you could explain this behavior by understanding that in Asian culture, direct eye contact is considered a sign of disrespect. Such cultural understanding is the inter-pretive framework that helps you understand the behavior.

A second effect that culture has on interpretation has essentially to do with your own reactions to the behaviors you observe. This effect more likely will occur if you are not knowledgeable about cultural differences. In the case of Soo Lin, if you are unaware of the perspective that Soo Lin's culture holds regarding direct eye contact, you could interpret her behavior as a sign of shyness, anxiety, or lack of interest in what an adult is saying. Moreover, in some instances, your perception of a child like Soo Lin could become negative and derogatory, especially if you believe that people—whether children or adults—should look each other in the eye when conversing. Therefore, the first effect is the desired one because it is based on knowledge of cultural differences, and it promotes an effective relationship with children and a more accurate interpretation of their behavior. The second effect is not desirable because it can lead to misunderstanding, conflict, and misinterpretation.

Culture: Some Considerations

Culture is an inevitable, inescapable companion that follows us through our lives. Usually we are more or less unaware of the influences of our own culture, much as a fish is unaware that it lives in water. But take that fish out of the water, and it becomes very "aware" of the dramatic change in its surroundings. Put us into a culture very different from our own, and we, too, become aware of the dramatic change in how things are done, in the language used to communicate, and in various customs, among other considerations. But we do not have to go to another culture to notice such differences. People of other cultures come to us, and we interact with them here in our own country and culture. We sometimes see people from different backgrounds as strange, wrong, or funny in some way, and their perceived strangeness can sometimes cause us problems in relating to them.

The United States is a multicultural society, which is a society that reflects cultural diversity. This means that in any child care setting, you are very likely to meet parents who hold views and opinions that are quite different from your own. These perspectives will include beliefs about what a child is, what he or she best needs for optimal growth and development, and a host of other concerns that might not occur to you until you are confronted with them.

Cultural diversity or multiculturalism is an important issue these days, but unfortunately it is an area that is not well understood by very many people. Even as knowledgeable a writer on this subject as Janet Gonzalez-Mena (1997) freely admits that understanding the ways of other cultures is not an easy task and that it requires much observation and dialogue with people who come from other ethnic and cultural backgrounds.

Nonetheless, the importance of understanding the different cultures from which children come cannot be denied, no matter how difficult the task may be. Although we cannot deal exhaustively with multiculturalism, we do want to give you some information that we hope will be useful when, as you almost inevitably will, you come into contact with children and parents from cultures different from your own.

Perhaps the best place to begin is to give you a conceptual framework within which to think about culture, what it is, and how it affects all of our behavior. Let us begin with a brief discussion of what culture is and the several different ways it affects development:

> Bredekamp and Copple (1997), in their revised edition of *Developmentally Appropriate Practice in Early Childhood Programs*, discuss culture as consisting of *a set of rules* or expectations for the behavior of group members that are passed on from one generation to the next. Cultural experiences are not limited to the artifacts or products of culture, such as holiday celebrations, foods, or music. These products are what can be seen easily, but they are not the culture itself, which is that set of underlying rules of custom or habit that yield or shape the visible products. Understanding culture requires an understanding of the rules that influence behavior, rules that give meaning to events and experiences in families and communities. (pp. 41–42, italics added)

Culture, therefore, is a set of rules that prescribe (allow or require) or proscribe (disallow or prohibit) certain behaviors. Bredekamp and Copple (1997) enumerate some of the rules that culture requires children to learn:

> Among the rules they learn are how to show respect, how to interact with people they know well as compared to those they just met, how to organize time and personal space, how to dress, what and when to eat, how to respond to major life transitions or celebrations, how to worship, and countless other behaviors that humans perform with little apparent thought every day. (p. 42)

Cultural understanding is the interpretive framework that helps you understand behavior.

Thomas J. Berndt (1997) discusses the significance of culture as an issue that "cuts across major theories or development" (p. 13). He cites two views of the role of culture in human development: cultural specificity and developmental universals. Cultural specificity asserts that "the most accurate descriptions and explanations of children's development will vary across cultures" (p. 13). The way different cultures view and treat children powerfully influences their development in such ways as "when (or if) children develop certain skills and which influences on their development are most powerful" (p. 13). The opposing point of view, referred to as developmental universals, assumes that cultural differences essentially have no appreciable effect on the development of various skills. All children go through the same universal set of processes at roughly the same ages (Berndt, 1997, p. 13).

Berndt introduces the concept of a *niche*, which he defines as "the place within an environment where an organism makes its home and to which it is adapted" (p. 14). Culture is a developmental niche in the strongest sense of the term. Every culture makes certain demands on, and holds out certain expectations for, its members. In this view, children have to learn and perform in accordance with the requirements of their respective cultures.

Super and Harkness (as cited in Berndt, 1997) propose three major components of a developmental niche. The first of these is the children's physical and social setting, a factor—especially the social setting—on which Vygotsky placed a great deal of importance in children's mental development. The second component entails a particular culture's customs regarding child care and child-rearing. Sleeping patterns, for example, are included in this component. Finally, there is what Berndt calls the *"psychology of the adults who care for children"* (p. 14, italics added). This includes *"what parents believe children need to be taught"* (p. 14, italics added). Probably any number of other factors could be added to this last component, factors that constitute parents' perspectives.

However, it should be noted that cultural diversity has different implications depending upon your objectives and the role(s) you play in the observation setting. Early childhood educators and professional child care providers are required to deal effectively with children who come from different cultural and ethnic backgrounds. For observers who have no direct role in interacting with children, cultural diversity or multiculturalism best provides a context or framework within which to observe, interpret, and understand children's behavior. It is important to keep this distinction in mind, especially because the focus of this text is on the behavior of children and not on the operation of the early childhood education classroom or child care facility.

A brief illustration of how a child's cultural background can figure in your observing and interpreting her behavior should be helpful. Gonzalez-Mena (1997) describes two children "who encounter similar situations in two different cultures" (p. 267). She asks her readers to imagine a cautious, shy, fearful three-year-old girl who lives in Italy and who arrives for her first day at preschool. When the girl comes to the classroom, she does not look at the teacher, who is there ready to greet her. Although the girl's shyness will be taken into account, because children are expected to greet adults in a socially acceptable way, she will still be expected to show the proper respect to her elders by greeting her teacher in the proper way.

The second girl is also a cautious, shy, fearful three-year-old, but she lives in the United States. On her first day at preschool she enters the room with her head down and does not greet or speak to the teacher. In this scene, the teacher says hello but does not press the girl for an answer. As Gonzalez-Mena points out, the teacher "will excuse the girl in her own mind, both because the child is shy and because she is young" (p. 267).

These two brief examples nicely illustrate two different frameworks within which an observer conceivably might interpret these two girls' behaviors. The objective characteristics of the two scenarios are fundamentally the same, yet different conclusions can be drawn regarding the meaning and significance of the girls' shyness. Such meaning and significance is provided by each girl's culture. In the case of the Italian girl, her shyness and failure to greet the adult at the door will not be completely condoned or overlooked, because in the Italian culture respect for one's elders is valued very highly. In the case of the American girl, her shyness is overlooked, and her failure to greet the adult at the door is not met with disapproval or immediate attempts to correct her behavior. Her age and her shyness are taken into account and are accepted as legitimate reasons for her behavior. This is not to say that the preschool staff might not at some time endeavor to help the little girl overcome some of her shyness.

However, this example must be placed in a context that is relevant to your purposes. With respect to understanding and interpreting properly, one must not give undue emphasis to the reactions of the adults in the two preschool facilities. Greater emphasis belongs on the girls' behaviors and, possibly, on how the girls subsequently respond to efforts to bring them out of their shyness and make them more outgoing.

Consequently, a child's cultural background is an important consideration when trying to understand behavior in particular situations. The preceding discussion is only the tip of the iceberg that constitutes cultural diversity. Nonetheless, even a brief discussion should make you aware that children have different experiences and that different expectations are held out for them as a consequence of their belonging to a particular cultural/ethnic group. Use the knowledge that you already possess and the knowledge that you will gain as you observe and work with children in various settings to help you interpret children's behavior more accurately than might otherwise be possible without such knowledge of cultural differences.

One immediately relevant piece of information you can use in your observations and interpretations is the set of cultural rules proposed by Bredekamp and Copple (1997 [see page 000]). These have an immediately practical application in the child care setting. This does not mean that you need make no further efforts to educate yourself regarding cultural diversity. Our recommendation merely gives you a place to begin your observations and interpretations. Look again at the cultural rules cited by Bredekamp and Copple (1997).

Early childhood educators and professional child care providers are required to deal effectively with children who come from many different cultural and ethnic backgrounds.

Not all of these rules will serve your reasons for observing in whatever setting. It is probably unlikely that you will have an opportunity to observe how children worship or how they respond to major life transitions or celebrations (although parents' divorcing would be a major life transition in many children's lives). But the remaining rules or cultural expectations will undoubtedly be observable at some time. You must be alert to them and to their manifestation in a variety of situations and circumstances.

Another Perspective on Diversity

Our discussion of diversity is not quite complete. The material just presented focuses on those various aspects of culture and diversity that might be relatively unfamiliar to some readers. But there is one other aspect, most broadly construed, that needs to be considered when using the concept of diversity as a tool for observing and understanding children's behavior. Allen and Marotz (2007) offer some important insights into the issue of cultural diversity in particular, and diversity in general: "In the broadest sense, the term diversity is inclusive, referring to a wide range of similarities, as well as differences. Dimensions that are most commonly described include: age, gender, race and ethnic background, socioeconomic class, language, abilities" (see, in Allen & Marotz, inserted material following p. 76). Even more instructive is the qualification they add to the discussion of diversity issues:

> However, diversity issues extend well beyond simple categorization. Family systems, communication styles, religious preferences, education, parenting practices, and community values all play important roles in shaping a child's unique heritage. They also influence a child's sense of identity, or self-concept. Each life experience affects the view children have of themselves. Therefore, efforts must be made to avoid simplistic assumptions and generalizations about aspects of diversity because there are often many variations associated with each dimension. For example, a child who speaks Spanish may come from any number of geographical locations or cultures. Categorizing the child as "Latino" fails to acknowledge individual and cultural differences and, thus, promotes stereotyping. (Allen & Marotz, 2003; see inserted material following p. 76)

An important message in this passage is that most, if not all, human behavior consists of, and is influenced by, an array of interacting variables, conditions, circumstances, and contexts. The issue of cultural diversity can have the undesirable effect of diverting your attention to cultural/ethnic categories to the exclusion of the many other variables that influence and determine an individual's behavior. In the example of the two shy three-year-olds presented earlier, it is not enough merely to know that one of them is Italian and the other is American. The fact that they are three years of age, not older or younger, that they are girls, not boys, that there was no information given about their particular and unique family backgrounds—in short, the brief information that was given, and other information that was absent—can serve to clarify or to confuse one's understanding and interpretation of children's behavior.

Culture and Nonverbal Communication

There is another aspect of cultural diversity that can be particularly useful for understanding and interpreting behavior. In her 1997 text *Multicultural Issues in Child Care*, Janet Gonzalez-Mena offers the following cogent advice:

> So it is important for teachers and caregivers who work with families whose culture differs from their own to take a good long look at where the parents are coming from when differences arise over issues of dependence and independence, feeding, toileting, napping, holding, comforting, "spoiling," discipline, and setting up the environment for play. (p. 21)

Of special interest is Gonzalez-Mena's emphasis on the importance of observation in learning about other cultures:

> I can't emphasize enough the importance of educating yourself when dealing with a person of a culture different from your own. I don't mean read books, though that may help. *I do mean observe closely.* (p. 21, italics added)

She goes on to identify five areas of nonverbal communication that can lead to faulty communication or miscommunication when dealing with parents and children from other cultures.

Personal Space

Personal space is the amount of distance we like to keep between other people and ourselves. It is very much like culture, in that we are largely unaware that we gauge how far we are from others based on how well we know them, and we try to maintain that distance. This phenomenon is called proxemics.

An important point about personal space is that when we sit or stand too close to others, they feel uncomfortable, just as we do when other people invade our space. Do not take it for granted that everyone else's sense of personal space is the same as yours. It is also interesting that in some cultures, a white Anglo- or European-American's view of appropriate distance is too far and indicates unfriendliness or coldness. Assume that children also possess a sense of personal space. Adults often believe it is perfectly all right to "get in a child's face," possibly thinking that getting physically very close to a child instills in him or her a sense of trust or intimacy. If a child's response to someone getting too close is not what you expect or think is proper, reassess your own response with respect to the child's cultural background.

Smiling

Smiling is probably one of those actions that most mainstream Americans assume means the same everywhere. But as Gonzalez-Mena points out, smiling, along with touch and eye contact, are culture-specific. In some cultures such as Russia, people smile when they are happy, not to show friendliness. A smile can also be a sign of embarrassment.

Gonzalez-Mena's (1998) description of the meaning that smiling has for the Vietnamese is highly instructive:

> Almost anyone who has visited Vietnam or come in contact with the Vietnamese has noticed … a perpetual and enigmatic smile in all circumstances, unhappy as well as happy…. Many foreign teachers in Vietnam have been irritated and frustrated when Vietnamese students smile in what appears to be the wrong time and place. They cannot understand how the students smile when reprimanded, when not understanding the lessons being explained, and especially when they should have given an answer to the question instead of sitting still and smiling quietly. These teachers often thought the students were not only stupid and disobedient, but insolent as well. One thing they did not understand was that the students often smiled to show their teachers that they did not mind being reprimanded, or that they were indeed stupid for not being able to understand the lesson. Smiling at all times and places is a common characteristic of Vietnamese. There are, however, no guidelines to tell foreigners what meaning each smile represents in each situation…. The Vietnamese smile may mean almost anything. (p. 61)

Eye Contact

Gonzalez-Mena asks whether it is important "to look people in the eye or to look away when you talk to them" (2005, p. 23). When cultures share the same beliefs about eye contact, people feel comfortable with each other. In our American culture we often think that a person who does not look us in the eye when talking with us is shifty or dishonest or has something to hide. Other considerations also apply. As Gonzalez-Mena reports, "Eye contact in the Western culture is considered as an indication of attentiveness, although in the Asian culture, it may be viewed as a sign of lack of respect or deference" (p. 23). She also notes that for Native Americans, "prolonged eye contact is extremely disrespectful" (p. 23).

In light of the preceding, it would be extremely easy to interpret incorrectly a child's pattern of eye contact, thereby coming to the conclusion that the child is inattentive or disrespectful, or possesses some other undesirable trait or characteristic.

Touch

Touch might well be a form of nonverbal communication that has received more attention than any other discussed thus far. Concerns about sexual harassment or child molestation, for example, place inappropriate touching in the forefront of many people's thinking. Some people appear to have a natural urge to touch others, while some also like to be touched by others. For them, touch expresses friendliness and intimacy, or perhaps touch is intended to give the other person a sense of security. It has become well known that individuals in positions of authority or high status tend to touch other individuals who are of a lower status than themselves. As Gonzalez-Mena puts it, "in mainstream Canadian and American culture, bosses touch their secretaries much more often than secretaries touch their bosses" (p. 23).

Touching someone on the head should be done with particular caution: "Consider the unwritten rules that white, mainstream, Canadian and American culture have about touching on the head. Anyone who touches someone else on the head is superior in some way—only inferiors (or intimates) are touched on the head" (Gonzalez-Mena, 1997, p. 23). It might seem appropriate to touch or pat a child on the head, which adults often do presumably as a sign of affection. Nonetheless, children also deserve to be shown proper respect, and if a child's culture deems head patting as offensive or disrespectful, it should not be done. With respect to interpretation, therefore, children's reactions to being touched, whether on the head or elsewhere, need to be put in the context of their cultural background.

Time Concepts

The reckoning or keeping of time is a human invention and activity. Young children do not think of time the way adults do, nor are they concerned about such things as being on time for appointments or scheduled activities. But with increasing intellectual and social development, children do become aware of time, and they probably, initially at least, adopt their parents' concept of time and how time should be handled in social situations. Gonzalez-Mena discusses time primarily with respect to staff and parents, an emphasis that is not of direct importance to our purposes. But even if you are only an observer having no official dealings with parents or staff, your perception of children can be unduly influenced by the way that their parents treat time. Perhaps it is analogous to being annoyed or angered by a child's misbehavior when, if you were objective about the situation, responsibility would be placed more with the parents than with the child.

A Final Summary

The central point to keep in mind from this entire discussion is that you must be vigilant when you observe and interpret children's behavior. You have an obligation to be as honest and accurate as humanly possible when forming conclusions about children. Recall the discussion of evaluation in Chapter 3, where it was noted that of all the purposes associated with observation, evaluation could be the most "dangerous" or potentially damaging to a child. This is because evaluations are frequently used to form judgments about such things as children's personalities, characters, and self-worth. Therefore, culturally influenced or culturally determined behaviors could be inappropriately used as a basis for disparaging comments about a child or for making inappropriate curriculum decisions that affect a child's experiences in a child care facility or early education classroom.

IMPLEMENTATION OF FINDINGS

We have included a discussion of implementation of findings primarily because observing behavior—certainly for child care professionals and parents—usually has a purpose or number of purposes. One purpose is to understand children's behavior and how they are growing and developing. Such understanding requires some interpretation of the data acquired through the observation and recording processes. Interpretation extends beyond observation per se because many interpretations are subjective and because, although based on reasonably objective observations, the meaning given to any behavior is not directly observable. Thus, one does not directly observe dependency, for example, but only certain behaviors from which dependency may be inferred.

Another purpose for observing children's behavior and development is to use observational data in ways that will benefit the children in the child care center, early education classroom, or home. Findings, as we call them, are the conclusions one reaches based on the interpretation of observational data. The implementation of findings is putting observational data to some appropriate use. Proper implementation depends upon sound observations and sound interpretations. However, we cannot tell you how to implement what you learn about children's behavior, because implementation is highly specific to particular purposes and situations. We could not possibly anticipate all the contingencies that you might face as you work with children. But you do need to understand how observation figures in any implementation process. To make curriculum changes or to try to change a child's behavior without having a rationale for such changes based on accurate, reliable, observational data would be foolhardy and probably a waste of time and effort. To observe with the intention of implementing your observational findings is to observe with a prespecified plan or purpose. You must know why you are going to observe before you set foot in the observation site (see Chapter 3). Again, properly practiced, observation never involves a situation where you go to the observation site and then ask yourself, "Now that I'm here, what am I supposed to do?"

Implementation is a broad topic. It is probably as broad as the number of reasons for observing and the number of observation methods you can use. This statement is based on the assumption that your reasons for observing should be determined before entering the child's behavior stream. The phrase *implementation of findings* implies a predesignated purpose and method. In this respect, observation, whether formal or informal, is not very different from a research study or experiment.

A researcher must know what his research topic or question is going to be and how he is going to gather and analyze his data.

Your observations, of course, are not likely to be as complicated as a formal research study, but the same fundamental principles apply to observation as to formal research: You have to know why you are observing before you "throw your net into the child's behavior stream." This principle was expressed in an earlier chapter by the statement that observation is not just casually looking *at* something; rather, it is looking *for* something.

To implement means to put to some practical use, to perform some action, or to satisfy the conditions of something. Implementing a plan, for example, means to put that plan into action or to perform the behaviors that are required for the plan to work. This is a very inclusive definition because there are broad limits to what one can perform, put into effect, or satisfy the conditions of. For that reason, implementation of findings at some point has to be considered in the specific context of your own observation purposes. For instance, you could satisfy the conditions of an observation exercise by obtaining a narrative description of a child's behavior during school recess. You might do nothing further with the record, but still have accomplished the goal of gaining experience in describing behavior in a detailed, narrative form. However, a teacher might use the record to monitor a child's progress in various developmental areas or to establish the basis for modifying the child's behavior.

The word *findings* must be carefully considered. If *findings* is given too limited a meaning, observation will predominantly serve to support research. This would rule out observing children simply to learn about them, to see if they behave as psychologists describe. In this sense, *findings* takes on a much broader meaning and can perhaps even be defined as "objectives" or "purposes." Implementation of a purpose can be accomplished when you satisfy the condition of learning how Adam responds to the social behaviors of his peers, or when you learn the characteristics of Margaret's speech.

Ongoing Evaluation

Making judgments is an unavoidable activity we all do for various reasons. To evaluate is to make a judgment, and to make a judgment is to make a comparison between some event, object, or behavior, and a standard or criterion. The notion of comparison seems obvious even in the simplest of circumstances. For example, you try a different route to class or work, but you decide that your old route is better than the new one. It is quicker, it is more scenic, and it passes by a store where you sometimes shop. Your standards here, among possible others, are time, aesthetic pleasure, and the convenience of not having to go out of your way to shop.

Comparisons are essential, for without them we could not perceive or know anything; we could not even distinguish the familiar from the unfamiliar. We must make comparisons with what we already know to recognize what we do not know. The critical factor in all of this is the selection of the standard. Selection is the basis of observation itself, of any implementation of findings, as well as of ongoing evaluation. All three of these activities require comparison with a standard. In this general sense, therefore, a standard is any framework or context within which one can make a judgment, decision, or comparison.

Let us return to some familiar territory. Some of our standards are determined by our personalities. We have standards of conduct, for example, by which we judge the acceptability of our own and others' behavior. Such standards could be part of our personality, the result of our upbringing, values, and attitudes. A theory is also a standard by which comparisons, judgments, and decisions are made. Standards based on theory might involve assessing a child's level of cognitive development using knowledge of Piaget's theory: What behaviors are typical of a sensorimotor child—these form the standards or bases of comparison—and how does the child you are observing behave or function in relation to those typical behaviors or standards? A theory is a formal standard, whereas our personalities might be called informal standards.

If evaluation involves comparison with a standard, then ongoing evaluation is a continuous comparison, with the implication that whatever is being evaluated can or will change. It is also possible for the standard to change. Indeed, when evaluating children, the standard has to change. Parents' expectations and demands regarding their child's behavior change as the child's abilities change with maturation and experience. Demands and expectations are therefore standards that are modified to keep step with the child's ability to meet them.

Selection of the standard, as previously mentioned, is critical in many cases, because the standard will determine whether the child's performance satisfies the adult's conception of what she can and should be able to do. For example, standards governing toilet training are applied by parents in relation to the child's bowel and bladder control. If the parents are realistic in their assessment of the child's physiological maturity, there may be no problem. The parents will adjust their standard to fit the child. In contrast, the parents could have unrealistic expectations (standards) for their child's toileting behavior, and they could misapply the standard—or apply the wrong standard. They could demand that she sit on the potty, not wet or soil her pants, and tell them when she has to go to the toilet, when the child is simply not capable of such behavior.

Matching the standard to the child's capabilities involves several factors. First, the parents have to know the approximate age that a child can be successfully toilet trained. This could be thought to involve an explanation or interpretation, in the sense that success is explained by the concept of maturational readiness. Second, implementation of findings is the result of learning about this maturational readiness, evaluating the child's present level of readiness, and then either applying or not applying the standard, depending on the outcome of the evaluation. If the child is not deemed ready for serious toilet training, further evaluation is necessary. The parents might reevaluate her a month or so later, updating their information and making another comparison between the child's apparent readiness and their standards for toileting behavior.

This example is a simple one. Ongoing evaluation occurs in much more complex ways, but regardless of the level of complexity, the same process occurs as in the toilet training illustration.

Some Practical Examples of Implementation

Although implementation of findings is a broad topic, it does have very specific and very practical effects. Let us look at some hypothetical examples of how observational findings could be used in various contexts.

Illustration 1

Mrs. Parrish wants to encourage independent behavior among the children in her preschool classroom. She is new to this particular setting, however, and she does not yet know the children and how they play or use the equipment and materials. She believes that independent behavior can be encouraged and fostered by the type and arrangement of the physical objects in the environment. Therefore, Mrs. Parrish decides to observe the children's play activities and, using an event sampling technique, record instances of dependent behavior displayed by the children. She chooses to observe dependent behavior first in order to identify the conditions under which such behavior occurs. She then hopes to modify those conditions in a way that will foster independent behavior.

Mrs. Parrish notices very quickly that every time any child wants to play with a puzzle, the alphabet game, record player, or paints, she has to ask an adult for help. When these materials are involved, the children almost invariably exhibit dependent behavior, simply because the shelves are too high for them to reach. If an adult must hand the materials to the children, Mrs. Parrish concludes, that hardly fosters independence and self-sufficiency.

As a result of this extremely simple observation and interpretation, Mrs. Parrish has the storage shelves lowered to a height accessible to the children. Ongoing evaluation finds that the incidents of children asking for help getting equipment are reduced almost to zero.

Illustration 2

Most preschools want to encourage cooperation and sharing among the children in their programs. Cooperation and sharing are learned behaviors, however, and one cannot count on them to occur simply as a matter of course. Ms. Crenshaw, the teacher of a class of four-year-olds, knew this, but she had to plan ways to allow the children to learn to cooperate. She had to determine how to arrange various classroom situations to bring about cooperative rather than competitive interactions among the children. She decided to observe the children and her staff to see what kinds of situations led to cooperation or competition.

The following scene was observed by Ms. Crenshaw on the morning following her decision to look for instances of cooperative and competitive behavior:

9:30 A.M. It was time for rhythm band activity, and Mrs. Wilson was in charge. She placed the box containing the rhythm instruments on the floor and told the children to get the instruments they wanted to play. (The box contained six triangles, one tambourine, one block and drumstick, and two rattles.) Immediately, there was a scramble toward the box. Martin got there first and grabbed a tambourine. Sally was right behind him, and she got her hand on the same tambourine. Martin tugged against Sally's grasp, saying, "It's mine; I got it first." "But I want to play it today," Sally responded. While this battle was going on between Sally and Martin, eight other children were milling around the box trying to get an instrument. Juan picked out the only wooden block and drumstick and ran over to the corner of the room. Carlisle had picked out one of the triangles. Willard also grabbed a triangle, but there were six of those, and so no arguments broke out over that particular instrument. Mrs. Wilson finally had to break up the fight between Sally and Martin. She asked Sally to let Martin play the tambourine today and said that she could play it tomorrow. Sally reluctantly agreed. Martin walked off, a big smile on his face. Sally picked out the last remaining triangle and walked over and stood beside the children who had gotten their instruments. After nearly two minutes of rather frantic activity, each child got an instrument, although not without some continued grumbling from the two or three children who did not get the one they desired.

From this observation, Ms. Crenshaw decided there must be a better way to start the rhythm band activity than by putting the box of instruments in the middle of the floor. She came to the conclusion that rather than foster cooperation and sharing, this approach really created competition. After all, thought Ms. Crenshaw, what other message could the children get when, in effect, they were told "OK, kids, it's first come, first served, and the fastest and strongest among you will get the instruments you want"? She instructed Mrs. Wilson that in the future, the box was to be passed among the children, permitting each child to choose the instrument he or she wanted that day. The teacher was also to explain that the next time, another child could pick an instrument that he or she was unable to choose the time before. In this way, every child would eventually get to play the instrument that he or she desired.

Subsequent observation of this activity confirmed Ms. Crenshaw's interpretation. Except for an occasional complaint from a child who did not want to wait until the next day to play his favorite instrument, the children accepted the new routine.

There were even instances when a child would relinquish her turn with an instrument and give it to a friend.

Illustration 3

Mrs. Gonzales believes that children are active participants in their own development, and therefore should be allowed to direct many of their own activities. Her preschool classroom has a wide variety of equipment and materials selected purposely to accommodate children who vary widely in interests and skills. Mrs. Gonzales also believes that children should be encouraged to "stretch" beyond their present level of ability to promote the development of new skills and interests. Consequently, she uses her observation skills to document each child's behavior and activities in various parts of the classroom. She observes and records data about the equipment and materials that the child uses and the skills and knowledge that they require of the child. She also observes how long and how often the child plays in any given area. Mrs. Gonzales would like the children to strike a reasonable balance in their use of materials and activities, believing that such a balance will further their overall development.

In the course of her observations, Mrs. Gonzales notices that Victor, a new boy in her class of five-year-olds, plays with the other children using equipment and materials that demand gross motor skills, but he avoids fine motor activities unless he is by himself. From time to time, Victor will watch some of the children as they play with small puzzles, cut out pictures with scissors, or string beads, but he never joins them. If, when he is by himself and in the middle of a fine motor activity, another child approaches, he immediately stops what he is doing and walks away. However, Mrs. Gonzales also notices that Victor's fine motor skills are quite good, so she tentatively rules out poor coordination as a cause of Victor's behavior. Because she cannot identify anything in the classroom that might contribute to his avoidance of these activities with other children, she decides to consult with Victor's mother or father. She recognizes that a child's experiences at home can affect his behavior at school.

From a conference with Victor's mother, Mrs. Gonzales learns that Victor's older brother (seven years old) is an exceptionally well-coordinated youngster, with motor abilities that are ahead of what one would predict for his age. Unfortunately, however, the brother ridicules Victor's less well-developed fine motor skills, even though Victor holds his own when it comes to running, jumping, climbing, and wrestling. Mrs. Gonzales tentatively concludes (infers) that Victor's self-image is poor in this area because of his brother's frequent disparaging remarks. Apparently, Victor refuses to play with the other children in these activities for fear they will also ridicule him.

Mrs. Gonzalez decides to test her interpretation, to implement her findings regarding Victor's home situation. Over the course of several weeks, she manages to draw Victor into a series of activities that increasingly involve fine motor abilities. She always makes it a point to comment favorably on Victor's performance, as well as on the performances of the other children. She has no real concern that anyone will make fun of Victor's fine motor abilities because she knows that his are as good as most of the other children's in the class. Ongoing observation and evaluation confirm Mrs. Gonzalez's interpretation. Within a month, Victor plays with other children in both large and small muscle activities. Now, Mrs. Gonzales notes, Victor is striking more of that balance she thinks is so important.

The first illustration might seem the simplest scenario one could paint. Mrs. Parrish notices that the children cannot reach some of the toys because the shelves are too high. She defines their asking for adults' help in getting the toys as dependency behavior. She then reasons that changing the conditions under which toys can be gotten will change the children's behavior. The shelves are lowered, and the children act independently.

The finding in this first illustration was the relationship Mrs. Parrish saw between shelf height and dependent behavior. She implemented her finding by changing the nature of the relationship from high shelves and high dependency to lower shelves and independence. However, what is important to note here is that the finding was given a particular meaning; children asking an adult for help in getting toys was interpreted as dependency behavior and evaluated as undesirable. Another teacher might have thought differently, possibly believing that the interests and goals of the preschool are better served by the staff maintaining control over equipment and materials. This second teacher would have looked for dependency in other kinds of behaviors.

The second illustration is only a little more complicated than the first. Much depended on the meaning Ms. Crenshaw put on the children's scrambling for the band instruments. The connection between placing the box on the floor and the children's behavior is not difficult to see. However, two key elements are the meaning of the children's responses and how they should be handled. Ms. Crenshaw saw the milling, shoving, and arguing as unacceptable behaviors that contradicted her goal of fostering cooperation and sharing. She implemented her finding (the connection just mentioned) by structuring the distribution of instruments so that the children had to take turns.

Another teacher might have seen the children's scrambling for the instruments as a natural part of growing up and of learning not only to share but also to assert themselves. He may have allowed some competition because he believes that competition is an inevitable part of life. A second possibility is that the other teacher agrees with Ms. Crenshaw's objective of promoting sharing and cooperation among the children, but disagrees with her method. He might implement his finding by trying to teach the children general rules of conduct. Instead of making it impossible to compete by giving each child an instrument, the second teacher might use suggestions or reminders of the rules. As Sally and Martin fought over the tambourine, he might have said something like "Now, Sally, Martin got the tambourine first. What did I tell you children about sharing toys? If someone gets a toy before you do, you have to wait until he is done playing with it, and then it is your turn." The second teacher would be counting on the children to internalize the rules and eventually behave cooperatively because it is the appropriate thing to do. In either case, ongoing observation and evaluation would determine the effectiveness of the two teachers' ways of interpreting and implementing their findings.

The final illustration involves more observational data and inferences than the other two illustrations. Mrs. Gonzales sees the children's behavior through her philosophy (and filter) of balanced activities and providing experiences that help the children progress beyond their current level of ability and development. Within that philosophy, Victor's failure to participate in fine motor activities with the other children violated the balance she thought so important. She progressively, though tentatively, ruled out various possible explanations of Victor's behavior. She finally made the inference that some situation at home might be the cause. When she learned about Victor's brother, she interpreted Victor's behavior as being a result of a poor self-image and fear of being ridiculed by his peers in school. She acted on that interpretation (implemented her finding) by gradually involving Victor in activities that increasingly required small muscle skills. When he learned that the other children did not make fun of him as his brother did, Victor became a regular participant in fine motor activities.

SUMMARY

Interpretation can be thought of in terms of personality and formal theory. In either case, interpretation is the foundation of implementation of findings and ongoing evaluation. A finding is a finding only if it has some meaning that can then be applied to a specific situation or problem. Ongoing evaluation depends on interpretation because evaluation involves making a comparison between something observed and a standard. This, in turn, requires making sense out of your observational data and seeing the relationship between the data and the standard you have selected. Ongoing evaluation also requires comparisons. Comparisons are essential because without them we could not perceive or know anything. Selection of the standard is critical to observation, implementation, and evaluation; all these activities require some sort of standard. A standard is any framework within which one can make a judgment, decision, or comparison. Our personalities are informal standards, and theories are formal ones. Ongoing evaluation often necessitates modifying the standard that one applies to a situation. This is especially true when evaluating children's behavior, which naturally changes as children grow and develop.

Implementation involves a performance, satisfying the conditions of something, or putting something into effect. If you find that Fred fights with Elizabeth whenever they are together in the big block area, you might implement that finding by directing one of them into a different activity. Your response implies that you have certain objectives for the children's behavior and that you interpret or see their behavior in terms of those objectives. Therefore, implementation is based on a predetermined purpose.

STUDY QUESTIONS

1. How do observation, interpretation, implementation of findings, and ongoing evaluation depend on one another? Describe their interrelationship.

2. What is meant by the term *bias* as it is used in this chapter? List some of your biases, and describe how they might affect what you see when you observe children and how they might affect your interpretations of your observations.

3. What happens when an observational finding is implemented? Describe the steps involved and the roles of observation and interpretation.

OBSERVATION EXERCISES

INTRODUCTION AND PREPARATION

Your observation exercises emphasize behavior and development. The major goal of the exercises will always be to learn about the child, whether from a broad developmental viewpoint or the immediate and narrower viewpoint of the child's situation and setting. A related goal will be to enable you to do something with the information you gain from the observations. What you do with that information depends on your reasons for observing and the meaning the information has for you.

Many textbooks on children divide the life span into developmental or functional areas such as physical, motor, social, emotional, and language. This way of studying the child might give the impression that these areas are independent of one another. This is not the case. It is for the convenience of the psychologist, teacher, and others who are involved with children that the child's development is segmented in this way. This procedure is useful and perhaps even necessary because it brings the study of the child down to a manageable size. No one can examine simultaneously every facet of development and behavior. Nonetheless, a child is a unified, integrated whole, and his physical self is part of his intellectual self, which are parts of his social self, and so on.

As you observe children of different ages, you will be conducting something similar to a cross-sectional study. You will be gathering data that could be used to compare, for example, children's language development from infancy to about six years of age. You could also use this data to determine how closely a particular child's behavior matches the norms for that behavior. For example, does eighteen-month-old Jamie walk by himself, as norms predict he probably will? Do the social behaviors of four-year-old Christine agree with normative descriptions of four-year-olds?

There is one other important feature of your exercises. Extensive use is made of questions, which serve at least two purposes. First, they give you information about some of the specific content of the developmental areas. They help you focus on specific behaviors as targets of observation and recording, However, remember that such a focus may not always be necessary, depending on the methods you use. Consider the narrative description, where any behaviors the child exhibits while you are in her "stream" are suitable for recording.

A second reason is that the questions can be useful aids in interpreting or classifying recorded behaviors. For example, the question "How capable is the child of balancing?" not only gives you information about an observable feature of motor behavior; it also suggests that if you observe a child walk across a balance beam, you could make some interpretive comments about his coordination and control in that activity. Asking questions is an important part of the observation process.

The observation exercises begin with the period of infancy. You will be asked to observe a newborn (birth to one month of age) and a fifteen- to eighteen-month-old infant. There are several observation exercises dealing with certain aspects of development and behavior for each age period.

The second set of observation exercises covers early childhood, or what is often called the preschool years. This portion of the life span begins at age two and goes up through age five. The changes that occur after infancy in areas such as physical growth are relatively slower and steadier than during infancy. Generally speaking, you will see greater differences between a six-month-old and an eighteen-month-old than you will between a two-year-old and a three-year-old. Therefore, in Chapter 16 you will observe children at intervals of years.

Each observation exercise also provides some brief background information concerning the specific developmental or behavioral area covered.

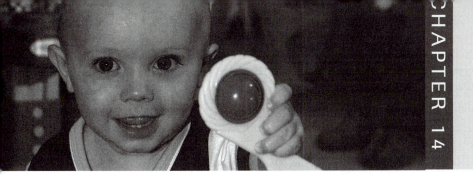

CHAPTER 14

Observing the Newborn: Birth to One Month

states

spontaneous behaviors

soothability

temperament

habituation

EXERCISE 14-1: PHYSICAL CHARACTERISTICS OF THE NEWBORN

Background Information

A newborn's physical appearance is easily recognized and typical of most newborns (Table 14-1). The birth weight of the average full-term baby ranges between 5.5 and 9.5 pounds, and the average length between 19 and 22 inches. Characteristically, the skin is wrinkled, blotchy, and covered with fine hairs (lanugo) that fall out during the first month. At birth, the skin may be pale to pink, or it may have a yellowish appearance because of what is called normal physiological jaundice. The eyes of Caucasian babies are generally blue and do not take on their true color until sometime during the first year.

The head may have a misshapen appearance created by passage through the narrow birth canal, but this disappears by the end of the second week. The head constitutes about one-fourth of the newborn's total length, which creates a disproportional appearance. The neonate has a very short neck, no chin, and a flattened nose—what some refer to as a "baby face." There are six soft spots or fontanels on top of the newborn's head. These allow the head to change its shape during the birth process, and they allow for brain growth during the first years of life. They close by around 18 months of age.

The external genitalia of both sexes may look enlarged, a temporary condition caused by the mother's female hormones passing to the baby during pregnancy. The newborn's legs are bowed slightly, and the feet turn inward at the ankles until the soles are almost parallel.

Table 14-1 Physical Characteristics of the Newborn	
Body Area	**Characteristics**
Body Weight	Average newborn weighs 5.5 to 9.5 pounds.
Length	Average length is 19 to 22 inches.
Skin	Wrinkled and blotchy; covered with fine hairs (lanugo). At birth, skin is pale pink or may have yellowish appearance due to normal physiological jaundice.
Eyes	Generally blue; take on true color during the first year.
Head	Has misshapen appearance that is gone by the end of the second week. Head constitutes one-fourth of total length. Short neck, no chin, flattened nose. Six soft spots (fontanels) on top of head (allow skull to grow) that close by about 18 months of age.
External Genitalia	Look enlarged in both sexes.
Legs and Feet	Legs bowed slightly. Feet turn inward at ankles; soles are nearly parallel.

Observation Objectives

To observe and describe the newborn infant's physical characteristics, with the eventual objective of comparing them with an older infant.

Procedure

Describe in as much detail as you can the physical characteristics of a newborn (one month old or less). You will need a measuring tape to measure certain physical features. We suggest that you write your original notes on ordinary paper, and then transfer them to a more formal observation sheet that follows the format provided at the end of the chapter. (See Observation Exercise 14-1 at the end of this chapter and in the Online Companion™.)

Question Guides

1. What are the newborn's most noticeable physical characteristics? How would you describe her body proportions? Facial features? The shape of her legs and their typical positioning?

2. Is there anything about the newborn's physical features that a parent or caregiver might find attractive or that might motivate a parent or caregiver to feel protective of the newborn? If so, explain.

3. Is there anything about the newborn's appearance that strikes you as unusual? If so, explain.

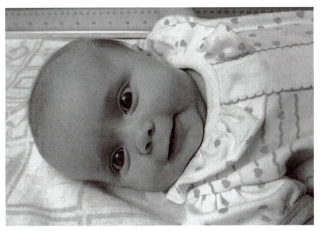

Face of a newborn. Note the relatively large head, short neck, and flat nose.

EXERCISE 14-2: INFANT STATES AND RESPONSIVENESS TO STIMULATION

Background Information

states

Levels of arousal such as asleep, alert, drowsy, and crying; they are behavioral conditions that (1) are stable over a period of time, (2) occur repeatedly in an individual infant, and (3) are encountered in similar form in other individuals.

The newborn is frequently described in terms of **states**, which are levels of arousal such as asleep, drowsy, alert, and crying (see Table 14-2). In an earlier edition of *A Child's World: Infancy Through Adolescence*, Papalia and Olds (1993) define *state* as "a periodic variation in an infant's cycle of wakefulness, sleep, and activity" (p. 136). A state has three important characteristics: It is "a behavioral condition that (1) is stable over a period of time, (2) occurs repeatedly in an individual infant, and (3) is encountered in very similar forms in other individuals" (Hutt, Lenard, & Prechtl, 1969, cited in Papalia & Olds, 1979). In their most recent edition of *A Child's World*, Papalia and Olds (2006) use the term *state of arousal* rather than just *state*, and although both terms mean essentially the same thing, *state of arousal* seems to provide more information than *state*. These authors define *state of arousal* as the "[i]nfant's physiological and behavioral status at a given moment in the periodic daily cycle of wakefulness, sleep, and activity" (p. 117).

Whichever term you prefer, states are important to the study of the neonate and young infant for several reasons: (1) states describe all infants, which make them consistent patterns of behaviors, and (2) the infant's state affects the abilities she exhibits and the responses she makes to stimulation at any given time. Besides the characteristics of these states, one can also consider such factors as (1) how frequently a newborn is in a particular state, (2) for how long, (3) what kinds of stimulation put her there, and (4) what amount of stimulation is necessary to arouse her.

Table 14-2 Infant States	
Regular Sleep (quiet sleep)	This state is characterized by closed eyes, regular breathing, and a lack of muscle or eye movements, except for sudden generalized startle responses. Mild stimuli will not arouse the infant who is in this state, which makes regular sleep the low point on the arousal continuum.
Irregular Sleep (active sleep)	The infant's eyes are still closed, but breathing is irregular and more rapid than during regular sleep. There are slight muscle movements or stirrings from time to time, but no generalized movements. The infant may exhibit facial grimaces, smiles, mouthing movements, and puckering of the lips. There may also be eye movements, which can be discerned through the closed lids.
Periodic Sleep	This state falls between regular and irregular sleep. The infant displays sudden bursts of facial and body movements; there are also changes in the rate of breathing.
Drowsiness	This condition typically occurs when the infant is waking up or falling asleep—what is sometimes called the "twilight zone." The eyelids open and close. If the lids are open, the eyes are unfocused and appear dull or glazed. An infant in the drowsy state will exhibit more activity than when in regular sleep, but less activity than when in irregular or periodic sleep.
Alert Inactivity	Here the infant is awake but not very active. The eyes have a bright and shiny appearance. A state of alert activity can usually be seen after three or four weeks of age. This state is similar to alert inactivity except that the infant displays considerably more motor activity.
Waking Activity or Active Alert (Krantz, 1994, p. 134)	In this state one sees frequent bursts of generalized motor activity; the eyes are open; the infant does not cry but may utter other vocalizations such as moans, grunts, or whimpers. Breathing is quite irregular.
Crying	Crying here refers to a sustained or prolonged cry. Facial grimaces, flushing of the face, and closed eyes may accompany the crying. There is frequently generalized motor activity—"vigorous kicking and flailing arm movements w/agitated crying" (Krantz, 1994, p. 134).

There are several forms of stimulation or interaction that are known to quiet a crying baby. Papalia and Olds (1992) note that "the age-old way to soothe crying babies involves steady stimulation—rocking or walking them, wrapping them snugly, or letting them hear rhythmic sounds or suck on pacifiers" (p. 96).

For another perspective on infant states, see, for example, Berk's *Infants, Children, and Adolescence* (2005, pp. 150ff).

Observation Objectives

To observe states of arousal of the newborn, to describe some of their defining characteristics, and to observe and record how a newborn's state affects his responses to the environment.

Procedure

As a first step, carefully describe characteristics of the physical and social environment that could be sources of stimulation for the newborn—for example, background noises, talking, objects within sight or reach of the baby, direct stimulation provided by the caretaker (talking to him, caressing him), and so on. This description of the environment is the background against which you will assess the newborn's responsiveness when in various states. As a second step, describe in detail the newborn's behaviors using the narrative description technique. Make note of the small components of responses, such as respiration rate and rhythm, muscle movements, facial expressions, and eye movements (as seen through closed lids if asleep). Classify the behaviors according to the categories defined in Table 14-2.

It is suggested that you observe for about five minutes at a time, striving for at least three five-minute sessions over a total period of an hour to an hour and a half. Because newborns tend to sleep a good part of the day, spacing out your recording sessions will help reduce fatigue and increase your chances of seeing the child in more than one state. (See Observation Exercise 14-2 at the end of this chapter and in the Online Companion™.)

Question Guides

1. How many different states of arousal does the newborn exhibit during your observation of him?

2. How long does he remain in each state?

3. Is he in one state more than any other? Which one?

4. Is there any one feature of each state observed that best distinguishes it from other states? What is that feature?

5. What, if any, stimulation changes the newborn's state? How does his state affect his response to stimulation—is there an apparent general relationship between state and responsiveness to stimulation? What is it?

6. How does the parent or caregiver respond to the newborn while he is in various states? Is the parent or caregiver aware of the newborn's differing sensitivity to stimulation when in various states? Explain.

EXERCISE 14-3: INDIVIDUAL DIFFERENCES AND THE NEWBORN

Background Information

Psychologists speak of individual differences even among newborns. Individual differences exist in such areas as **spontaneous behaviors**, **soothability** states, physical characteristics, and **temperament**.

spontaneous behaviors
Behaviors that are internally generated and not responses to outside stimuli; they include behaviors such as random startles, fleeting smiles, and erections.

soothability
The ability of a crying or upset infant to be quieted by such adult responses as rocking, holding, swaddling, or giving a pacifier.

temperament
A child's characteristic ways of responding to various situations; temperament is described by the child's responses on six personality dimensions: activity level, rhythmicity, approach/withdrawal, adaptability, intensity of reaction, and quality of mood.

Spontaneous behaviors are internally generated rather than responses to outside stimuli. They include such observable behaviors as "random startles, fleeting smiles, kicking, erections, and random mouthing and sucking movements" (Gander & Gardner, 1981). As Gander and Gardner note, infants differ markedly in how often these behaviors occur, their type, and the sequences in which they occur. Soothability refers to how easily a crying or upset infant is comforted by such adult responses as holding, rocking, swaddling, warming, or giving a pacifier.

Perhaps the most interesting assessment of individual differences was made by the research team of Thomas, Chess, and Birch (1968, 1970). They describe infants by the terms "easy," "slow-to-warm-up," and "difficult." These descriptions are the result of infants' and children's responses on six personality dimensions: activity level, rhythmicity, approach/withdrawal, adaptability, intensity of reaction, and quality of mood. The infant or child is rated as either high or low on each dimension, depending on the characteristic ways she responds to various situations. These characteristic responses identify the child's temperament. Temperament is an important concept because the infant's response tendencies can interact with the personalities of the parents and with the environment. This interaction can result in either a compatible or an incompatible relationship between the infant and her physical and social environment. For example, imagine a child with a vigorous, physically active temperament born to parents who are inactive physically. Of course, the relationship would not be determined solely by the parents' and the child's temperaments. Nonetheless, temperament can have an effect on the child's development and behavior, and because qualities of temperament seem to be stable over the first 10 years of life, they deserve attention. Table 14-3 presents the responses of a two-month-old who would be rated high and low on each of the six personality dimensions identified by Thomas and colleagues.

Observation Objectives

To observe the differences in the soothability, spontaneous behaviors, and the temperaments of two newborns.

Procedure

This exercise ideally requires you to observe two newborns; however, if that is not possible, you can complete the exercise with just one newborn. Although the behaviors you will be observing are useful for studying individual differences, they will also give you information about a single child. It is suggested that you use the narrative description format for observing and recording. Observe each of the two newborns for at least three 5- to 10-minute sessions within a total period of 60 to 90 minutes in each case. If you find it difficult to obtain much information on each newborn's temperamental qualities just by observing, you may ask the parent or caregiver about the

Temperament	Rating	Behavioral Characteristics
Activity level: The way the infant moves and how much she moves.	Low	Displays no movement while being dressed or while asleep, for example.
	High	A lot of movement during sleep; wiggles or squirms during some caretaking activities (e.g., diapering).
Rhythmicity: Concerns the "predict-ability of biological cycles such as hunger, sleep, and elimination."	Regular	Has been on a regular feeding schedule since birth; bowel movements are regular; sleep patterns are consistent.
	Irregular	Does not awake at the same time each morning. Food eaten varies in amount from meal to meal.
Approach/Withdrawal: How the infant initially reacts to new situations or stimuli such as food, objects, and persons.	Positive	Responds smilingly to caretaking activities such as face washing; has never rejected the bottle; no negative or fearful reactions to strangers.
	Negative	May reject food the first time. Shows distress at the approach of strangers.
Adaptability: How easily or quickly child's initial response to new situation can change "in a desired direction."	Adaptive	Passive response to some activity (e.g., bathing) changes to enjoyment after initial response.
	Not adaptive	Retains startle response to sudden noises; continues to resist such caretaking activities as diapering and bathing.
Intensity of Reaction: How vigorously infant responds.	Mild	Does not cry when experiencing mild discomfort (e.g., wet diapers). Hunger evokes whimpering but not crying.
	Intense	Cries when experiencing mild discomfort such as wet diapers or hunger; vigorously rejects food when not hungry.
Quality of Mood: Is the infant's beha-vior typically pleasant and friendly, or is it unhappy and unfriendly?	Positive	Smiles at familiar others. Shows a positive response to a new food—e.g., "smacks lips" (Dworetzky, 1987, p. 110).
	Negative	Is fussy after eating. Some activities/experiences cause crying—e.g., "rocking the carriage" (Dworetzky, 1987, p. 110).

Adapted from Papalia and Olds, 1996, pp. 266–267; and Dworetzky, 1987, p. 110.

child's typical responses in various situations. For this, see Table 14-4, which provides a general description of behaviors related to the six personality dimensions identified by Thomas and colleagues (also refer to Table 14-3). (See Observation Exercise 14-3 at the end of this chapter and in the Online Companion™.)

Table 14-4 Temperamental Qualities	
Activity Level	Activity can begin in the uterus, where an active fetus can kick frequently. Active babies move around in their cribs or basinets; they prefer to climb or run rather than engage in more placid activities. Other babies show much less vigorous activity levels.
Rhythmicity	Rhythmicity is characterized by regular cycles of activity—eating, sleeping, and bowel movements that occur pretty much on schedule. Other infants are not as predictable.
Approach/Withdrawal	Approach is an attitude of delight or acceptance when confronted with something new—laughter at first bath, readily eating new food. Withdrawal is a refusal to accept new situations.
Adaptability	Characterized by rapid adjustment to change; no severe negative reactions to disruption of normal routines. Some babies do not easily tolerate change or deviations from the familiar.
Intensity of Reaction	Some children laugh loudly, scream when they cry. Others merely smile, whimper, or cry softly.
Quality of Mood	Some children are generally bright and cheerful; they smile easily. Other children seem generally unhappy and discontent, seem constantly to complain.

Question Guides

1. What spontaneous behaviors does the newborn exhibit? How frequently do these occur? About how long do they last? Do they seem to follow a recurring sequence or pattern? If so, describe.

2. Does the parent or caregiver respond to any of the spontaneous behaviors exhibited? If so, describe.

3. Is the newborn easily soothed or comforted? What seems to soothe her the most? What different tactics does the parent or caregiver use to comfort the baby?

4. What temperamental qualities characterize the baby? Under what circumstances do you observe indications of the newborn's temperament?

5. Does the parent or caregiver seem aware of the baby's unique responses to situations? If so, how? Do the parents or caregivers of the two newborns observed differ in their responses to the babies' temperaments? How?

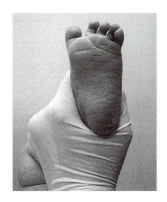

The Babinski reflex.
Note the spread toes.

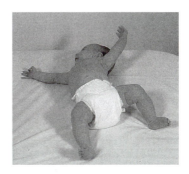

The Moro reflex.

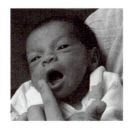

The rooting reflex.

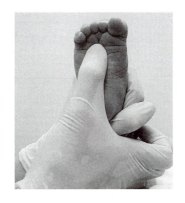

The plantar reflex.

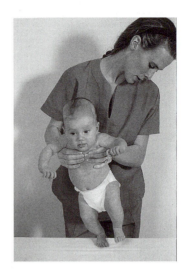

The stepping reflex.

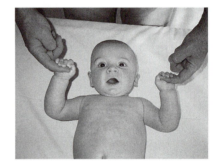

Grasping.

EXERCISE 14-4: MOTOR RESPONSES OF THE NEWBORN

Background Information

The newborn's motor abilities are best characterized as reflexive. Discussion of the newborn or infant would be incomplete without mentioning these built-in motor patterns. You may see several of these reflexes during your observations, especially the more common ones such as the startle, orienting, rooting, sucking, swallowing, eye blink, and grasp reflexes (see Table 14-5). Some of these reflexes have survival value; they protect the newborn and young infant from potential harm and enable her to take advantage of the caregiver's efforts to keep her alive. The rooting, sucking, and swallowing reflexes, for example, permit the newborn to eat; the vomiting and eye

	Table 14-5 Infant Reflexes		
Reflex	**Eliciting Stimulus**	**Response**	**Age Ceases**
Rooting	Stroking of the cheek with a finger or a nipple.	Infant turns head, opens his mouth, and starts sucking.	9 mos.
Moro	Sudden stimulus such as a loud noise or being dropped.	Infant extends her arms, legs, and fingers; she arches her back and throws her head back.	3 mos.
Grasping	Stroking the palm of the hand.	Fingers close in a strong fist— strong enough for infant to be pulled to an upright position while holding on to something like a stick or one's fingers.	2–3 mos.
Tonic Neck	Infant is put into a supine position (i.e., on his back).	Infant turns his head to one side, extends arms and legs on the preferred side while flexing limbs on the opposite side (so-called "fencer" position).	2–3 mos.
Babinski	Stroke one side of the foot.	Toes fan out and big toe turns upward while foot twists inward.	6–9 mos.
Walking	Hold infant under arms and have his bare feet touch a flat surface.	Makes stepping movements that resemble coordinated walking.	4–8 wks.
Eye Blink	Elicited by a puff of air in the face, a strong odor, a bright light, a loud noise.	Infant blinks eyes.	

blink reflexes are protective in nature. Other reflexes appear to serve no special purpose, although pediatricians use them as indications of the child's neurological development. For example, if the Babinski reflex (in which the toes curl upward and fan out when the sole of the foot is stroked) persists beyond six months or so of age, it could indicate damage to the central nervous system.

The newborn's voluntary gross (large) motor activities are limited to lifting up his head while lying on his stomach. Some newborns can lift their heads to about a 45-degree angle (Denver Developmental Screening Test, 1969). Hand functions are limited mainly to the grasp reflex. General, undifferentiated body movements are prominent in the newborn. Even his reactions to focused stimulation, such as a pinprick to the foot, typically involve overall movements of the arms, legs, and torso rather than withdrawal of just the stimulated foot and leg.

Keep in mind the general principles that govern motor development. Muscle control proceeds from the head to the feet (cephalocaudal principle) and from the midline of the body to the outer extremities (proximodistal principle). Thus, control of the head and neck (which includes the eyes, mouth, lips, and tongue) comes before control of the trunk, legs, and feet. The infant gains control over the larger arm and shoulder (midline) movements before he can grasp small objects between thumb and forefinger (extremities).

Observation Objectives

To observe and record a newborn's reflexive and voluntary motor responses.

Procedure

In this exercise, you will be asked to deviate from a totally naturalistic approach and try to elicit some common reflexes. It is recommended that the parent or caregiver stimulate the reflexes so that you will be free to carefully observe and record the responses while they are occurring. Do not overstimulate the baby, especially when eliciting reflexes that require loud noises or sudden withdrawal of physical support. You will also observe and record the newborn's voluntary movements and motor patterns. For this, you will use a narrative descriptive format because movements of some kind are likely to occur for much of the time. Observe for five minutes at a time, and try for at least three, five-minute sessions over a total period of an hour to an hour and a half. (See Observation Exercise 14-4 at the end of this chapter and in the Online Companion™.)

Question Guides

1. What reflexes does the newborn exhibit? What specific stimuli elicit the responses? Does he get used to (**habituate**) and stop responding to any stimuli that initially cause reflex responses?

2. What nonreflexive movements does the newborn display? What are the characteristics of these movements—smooth? Jerky or thrashing about? Coordinated? Are movements related to one another, or are they seemingly independent? Do his movements bring him into any contact with the physical environment? If so, does such contact seem to affect or influence further movements? Explain your answers.

3. Does the newborn have control over his general movements? Over individual parts of his body? Does he have more control over some body parts than others? If so, how might this difference in control be explained?

4. Does the parent or caregiver respond to his movements? Does he try to encourage them? Explain.

EXERCISE 14-5: PERCEPTUAL RESPONSES OF THE NEWBORN

Background Information

Vision

Vision is the sense on which the majority of us depend the most. As Berk (2005) puts it, "More than any other sense, humans depend on vision for active exploration of the environment" (p. 194). It is also true that of all the newborn baby's senses, vision is the least mature. However, this does not mean that newborns are totally incompetent visually. Although their visual acuity is far from what it will be at a later age, newborns can see. What adults can perceive at 660 feet, for example, newborns can perceive at only about 20 feet. Stated in more practical terms, the newborn's optimal range of vision is about 6 to 8 inches. Yet, despite their limited acuity, newborns still actively explore their environment by scanning the visual field for interesting things, and they will try to track moving objects, albeit with slow, inaccurate eye movements.

Bukatko and Daehler (1995) make an interesting and informative observation about newborns' visual capacity and its role in the active exploration of the environment:

> Because newborns have limited motor skills, we are often tempted to assume that their sensory systems—their eyes, ears, nose, mouth, and skin—must be passive receptors awaiting stimulation. But Eleanor J. Gibson and James J. Gibson convincingly argue that perceiving is an active "process of *obtaining* information about the world" (J. J. Gibson, 1966, italics original). We don't simply see, we "look." ... even neonates mobilize sensory receptors to respond to stimulation flowing from their bustling environment. (p. 218)

Newborns also appear to have some visual preferences and can discriminate between some different visual stimuli. The early work of Fantz (1963), for instance, showed that babies can discern the difference between such patterned visual stimuli as a face, concentric circles, and a newspaper, and such unpatterned stimuli as simple patches of color. Newborns as young as 10 hours to 5 days of age looked at the patterned displays longer than at the unpatterned ones; of the patterned stimuli, they most preferred the face (Schickedanz et al., 1993, p. 135). Willemsen (1979) reports that newborns can "discriminate between solid gray patterns and those composed of five gray stripes."

One final feature of the newborn's vision that we want to mention is that infants younger than about two months of age tend to focus their attention on the outer aspects or contours of a complex stimulus, whereas the older infant tends to look at the internal features of a complex stimulus as well as the outer ones. (See, e.g., Bukatko & Daehler, 1995, for a discussion of this phenomenon.)

Newborns are sensitive to changes in the brightness of the surrounding lighting (Willemsen, 1979). Not all psychologists agree on the newborn's visual preferences. Writers such as Craig (1989) report that "infants are selective about what they look at from the beginning. They look at novel and moderately complex patterns and at human faces" (p. 156). Craig (1989) notes that the newborn's preference for the edges of a face changes, with development, to an interest in "the eyes, and even later, at the mouth of a person talking" (p. 156). There does seem to be agreement that newborns prefer to scan the edges and outlines of objects, especially curved outlines. Interestingly, there is evidence that newborns as young as two weeks of age can show a preference for their mothers' faces, even when presented as pictures rather than live (Carpenter, 1974, cited in Craig, 1989).

Hearing

It was once believed that newborns were deaf, but it is now known that they are sensitive to some aspects of sound. Indeed, Willemsen (1979) notes that they "react to all the major aspects of auditory stimulation—that is, pitch, loudness, timbre, and pattern (rhythm)." Papalia and Olds (1979) report that "the greater the sound intensity, the greater the babies' increase in heart rate and movement," where such increases indicate awareness of the stimulation. Their responses to intense sound helps explain why newborns and babies in general pay attention to high-pitched voices and why adults speak to them in that way. There is also evidence to suggest that newborns can distinguish their mother's voice from that of another female (Fogel, 1984). Papalia and Olds (1987) suggest that the infant's "early preference for the mother's voice may be an important mechanism for initiating bonding between a mother and a baby" (p. 161).

Habituation

Habituation, another important component of a newborn's response capability, occurs when, after exposure to a physical stimulus that originally evokes response, the newborn ceases to respond. She gets used to it, and it no longer interests her. As Berk (2005) puts it, "**Habituation** refers to a gradual reduction in the strength of a response due to repetitive stimulation" (p. 184, emphasis original). To round out the concept of habituation, Berk further writes: "Once this has occurred, a new stimulus—some kind of change in the environment—causes responsiveness to return to a higher level, an increase called *recovery*" (p. 184, emphasis original). The term *dishabituation* is interchangeable with the term *recovery*. There are two basic reactions to novel sounds (Papalia & Olds, 1979). First, the newborn will exhibit an orienting response by turning her head toward the source of the sound. Second, if she is doing anything else at the time, she will stop or inhibit that activity. It is as though she can do only one

habituation
After being exposed to a physical stimulus that originally evokes a response, the individual ceases paying attention to it; get used to stimulus and lose interest in it.

An infant's early preference for the mother's voice may be an important mechanism for initiating bonding between a mother and a baby.

thing at a time, and the novel sound is more important than something that may already be familiar to her. But, as Papalia and Olds (1979) point out, it might be difficult to observe an orienting response because the newborn does not have good control of her eye and muscle movements. Therefore, inhibition of an activity (such as sucking) following a sound indicates that the newborn is orienting. The inhibitory response reliably accompanies the orienting reflex.

Observation Objectives

To observe and record some of the newborn's behaviors that reflect her perceptual response capabilities.

Procedure

This exercise has two parts. In Part I, you will be eliciting some responses from the newborn. Perform the simple stimulation tasks outlined below, and record on the checklist provided whether or not the baby responded. Immediately follow with a detailed but concise description of the response. You will need a small flashlight (a penlight is preferable) to test several of the newborn's visual responses. (See Observation Exercise 14-5 at the end of this chapter and in the Online Companion™.)

In Part II, using a form of event sampling, observe the newborn for any of the perceptual responses discussed in the section on Background Information. Especially look for behaviors such as the orienting and habituation responses. Notice how the parent or caregiver responds to and stimulates the baby. You may want to perform some casual testing by speaking to the newborn and comparing her reactions to your voice with her reactions to the voice of a familiar person. If there are objects hanging above the crib, observe whether she visually responds to them.

Question Guides

1. Are there any objects within the newborn's line and range of vision? Does he visually respond to these objects? Does he gaze at it or follow it with his eyes if it is moved slowly in front of his face?

2. Does the newborn respond visually to the general environment? Does the newborn appear to scan the area immediately above him (assuming there are no objects suspended above his crib or basinet) or to either side of him? If he is held, does he look around the room, as though trying to visually take in his surroundings? What leads you to believe that the newborn has made responses to particular stimuli?

3. Do some body positions seem to evoke more responses to the environment than other positions (e.g., lying on his back, held over an adult's shoulder, or on an adult's lap)?

4. Is there any apparent mismatch between the newborn's visual competence and the visual stimuli provided for her? For instance, is there a complicated mobile hanging above her crib when a simple square, circle, or diamond shape might be more appropriate to her ability to process visual information?

5. Does the newborn respond to background sounds? Are there any orienting responses? Has she habituated to these general noises? Why do you think she has made a recognizable response to this aspect of her physical environment?

6. Does the newborn respond to sounds that are not always present in the background? Does she orient? Does she eventually habituate? What leads you to

conclude she oriented or habituated to any sounds? To what sounds are these responses made?

7. Does the newborn respond differently to continuous as opposed to intermittent sounds? If so, what are the differences, and what are the specific sounds he responds to?

8. Does the newborn respond to voices? Does she give any indication that she prefers her mother's voice to someone else's voice? If you think so, how does she demonstrate her preference?

EXERCISE 14-6: EMOTIONAL FUNCTIONING OF THE NEWBORN

Background Information

This last exercise is intended only as a very brief introduction to the area of emotional behavior and functioning, a topic that is continued in Chapter 15 and Chapter 16. We draw here on the work of Stanley and Nancy Greenspan (1985), who identified six emotional milestones. We are primarily concerned in this chapter with the first of these six milestones, or stages, but for the sake of providing you with a feeling of continuity and with a larger context, we include the second stage as well.

The first two of these stages, or milestones, concern the capacities of self-regulation and the use of the senses to take an interest in the world. The Greenspans refer to these milestones as "two simultaneous challenges" (Greenspan & Greenspan, 1985, p. 4). They are challenges because the newborn, after nine months in the darkness and relative quiet of the womb, is suddenly catapulted, as it were, into a world filled with a variety of sensations that are completely new to her. In the first milestone, which takes place between birth and three months of age, the newborn must organize these sensations and at the same time feel comfortable in their presence and actively engage them in ways that are appropriate to her level of developmental maturity—for example, show interest in the sights and sounds around her and not find them painful.

This then permits achievement of the second milestone (two to seven months), which is that of "taking a highly specialized interest in the *human* world" (p. 5, italics original). An assumption here is that if the baby does not find these environmental stimuli pleasurable, he may be unlikely to progress to the stage where the world of human beings "is seen as the most enticing, pleasurable, and exciting of all experiences" (p. 4). The pleasure that one wants the baby to feel, write the Greenspans, can be seen in her "enraptured smiles and eager joyfulness" as she "gazes excitedly at your face" while she feels the movements of your body and hears your voice.

Observation Objectives

Your objectives here are quite abbreviated relative to the preceding exercises. We simply want you to attempt to assess how well a newborn is achieving the Greenspans' first emotional milestone. Your objective is to observe and record the newborn's interest in and responsiveness to the sounds, sights, and things that are in his environment. We are aware that responsiveness is already heavily involved in the other exercises in this chapter. Nonetheless, we want to place emphasis on emotions and, in the case of the newborn, on the foundation or precursors of his subsequent emotional growth, development, and behavior.

Procedure

In this exercise, use the event sampling technique. Watch a newborn (a child between birth and one month of age and no older) for any behavioral evidence that she is spontaneously interested in the sights and sounds around her and that she does not "find them painful" (i.e., she does not appear disturbed or distressed by them). *Spontaneously* means that the newborn is not reacting to your efforts to evoke some kind of response from her; she is responding on her own. (See Observation Exercise 14-6 at the end of this chapter and in the Online Companion™.)

Observe for about five minutes at a time over three separate sessions. Pool or combine the information from the three sessions to draw your conclusions or inferences.

OBSERVATION EXERCISE **14-1**

The Physical Characteristics of the Newborn

Observer's Name _____

Child/Children Observed _____

Child's/Children's Age(s) _____ Child's/Children's Sex _____

Observation Context (home, child care center, preschool, school) _____

Date of Observation _____ Time Begun _____ Time Ended _____

Brief Description of Physical and Social Characteristics of Observation Setting:

Objective Behavioral Descriptions (OBDs): *Modified Narrative Description*

Total Length of Newborn _____ Weight of Newborn _____

Length of Head _____ Ratio of Head to Total Body Length _____

Length of Trunk _____ Ratio of Head to Trunk _____

Describe the characteristics of the following:

HEAD and FACE (shape, eyes, ears, mouth, nose):

TRUNK (e.g., size in relation to head, overall appearance):

ARMS and LEGS (positioning, shape):

HANDS and FINGERS (positioning, shape):

SKIN (color, texture, general appearance):

OBSERVATION EXERCISE **14-2**

Infant States and Responsiveness to Stimuli

Observer's Name _____

Child/Children Observed _____

Child's/Children's Age(s) _____ Child's/Children's Sex _____

Observation Context (home, child care center, preschool, school) _____

Date of Observation _____ Time Begun _____ Time Ended _____

Brief Description of Physical and Social Characteristics of Observation Setting:

Objective Behavioral Descriptions (OBDs): *Narrative Description*

OBD Session 1: [Time begun _____ Time ended _____]

Response to Stimulation

OBD Session 2: [Time begun _____ Time ended _____]

Response to Stimulation

OBD Session 3: [Time begun _____ Time ended _____]

Response to Stimulation

Parent's or Caregiver's Responses to Newborn's State Behaviors:

OBSERVATION EXERCISE **14-3**

Individual Differences in Newborns (Part I) (Newborn #1 of Two Newborns Observed)

Observer's Name _____

Child/Children Observed _____

Child's/Children's Age(s) ____ Child's/Children's Sex ___

Observation Context (home, child care center, preschool, school) _____

Date of Observation _____ Time Begun _____ Time Ended _____

Brief Description of Physical and Social Characteristics of Observation Setting:

....

Objective Behavioral Descriptions (OBDs): *Narrative Description*

OBD Session 1: [Time begun _____ Time ended _____]

Time ended _____]

OBD Session 2: [Time begun _____ Time ended _____]

OBD Session 3: [Time begun _____ Time ended _____]

PARENT'S REPORT (if needed, identify each area reported on):

....

Individual Differences in Newborns (Part II) (Newborn #2 of Two Newborns Observed)

Observer's Name _____

Child/Children Observed _____

Child's/Children's Age(s) _____ Child's/Children's Sex _____

Observation Context (home, child care center, preschool, school) _____

(continues)

PART THREE

OBSERVATION EXERCISE **14-3** (Continued)

Date of Observation _____ Time Begun _____ Time Ended _____

Brief Description of Physical and Social Characteristics of Observation Setting:

....

Objective Behavioral Descriptions (OBDs): *Narrative Description*

OBD Session 1: [Time begun _____ Time ended _____]

OBD Session 2: [Time begun _____ Time ended _____]

OBD Session 3: [Time begun _____ Time ended _____]

PARENT'S REPORT (if needed, identify each area reported):

....

Comparisons

Newborn #1: Summary Description

Newborn #2: Summary Description

Summary Description of Differences

Soothability:

Spontaneous Behaviors:

Temperaments:

OBSERVATION EXERCISE **14-4**

Motor Responses of the Newborn

Observer's Name _____

Child/Children Observed _____

Child's/Children's Age(s) _____ Child's/Children's Sex _____

Observation Context (home, child care center, preschool, school) _____

Date of Observation _____ Time Begun _____ Time Ended _____

Brief Description of Physical and Social Characteristics of Observation Setting:

Objective Behavioral Descriptions (OBDs): *Narrative Description*

Reflex Elicited _____ **(#1)**

Stimulation Used _____ **Response** _____

Reflex Elicited _____ **(#2)**

Stimulation Used _____ **Response** _____

Reflex Elicited _____ **(#3)**

Stimulation Used _____ **Response** _____

Reflex Elicited _____ **(#4)**

Stimulation Used _____ **Response** _____

Reflex Elicited _____ **(#5)**

Stimulation Used _____ **Response** _____

Reflex Elicited _____ **(#6)**

Stimulation Used _____ **Response** _____

Voluntary Responses (Describe):

Head:

Arms:

(continues)

PART THREE

OBSERVATION EXERCISE **14-4** (Continued)

Objective Behavioral Descriptions (OBDs): *Narrative Description* **Continued**

Legs:

Trunk:

Overall Description:

OBSERVATION EXERCISE **14-5**

Perceptual Responses of the Newborn

Observer's Name _____

Child/Children Observed _____

Child's/Children's Age(s) _____ Child's/Children's Sex _____

Observation Context (home, child care center, preschool, school) _____

Date of Observation _____ Time Begun _____ Time Ended _____

Brief Description of Physical and Social Characteristics of Observation Setting:

....

Part I: *Modified Checklist Technique*

Stimulation: Loud Hand Clap

Response: Yes _____ **No** _____ **Uncertain** _____

Description:

Stimulation: Soft Hand Clap

Response: Yes _____ **No** _____ **Uncertain** _____

Description:

Stimulation: Loud Voice

Response: Yes _____ **No** _____ **Uncertain** _____

Description:

Stimulation: Soft Voice

Response: Yes _____ **No** _____ **Uncertain** _____

Description:

Stimulation: Object 6 Inches from Eyes

Response: Yes _____ **No** _____ **Uncertain** _____

Description:

Stimulation: Object 15 Inches from Eyes

Response: Yes _____ **No** _____ **Uncertain** _____

Description:

(continues)

OBSERVATION EXERCISE **14-5** (Continued)

Stimulation: Tracks Moving Light

Response: Yes _____ **No** _____ **Uncertain** _____

Description:

Part II: *Event Sampling*

Event Observed _____

Description:

OBSERVATION EXERCISE **14-6**

Emotional Functioning of the Newborn

Observer's Name _____

Child/Children Observed _____

Child's/Children's Age(s) _____ Child's/Children's Sex _____

Observation Context (home, child care center, preschool, school) _____

Date of Observation _____ Time Begun _____ Time Ended _____

Brief Description of Physical and Social Characteristics of Observation Setting:

Objective Behavioral Descriptions (OBDs): *Event Sampling*

OBD Session 1: [Time begun _____ Time ended _____]

Interpretation 1:

OBD Session 2: [Time begun _____ Time ended _____]

Interpretation 2:

Continue with as many OBDs and interpretations as are needed or desired.

Summary Comments on Newborn's Emotional Functioning

(use the Greenspans' first emotional milestone):

CHAPTER 15

Observing the Infant: 1 to 24 Months

KEY TERMS

attachment

object permanence

linguistic

visible displacement

invisible displacement

INTRODUCTION

In the Preface of his *A Primer of Human Development*, T. G. R. Bower (1977), a well-known psychologist, researcher, and writer, claims the following:

> Few would dissent from the proposition that infancy is the most critical period of human development, the period in which the basic frameworks for later development are established.

It is not our major concern whether or not infancy is, as Bower claims, "the most critical period of human development." However, we do recognize that researchers and theorists alike deem this initial period of the human life span at least to be extremely important.

There are, we suppose, any number of reasons why this is so. We suppose further that some of these reasons are affected or determined by the particular definition of *infancy* that the researcher or theorist is using. Let us look briefly at some definitions or meanings of *infancy* before we discuss further why this period is important.

The first such definitions we offer are based on age or developmental level. We view these definitions as more or less conventional; they are similar to an antique dealer assessing the value of an object on the basis of its age while essentially disregarding the object's purpose or function per se. In some contrast, we offer two additional bases for defining *infancy*. For these we are indebted to the work of Alan Fogel (1984), a psychologist and writer. First, we briefly present Fogel's description of the parental attitudes toward, or perspectives on, children that prevailed in the Western world during the nineteenth century and that prevail today. These attitudes can be thought of as behavioral definitions. A behavioral definition is a meaning assigned to something (object, person, or event) based on how that thing is treated or dealt with by the individual doing the defining. The meaning is determined by how he literally behaves toward, or relates to, the object. For instance, a *chair* might be defined behaviorally as not only something one sits on, but also as something one stands on to change a light bulb, or as something with which to prop open a door, and so on. In like fashion, an individual's behavioral definition of *child* can be discerned by how he actually behaves toward *child*, with the meaning of *behaves toward* left undefined at this time.

We then turn to a discussion of what Fogel calls nine "areas of competency or types of skill that infants are trying to develop" (p. 5) as a form of definition based on function. However, you should keep in mind that infancy's functions are not separable, at least not easily, from its genetically patterned developmental period from birth to two or three years. Put another way, whereas the adult function or task, let's say, of establishing a family through marriage might typically occur during the period of young adulthood, a middle-aged couple can also establish a family, even for the first time. The infant seems destined to accomplish his or her developmental tasks only or predominantly during this relatively short time we call infancy. This reference to a developmental time frame applies to what we call normal development. Delays do occur that put some children behind their age peers, just as there are precocious children who move through certain developmental areas at a faster rate than their peers. However, this text is interested in the typical rate and path of development, not the atypical ones. Nonetheless, this emphasis does not rule out the possibility that you may be interested in observing and recording non-normative developmental patterns; we simply do not deal with them here. You will, of course, recognize this requirement or time constraint as being a characteristic of a stage.

What Is an Infant?

As Bower (1977) states, "An infant is literally someone who does not talk" (p. 1). On this view, according to Bower, "The normal duration of infancy, in this strict sense, is about eighteen months" (p. 1). Alan Fogel (1984) is not as definitive or as dogmatic as Bower: "The definition of infancy varies, depending upon whom you talk to" (p. 1). He clearly disagrees with Bower regarding the age range of the infancy period: "Few experts would answer that infancy covers the period from birth to two years of age" (p. 1). Importantly, however, he also asserts, "Few people in our society would say that a three-year-old is a baby" (p. 1). Fogel decides that his book "will cover human development from birth up to the age of three years" (p. 1). But Fogel also recognizes that simply knowing the ages that define the period of infancy is not sufficient to understanding this segment of the life span. We agree. But we must also settle on some age range within which to confine our remarks. Consequently, we have struck a compromise of sorts between Bower's 18 months and Fogel's 36 months. We define infancy chronologically as approximately the first 24 months of life following birth. This is also in keeping with our treatment of the preschool period (Chapter 16) as comprising the ages two to five years.

We can probably agree that infancy is a significant period of human development. We nonetheless might want to deal a bit further with the question of what an infant is. Any answer certainly has to do with how one sees an infant—with one's perspective on such matters. Alan Fogel (1984) devotes an entire introductory chapter to the question of what is an infant, and we have already touched on some of his ideas on this topic in our earlier comments. Part of Fogel's treatment incorporates an interesting tracing of historical views of children held by the Western world over the past 2,400 years. Drawing on the work of Lloyd de Mause (1974), Fogel describes six stages that have characterized parent–child relations in Western civilization from ancient times to the present day. We mention only the last two of these stages, which began in the nineteenth century. Fogel refers to the stages as "modes," which "represent prevailing attitudes of parents toward infants and children" (p. 2).

The socialization mode (nineteenth to mid-twentieth centuries) emphasized children's conformity to the "goals and standards of adult society," and children were "to be trained and taught in proper ways" (Fogel, 1984, p. 3). Of particular interest is that "parents believed that children should be loved according to how ' good' or ' bad' they have been" (p. 3). The current mode (mid-twentieth century) is called the helping mode and is characterized by the belief that children are "active, creative, and intrinsically valuable" (p. 4). In this context, according to Fogel, "Children should be loved no matter how they behave, and parents should be able to empathize with the child in order to provide whatever is necessary for the child's well-being" (p. 4). In short, the essence of modern parent–child relationships might be said to be involvement and "increasing awareness of children and concern for their welfare" (p. 4).

It should be clear to you that these modes are ways of seeing children, and, as earlier modes have done for the historical periods in which they were prevalent, these last two modes form a foundation for present-day treatment of children. Let us move on to further discussion of a definition of *infancy*.

We hold that a phenomenon (object or event) can be defined according to what it does, what its functions are, or what actions or behaviors are part of its inherent features or attributes. Fogel, again, very nicely provides us with just such a definition according to function. He refers to nine competency areas or "types of skill that infants are trying to develop" that are requisite to the child's becoming "an active, functional member of her society, family, and community" (p. 5). (Please bear in mind that Bower's description of the infant's accomplishments [p. 161] are equally relevant to, though less detailed than, the present discussion.) As it turns out, these areas also afford us a convenient basis for observing infants' behavior and for making judgments concerning their abilities and levels of development. Let us treat these nine areas very briefly.

Perceptual/Sensorial Skills

Involved here are the infant's sensory capacities of hearing, sight, touch, smell, taste, and those distinctly interior senses that pertain to balance and to awareness of the location of one's body and its various parts (arms, legs, and so on). Also involved is the way she uses these senses to gain knowledge about the environment. The development (progressive change over time) of the infant's perceptual and sensory skills should be of special interest to you as an observer.

The development of the infant's perceptual and sensory skills should be of special interest to you as an observer.

Sensorimotor/Tool-Using Skills

Most simply put, this competence area has to do with the development of motor skills, which include such actions as rolling over, sitting up, standing, walking, and running. Fogel includes Jerome Bruner's (1975) ideas on tool-using skills as "a manifestation of the infant's capacity to understand and manipulate the environment" (Fogel, 1984, p. 6). *Tools* is to be broadly understood as anything that can help accomplish some purpose. Do not restrict your notion of tools to such better-known objects as hammers, wrenches, screwdrivers, and the like. In the broad meaning of *tool*, a stick could be used to pull a toy closer to oneself, thereby making that stick a tool.

Conceptual/Thinking

At about six months of age, infants show the start of an ability to make "conceptual differentiations between classes of objects" (Fogel, 1984, p. 6). A beginning awareness of object permanence, which is the understanding that an object's existence does not depend on its being evident to the physical senses, appears at about nine months of age. Fogel notes that (mental) behavior that reflects actual thinking, reasoning, and planning is not evident much before the last part of the second year. Until then, what predominates is trial-and-error "thinking" in the form of overt acting out rather than mental or internalized selection of courses of action (p. 6). "Internalized selection of courses of action" simply means that the individual can mentally rehearse or anticipate the consequences of various behaviors without actually performing them. Therefore, he can choose an action based on its predicted outcome or effect, although this ability does not rule out the possibility of error.

Memory

Memory is a critical component of the infant's developing cognitive abilities. Jerome Kagan (1984), a well-known psychologist and author, makes a strong claim for the importance of memory: "The ability to relate an experience in the present to relevant schemata is one of the central maturing functions of the first year of life. In plainer language, the child becomes able to remember the past" (p. 40). (*Schemata* is the plural of *schema*, which Kagan defines as "a representation of experience that bears a relation to an original event" [p. 35].) Fogel (1984) notes that "nine months of age marks a significant shift in the infant's ability to remember" (p. 6), a shift that leads or contributes to the concept of object permanence and the ability to compare objects in "space, time, and quality" (p. 6).

Kagan (1984) discusses three aspects of memory development that constitute the overall ability to remember the past. He refers to these aspects as "recognition of the past, retrieval of the past, and the ability to compare past and present on the stage of active memory" (p. 40). Let us look briefly at these with respect to some normative ages of particular accomplishments.

First Aspect of Memory Development: Recognition of the Past

Kagan says that the three-month-old infant "can recognize a familiar event in her perceptual field because it shares properties with her schemata" (p. 40). Sharing properties with her schemata means that the familiar event previously encountered by the infant is perceived as being similar in some respects to her memory of that event. During the first six months, however, this recognition will disappear if too much time passes between successive experiences of the event.

Second Aspect of Memory Development: Retrieval of the Past

The second element of memory development, the ability "to retrieve a schema when there are minimal clues … in the immediate field" (p. 40), becomes functional, Kagan says, after the first six months. This ability to retrieve a schema can be measured by hiding an attractive toy and making the infant wait before he is allowed to reach for it. Kagan cites research that found that in a group of infants studied from the ages of 8 to 12 months, "no eight-month-old was able to remember the toy's location with a one-second delay" (p. 41). By 12 months of age, all the infants could find the toy when their search for it was delayed for three seconds, and a majority could perform this task even with a seven-second delay.

Third Aspect of Memory Development: Comparing Past and Present

The third memory achievement involves the ability to retrieve the past over longer and longer lapses of time. As Kagan notes, "When older children and adults read a sentence or listen to a conversation, they are able to integrate the incoming information with their knowledge over a period of time that can last as long as thirty seconds" (p. 42). Kagan calls this process of integration "active memory," which, he says, becomes stronger and more functional around eight months of age (p. 42). Thus it is that "the infant now automatically relates the present to the immediate past, which means she is comparing information from two sources" (p. 42).

Representational/Symbolic

Representation, which is having one thing stand for another, possibly quite different thing, is, says Fogel (1984), the "crowning achievement of cognitive development in the first three years of life" (p. 6). He also includes symbolic thinking, the most significant of which is the use of language. (For a detailed discussion of representational ability, see Chapter 17, Exercise 17-3.) Of course, one major function of linguistic symbols is precisely to represent something else: The word *chair* stands for the actual object we sit in; *dog* can stand for a particular furry, four-legged animal we pass every day on our way to work (or perhaps "Rover" stands for our dog). Fogel indicates that it is late into the second year of life before most children can grasp "the relation between the symbol and the actual object" (p. 6). This simply means that symbol use is essentially "unthinking" or "uncritical" and that it serves predominantly practical purposes, such as in the practical connection between, say, the word *milk* and the actual glass of white liquid that the parent gives the child following his utterance of the word.

Communicative/Linguistic

This competency area is close to the representational/symbolic competency just discussed. One important difference is emphasis on the use of language to communicate.

There is, of course, the complicated business of learning the meaning of words, proper grammar, and so on, but the ultimate use of language is to convey one's ideas, thoughts, and feelings to other people. Communication also involves knowing when to speak and when to listen (the reciprocal character of communication), learning about the environment, understanding what others are trying to make known, and making known one's own messages in socially appropriate ways. In short, language is a social skill as well as an intellectual skill.

Social/Interactive

Fogel (1984) initially emphasizes social/interactive competence in the context of language usage, especially the skill of taking turns in conversation. He mentions the naturally occurring "bursts and pauses in their behavior" as potential forerunners of such conversational skills, but he quickly points out that "any semblance of taking turns seems to be created by the adult partner who learns to skillfully insert her smiles, coos, and words into the natural silences left by the infant" (p. 7). Fogel indicates that the infant's awareness of his or her role as a partner in an interaction with an adult does not come about before the age of five or six months. Although there are other facets of social competence, of course (the next basic competency area is one of these other facets), it is important to recognize that infants start to learn social skills far ahead of any learning of words.

Expressive/Emotive

Feeling and expressing certain kinds of emotional states is an important element of the infant's social skills (Fogel, 1984, p. 7). What emotions an infant can experience apparently depends upon age or developmental level. Fogel says there is general agreement that "infants do not know the feeling of fear before about eight months, and they cannot experience complex feelings like guilt, pride, or shame until they are almost three years old" (p. 7). Control of the kinds of emotions they want to express is not achieved before two or three years of age (p. 7). Kagan (1984) offers some informative comments on the relationship between emotional states and age, as well as on the general development of emotion:

> The popular belief that a child's emotions do not change with growth requires the improbable assumption that maturational changes in the brain that produce new cognitive evaluations and special feeling tones have no influence on the older person's emotional experiences. However, because one often uses the same language to name emotions in two- and twenty-two-year-olds, it is easy to believe that the emotional experiences are the same. American mothers also assume, incorrectly I believe, that three-month-olds can experience the emotions of interest, anger, joy, or fear that are attributed to adults. (p. 172)

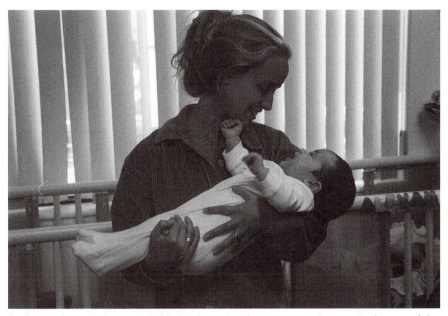

Feeling and expressing certain kinds of emotional states are an important element of the infant's social skills.

Self-Regulatory/Coping

Whether consciously aware of it or not, parents, teachers, caregivers, and other adults who work with children are concerned over the practical issues of a child's self-control and her ability to deal constructively with various aspects of the environment; they are also pleased (if not downright relieved) when a child in fact achieves these abilities. As Fogel (1984) puts it, "The development of self-regulatory skills is greeted by parents with a sense of relief that goes beyond delight. The ability of an infant to cope with the stresses of everyday life takes from the parent's shoulders a considerable burden" (p. 7). Among the indicators of "successful self-regulation," Fogel lists "sleeping through the night, waiting patiently while a meal is being prepared, handling the fear and distress of separation from the parents, fighting assertively to retrieve a toy from a meddling older sibling" (p. 7).

Although Fogel's indicators of successful self-regulation might suffice to make his point, we want to point out that the infant's ability "to cope with the stresses of everyday life" should not be taken to mean that the infant is stress free. It more accurately means that overall, and on average, the infant is able to handle those normal stresses that are characteristic of, and appropriate to, his or her developmental stage. It is also the case with adults that possessing effective strategies for coping with some kinds of stress does not preclude being faced with stress with which they cannot adequately cope.

These skills can be put into the general category of autonomy, which, of course, tends to free adults from some of the tasks associated with being a child's parent or caregiver (see Fogel, 1984, p. 8). This freedom gives credence to the relief and delight that adults feel when the child achieves self-regulatory and coping skills.

Some of the preceding descriptions have a Piagetian focus. More recently, however, the theoretical concepts of Lev Vygotsky have come to psychologists' attention. Indeed, his ideas are now competing with Piaget's theory and with an information processing theory. Berk (2005), for example, while praising Piaget for his contributions to our understanding of children's cognitive development, points out that Piaget's theory has not gone unchallenged:

> Research indicates that Piaget underestimated the competencies of infants and preschoolers. When young children are given tasks scaled down in difficulty, their understanding appears closer to that of the older child and adult than Piaget assumed. This discovery has led many researchers to conclude that the maturity of children's thinking may depend on their familiarity with the task presented and the complexity of knowledge sampled. Furthermore, many studies show that children's performance on Piagetian problems can be improved with training—findings that call into question Piaget's assumption that discovery learning rather than adult teaching is the best way to foster development. (p. 22)

Berk (2005) also acknowledges the contribution of information-processing theory, noting that "A great strength of the information-processing approach is its commitment to careful, rigorous research methods." But she notes further that "information processing has fallen short in some respects. Although good at analyzing thinking into its components, it has difficulty putting them back together into a comprehensive theory" (p. 24).

The relevance of Vygotsky's theory lies in its emphasis on the role of the social context in cognitive development. An informative and interesting discussion of Vygotsky's theoretical position is offered by the writing team of Bukatko and Daehler (1995):

> A central tenet of Vygotsky's sociohistorical theory is that as children become exposed to and participate in their culture, they begin to internalize and adopt, often with the guidance of a skilled partner such as a caregiver or teacher, more mature and effective ways of thinking and solving problems with respect to their circumstances. Infants, of course, are not born with the tools and ways of thinking that are part of a community's history. These, however, can be transferred to children by those who are skilled or knowledgeable in their use. (pp. 64–65)

These authors go on to say that a critical component of a child's learning consists of social interactions that involve observing how others communicate and solve problems using the resources available to the child's particular culture. Vygotsky also viewed language as a very important cultural tool because the child internalizes language and uses it to think and to solve problems. Indeed, there is a circular or reciprocal aspect to language use. As the child uses language to think and solve problems, these very activities in turn promote and enhance further development of language skills that, again in turn, can be used to think in more complex ways and to solve more complex problems.

Why Is Infancy Important?

Let us get back briefly to the reasons that infancy is such an important topic of study. Here we follow Bower's (1977) lead because he also asks the same question. "Why," he asks, "should 2 percent of life span merit such attention?" (p. 1; "such attention" refers, among other things, to his own book on infancy). We like his answers because they are ones over which probably few would quibble. We offer you an extensive passage from his *Primer:*

> Probably more of the skills that separate human beings from other animals are acquired in infancy than in all the rest of childhood together. By the end of infancy the baby is sociable and cooperative. He has learned what is necessary for language, possibly the most important of all human skills. He can walk on his own two feet. He has refined the manual skills that man shares with no other animal. He can use tools to a limited extent, but an extent greater than any nonhuman. He has acquired some very basic and important concepts of space, causality, number. All this happened in eighteen months, grown from what look like most unpromising beginnings. (pp. 1–2)

David Elkind (1981), a well-known author and professor of child study at Tufts University, also specifies the particular concerns, and therefore the potential accomplishments, of the infancy period:

> From birth until about two years of age infants are concerned with constructing a world of permanent objects, attaching themselves to significant others, and establishing what now retired Harvard professor Erik Erikson called a sense of "trust." These three attainments constitute the major intellectual, social, and emotional developments of the infancy period. (p. 98)

Have you any doubt that all these cited accomplishments are indeed important and that they form the very foundation for everything that is to come in subsequent developmental periods?

Of course, the nine competency areas just discussed are, in and of themselves, the occasions for celebrating this first portion of the life span. Although one could argue that the adult also functions within, as well as adds to, these skill areas, he or she does not do so for the first time as an adult (or older child). Let us turn now to a practical application of these ideas.

EXERCISE 15-1: PHYSICAL CHARACTERISTICS AND MOTOR ABILITIES OF THE INFANT/TODDLER (1 to 24 MONTHS)

Background Information

Physical Characteristics

You will find some striking differences in physical appearance between the newborn and the 15- to 24-month-old infant or toddler. Indeed, you need not wait very long before seeing some dramatic changes. Let's first look briefly at the changes that take place in the child's weight and height. Faw and Belkin (1989), in their excellent college review book on child psychology, report that the first four months of life result in a doubling of birth weight, which brings the infant up to a weight of 14 or 15 pounds. (Craig [1989] indicates a range from 12 to 15 pounds. We mention this only to point out that such norms will vary at least slightly from source to source; any specific norm probably should not be considered a precise figure.) Papalia, Olds, and Feldman (2006) report that by the end of the first year, the average baby boy weighs 23 pounds, and the average baby girl weighs about a pound less. Interestingly enough, subsequent weight gain during the whole second year, according to Faw and Belkin, amounts to only about 5 pounds. This sharp decrease in gain is attributed to the child's increased physical activity and resulting increased use of calories.

Height gains during the first four months come to about 3 to 4 inches (Faw & Belkin, 1989, p. 130). By the end of the first year, the child grows yet another 6 inches, achieving a length (on average) of 29 to 31 inches. As with weight increases, growth in height slows down during the second year to a mere 4 (to 5) inches. The height of the average two-year-old is 33 to 35 inches (p. 130). Height of the two-year-old, by the way, is approximately one-half of what it will be when he or she is an adult. Recall from Chapter 14 that the newborn's head is misshapen and disproportionately large relative to her body, which gives the child an appearance that is peculiar if not outright distorted. The growth following this first month or two of life is, say Faw and Belkin, an attempt of the body to "'catch up with' the head" (p. 131). The trunk gains some 50 percent in length during the first two years; the arms increase their length by 60 to 75 percent (p. 131).

Motor Characteristics and Abilities

At one month, the newborn exhibits a number of involuntary reflex responses, and his voluntary movements are random and poorly controlled. This random aspect of early muscle movement is referred to as mass action and is the opposite of the specific action that refers to the older child's more coordinated muscle movements. Use of the hands is limited to a grasp reflex, and he seems totally unaware that he even has hands. By 18 months, the infant has accumulated the achievements of head control, sitting, rolling over, crawling, creeping, standing, walking, and running. His ability to reach for, grasp, and manipulate objects has also undergone dramatic change. By about 3 months of age, he begins swiping at objects and becomes aware of his hands; by 18 months, he can turn pages of a book one at a time. At 1 month, his only way to communicate is to cry; by 18 months, he uses words and exhibits other true social behaviors. (See Tables 15-1, 15-2, and 15-3.) Of course, all these accomplishments have depended on the development and maturation of the nervous system, which in turn have depended on many other factors, not the least of which was a supporting and nurturant physical and social environment.

Craig (1989) offers a useful "overview" of an infant's competencies at the ages of 4, 8, 12, 18, and 24 months. For the area of motor competencies, we take advantage of Craig's format and briefly present some of the developmental milestones that are typical at the ages just indicated.

Four Months

The infant can usually hold up his chest when in the prone (on the stomach) position. The four-month-old can also hold his head steady while sitting up supported by an adult. He can roll over from front to back and vice versa. Craig notes that "most four-month-olds can reach and grasp for an object, although they frequently do not make contact" (p. 145). Faw and Belkin (1989) say that the infant of two and one-half months of age is in what they call the "early reaching period," in which she reaches for objects she sees but does so with very poor coordination and control, and frequently her efforts fail. (The development of reaching and grasping behavior is discussed in greater detail later in a separate section.) These authors report that by the age of four months, "visual reaching and hand reaching become coordinated" (p. 145). This skill is evidenced by infants "visually following their hand and arm as they reach for an object, and their attention alternates between the object to be grasped and the grasping hand itself" (p. 145). Incidentally, Faw and Belkin view visual tracking as a form of visual reaching, even though it is not coordinated with hand and arm movements. Visual tracking is following an object with the eyes, and it appears at about three and one-half months of age.

Eight Months

Craig (1989) reports that most eight-month-olds can get into a sitting position on their own, and almost all infants of this age can maintain a sitting posture once they are put into it by another person. Faw and Belkin (1989) note that most six- to seven-month-olds can sit in a high chair, but that accomplishment comes slightly before the ability to sit without external support. Craig (1989) indicates that more than half of all eight-month-olds can stand while holding on to a support, and about half can bring themselves to a standing position (p. 147). Some smaller proportion can move about in a sidewise stepping motion while holding on to the sides of a crib or playpen; some

Table 15-1 Developmental Checklist—12 Months

Child's Name _____   Age _____

Observer _____   Date _____

Developmental Checklist	Yes	No	Sometimes
By 12 months, does the child:			
Walk with assistance?			
Roll a ball in imitation of an adult?			
Pick up objects with thumb and forefinger?			
Transfer objects from one hand to other hand?			
Pick up dropped toys?			
Look directly at adult's face?			
Imitate gestures: peek-a-boo, bye-bye, pat-a-cake?			
Find object hidden under a cup?			
Feed self crackers (munching, not sucking on them)?			
Hold cup with two hands; drink with assistance?			
Smile spontaneously?			
Pay attention to own name?			
Respond to "no"?			
Respond differently to strangers and familiar persons?			
Respond differently to sounds: vacuum, phone, door?			
Look at person who speaks to him or her?			
Respond to simple directions accompanied by gestures?			
Make several consonant–vowel combination sounds?			
Vocalize back to person who has talked to him or her?			
Use intonation patterns that sound like scolding, asking, exclaiming?			
Say "da-da" or "ma-ma"?			

Table 15-2 Developmental Checklist—2 Years

Child's Name _____   Age _____

Observer _____   Date _____

Developmental Checklist	Yes	No	Sometimes
By 2 years, does the child:			
Walk alone?			
Bend over and pick up toy without falling over?			
Seat self in child-sized chair? Walk up and down stairs with assistance?			
Place several rings on a stick?			
Place 5 pegs in a peg-board?			
Turn pages 2 or 3 at a time?			
Scribble?			
Follow one-step direction involving something familiar: "Give me _." "Show me_." "Get a _."			
Match familiar objects?			
Use spoon with some spilling?			
Drink from cup holding it with one hand, unassisted?			
Chew food?			
Take off coat, shoe, sock?			
Zip and unzip large zipper?			
Recognize self in mirror or picture?			
Refer to self by name?			
Imitate adult behaviors in play—for example, feeds "baby"?			
Help put things away?			
Respond to specific words by showing what was named: toy, pet, family member?			
Ask for desired items by name: (cookie)?			
Answer with name of object when asked "What's that"?			
Make some 2-word statements: "Daddy bye-bye"?			

Table 15-3 Age (in Months) of Acquisition of Selected Motor Abilities of Infants and Toddlers (Summary of Craig's [1989] Data Discussed in This Chapter)				
4 Months	**8 Months**	**12 Months**	**18 Months**	**24 Months**
Holds chest up from stomach position	Gets into sitting position on his/her own; can maintain sitting posture if put there by another person	Typically takes first unsupported steps	Almost certainly can walk alone; can carry things in his/her hands while walking	Can walk and run, pedal a tricycle, jump in place with both feet, balance short time on one foot, throw over-hand fairly well
Holds head steady while sitting sup-ported by an adult	Half of all eight-month-olds can stand holding on to a support as well as bring self to a standing position	Can manipulate a number of objects (undo latches, open cabinets, pull toys, twist lamp cords)	Usually can stack from 2 to 4 blocks to build a tower; can scribble with crayon or pencil	Climbs steps and sometimes comes down with help; crawls into, over, around, and under various objects
Reaches and grasps for an object—con-tact infrequent	Typically can crawl or creep on hands and knees	Acquires pincer grasp—opposition of thumb and fore-finger	Increasing ability to feed self; can partly undress self	Places things into and takes things out of containers; pours water, molds clay, generally ma-nipulates objects to the fullest extent
Visual tracking be-gins at about 3 1/2 months	Most can pass objects from hand to hand; some can use thumb and fore-finger to grasp; most can hand objects back and forth to an adult			Transports items in carts, wagons, carriages, or trucks; explores, tests, and probes

even have the early ability to walk while holding on to a piece of furniture for support, an ability sometimes referred to as cruising.

The typical eight-month-old can move from place to place by crawling (with the body on the ground) or by creeping on the hands and knees (Craig, 1989, p. 147). Faw and Belkin (1989) note that at about seven months, infants might thrust "one knee forward as they lie on their stomach." This, say Faw and Belkin, "is the initial step in learning to crawl" (p. 40). These authors claim that by eight months ("34 weeks"), the average child has the capacity to crawl, but they point out that because there is not sufficient arm and leg strength, he cannot yet keep the stomach off the ground by creeping on the hands and knees.

With regard to hand and arm control, Craig (1989) indicates that most eight-month-olds can "pass objects from hand to hand, and some are able to use the thumb and

By the age of eight months, most infants can maintain a sitting posture, and more than half can stand if supported.

The typical eight-month-old moves from place to place by crawling.

finger to grasp" (p. 149). She also reports that infants of this age can usually "bang two objects together" (p. 149). Craig also notes that most eight-month-olds can hand an object back and forth to an adult, an activity they very much enjoy doing.

Twelve Months

Faw and Belkin (1989), distinguishing between "supported walking" and "independent walking" (p. 141), report that children typically take their first unsupported (independent), albeit unsteady, steps a short time after their first birthday. Subsequent development of the ability to locomote progresses quickly from that milestone accomplishment, say Faw and Belkin. Craig (1989) writes that 12-month-olds "actively manipulate the environment. They are able to undo latches, open cabinets, pull toys, and twist lamp cords" (p. 149). She also mentions the acquisition of a pincer grasp, which should be distinguished from the ulnar grasp, which Berk (2006) describes as "a clumsy motion in which the fingers close against the palm" (p. 147). The pincer grasp enables the infant to oppose the thumb and forefinger. This cortical opposition ability, in turn, enables the child to pick up quite small objects such as hairs, pins, coins, and so on. With this and other new abilities, however, the child can also get into many more things (and much more trouble) than she could heretofore: She can "turn on the television set and the stove, … explore kitchen cupboards, open windows, and poke things into electrical outlets" (Craig, 1989, p. 149).

Eighteen Months

Children 18 months of age are almost without exception walking alone. They often like to carry things in their hands or push or pull some kind of object as they walk (Craig, 1989, p. 150). They have a very hard time as yet doing such things as kicking a ball, jumping, or pedaling a tricycle (p. 150).

Eighteen-month-olds, according to Craig, are generally capable of "stacking from two to four blocks to build a tower, and often they can manage to scribble with crayon or pencil" (p. 150). At this age, children frequently show increased ability to feed themselves and can even partly undress themselves (p. 150). However, dressing oneself is apparently an appreciably more difficult task than taking clothes off, and for that reason, dressing comes later in development.

Twenty-Four Months

The gains in abilities between 18 and 24 months of age seem quite astonishing. As Craig (1989) puts it,

> Two-year-olds can not only walk and run, but they can usually pedal a tricycle, jump in place on both feet, balance briefly on one foot, and accomplish a fairly good overhand throw. They climb up steps and, sometimes, come down again with assistance. They crawl into, under, around, and over objects and furniture; they manipulate, carry, handle, push, or pull anything they see. They put things into and take things out of large containers. They pour water, mold clay, stretch the stretchable, and bend the bendable. They transport items in carts, wagons, carriages, or trucks. They explore, test, and probe. (p. 151)

Perhaps her concluding statement is of the greatest importance: "All this exploration provides a vital learning experience about the nature and possibilities of their physical world" (p. 151). This, of course, is what development is all about.

To bring this section of this first exercise or unit to a close, we present in summary form Faw and Belkin's discussion of the "phases of object manipulation." We do this because the ability to reach for, grasp, and manipulate objects is so critical. Indeed, it could be argued that our hand or manual dexterity is among the central attributes that set us apart from the rest of the animal kingdom, with language or symbol use certainly being another key distinguishing characteristic of human behavior and ability.

The authors identify a "prereaching period" and an "early reaching period" (Faw & Belkin, 1989, p. 144). The first period comprises about the first two or two and one-half months, during which time the newborn or infant does not reach for objects but merely stares at them if they come into view. (See also Berk [1989] for reference to, and a discussion of, prereaching.) The second, early reaching period, begins at about two and one-half months of age, when "children begin to reach for objects that they see" (p. 144). Again, however, such behavior is poorly controlled and usually fails to hit the intended target. Let's look now at the two phases discussed by Faw and Belkin.

Phase I, say Faw and Belkin, evidences "various stages of object manipulation," but they write in terms of the characteristics of the skills that represent those stages. Phase I characteristics follow:

Phase I

1. Reaching and grasping are not engaged in as separate acts. That is to say, they lack differentiation and demonstrate instead the characteristics of mass action. Faw and Belkin also point out that this aspect of hand use demonstrates the principle of proximodistal development. This is simply development that proceeds from the midline (proximo) of the body outwards to the extremities (distal).

2. The infant in Phase I cannot yet use two arms at the same time.

3. Control of hand and arm movements is relatively absent. Once initiated, the infant in Phase I cannot stop a reaching movement, nor can she adjust a reaching movement if it is inaccurate and off target.

4. Grasping in Phase I is not performed in conjunction with how the object feels to the infant. Instead, reaching and grasping are directed by the visual presence of the object as well as by the object's visual relationship to the hand.

Adapted from Faw and Belkin, 1989, p. 144.

Faw and Belkin indicate that the "obvious switching of attention back and forth between the grasping hand and the object to be grasped" ends by five months of age, and the infant now "moves his or her hand directly to the object" (p. 145). The authors note that although the movements are well coordinated, they nonetheless still belong in Phase I because "the reach and grasp are controlled by the visual presence of the object sought and are a unitary action rather than two separate actions" (p. 145). They also note, importantly, that a grasping response will still be made once the reaching is initiated, even if the hand does not actually touch the object. This phenomenon occurs because the infant cannot yet completely control bodily actions. It is as though once begun, a movement or gesture simply must be finished, despite the fact that nothing will be accomplished by it.

Five months of age, say Faw and Belkin, denotes the division or transition between Phase I and Phase II. Phase II has the following characteristics:

Phase II

1. In this phase, infants reach and grasp with two hands, not just one.

2. Infants are able to correct errors in reaching once they are detected.

3. Reaching and grasping now become separable activities, and each can be engaged in independently of the other.

4. Visual presence of the object is no longer the primary impetus for grasping; now contact with the object is the controlling factor.

Adapted from Faw and Belkin, 1989, p. 146.

Some of the objectives found in this chapter will provide you with a number of options that are absent in the other exercise chapters. The age span from 1 to 24 months comprises a large number of developmental changes that cannot be observed and recorded by any single individual. Moreover, it is also likely that you will have less opportunity to observe infants and toddlers than you will children of preschool age. This fact almost necessitates that we give you enough alternatives so that you can observe the behavior of at least one child in this important first stage of life.

Observation Objectives

(1) To observe and describe the physical characteristics of a child anywhere between 1 month and 24 months of age and compare them with the physical characteristics of the newborn observed in Exercise 15-1, and/or (2) to observe and record the motor behavior of an infant between 1 and 24 months of age. This objective should be done in conjunction with objective (1), which means that you can observe the same infant for both parts of the assignment, and/or (3) to compare and contrast the motor skills of at least two infants who are of appreciably different ages (e.g., 10 months and

18 months)—the goal here is to chart, in a cross-sectional way, the developmental progress that an infant makes over the space of several months.

Procedure

For Objective (1) of this exercise, measure the child's weight, total height, and the length of the head, trunk, and legs. Compare these measurements with those you obtained on a newborn, and summarize the differences. If a comparison with a

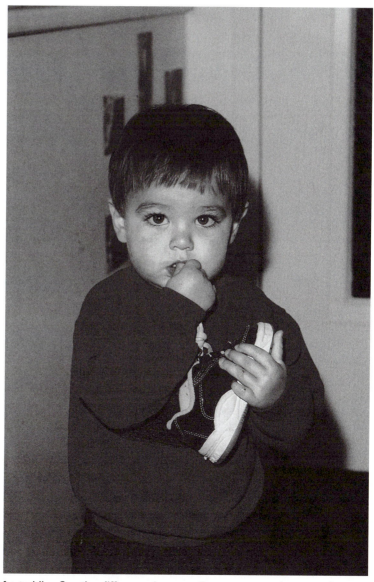

Face of a toddler. See the difference in proportion as compared to a newborn.

newborn is not possible, simply determine whether the infant's physical characteristics correspond to what you would normatively expect for his or her age.

For Objective (2) of this exercise, use the event sampling format and observe and record all the infant's motor behaviors for two or three five-minute periods. Distribute your observations to get a varied sample of the infant's abilities rather than an extended display of pretty much the same behaviors. In other words, try to get examples of reaching and grasping, crawling or creeping, walking, cruising, and so on, depending on the infant's age or developmental level. Compare the infant's abilities with norms for his or her age.

For Objective (3), you will observe and record in event sampling format two infants' large and fine motor skills as specified in the observation exercise sheet. You may have to encourage the infants to exhibit some of the skills listed if they do not display them spontaneously. *Encourage* here means demonstrating what you want them to do. We permit such encouragement in this instance because we want you to compare and contrast the two infants' abilities on the same tasks.

You should have on hand such items as a few raisins, four to six small blocks, a small container with lid (large enough to hold several of the blocks), beads and a piece of string, a book or magazine, play dough, and a crayon. Some of these items may already be part of the infants' or toddlers' toy collection. Observe and record the following fine motor tasks: (1) stacking several blocks (determine how many they can stack); (2) picking up a raisin (what grasping technique do they use?); (3) placing some of the blocks in the container and removing them again; (4) pulling, squeezing, or pounding play dough; (5) turning the pages of a book; and (6) scribbling with a crayon. The larger motor skills you are to observe are self-explanatory. Ideally, pick subjects who are old enough to display at least some of the behaviors described here but who are sufficiently different in age to show developmental differences in performance or competence.

This exercise falls under Fogel's sensorimotor/tool-using competency area. Can you observe the infants using an object in any way that qualifies as tool use? Naturally, the probability of tool-using behavior increases as the infant's age increases. Therefore, do not look for such behavior in a very young infant.

There is no set amount of time you are to observe, but complete the exercise. (See Observation Exercise 15-1.)

Question Guides

The following questions use language that seemingly emphasizes the observation of two infants. If you cannot perform that objective, simply refer to the questions in terms of one infant; none of the meaning will be lost.

1. If you observe a toddler, does he possess any physical–motor characteristics that might explain the term *toddler*? Explain.

2. What is the overall character or quality of the two infants' large muscle actions? Generally smooth and accurate, or rough and imprecise? How do they differ?

What differences would you predict based on their respective ages or developmental levels?

3. Are there large muscle actions that the infants perform easily and others they have difficulty with? Is there any apparent relationship between their abilities and the kinds of activities they choose? That is, do they try things that they do not do very well, or do they seem to stay with those activities they do best? Elaborate on your answers.

4. Do the infants show any signs of preferring one foot over the other? One hand over the other? If so, how do they demonstrate their preference (e.g., kicking a ball, the foot they lead with when stepping up a stair, the hand they use to pick up objects)?

5. How many blocks can the infants stack? What best characterizes their efforts to stack blocks? Quick and sure? Slow and uncertain?

6. When picking up a small object such as a raisin, which fingers do the infants use? What part do their thumbs play? Are they at first unsuccessful in their efforts and then succeed by changing their approach or grasping style?

7. Are there any differences between the way the infants grasp a large object such as a block and a small object such as a raisin? Explain such differences.

8. How do their large and fine motor skills compare with the norms for children their age? What skills or responses would you predict they could do fairly well, and which would you predict they could not do at all? Can you rank them in order of increasing difficulty, based on the norms provided, and then rank them based on how well they actually performed? How do the two rankings compare with each other?

9. What locomotor skills do the infants exhibit? If an infant is just beginning to walk, what proportion of time does she spend walking as opposed to crawling or creeping?

10. Which of Faw and Belkin's phases of reaching and grasping development describe the two infants? On what specific behaviors do you base your conclusion?

EXERCISE 15-2: SOCIAL BEHAVIOR OF THE INFANT (1 to 24 MONTHS)

Background Information

When two or more persons take each other into account and influence each other in some way, their behavior is social behavior. The infant most assuredly influences others, and, in an elementary way, he also takes others into account. The infant exerts influence every time an adult responds to his crying, smiling, and vocalizing. When the child changes his behavior to adjust to someone else's characteristics and responses, he is taking that person into account.

There are a few infant behaviors that adults consider especially significant socially. Crying is an important response from the moment of birth; it signals that something is wrong and requires attention. Throughout childhood, crying continues to be a form of communication; it is often disturbing to adults, who take quick action to stop it. Smiling, along with specific eye contact, is particularly gratifying to adults, and the first true social smile—which appears by around six weeks—often makes parents ecstatic. Bower (1977) offers several reasons why infants smile: "(1) ... human beings around them. (2) ... any high contrast stimuli, which elicits attention from those around them and causes the infant to link the human face with pleasure. (3) ... at discovering a relationship between their behavior and events in the external world" (as cited in Travers, 1982, p. 56). Discussions of the infant's social behavior and competence often include the subject of **attachment**. Attachment is considered present when one person is dependent on another person for emotional satisfaction. One psychologist defines *attachment* as "an affectional tie that one person forms to another specific person, binding them together in space and enduring over time" (Ainsworth, 1973, p. 1, cited in Travers, 1982, p. 329). Seifert and Hoffnung (1987), also citing Ainsworth, emphasize an additional aspect of attachment by indicating that attachment is "a relationship that is characterized by reciprocal affection and *a shared desire to maintain physical closeness*" (p. 271, italics added).

Attachment develops in stages that have been described by a number of researchers. It is thought to be essential to healthy development, and some psychologists believe that attachment forms the basic foundation for much of the child's future social development and relationships. Table 15-4 depicts some typical characteristics and behaviors associated with attachment, and Table 15-5 presents Mary Ainsworth's (1967, 1973) three stages in the development of attachment (adapted from Travers, 1982, p. 331).

The concept of basic trust versus mistrust is another aspect of social behavior. Trust versus mistrust is the first of eight psychosocial stages in Erik Erikson's theory of personality development. Psychosocial stages, according to Craig (1989), are "periods in life during which the individual's capacities for experience dictate that he or she must make major adjustments to the social environment and the self" (p. 41). However, the adjustment to be made is determined by the individual's developmental level and receptiveness to experience. Basic trust versus mistrust should be resolved during the first 18 months to 2 years. If things go well, the infant will resolve this first conflict by establishing a stronger sense of trust than of mistrust in his physical–social environment. Whether trust or mistrust becomes the stronger feeling depends on how the infant is treated and on whether or not he sees the world as a predominantly safe, nurturing, and reliable place. Achieving feelings of trust requires interactions between

attachment
A condition process in which one person is dependent on another for emotional satisfaction and support; attachment forms with specific other persons and is enduring over time.

Table 15-4 The Development of Attachment: Bowlby's Four Phases		
Age	**Attachment Phase**	**Behavioral Characteristics**
0 to 6 wks.	Preattachment phase	Infant displays a number of signals that bring the caregiver into close proximity—smiling, crying, grasping, visual contact. The infant's positive responses to the caregiver—feeling comforted, cessation of crying—motivates her to stay with the infant and to continue the caregiving activities. Infant not yet attached, however, because he does not mind being left with an unfamiliar person or the mother's absence (shows no stranger or separation anxiety).
6 wks. to 6-8 mos.	Attachment-in-the-making phase	Now infant evidences different responses to a familiar caregiver(s) than to a stranger; she responds to mother in ways that clearly demonstrate recognition of the mother. Infant begins to learn a sort of cause-and-effect relationship between what she does and her mother's responses to her behaviors—she is learning that she has an effect on her environment. Also begins to develop Erikson's sense of trust. A clear-cut attachment still not present, however, because child does not yet show separation anxiety in the mother's absence.
6-8 mos. to 18-24 mos.	Clear-cut attachment phase	Infant shows unequivocal signs of separation anxiety. This reaction indicates that the infant has the concept of object (person) permanence. Child uses mother or other attachment target as a secure physical and psychological base from which to explore the environment and from which to receive emotional support and assurance. Child makes deliberate efforts to keep mother/attachment figure close to him.
18 mos. to 24 mos. and beyond	Formation of a reciprocal goal-directed relationship or partnership	Child's increasing cognitive skills enable her to understand some of the factors that play a role in the parents' activities and responses to the child. These beyond cognitive and social skills permit more of a negotiating style of interacting with the parent rather than protesting, crying, or constantly seeking physical proximity to the parent in order to get what the child wants.

Based on the work of Bowlby (1969). Table adapted from Berk, 1996, pp. 266–267.

the adult and child that are consistent and effectively match the psychological characteristics of both of them. As Gander and Gardner (1981) put it, "Trust results when mother and infants coordinate their behaviors to one another's temperaments and needs and are consistent and reasonable" (p. 201). The physical environment must also be perceived as reasonably safe and predictable. This perception is affected by the infant's learning that his behaviors have predictable consequences. For example, he shakes his crib, and a mobile above him moves. Or, as he learns to control his body, he increases his sense of security and confidence as he functions in a world of space, objects, and natural laws.

Table 15-5 Stages in the Development of Attachment	
Stage	**Characteristics**
1	During the first months after birth, there is increasing social responsiveness on the part of the infant. She does not yet distinguish her primary caregiver from others in the environment who may pick her up or care for her.
2	At about six months, the infant engages in active proximity seeking, which is evidenced by such responses as consistently seeking attention and contact with the mother or other primary caregiver, and/or by stranger anxiety. This behavior continues through the second year.
3	Near the age of three years, child exhibits partnership behavior; she tries to participate in the mutual give-and-take aspects of social interactions. Also has an identity separate from the parent.

Observation Objectives

To observe and record (1) the infant's general social behaviors and interaction patterns with others, (2) behaviors that indicate attachment, and (3) the effect of observed and reported qualities of the infant's temperament on the interactions between her and others in her familiar surroundings. Also, to use data from different recording methods to draw conclusions about the child's social behavior and temperament, and about the usefulness of different methods in a particular situation.

Procedures

This is a three-part exercise, although each part can stand as an independent exercise. In Part I, you will use the narrative description method of recording. You should observe for about three 10-minute sessions within a 60- to 90-minute period, depending on your circumstances. Refer to the guide questions that are provided. You will be asked to record your interpretive comments. Make certain that your inferences are related to your observed data: Do not make an interpretation that is not supported by your objective behavioral description. The information from Part I will also be used in Parts II and III.

In Part II, you will use a time sampling and frequency count format. You will also be using the observation data obtained in Part I. You will note on the checklist whether the infant displays attachment behaviors during the specified time intervals. In this part of the exercise, you are asked to determine the observing and recording intervals to be used. As a general procedure, you may want to divide your recording time into a series of equal intervals, such as ten 10-second periods. Choose another short period of time (e.g., 10 seconds) between each recording interval during which you will only observe. Wait for a time (perhaps five minutes), and repeat the process at least twice more. For this part of the exercise, the parent or another familiar caregiver must be with the child, or he is not likely to show attachment behaviors. After you have collected your data, answer the questions that follow Part II.

Part III requires you to integrate information on the infant's general social responses and interaction patterns, which you will have obtained in Part I, and information on the child's temperament. Data on temperament will be acquired from your observations and the parent's report. Table 15-6 describes the characteristics of various temperaments. First observe and record the infant's behavior over two or three 10-minute sessions using the narrative description format. When the data are collected, analyze the record for examples of behaviors and descriptions of characteristics that fit any of the information on temperament in Table 15-7. In the second phase of this exercise, ask the parent specific questions about the child's temperament. The information given in Table 15-6 and Table 15-7 can help you formulate these questions.

Finally, answer the questions that follow Part III. It is in answering these questions that you will integrate the two sets of information. (See Observation Exercise 15-2.)

Table 15-6 Temperamental Qualities	
Activity Level	Activity can begin in the uterus, where an active fetus can kick frequently. Active babies move around in their cribs or basinets; they prefer to climb or run rather than engage in more placid activities. Other babies show much less vigorous activity levels.
Rhythmicity	Rhythmicity is characterized by regular cycles of activity—eating, sleeping, and bowel movements that occur pretty much on schedule. Other infants are not as predictable.
Approach/ Withdrawal	Approach is an attitude of delight or acceptance when confronted with something new—laughter at first bath, readily eating new food. Withdrawal is a refusal to accept new situations.
Adaptability	Characterized by rapid adjustment to change; no severe negative reactions to disruption of normal routines. Some babies do not easily tolerate change or deviations from the familiar.
Intensity of Reaction	Some children laugh loudly, scream when they cry. Others merely smile, whimper, or cry softly.
Quality of Mood	Some children are generally bright and cheerful; they smile easily. Other children seem generally unhappy and discontent, seem constantly to complain.

Adapted from Berger, 1980, pp. 91.

Table 15-7 Temperamental Qualities at One and Two Years			
Temperamental Quality	**Rating**	**Behavioral Characteristics**	
		One Year	**Two Years**
Activity Level	Low	Slow to finish bottle; falls asleep without a fuss; does not resist caretaking activities such as diapering or nail cutting.	Plays quietly with toys; can attend to an activity for long period of time (e.g., listening to a record or watching TV).
	High	Moves quickly, enjoys eating; gets into everything—climbing, crawling, and so on.	Still gets into everything; curious about things, explores; may do such things as resist going to bed by repeatedly getting up out of the bed (Dworetzky, 1987, p. 111).
Rhythmicity	Regular	Regularly naps after a meal and takes a bottle before bedtime. Shows similar regularity and predictability of other bodily functions—bowel movements, waking, and sleeping.	Eating patterns regular and predictable; eats heartily every day, snacks before bedtime.
	Irregular	Very slow in falling asleep; bowel movements unpredictable. Other bodily functions also unpredictable.	Inconsistent nap times. Unpredictable bowel movements make toilet training difficult (Dworetzky, 1987, p. 111).
Approach/Withdrawal	Positive	Not afraid of strangers; not leery of new foods, objects. Sleep not disturbed by new surroundings.	"Slept well the first time he stayed overnight at grandparents' house" (Dworetzky, 1987, p. 111).
	Negative	Cries at new activities, experiences. Sleep disturbed by strange surroundings. Cries or withdraws at presence of strangers.	Resists new experiences. Does not readily interact with strange children. "Whimpers first time at beach. Will not go into water" (Dworetzky, 1987, p. 111).
Adaptability	Adaptive	Initial fear or hesitation with strange toys or objects fairly quickly overcome. Initial rejection of new food also replaced by acceptance.	"Obeys quickly" (Dworetzky, 1987, p. 111). Will remain in a place for a long time without feeling anxious—e.g., "stays contentedly with grandparents for a week" (Dworetzky, 1987, p. 111).

(continues)

		One Year	Two Years
	Not Adaptive	New foods, experiences continue to be resisted, rejected. Generally lacks positive response to new things.	"Obedience lacking or not readily displayed" (Dworetzky, 1987, p. 111). Strongly resists some caretaking activities—e.g., getting haircut (p 111).
Intensity of Reaction	Mild	Response to various experiences is not strong or vigorous; does not protest having things done to him or her—e.g., clothing pulled over head (Dworetzky, 1987, p. 111).	Responds mildly to other's behavior directed at him or her, for example, being hit, having a toy snatched away (Dworetzky, 1987, p. 111).
	Intense	Emotional and behavioral responses generally strong, vigorous. Rough-and-tumble play evokes loud laughter, screaming; also resists such things as having temperature taken (Dworetzky, 1987, p. 111).	Loudly displays excitement when playing or pleased with something. Shows strong protest if denied something such as a toy.
Quality of Mood	Positive	Enjoys eating; reaches for bottle and shows positive affect. Strong reaction to interaction games such as peek-a-boo (Dworetzky, 1987, p. 111).	Plays with siblings and shows positive feelings. Displays satisfaction when successful at accomplishing a task—e.g., putting shoes on (Dworetzky, 1987, p. 111).
	Negative	Does not like being left alone. Cries at mildly painful experiences such as injections (Dworetzky, 1987, p. 111).	Resists such experiences as haircuts; displays separation anxiety when mother leaves.

Table 15-7 Temperamental Qualities at One and Two Years (Continued)

Adapted from Dworetzky, 1987, p. 111.

Questions, Part I

1. Does the infant initiate social contacts with others in the environment? How does he go about it? By verbalizing? By establishing physical contact? By crying? By sharing a toy?

2. How does the other person react to the infant's social behaviors? Does the adult focus her attention on the infant and try to sustain the interaction, or does she cut short her response to him as though his overtures were an inconvenience? Explain.

3. Does the infant smile? How frequently, and at what? How do others react to his smiling? Does their reaction have any observable effect on the child's subsequent behaviors? Explain.

4. How does the infant respond to you, the observer? Does he show fear and uncertainty? Withdrawal? Does he approach and try to engage you in play or other interaction? If he approaches you, how long does it take him to do so? Is there a period of adjustment on his part? How long is that period?

5. Which physical features of the infant or toddler do you think may be attractive to the adult in his setting or to adults in general? Does the adult present during your observations make any comments about baby features she finds appealing? If so, does she respond in any way to those features? How?

6. What is the adult's response to the child's crying? How tolerant does the adult seem to be of the baby's crying? Is the adult's response immediate, delayed slightly, delayed for a long time? How does the infant respond to the adult's efforts to stop his crying? If the adult is successful, does she stop her interactions with the child, or does she take the opportunity to engage in further social contacts? Does the child seem to cry excessively?

7. Is there specific eye-to-eye contact between the adult and the infant? How does each respond to such contact? How long does the baby maintain this contact? How and for how long does the adult try to establish contact if he is not immediately successful?

8. Where does the child fit in terms of Fogel's social/interactive area of competence? Does the infant have any concept of sharing or taking turns? Is the infant old enough to be aware of his role as "a partner in an interaction with an adult"? Explain.

Questions, Part II

(These are not guide questions. They are questions you are to answer in writing.)

1. What percentage of the total time observed did the infant exhibit each of the attachment behaviors sampled? What percentage of the total time observed did the child exhibit nonattachment behaviors? How do these frequencies compare with each other, and what is the ratio between them?

2. Analyze your narrative description data (from Part I) for attachment behaviors. If there are any, count how often they occurred. How does this frequency count compare with the count obtained from your time sample? Do you feel more comfortable with one set of figures than with the other? If so, why? Was time sampling an appropriate method to use under the circumstances? Why or why not?

3. On the basis of Ainsworth's three stages of attachment (Table 15-5) and the information given in Table 15-5, can you tell from your time-sampled data which stage of attachment the infant is in? Can you tell from your narrative description? Is one a better basis for judgment than the other? If so, which one, and why?

Questions, Part III

(These questions are to be answered in writing.)

1. How do your decisions or judgments regarding the child's temperament compare with the parent's reported descriptions of her temperament? Going back to your narrative description data, whose conclusions about the child's temperament seem more accurate?

2. Does the child's behavior as you observed it correspond with the parent's report? That is, could you have used the parent's perceptions of the child to predict the infant's behaviors with reasonable accuracy? Explain.

3. What general conclusions do you reach about the usefulness of the concept of temperament? Why do you draw the conclusions you do?

EXERCISE 15-3: COGNITIVE AND LANGUAGE BEHAVIOR OF THE INFANT (1 to 24 MONTHS)

Background Information

Many of the behaviors you have observed to this point are related to the infant's cognitive and language development. From Piaget's theoretical perspective, motor and perceptual functions (the essential components of the sensorimotor period) are the foundation of cognitive development. Early motor responses first allow the infant to handle objects, to bang, pull, push, drop, and roll them. These are necessary activities, says Piaget, because the child learns about objects by doing something with them. He cannot yet learn about the world by thinking and reasoning. Eventually, the infant becomes mobile, which puts him into more direct contact with the environment. Progressing from having objects brought to him to going to objects on his own changes both the quantity and the quality of his experiences.

The infant, like everyone else, gets information about his world through seeing, hearing, touching, tasting, and smelling. But merely receiving information is not enough; he must do something with it. Language and cognition, which includes thinking, knowledge, memory, problem solving, reasoning, and concepts, provide the means of processing and using information.

There are several aspects of cognitive behavior that are relevant to the infant. One aspect is concept. As Gander and Gardner (1981) write, "A *concept* may be thought of as a mental representation or memory of something" (p. 143, italics original). Ault (1977) notes that concepts "represent the attributes common to several different events" (p. 89). Piaget's schema is a mental representation of events in the world. Concepts, however defined, provide ways of classifying and organizing our sensory information; they bring together features and qualities that are shared by concrete things or abstract ideas. For example, "dog" is a concept. When someone says "dog," we might think of such things as many different species (collie, German shepherd, terrier); four-legged animal; furbearing, carnivorous, domesticated house pet; and "Rover."

It is generally assumed that infants do not have the same kinds of concepts as adults do, that the infant's concepts are not as sophisticated or as abstract as those of adults. If babies can think, Piaget argued that they do so primarily in sensorimotor ways—that is, through active hands-on involvement with objects in their environment —without the benefit of mental operations or use of the symbolic function (language). We do not debate the issue here, but it is not unreasonable to maintain that infants do have and use at least rudimentary concepts. Certainly they can distinguish among many objects and people in their surroundings: They know their parents from strangers or friends, food that they may eat from things that they may only be able or allowed to put in their mouth, and so on.

Habituation is used by some psychologists (see Willemsen [1979] or Sroufe and Cooper [1988], for example) to infer the presence of concepts or memory even in the newborn. "When something new is perceived in the environment," write Sroufe and Cooper (1988), "attention tends to be focused on it. If it is repeated over and over, it loses its ability to draw attention" (p. 149). This is the phenomenon of habituation. If the infant (or anyone else) reorients to a new stimulus, it is logical to believe that he must have a concept of the first stimulus to know that the second one is different in some way. Sroufe and Cooper (1988) note that habituation "has provided the basis for a very powerful research technique used to study infants" (p. 150). Stranger anxiety also requires the possession of concepts. The child has to recognize that what he perceives about a stranger is somehow different from his concept of a familiar person.

object permanence
The understanding that objects continue to exist even when out of sight or hearing; this is the most important achievement of the sensorimotor period.

For Piaget, **object permanence** is the crowning achievement of the sensorimotor period and provides the basis for all further cognitive development. When a child has the concept of object permanence, he understands that objects continue to exist even when out of sight or hearing. "Out of sight, out of mind" characterizes the infant who has not yet achieved object permanence. Object permanence develops through a series of stages (see Table 15-8) and is complete by the end of the sensorimotor period at about two years of age.

The sensorimotor period is divided into the six subperiods depicted in Table 15-9. Piaget used the idea of sensorimotor schemes, which are organized actions or sequences of actions that permit the individual to interact with the environment. Schemes become modified through learning and provide the foundation for more complex schemes and learning.

Table 15-8 Piaget's Stages of Object Permanence

Stage	Approximate Ages	Chief Characteristics
I.	0 to 1 month	No object permanence
II.	1 to 4 months	No object permanence or organization of space
III.	4 to 8 months	Start of permanence; infant begins to grasp for objects but does not continue to search for hidden objects
IV.	8 to 12 months	Continues search for hidden objects but in a random, haphazard fashion
V.	12 to 18 months	Searches for hidden objects in correct place but is confused if object's location is changed
VI.	18 months up	Has image of object and searches for it in various places

Adapted from Travers, 1982, p. 234.

Table 15-9 The Six Substages of Piaget's Sensorimotor Period (Including the Stages of Object Permanence)

Substage	Age	Principal Characteristics
I: Reflexive substage	0 to 1 mos.	Infant mostly uses his reflexes, over which he gradually gains control. He cannot yet demonstrate sensory coordination—i.e., he cannot, for example, recognize the same object by using information coming from two or more of the five physical senses at the same time. No evidence of object permanence.
II: Primary Circular Reactions	1 to 4 mos.	Infant capitalizes on chance occurrences of actions. He engages in repetitive behaviors (thus the term *circular*) that primarily involve his own body—e.g., sucking the fingers, watching his hands and feet—rather than the external environment. No evidence of object permanence.
III: Secondary Circular Reactions	4 to 8 mos.	Interactions with the external environment assume importance. Infant repeats behaviors that involve objects in the environment. Infant shows the beginning of intentional behavior, which he repeats because he enjoys the consequences of his actions. Infant shows the beginning of object permanence by starting to grasp for objects, although he will not continue to search for an object that is hidden.
IV: Coordination of Secondary Schema	8 to 12 mos.	Infant now combines existing behaviors in order to achieve some goal. He uses specific behaviors as a means to achieve a goal (ends). Infant will now continue to search for hidden objects, but his search is not organized or methodical; it is random and haphazard.

(continues)

Table 15-9 The Six Substages of Piaget's Sensorimotor Period (Including the Stages of Object Permanence) (Continued)		
Substage	**Age**	**Principal Characteristics**
V: Tertiary Reactions	12 to 18 mos.	Infant repeats actions because they are novel or unfamiliar. He devises and experiments with new means to achieve various ends. Infant can search for and successfully find hidden objects in one location but is confused if the object is moved to a different place.
VI: Beginning of Thought	18 to 24 mos.	Infant is ready to enter the preoperational stage of cognitive development. He moves from sensorimotor intelligence to representational intelligence, which means he can deal with symbolic or mental representations of objects. He uses thought to develop and achieve new goals. Infant has a true concept of the object and will search for it even if it is moved from one location to another and he does not witness the transfer.

Adapted from Travers (1982) and Wadsworth (1984).

There are two other Piagetian concepts that help explain cognitive development and behavior throughout the life span: assimilation and accommodation. **Assimilation** occurs when the person attempts to make a stimulus or event fit what she already knows or knows how to do. The infant deals with reality by using existing sensorimotor schemes. For example, if an infant can pick up objects with a palmar grasp, she may try to pick up small, flat ones in the same way. But, if efforts to assimilate do not succeed, then progress depends on the infant making changes in her sensorimotor scheme. The infant has to **accommodate** to the novel features of the situation. The infant in this example will have accommodated if the infant changes the grasping scheme from a palmar grasp to a thumb and forefinger (pincer) grasp to pick up the small, flat object. Accommodation does not occur automatically; the child must be developmentally ready for it.

The reinforcement theory of learning has also had a significant impact on developmental psychology. This view holds that individuals behave as they do because their behavior has led to consequences they found rewarding: The response is reinforced. This form of learning is known as operant conditioning. A key point about operant conditioning is that an individual is more likely to repeat a behavior if its consequences are satisfying than if they are unpleasant and punishing.

A second major type of learning is classical conditioning. An important aspect of classical conditioning is that it involves involuntary behavior, which is behavior over which we have little to no control. What is especially significant about classical conditioning is that emotional responses can be learned in this way. Classical conditioning begins with an event that naturally causes a response (as when hunger causes a dog to salivate in the presence of food). This event can become associated with a second event that does not cause the response (e.g., the sound of a bell does not

Sensorimotor behavior is displayed by the child using this stacking toy.

cause salivation). Through a pairing of these two events, the second event (the bell) can acquire the ability to produce the response (the salivation) originally produced only by the first event (hunger). Imagine a child who is constantly punished by her uncle. Punishment causes anxiety and fear. Those emotions become associated with the uncle, and eventually his mere presence makes the child anxious and fearful.

Language

Language could be the single most significant accomplishment of the human species. Language is a complex set of written or spoken symbols that are combined according to special rules of grammar or syntax to communicate various kinds of information.

Table 15-10 Stages in the Development of Language	
Prelinguistic Speech	**Characteristics**
Undifferentiated Crying	A reflexive action; form of communication by which infant signals her needs.
Differentiated Crying	After one month, crying more precise; different patterns, intonations, intensities, and pitches reflect different emotional states.
Cooing	Six weeks, chance utterances of vowel sounds occur; become part of infant's expression of contentment.
Babbling	About 3 to 4 months, playful repetition of simple consonant and vowel sounds (ma-ma-ma, ba-ba-ba, etc.).
Echolalia	About 9 to 10 months, infant consciously imitates sounds of others, but without understanding.
Linguistic Speech	**Characteristics**
Holophrases	About 12 months, uses single word to express a thought ("ball" to mean "play ball with me," or "this is a ball," etc.). Average 1-year-old has 4- to 5-word vocabulary; 10-word vocabulary at about 15 months, and 50-word vocabulary by 19 months, by some studies (Nelson, 1973).
Telegraphic Speech	At about 24 months, child strings 2 or 3 words together to form a sentence. Only essential nouns and verbs are used.
Grammatically Correct Speech	By around 3 years, child may have a vocabulary of some 900 words; uses longer sentences with all parts of speech. Has grasp of grammatical principles, although his sentence constructions follow the rules too literally.

linguistic
Vocalizations that include actual words.

Language is acquired in a predictable series of stages that can be distinguished according to whether or not the child speaks intelligible words. Vocalizations that occur prior to speech are called *prelinguistic*, and those that include true words are called **linguistic**. Thus, we have two distinct periods of language development that are further subdivided into stages. These periods and stages are depicted in Table 15-10 and Table 15-11.

Observation Objectives

To observe and record various behaviors that indicate the level and characteristics of the infant's cognitive and language functioning, including such abilities as memory and conceptual thinking. To identify situations in which operant and classical conditioning might be occurring.

Age in Months	Manipulative Ability
	Table 15-11 Summary of Development of Eye–Hand Skills
1.5	Manual control consists only of grasp reflex; no coordinated grasping possible at this stage.
3	Uncoordinated swiping at objects is now possible. Infant also observes her own hands.
5.5	Infant can now reach for and grasp an object and bring it to the mouth. Might hold a bottle; bangs toys, manipulates such objects as a rattle.
6.5	Increased manipulation of objects; done with greater skill and coordination.
9.5	Shows the start of the pincer grasp, i.e., infant opposes the thumb and forefinger and can pick up relatively small objects.
10	Gains a number of new skills: can take the lid off a box; pokes or points with the index finger; has the ability to let go of objects intentionally; can begin to show a preference for the right or the left hand.
11.5	Infant can hold a crayon; she can remove small objects from a container such as a cup; intentional release of an object now easily accomplished and can be done for a purpose; can imitate scribbling.
13	Infant can now put small objects into a container as well as take them out; can build a tower 2 to 3 blocks high.
16	Infant can build a tower of 3 to 4 blocks; she can scribble with a crayon or pencil; turns pages of a book, but does so 2 to 3 pages at a time.
18 to 24	Infant now has a definite preference for one hand over the other; tower building increases to 4 to 6 blocks; can turn one page at a time.
24 to 30	Infant can now put a few beads on a string; she can mold clay by rolling, pounding, squeezing, and so on.

Adapted from Gander and Gardner, 1981, pp. 125–126.

Procedure

This exercise has three parts. In Part I, you will test the infant's concept of object permanence. You will need an attractive toy and two pieces of cloth large enough to completely cover the toy. Your test consists of the following steps: Step 1—seat the child in a chair and, after holding a toy in front of her so that she can see it, drop the toy on the floor. Observe and record her response (refer to the Guide Questions). Step 2—seat the child at a flat surface. Show the child the toy, making certain she sees it; then place the toy under the cloth while the child watches you do it. Observe and record the response.

visible displacement
Taking an object from one place of concealment (such as under a cloth) and moving it to another, allowing the child to watch you make the change. This is a technique used to test a child's concept of object permanence.

invisible displacement
Taking an object from one place of concealment (such as under a piece of cloth) and moving it to another, but not allowing the child to watch you make the change; this is a technique used to test a child's concept of object permanence.

Step 3—as the child watches, move the toy from under the first cloth and hide it under the second cloth (**visible displacement**). Observe and record the child's response. Step 4—hide the toy under the cloth as the child watches. Then, while the child cannot see what you are doing, hide the toy under the second cloth, but leave the first cloth in its original position (**invisible displacement**). Observe and record the child's response. (In all these steps, refer to the Question Guides for Part I.)

In Part II, observe the child for two to three 10-minute sessions and record in narrative description form the child's behaviors and relevant characteristics of the context. When you have completed your observations, analyze the narrative description for behaviors that indicate anything about what she has learned and her level of cognitive functioning. Look for behaviors that indicate whether the child is in Piaget's sensorimotor period; look for behaviors that identify which substage of the sensorimotor period the child is in. Also look for occasions when operant or classical conditioning might be occurring, such as when the parent responds with "Good girl, Mary!" when the child brings her a favorite toy, or when the parent punishes the child. (Refer to the Question Guides for Part II.)

In Part III you will be using an event sampling procedure to observe and record the infant's language behavior. Spend about 20 or 30 minutes in the child's context, but remain as inconspicuous as possible. Record verbatim the child's speech, to whom she speaks and under what circumstances, and the reactions of others to her communications. Also note behaviors that reflect the child's speech reception abilities—how much speech she understands. Also take note of the physical gestures the child might use in her efforts to communicate. (Refer to the Question Guides for Part III.) (See Observation Exercise 15-3.)

Question Guides, Part I

1. How does the child respond visually when the toy is dropped? Does she look for it? Does she look in the right place? That is, does she seem to know the path the toy will take as it falls? Explain.

2. How does the child respond when you hide the toy under the cloth in Step 2? Does she look for the toy under the cloth or somewhere else? Does she make any emotional or motor responses—for example, facial expressions that indicate delight or amusement, or gross muscle movements that indicate excitement?

3. How does the child respond to Step 3? Does she continue to look under the first cloth where she first saw you hide the toy, or does she look under the second cloth? Again, what emotional or motor responses does she make as she participates in this game?

4. How does the child respond to the invisible displacement of the toy? Does she persist in looking under the first cloth, or does she go immediately to the second cloth?

5. Given the child's age, what responses would you predict from her in the area of object permanence? (What do the norms indicate about her probable level of response?) What stage is the child in with respect to the development of object permanence?

Question Guides, Part II

1. What evidence is there that the infant is in Piaget's sensorimotor stage of cognitive development? That is, what responses seem typical of the infant, and how do these responses fit into Piaget's theory?

2. What responses does the infant make that are classifiable as sensorimotor schemes? Why do they fit that category rather than the category of random or unpatterned activity?

3. Are there any indications that the infant possesses concepts? What behaviors can be interpreted as showing possession of concepts?

4. What evidence does the infant show that she remembers?

5. Are the infant's behaviors being reinforced in any way? What responses are reinforced, and how does the reinforcement occur—by a smile from the adult, by picking the child up and making a fuss over her? What behavior changes result from the reinforcement (changes in the basic nature of the behavior)? In its frequency?

6. Are there any indications that classical conditioning could be taking place? What are the circumstances of the conditioning process? What is the originally neutral stimulus, and what stimulus is substituted for it? What is the resulting change in behavior? Emotional changes? Changes in motor activity? Avoidance of an object or person?

7. Does the infant give evidence of accommodation? For example, does she change her approach to a problem when the initial approach does not succeed? If the child accommodates, how does her behavior change as a result? What behaviors indicate that assimilation is occurring? Does the infant show signs of Fogel's "internalized selection of courses of action"? Explain.

8. Are there any occasions for learning created just by the adult's normal caregiving activities—for example, verbalizing about an event or object while she changes the infant's diapers? What kind of learning might be taking place? What specific adult activities contribute to the infant's learning opportunities?

Question Guides, Part III

1. What in the physical or social environment stimulates vocalizations? Inhibits them? What are some possible explanations for either of these effects?

2. What are the main characteristics of the infant's vocalizations? Are they babbling sounds? One-word phrases? Telegraphic speech? What effect do these vocalizations have on others? How do they respond? Do their responses affect the infant's subsequent vocalizations?

3. When does the infant cry? What happens when she cries? Do the effects on adults of her crying change the crying pattern? Does she use crying often as a means of communication, or does she more often use language to communicate?

4. What physical gestures does the infant use to try to get her meaning across to others? Does she point? Take the person by the hand and lead her to the "situation"? Do her gestures seem to match or fit her verbalizations? That is, does she seem to coordinate the timing of her gestures with her speech?

5. What responses give evidence of the infant's ability to understand language? That is, what are her receptive skills? What commands and directions is she able to understand and obey? Are her reception and production abilities different from each other? Does the infant understand more than she can speak, or the opposite?

EXERCISE 15-4: EMOTIONAL DEVELOPMENT AND BEHAVIOR IN THE INFANT (2 to 18 MONTHS)

Background Information

Emotions are an extremely important part of human behavior, and as Greenspan and Greenspan (1985) make clear, emotional development begins almost from the moment of birth. Recall from Chapter 14 that the first milestone of emotional development (which occurs between birth and three months of age) involves the newborn's capacity of self-regulation. This first milestone also involves the infant's taking an interest in the world. The Greenspans put it this way:

> Your newborn is faced with two fundamental and simultaneous challenges during the first weeks of life. The first is self-regulation—the ability to feel calm and relaxed, not overwhelmed by his new environment. The second is to become interested in the world through his senses—what he hears, sees, smells, tastes, and touches, and what he experiences through his sense of movement. (p. 14)

These tasks are challenges because the newborn, after nine months in the "darkness and relative quiet of the womb," is suddenly catapulted, as it were, into a world filled with a variety of sensations that are completely new to him. The newborn must organize these sensations and at the same time feel comfortable in their presence and actively engage them in ways that are appropriate to his level of developmental maturity—for example, show interest in the sights and sounds around him and not find them painful (Greenspan & Greenspan, 1985). This then permits achievement of the second milestone, which is that of "taking a highly specialized interest in the *human* world" (p. 5, italics original).

The second milestone (from about two to seven months) is described by the Greenspans as "falling in love":

> As your newborn moves along into the second, third, and fourth months of life, she will begin to show selective interest in the most special part of her world, namely, you. (p. 41)

It is assumed that if the baby does not find environmental stimuli pleasurable, he may be unlikely to progress to the stage where the world of human beings "is seen as the most enticing, pleasurable, and exciting of all experiences" (p. 4). The pleasure that one wants the baby to feel, say the Greenspans, can be seen in the baby's "enraptured smiles and eager joyfulness" as he or she "gazes excitedly at your face" while feeling the movements of your body and hearing your voice. They indicate further that the "baby is now becoming more responsive to external social interactions, whereas earlier she was more influenced by her inner physical sensations (e.g., hunger, gas bubbles)" (p. 41).

The third milestone, which occurs between 3 and 10 months of age, is founded on this special interest in the human world, but now the baby in effect says "Love alone is not enough—I now want a dialogue" (p. 4). Dialogue here does not mean sitting down and talking with the adult. It refers instead to such things as the baby smiling in response to the parent's smile, or reaching for an object that is held out to him, or making sounds in response to the parent talking to him. The baby is communicating in his own way, and the communication is intentional. Indeed, the authors call this milestone "developing intentional communication." The Greenspans also note that the baby is learning that the world is "a cause-and-effect world" (p. 5) (also a cognitive achievement on the baby's part), which means he learns that his behaviors lead to behaviors from others—when he smiles, for example, so does his mother or father. The child is also learning some negative emotions, such as anger when you try to take away a toy.

The fourth milestone, which occurs between 9 and 18 months of age, is characterized as the "emergence of an organized sense of self" (p. 83). In this stage the child extends her "emotional dialogue" another step and "learns to connect small units of feeling and social behavior into large, complicated, orchestrated patterns" (p. 5). The increased skill becomes especially evident near the middle of the fourth stage, which is at 14 or 15 months of age, when the child can integrate or combine newer and more complex behaviors with behaviors accomplished earlier. If Susan wants to play, for instance, she is no longer confined to pointing to a toy and making sounds that her mother may or may not understand. Instead, Susan can pick up the toy and carry it to her mother, thereby making her intentions rather clear.

The ability to combine relatively complex social and emotional patterns also indicates increasing cognitive abilities. As the Greenspans write, "The emerging ability to piece together many small activities and emotions into a pattern, known as the ability to organize, is crucial to the development of higher-level thinking and planning" (pp. 83–84). In the example of Susan, she demonstrated that she knew the meaning of objects, the toy, in this case, and of the action of taking the toy to her mother to play. Again, as the Greenspans put it, "This is the beginning of a 'conceptual' attitude toward the world. Objects now have functions" (p. 5). Equally important, however, people, especially parents, also come to have functions for the child; they serve special purposes. Furthermore, they "take on attributes" (p. 5). Parents show feelings and display actions whose functions or meanings the child eventually recognizes.

Observation Objectives

The objective of Part I is to observe and record behaviors that indicate an infant's level of emotional development according to Greenspan and Greenspan's (1985) second, third, and fourth emotional milestones. The objective of Part II is simply to observe and record the general emotional responses or behaviors of two infants between 2 and 18 months of age. Here, the focus is not on Greenspans' emotional milestones, but rather on what most of us would think of as a baby's normal feelings as expressed in crying (for various reasons), smiling, cooing, looking about with curiosity, and the like.

Procedure

We suggest that you observe an infant between the ages of 2 and 18 months to maximize the possibility of getting data that are relevant to the stages of emotional development specified in the observation objectives.

We suggest that you use the event sampling technique. Specifically, look for those behaviors or capacities that define the emotional milestone (stage) that corresponds to the age of the infant you have chosen. We suggest that you observe for at least three or four 10-minute periods; this should give you ample opportunity to see the behaviors that are of interest to you. Try to get a varied sampling of emotional behaviors, behaviors that demonstrate more than just one aspect of your particular infant's stage of emotional development. In Part II, use the event sampling technique to record the general emotional responses of at least two infants between the ages of 2 and 18 months. In this exercise, focus on such things as crying, displays of anger or annoyance, fear responses, contentment or delight, and so on. Be sure to record the circumstances or contexts in which these responses occurred. Then compare and contrast the emotional behaviors of the two infants: How did they differ? How were they alike? If you could observe them under the same or similar circumstances, did the two infants behave differently or similarly under relatively the same conditions? (See Observation Exercise 15-4.)

Question Guides

1. What specific behaviors did the infant exhibit that led you to classify her level of emotional development as you did?

2. Did the infant exhibit any behaviors that are found in the next higher stage? If so, were they too infrequent to allow you to put her into that next stage? Or did you classify the infant in the lower stage because of her age?

3. Was the infant ahead of her age with respect to emotional development? Was she behind?

OBSERVATION EXERCISE **15-1**

Physical/Motor Characteristics and Skills of the Infant or Toddler (1 to 24 months)

Observer's Name _____

Child/Children Observed _____

Child's/Children's Age(s) _____ Child's/Children's Sex _____

Observation Context (home, child care center, preschool, school) _____

Date of Observation _____ Time Begun _____ Time Ended _____

Brief Description of Physical and Social Characteristics of Observation Setting:

Objective 1: Physical Characteristics

Total Length of Newborn _____ Weight of Newborn _____

Length of Head _____ Ratio of Head to Total Body Length _____

Length of Trunk _____ Ratio of Head to Trunk _____

Describe the characteristics of the following:

HEAD and FACE (shape, eyes, ears, mouth, nose, etc.):

TRUNK (e.g., size in relation to head, overall appearance, etc.):

ARMS and LEGS (positioning, shape):

HANDS AND FINGERS:

Comparisons with newborns (these may be made using established norms if actual observations of a newborn are not possible or wanted):

Length:

Weight:

Ratio head to total body length:

(continues)

OBSERVATION EXERCISE **15-1** (Continued)

Objective 1 Continued

Ratio head to trunk:

Child's height and weight relative to norms cited:

Objective 2: Motor Skills of the Infant (1 to 24 months)

Observer's Name _____

Child/Children Observed _____

Child's/Children's Age(s) _____ Child's/Children's Sex _____

Observation Context (home, child care center, preschool, school) _____

Date of Observation _____ Time Begun _____ Time Ended _____

Brief Description of Physical and Social Characteristics of Observation Setting:

Objective Behavioral Descriptions (OBDs) and Interpretations: *Event Sampling*

OBD Session 1: [Time begun _____ Time ended _____]

Interpretation 1:

OBD Session 2: [Time begun _____ Time ended _____]

Interpretation 2:

Continue with OBDs and interpretations for as long as feasible or needed.

Comparison of Infant's Functioning with Age Norms:

OBSERVATION EXERCISE **15-1** (Continued)

Objective 3: Fine Motor Abilities (If children were tested by observer, describe how they were persuaded to perform.)

Fine Motor Tasks

Child 1: (Age___)

Event and Description of Response (OBD): *Event Sampling*

Stacking Blocks:

Picking up Raisin:

Putting Blocks in Container; Removing Them:

Stringing Beads:

Response to Play Dough:

Scribbling with Crayon:

Turning Pages:

Hand and Leg Preference:

Indications of Tool Use:

Child 2: (Age_____)

Stacking Blocks:

Picking up Raisin:

Putting Blocks in Container; Removing Them:

Stringing Beads:

Response to Play Dough:

Scribbling with Crayon:

Turning Pages:

Hand and Leg Preference:

Indications of Tool Use:

Comparison (Similarities) of Child 1 and Child 2:

Contrast (Differences) between Child 1 and Child 2:

OBSERVATION EXERCISE **15-1** (Continued)

Objective 3 (*continued*): *Gross Motor Abilities*

Gross Motor Abilities

Child 1: (Age_____)

Event and Description of Response (OBD): Event Sampling

Walking:

Running:

Climbing Stairs:

Walking Sideways, Backwards:

Jumping from Low Height (one step):

Other (crawling, creeping, scooting, etc.):

Child 2: (Age_____)

Event and Description of Response (OBD): Event Sampling

Walking:

Running:

Climbing Stairs:

Walking Sideways, Backwards:

Jumping from Low Height (one step):

Other (crawling, creeping, scooting, etc.):

Comparison of Child 1 and Child 2:

Contrast between Child 1 and Child 2:

PART THREE

OBSERVATION EXERCISE **15-2**

PART I: Social Behavior of the Infant (1 to 24 months)

Observer's Name _____

Child/Children Observed _____

Child's/Children's Age(s) _____ Child's/Children's Sex _____

Observation Context (home, child care center, preschool, school) _____

Date of Observation _____ Time Begun _____ Time Ended _____

Brief Description of Physical and Social Characteristics of Observation Setting:

Social Behaviors and Interaction Patterns

Objective Behavioral Descriptions (OBDs) and Interpretations:

Narrative Description

OBD Session 1: [Time begun _____ Time ended _____]

Interpretation 1:

OBD Session 2: [Time begun _____ Time ended _____]

Interpretation 2:

OBD Session 3: [Time begun _____ Time ended _____]

Interpretation 3:

Continue with OBDs and interpretations for as long as possible or needed.

OBSERVATION EXERCISE **15-2** (Continued)

PART II: Social Behavior of the Infant (1 to 24 months)

Observer's Name _____

Child/Children Observed _____

Child's/Children's Age(s) _____ Child's/Children's Sex _____

Observation Context (home, child care center, preschool, school) _____

Date of Observation _____ Time Begun _____ Time Ended _____

Brief Description of Physical and Social Characteristics of Observation Setting:

Time Sampling of Attachment Behaviors

Recording Intervals	1	2	3	4	5	6	7	8	9	10
Behavior Categories										
Looks at Caregiver										
Makes Physical Contact with Caregiver										
Smiles at Caregiver										
Shows Object to Caregiver										
Moves Closer to Caregiver										
Establishes Visual Contact with Caregiver										
Cries When Caregiver Leaves Room										
Negative Reaction to Stranger's Approach										

PART THREE

OBSERVATION EXERCISE **15-2** (Continued)

INTERPRETIVE COMMENTS:

Partly adapted from Willemsen, 1979, p. 250.

PART III: Social Behavior of the Infant (1 to 24 months)

Observer's Name _____

Child/Children Observed _____

Child's/Children's Age(s) _____ Child's/Children's Sex _____

Observation Context (home, child care center, preschool, school) _____

Date of Observation _____ Time Begun _____ Time Ended _____

Brief Description of Physical and Social Characteristics of Observation Setting:

Objective Behavioral Descriptions (OBDs): *Narrative Description*

Session 1: [Time begun _____ Time ended _____]

Qualities of Temperament Noted:

Session 2: [Time begun _____ Time ended _____]

Qualities of Temperament Noted:

Session 3: [Time begun _____ Time ended _____]

Qualities of Temperament Noted:

Parent Interview:

Question Asked Parent(s) (#1):

Parent's Response (#1):

Question Asked Parent(s) (#1):

Parent's Response (#1):

OBSERVATION EXERCISE **15-3**

PART I: Cognitive and Language Behavior of the Infant (1 to 24 months)

Observer's Name _____

Child/Children Observed _____

Child's/Children's Age(s) _____ Child's/Children's Sex _____

Observation Context (home, child care center, preschool, school) _____

Date of Observation _____ Time Begun _____ Time Ended _____

Brief Description of Physical and Social Characteristics of Observation Setting:

PART I: Object Permanence: *Event Sampling*

Tested Event and Description of Response Observed:

Step 1—Dropping the toy:

Step 2—Hiding the toy while the child watches:

Step 3—Visible displacement of the toy:

Step 4—Invisible displacement of the toy:

Comments:

PART II: Cognitive and Language Behavior of the Infant (1 to 24 months)

Observer's Name _____

Child/Children Observed _____

Child's/Children's Age(s) _____ Child's/Children's Sex _____

Observation Context (home, child care center, preschool, school) _____

(continues)

OBSERVATION EXERCISE **15-3** (Continued)

Date of Observation _____ Time Begun _____ Time Ended _____

Brief Description of Physical and Social Characteristics of Observation Setting:

Objective Behavioral Descriptions (OBDs) and Interpretations: *Narrative Description*

OBD Session 1: [Time begun _____ Time ended _____]

Interpretation 1:

ODB Session 2: [Time begun _____ Time ended _____]

Interpretation 2:

ODB Session 3: [Time begun _____ Time ended _____]

Interpretation 3:

Continue with OBDs and interpretations for as long as needed.

PART III: Cognitive and Language Behavior of the Infant (1 to 24 months)

Observer's Name _____

Child/Children Observed _____

Child's/Children's Age(s) _____ Child's/Children's Sex _____

Observation Context (home, child care center, preschool, school) _____

Date of Observation _____ Time Begun _____ Time Ended _____

Brief Description of Physical and Social Characteristics of Observation Setting:

OBSERVATION EXERCISE **15-3** (Continued)

PART III:
Language: *Event Sampling*

OBD Session 1: [Time begun _____ Time ended _____]

Interpretation 1:

ODB Session 2: [Time begun _____ Time ended _____]

Interpretation 2:

ODB Session 3: [Time begun _____ Time ended _____]

Interpretation 3:

Continue with OBDs and interpretations for as long as needed.

OBSERVATION EXERCISE **15-4**

Emotional Development of the Infant (2 to 18 months)

Observer's Name _____

Child/Children Observed _____

Child's/Children's Age(s) _____ Child's/Children's Sex _____

Observation Context (home, child care center, preschool, school) _____

Date of Observation _____ Time Begun _____ Time Ended _____

Brief Description of Physical and Social Characteristics of Observation Setting:

Objective Behavioral Descriptions (OBDs) and Interpretations: *Event Sampling*

OBD Session 1: [Time begun _____ Time ended _____]

Interpretation 1:

OBD Session 2: [Time begun _____ Time ended _____]

Interpretation 2:

Continue with as many OBDs as are feasible or needed.

Behavioral Summary:

Infant's Probable Emotional Stage:

Supporting Evidence:

OBSERVATION EXERCISE **15-4** (Continued)

**PART II:
Emotional
Development of
the Infant
(2 to 18 months)
(Alternate
Exercise)**

Observer's Name _____

Child/Children Observed _____

Child's/Children's Age(s) _____ Child's/Children's Sex _____

Observation Context (home, child care center, preschool, school) _____

Date of Observation _____ Time Begun _____ Time Ended _____

Brief Description of Physical and Social Characteristics of Observation Setting:

....

**Objective
Behavioral
Descriptions
(OBDs) and
Interpretations:**
Event Sampling

Context of OBD 1:

OBD Session 1 (Infant #1): [Time begun _____ Time ended _____]

Interpretation 1:

Context of OBD 2:

OBD Session 1 (Infant #2): [Time begun _____ Time ended _____]

Interpretation 2:

Context of OBD 3:

OBD Session 1 (Infant #3): [Time begun _____ Time ended _____]

Interpretation 1:

Continue for as many OBDs as are needed or desired.

Comparisons and Contrasts between Infants' Emotional Behaviors:

Summary Comments:

CHAPTER 16

Observing the Young Child: Ages Two through Five

INTRODUCTION

This chapter focuses your observations and recordings on the period referred to as the preschool years. Although many significant things occur during this span of four years, the rate of growth and developmental change seen during the 18 to 24 months of infancy probably will never again be equaled in any comparable period of time.

The observation exercises in this chapter are approached differently from those in the previous chapters. Unlike the period of infancy, the preschool period will not be divided up into smaller units such as four one-year periods, with separate exercises for each year. The entire preschool period is covered as a single entity, even though it comprises a greater amount of chronological time than infancy.

A second difference in approach concerns the organization of the material. The Question Guides are presented before the Exercise Sheets, and some of the background information is included among the questions rather than in a separate section. The background information is a starting point for your observations. There are other sources of information you can consult about child development and various theories as additional points of view from which to see, understand, and interpret children's behavior.

The numbered questions (Question Guides) from Exercises 16-2 on are based in part on the works of Lay and Dopyera (1977) and Lay-Dopyera and Dopyera (1982).

EXERCISE 16-1: THE PRESCHOOL CHILD IN THE PHYSICAL ENVIRONMENT

Background Information

Our physical surroundings exert a powerful influence on all of us. How much space we have, the objects and their arrangement in that space, and the social–psychological meaning of the space combine to determine and direct our behavior. A preschool classroom, a playground, or the child's home are particular spaces with equipment, materials, people, and arrangements that are used even if they are not designed for special purposes. As children's cognitive and language abilities become more sophisticated, children also come to understand that spaces have definitions. These definitions dictate what they may do in that space—that is, what others will allow them to do. However, also important is the children learning what they can do in the space because of the physical properties of the objects and materials it contains.

Observation Objectives

To familiarize you with the physical environment in which you are observing and to learn how children respond to and are influenced by their physical surroundings.

Procedure

Your first task is to draw a diagram of the indoor and outdoor environments. On each diagram, name the equipment and materials, and show their locations. With your diagram in hand, anyone should be able to walk into the observation setting and find anything that is there (bookshelves, toilets, art area). Similarly, the diagram of the outside environment should locate all the equipment and materials that are provided for the children's use. Contemporary outdoor environments for young children can be referred to as **playscapes**. With regard to these contemporary playground structures, Essa writes: "Most early childhood playgrounds come equipped with either traditional structures such as metal swings, slides, and climbers or with more contemporary **playscapes**, which combine a variety of materials and allow for a range of activities. Such equipment must meet standards of safety and developmental appropriateness. Beyond the immovable components of the outdoor space, however, various elements can enhance and expand children's play ..." (p. 201, emphasis original). Given such a potential variety of objects, it may not be enough simply to name them. It may be advisable to describe both the items that make up each piece of play equipment and the uses to which each item or object is put. For example, a drainage pipe should be described in reasonable detail not only with respect to its size and location but also with respect to how the children actually use it for their play activities: What do they do with such a pipe?

playscapes
A relatively recent term to describe contemporary playground structures that are innovative by combining "a variety of material" (Essa, 2007).

The second part of your assignment concerns how children use the areas available to them and how different areas have different effects on behavior. Begin by selecting two areas of the classroom or other setting that differ significantly in the activities and behaviors allowed there. For example, one would expect behavior in the big block area to be quite different from that in the dramatic play or storytelling area. The differences can be partly the result of the teacher's enforcement of rules governing behavior. But spaces themselves also affect behavior. What can be done in a given space is determined by what is there to do something with. If there are no blocks on hand, obviously there will be no playing with blocks. If puzzles are stored on shelves out of the children's reach, playing with puzzles will have to depend on an adult's help.

Observe and record the behavior of two children in the two areas; follow them as they move around the area. Then compare and contrast their behavior in one area with their behavior in the other. Note whether their actions are in keeping with the requirements and expectations of the location. Summarize the specific ways their behavior changes (if in fact it does) from one location to another. For this exercise, use the narrative description method because you are not looking for any particular event or behavior; you are interested in everything that occurs related to the child in the physical environment. (See Observation Exercise 16-1.)

Question Guides

1. Do the children's behaviors change from one location to another? If so, how?

2. What behaviors would you expect in each of the two locations where you observe the children? Do their behaviors conform to your expectations (or the space's definition)? If so, how? If not, why not? Does the caregiver have to remind the children of the appropriate behavior?

3. What in the environment holds the children's interest? How do they express that interest?

4. How would you assess the overall arrangement of the room or playscape? Is there enough space for the children to move around freely? To engage in the activities for which the space is intended?

EXERCISE 16-2: PHYSICAL GROWTH AND MOTOR FUNCTIONING

Background Information

Physical characteristics and motor abilities are probably the most noticeable and easily measurable aspects of human growth and development. These characteristics and abilities are often of major importance to parents, who point with pride to the gains their child makes in height, weight, and ability to walk, run, and manipulate objects. Because everything we do in some way involves a physical body, it makes sense to say that our physical and motor development and abilities form the foundation for our behavior.

In certain respects, this exercise will be easy to accomplish. Young children of normal ability are usually active physically, and many of their motor behaviors are obvious. On the other hand, there are some subtle aspects to motor behavior that can be overlooked. For example, all typical children walk and run, but each does so in her own unique style. For some, walking is smooth and well coordinated, with no significant peculiarities; for others, toes might point noticeably outward, feet may be somewhat widely spaced, or balance while running might be poor. Moreover, there are behaviors that do not have obvious physical–motor components. Sitting at the snack table eating is not a vigorous activity like free play in the big block areas. Yet there are things to be considered—for example, the child's posture (does he slouch, sit on one leg, cock his head to one side?) and the child's skill in handling eating utensils, pouring juice, or wiping crumbs from the table.

The behaviors of interest in this exercise fall into three general categories: (a) physical characteristics, (b) gross (large) motor movements or abilities, and (c) fine (small) motor movements or abilities. All of the child's physical–motor functioning will fall into one of these three categories. The questions that are provided throughout this chapter are intended to act as guides, as a means of directing your observations and your thinking as you approach each of the Observation Exercises. We do not intend that you actually answer every one of these questions. We also fully recognize that some of the questions will not be appropriate or applicable to two- and three-year-olds, and maybe not even to some four- or five-year-olds. It could therefore be argued that it makes no sense to look for behaviors that are not likely to occur because of a child's particular age or developmental level. Moreover, it could also be argued that it makes no sense to ask questions that are very likely to be answered "yes" precisely because the child is of an age or developmental level where particular behaviors or characteristics are commonly observed. In short, why bother to observe for behaviors, skills, or characteristics that are improbable, or for behaviors, skills, or characteristics that are almost certain to occur?

The most reasonable answer to these questions has to do with one of the basic purposes of observation, which is to discover important things about children. You may—perhaps should—look for improbable or unlikely behaviors, skills, or characteristics because you will not always be certain that the children you are observing cannot display such behaviors, skills, or characteristics. There can be exceptions, such as the precocious or advanced children who are able to demonstrate abilities that are beyond adults' expectations. In the same vein, you may—again perhaps should—look for behaviors, skills, and characteristics that are probable or likely, given the children's ages and developmental levels, because unless you actually witness these things, you cannot be absolutely certain the children possess them.

Think of the observation setting an as inhabited, but as yet unexplored, territory (at least initially), where you have come to learn about what is there and how the inhabitants behave and change over time. If you simply assume that the people living there can or cannot do certain things, then what is the point of your being there in the first place? Your observations would be unnecessary because you have already formed your conclusions about what you will or will not see.

This chapter concerns the ages from two through five years. In that span of time, most if not all of the guide questions presented could, in principle, be answered, or behaviors could be observed that will answer these questions. (Of course, no one individual is likely to see all of the behaviors and skills that are possessed by one or more children.) And there is also the issue of individual differences. One cannot assume that three-year-old Melinda will, or will not, in fact exhibit a certain ability simply because developmental norms for three-year-olds predict that she will or that she will not. Again, one of the general goals of observing young children's behavior is to learn what specific children are able to do, as well as to learn about children in general.

Consequently, suppose that you are observing, say, two-year-olds, and you refer to the question "What are the child's abilities to perform rhythmic movements?" If you restrict yourself to the examples of rhythmic movements given in the text, you may not be able to identify any such rhythmic ability. But the overall objective of the first exercise is to observe and record motor behaviors of any kind. Even the two-year-old can do some rhythmic things—walking, for instance, has a certain rhythm to it. Whatever the case, your goal is to look for all instances of motor behaviors and skills. If you cannot specifically respond to a particular question, it is not critical. What is critical is what you do observe and the sense or meaning you derive from your observation.

While observing children's motor skills—and all other areas of functioning—it is crucial to take their ages into consideration. It should not surprise you to observe that a two-year-old, who is likely to be two years and some months of age, might prefer large-muscle movements over small ones. This does not mean that a child this age cannot perform small-muscle movements and activities. Indeed, children considerably younger than two years do have some fine motor skills, although they are more rudimentary than those of their older counterparts. If, however, a five-year-old seems to prefer gross- over fine-muscle activities, several factors might be at play. The child may not be as skilled or well-developed motorically as his or her age peers, or maybe the child does not find the fine motor activities or opportunities that are available in the setting particularly interesting, which motivates him or her to play in the large motor areas. (See Tables 16-1, 16-2, 16-3, and 16-4 for summaries of motor skills of two- to five-year-olds.)

The procedure will be to observe at least two children of differing ages (a two- or three-year-old and a five-year-old would be good choices that, generally, would accentuate difference in motor skills). If you do not have access to children who fall into a two- to five-year range, pick two children who are reasonably active physically.

Table 16-1 Summary of Motor Skills of the Two-Year-Old Child

- Earlier wide stance while walking replaced by a heel-to-toe movement pattern; can now maneuver around obstacles
- Runs more confidently and with fewer falls
- Climbs stairs without help but cannot yet alternate feet
- Can balance on one foot for a brief time; will still fall when attempting to jump up and down
- Can throw a relatively large ball underhand and does not lose balance
- Can hold cup or glass in one hand
- Can unzip large zippers and unbutton large buttons
- Can turn doorknobs and open doors
- Can hold large crayon with fist; can also scribble (does so "enthusiastically on a large piece of paper")
- Can climb up on chair, turn around, and sit down
- Can pour and fill containers with sand, water
- Can stack 4 to 6 objects on top of one another
- Can propel wheeled toys with the feet

Table 16-2 Summary of Motor Skills of the Three-Year-Old Child

- Can walk up and down stairs without help; alternates feet; may jump from last step to the floor and land on both feet.
- Can briefly balance on one foot
- Can kick a large ball
- Can feed self without help or with "minimal assistance"
- Can jump in place
- Can pedal a small tricycle or other wheeled toy
- Can throw a ball overhand
- Can catch a bounced ball with outstretched arms
- Shows improved use/control of crayons and markers while drawing; can make vertical, horizontal, and circular motions
- Can hold a crayon or marker between the first two fingers and thumb, as opposed to the earlier use of the fist to grasp these objects

(continues)

PART THREE

Table 16-2 Summary of Motor Skills of the Three-Year-Old Child (Continued)

- Can turn pages of a book one at a time
- Likes to build with blocks
- Can build a tower with 8 or more blocks
- May show preference for either left or right hand
- Can carry a container of liquid without excessive spilling; can also pour from a pitcher into another container
- Can manipulate large buttons and zippers on clothing
- Can wash and dry hands; can brush teeth
- Normally achieves complete bladder control during third year

Adapted from Allen and Marotz, 2007, pp. 131–132.

Table 16-3 Summary of Motor Skills of the Four-Year-Old Child

- Can walk in a straight line (guided by "tape or chalk line on the floor") (p. 142)
- Can hop on one foot
- Can pedal and steer a wheeled toy with skill and confidence; can turn corners and avoid obstacles
- Can climb steps, ladders, trees, and playground equipment
- Can jump over objects 5 or 6 inches high or from a step; lands with both feet together
- Can run, start, stop, and move around obstacles without difficulty
- Can throw a ball overhand
- Can build a tower with 10 or more blocks; uses the dominant hand
- Can form shapes and objects out of clay
- Can reproduce some shapes and letters
- Holds a crayon or marker using first two fingers and the thumb ("tripod grasp")
- "Paints and draws with purpose; may have an idea in mind but often has trouble implementing it, so calls the creation something else" (p. 143)
- Hits nails and pegs more accurately with a hammer
- Can thread small wooden beads on a string

Adapted from Allen and Marotz, 2007, pp. 142–143.

Table 16-4 Summary of Motor Skills of the Five-Year-Old Child

- Can walk backwards heel-to-toe
- Can walk up and down stairs without help; alternates feet
- Is able to learn to do somersaults
- Can touch toes without bending at the knees
- Can walk a balance beam
- Can learn to skip with alternating feet
- Can catch a ball thrown from a distance of 3 feet
- Displays skilled riding of a tricycle; rides with speed and skillful steering. Some may learn to ride bicycles.
- Can jump or hop forward on both feet 10 times in succession without falling
- Can balance on either foot with good control for 10 seconds
- Can reproduce variety of shapes and letters: square, triangle, A, I, O, U, C, H, L, T, V
- Shows good control of pencil or marker; may start to color within the lines
- Cuts on the line with a scissors, although not perfectly
- Hand dominance pretty well established

Adapted from Allen and Marotz, 2007, p. 152.

Observation Objectives

To learn about preschool children's physical characteristics and motor abilities and how they are alike and how they are different from one another in these areas.

Procedure

If possible, select two children of differing ages (a two- or three-year-old and a five-year-old would be good choices). If that is not possible, simply select any two children who are reasonably active physically. Using an event sampling format, describe in detail (1) the children's physical appearances and (2) their motor activities as they play during the observation session. Observe each of the two children for about 10 to 15 minutes. To make the most productive use of your time, observe the children when they are most likely to display the motor behaviors that you want to see. If your objective concerns large motor activity, observe the children in those areas of the facility that promote or encourage large-muscle movements. Apply the same rationale to small-muscle activities. Then examine your data and compare and contrast (i.e., describe the similarities and differences between) the two children; draw some general conclusions as to their motor skills, degrees of coordination, and preferred activities. The Question Guide provided gives you information about the components of motor development and behavior and directs your observations and interpretations. (See Observation Exercise 16-2.)

Question Guides (Partly adapted from Lay and Dopyera [1977])

1. Is there anything about the child's body build that sets him apart from the rest of the group? If so, explain.

2. What can you say about how the child holds his body? For example, how does the child stand, sit, walk, and run? Is the child stoop-shouldered? Is the head carried high, or does the child look down?

Gross Movements and Abilities

Gross movements and abilities involve the large muscles of the body. Movements controlled by these muscles are large, sweeping movements such as climbing, swinging, walking, running, throwing, and jumping. There is an important consideration for this exercise. When children are just learning a skill, they tend to practice only that skill, isolating it from others already mastered. This process of learning and practicing a behavior is called differentiation. This is the process in which a new skill differentiates or separates out of old, existing skills. During differentiation, the children must devote their entire attention to the unfamiliar task. Once the task is perfected, however, they can combine the new skill with existing skills to form an integrated whole. These existing skills are not necessarily physical–motor skills, but may be verbal or cognitive skills. For instance, a child might climb up and down the jungle gym using the hands and feet in a number of different ways, while at the same time shouting to a friend, "Look at what I'm doing." This is an example of **integration**.

integration
Combining a newly learned skill with existing skills to form an integrated whole. The skills can be not only physical motor skills but also verbal or cognitive skills.

When you observe a motor behavior, note whether it is combined with other behaviors to form a more complex pattern (integration) or whether the behavior is exhibited by itself and in a repetitive manner (differentiation) (Lay & Dopyera, 1977).

Children are capable of a wide variety of motor actions, although individual differences exist. Some children will be able to run, jump, climb, intentionally fall down (with control), and do somersaults and cartwheels. Some of the child's motor behaviors are basic skills (e.g., walking and running), and certain children will be able to perform variations of these basic skills. For example, a child may be able to walk and run backwards or sideways. Be alert to the range or variety of motor actions the child can perform. Remember that developmental level, which is to some degree indicated by age, is a strong determinant of what a child can do.

3. How many different motor behaviors can the child perform?

Children demonstrate their ability to balance in many ways. They walk across balance beams elevated off the floor; they walk on cracks or lines on the ground; they walk

Gross motor skills, or use of large muscles, are demonstrated by these preschoolers on a riding toy.

stepping from one rock to another. When recording instances of these behaviors, try to indicate how much balancing ability is required. For example, how wide is the beam the child walks across? How quickly does she move on these balancing tasks? Can the child do these things without help, or must her hand be held? How does the child compare with the other children? Can the child perform other actions while balancing (integration)?

4. How well does the child perform balancing activities?

You may be able to gauge the child's strength only by seeing how much he or she can lift, pull, or push compared with peers. You may not be able to determine strength in terms of the *most* the child can lift, pull, or push. Children demonstrate their strength in a number of ways: They lift and stack blocks, pull each other in wagons, hang from ladders or jungle gyms, and wrestle with each other. What behaviors show the child's strength? How much strength is needed for a particular behavior? For example, how many blocks did the child lift at one time, how many children did he or she pull in the wagon at the same time, and so on.

5. How strong is the child?

Some children seem to do everything at their top rate of speed, whereas others have a more leisurely pace. How quickly does the child do various things such as walk, run, and climb? Does the rate of movement vary depending on the particular activity or piece of equipment used (keeping in mind that such things as rate of movement also depend upon the child's level of skill)? Are the child's movements coordinated and well timed, or does the child do things faster than his or her coordination will allow?

6. How quickly can the child move or perform various activities?

How long can the child perform a given activity without resting? Can the child go from one activity to another without seeming to get tired? How many times can the child perform a given movement without stopping to rest? Endurance may be partly determined by comparison with the child's peers.

7. How much endurance or stamina does the child appear to have?

Many activities require a sense of rhythm, an ability to move one's body in a properly timed sequence (e.g., in dancing). What evidence is there that the child has this rhythmic capacity? Can the child keep time with music and bounce a ball? Can the child hop or skip halfway across the room without losing the correct pattern of motion? Can the child perform one nonrhythmic activity while simultaneously performing a rhythmic one? For example, can he or she talk with someone while at the same time make dance movements to music?

8. What are the child's abilities to perform rhythmic movements?

Fine Motor Movements and Abilities

This category involves movements of the small muscles of the body—for example, those used in picking up small objects, zipping a jacket, writing with crayon or pencil, and buttoning a shirt. Fine motor behavior evolves or differentiates out of gross motor movements; it therefore occurs later in the motor development sequence.

9. What are the range and variety of the child's fine motor skills involved in self-help behavior?

The preschool environment is full of materials that provide opportunities for small-muscle activities. There might be tools such as screwdrivers, hammers, and pliers; jigsaw puzzles with small parts to be fitted together; small blocks to build. Simply turning the pages of a book requires fine-muscle skills. Be alert to the child's

Fine motor skills the use of small muscles, are demonstrated by this child.

functioning in these areas. Try to draw some conclusions regarding his skill in various activities, as well as the extensiveness of his small-muscle abilities.

10. What is the child's ability to handle and use various kinds of toys, objects, and tools? How extensive are his abilities in this area?

EXERCISE 16-3: COGNITIVE AND INTELLECTUAL DEVELOPMENT AND BEHAVIOR

Background Information

This exercise is concerned with the children's mental functioning: how they perceive and think about the world, and the factual knowledge they have and how they use it. Jean Piaget distinguishes between two kinds of knowledge: (1) knowledge of specific facts and information, which he called knowledge in the "narrow sense"; and (2) knowledge that involves children's thinking processes and how they reason about reality, which he called knowledge in the "broad sense." Knowledge in the broad sense also concerns the relationships that children form among the various facts they have learned in the narrow sense (see Kamii & DeVries, 1977).

egocentrism
The cognitive inability to take other people's points of view and to recognize their needs and interests; a preoccupation with one's own view of the world.

One of the characteristics of children's thinking has to do with what Piaget called egocentrism. **Egocentrism**, which is perhaps the best known of the cognitive contents, is concerned with the extent to which children view themselves as the center of reality. Charles Brainerd (1978) offers an interpretative rule of thumb: "Any behavior that suggests children are preoccupied with themselves and/or unconcerned with things going on around them may be termed egocentric" (p. 103). It is important to recognize that egocentrism results from young children's cognitive inability to take someone else's point of view or to separate themselves from various aspects of their environment. Do not confuse this with egotism, a label we usually reserve for older children or adults who are intellectually capable of seeing the world from another's perspective but for whatever reason choose not to do so.

Egocentrism can be expressed by the child who makes a remark about another child, not realizing that the remark could hurt that child's feelings. Or a child might tell you a story and mention names or describe events that only she knows about, yet the child assumes that you are as aware of these persons and events as she is.

1. Look for examples of egocentric behavior.

There are many cognitive abilities that adults take for granted. For the young child, however, these abilities must develop over a long period of time. Piaget argued that some abilities cannot be taught directly; rather, they are the result of maturation, a lot of general experience, learning from others (social transmission), and the processes of assimilation and accommodation.

One of these cognitive abilities is known as **classification**. This is the process of sorting objects into groups according to perceived similarities. Classification requires that the child notices similarities and differences in the properties of objects. Then he must group those objects on the basis of their similarity on a particular property—for example, color, size, shape, or function. Properties of objects are also called stimulus dimensions. There are many dimensions that can form the basis of classification.

2. Observe how the child sorts objects. How does the child perceive things to be alike or different? On what basis does the child note similarities and differences?

Another important cognitive ability concerns the concept of number. Number includes the ability to count, but it also involves such things as one-to-one correspondence and conservation of number. **One-to-one correspondence** is the process of matching two groups of objects, lining up one object of one group with one and only one object of the other group. A child who has this ability can, for example, give each child at the snack table one glass of juice or place a chair at the table for each child there. Note that this ability does not require counting, but only the ability to see that each child is to get one glass, one chair, or what have you.

Conservation of number is the understanding that the way objects are arranged in space has no effect on their quantity—if no objects are added to or subtracted from the group, their total number remains unchanged. For example, you show a child two equal rows of pennies (say, five in each row). The child agrees that the rows are the same. Then, while the child watches, you spread out the pennies in one row so they take up more space than the other row. If the child cannot conserve number, he or she will tell you the altered ("spread out") row has more pennies than

classification

A process of sorting objects into groups according to perceived similarities—for example, putting all green things into one group and all red things into another group. Objects (and ideas) can be classified according to a number of dimensions at the same time—for example, according to shape, size, and color.

one-to-one correspondence

A matching of two groups of objects in which one object of one group is paired with one and only one object of the other group; for example, a child who has this ability can give each child at the snack table one cookie and one napkin.

conservation of number

One of several conservation tasks or abilities, conservation of number refers to the fact that two numerically equal quantities of something remain equal even when one of them is changed in some way, provided that nothing has been added or taken away. Changes that do not affect the quantity of something are called irrelevant transformations.

the unaltered row. The child who can conserve number will not be fooled by the altered row's appearing to have more pennies and will tell you the two rows are still the same.

3. Can the child put objects into one-to-one correspondence? Can you give an example? Does the child have the concept of number? How does the child show that understanding? If he does not understand the number concept, what does he do that indicates the absence of the number concept?

seriation

A process of arranging objects in some order according to a particular dimension; seriation requires the ability to compare and coordinate differences between objects—for example, arranging a collection of rocks in order of increasing weight, from the lightest to the heaviest.

Another cognitive ability that interested Piaget is called **seriation**. Seriation involves the sequential arrangement of objects or ideas according to a particular attribute. Specifically, seriation requires that the child compare and coordinate differences among objects. Thus, arranging sticks of different lengths from shortest to longest is an example of object seriation. Knowing that if Billy is older than Tommy, and Tommy is older than Mary, then Billy is older than Mary is an example of an abstract seriation.

4. Can the child seriate? According to what criteria does the child arrange objects or events? How many objects can the child arrange in some kind of order?

A child may be able to arrange three sticks according to length but has difficulty with more than three sticks. He may simply put a larger group of sticks into several groups of three each, although each set of three may be seriated correctly. For example, given nine sticks of different lengths, the child may sort the sticks into three groups of three sticks each, but each smaller group may be seriated correctly.

Constructing a jigsaw puzzle illustrates the cognitive ability of seriation.

5. Does the child have any understanding of conservation of liquid and substance? How does she show this understanding?

The concepts of causality, space, and time are also important aspects of cognitive functioning. **Causality** is the child's comprehension of cause-and-effect relationships and how the child attempts to explain various phenomena. For example, does the child see the relation between the weather and how one should dress? Or how does the child try to explain why one object floats and another one sinks?

There are several aspects to preoperational children's concepts of causality that over the years have captured the interest of many writers and theorists. We briefly discuss two of these, namely **animism** and **artificialism**. But as with Piaget's views on egocentrism, contemporary writers and researchers do not all share Piaget's conclusions about preoperational children's conceptualizations of causality.

6. Does the child show animism or artificialism in his thinking? What behaviors give evidence for this kind of thinking? What evidence is there for the child's general understanding of causality, of cause-and-effect relationships?

The space concept involves awareness of how objects are located in space, of objects' relative positions, and of the amount of space needed to accommodate or contain an object. Some concept of space is needed just to move from place to place without bumping into things, or to find one's way without getting lost.

The concept of time involves an understanding of past, present, future, and duration, which is how long something lasts. Does the child refer to something he or she did yesterday or is going to do tomorrow? Does the child have a grasp of relational terms such as *before, during*, and *after*? Does the child say such things as "I have to wash my hands before I eat" or "Daddy always drinks coffee after he eats"?

7. Does the child demonstrate an understanding of space and time? How does he show this understanding? How complete does it seem to be?

You should also be alert to the child's factual knowledge. What general kinds of information does he have? Can the child name many objects, persons, or animals? Does he know where he lives (address, city)? Does he have knowledge of some events that are current in the news? This factual information is knowledge in the "narrow sense" and can be thought of as part of the child's intellectual development and behavior.

8. What factual information does the child have, and how does the child use those facts in his dealings with others?

There are other cognitive contents that are relevant to the preschool period of the life span, but we obviously cannot cover all of these. However, there is one other kind of ability that we feel is especially appropriate to your understanding of preschool children's intelligence: the ability to represent mentally the world and its various aspects. Ruth Saunders and Ann Bingham-Newman (1984) offer an excellent account

---

causality
The comprehension of cause-and-effect relationships.

animism
A belief that nonliving objects are actually alive and behave like humans.

artificialism
The belief that everything that exists has been created by human beings or by a god who builds things the way people do according to a plan or blueprint.

of six characteristics of representation ability. These characteristics can be said to identify the types or levels of representation that are possible for the preoperational child (and for older children and adults, as well). Let us look at these briefly (see also Saunders & Bingham-Newman, 1984, pp. 137–138).

(1) The ability to have three-dimensional objects represent or stand for other objects. This ability can be expressed under at least three conditions or circumstances: (a) when both objects are very much alike (p. 137), (b) when both objects are not much alike, and (c) when the child constructs a model of some real object by using a variety of other objects.

(2) The ability to recognize and use two-dimensional objects such as pictures or drawings to represent another real object or setting. The authors cite an example of "using a picture of a doctor's office to create the atmosphere for a dramatic play episode" (p. 137).

(3) The ability to denote objects by exhibiting actions that are usually performed on or with those objects, such as "making a pounding motion to stand for a hammer or a dribbling motion to stand for a basketball" (p. 137).

(4) The ability to represent beings that are alive by mimicking actions or behaviors that are associated with them—for example, moving one's arms to imitate an elephant's trunk (p. 137).

(5) The ability to represent a real event through the use of an abbreviated action or series of actions. This can involve making just a few movements to stand for a lot of movements that, in an actual situation, take a considerably longer period of time. Saunders and Bingham-Newman give the example of a child bringing "a spoon to the mouth three times to stand for eating breakfast" (p. 137).

(6) The ability to express an idea in a number of different ways.

Observation Objectives

To sensitize you to the way children think and to the kinds of information they might know and are capable of learning. To observe how children differ in their cognitive abilities and styles. To become aware of how preschool, preoperational children mentally represent their world.

Procedure

If you can, select two children of different ages as the subjects of your observations. A five-year-old and a two- or three-year-old would be best. If this is not possible, randomly select two children who are in the observation setting. Using the narrative description method, record in as much detail as you can the children's behaviors and the context of those behaviors. Devote about 10 or 15 minutes to each child. Then examine the narrative description and describe each child's cognitive characteristics. Write a summary cognitive profile of the two children. How well do the children fit Piaget's sensorimotor stage of development? What representational abilities do the children demonstrate? Describe specifically the behaviors or characteristics that, to you, indicate functioning within a particular category of representational ability. As a final step, compare the two children's level of mental functioning. What can the older child do that the younger one cannot? Which child demonstrates more egocentric behavior? How do they differ in the way they mentally represent the world and its objects or events? As well, how are they alike in all these areas of cognitive functioning? (See Observation Exercise 16-3.)

EXERCISE 16-4: LANGUAGE DEVELOPMENT

Background Information

Language is one of the more prominent behaviors in the preschool child. The preschooler is rapidly acquiring speech vocabulary and is refining his grammar and syntax to conform more closely to adult speech patterns. For many people, language is an indication of intellectual and social progress. In this exercise, you will be concerned with describing and analyzing the child's speech, determining such things as the depth and variety of his vocabulary, characteristic sentence structure, and the syntactical forms the child is capable of using. In later exercises, you will be asked to observe and record children's social uses of language beyond the present unit's emphasis on egocentric and **sociocentric speech**.

sociocentric (or socialized) speech
Public speech; speech that is intended to communicate with someone—each person takes into account what the others say, and each responds accordingly.

PIAGET'S AND VYGOTSKY'S VIEWS ON CHILDREN'S PRIVATE SPEECH: A BRIEF COMPARISON AND OVERVIEW

The theories of the Soviet psychologist Lev Vygotsky have assumed considerable importance in contemporary thinking about children's cognitive and language development. It appears that Vygotsky's interpretations of children's private speech have largely supplanted Piaget's interpretations of this topic. Berk (2006), for example, writes as follows: "Over the past three decades, almost all studies have supported Vygotsky's perspective.... As a result, children's self-directed speech is now called **private speech** instead of egocentric speech. Research shows that children use more of it when tasks are difficult, after they make errors, and when they are confused about how to proceed" (p. 259, emphasis original).

To begin to understand Vygotsky's theory and how it essentially differs from Piaget's, let us look at Berk and Winsler's (1995) description of the basic premise of Vygotsky's theory:

> Vygotsky's theory of child development assumes that social interaction and children's participation in authentic cultural activities are necessary for development to occur. Also similar to how, during evaluation, new mental abilities in the human species arose out of the need to communicate and function as a collective, Vygotsky's theory grants a special place to social interaction in ontogenesis as a means of developing all complex, higher mental functions. (pp. 4–5)

Miller (1993) begins her discussion of Vygotsky's theory by providing a brief historical perspective on how individuals' development was viewed in the past:

> Most of the theories that have influenced developmental research in the Western world have viewed individuals as separate from their social and physical environments. In these views, such as Piaget's, development is seen primarily as an individual activity and the environment as simply an "influence on" an individual's development.... In the Vygotskian–contextualist view, humans are embedded in a social matrix (context) and human behavior cannot be understood independently of this matrix. (p. 370)

Based on Vygotsky's emphasis on the influence of social context on development, he logically enough is sometimes referred to as a contextualist. Miller defines *contextualism* and speaks to the essential nature of Vygotsky's perspective on the child:

> The social-cultural-historical context defines and shapes any particular child and his experience. At the same time children affect their contexts. Because of this interrelatedness, looking at a child while ignoring his context distorts our concept of the nature of children. Focusing on a child alone tends to encourage us to look for causes of behavior within the child rather than in the context. In actuality, the same developmental processes can lead to different outcomes, depending on the circumstances. (p. 375)

The Core Ideas of Vygotsky's Theory

Berk and Winsler (1995) identify eight major ideas that form the substance of Vygotsky's theory. We deal with six of these ideas relatively briefly but in sufficient detail to provide you with some meaningful information that you can apply in your own observations and interpretations of children's cognitive and language behavior.

Cross-Cultural Variation

The first idea presented by Berk and Winsler is that of cross-cultural variation. This idea is relevant to the discussion of multiculturalism in this text. Cultures differ in what they emphasize as important and in the activities in which children are involved. Therefore, it is assumed that because cultures differ in the activities they stress as important, "higher mental functions in humans vary across cultures" (Berk & Winsler, 1995, p. 5). This idea is easy enough to understand if we accept the proposition that intelligence serves a survival or adaptive function. It is our intellect that enables us to meet and adapt to the demands made on us by our society and culture. Consequently, with our intellect as a tool, different cultures, with their different demands, require different, and to some degree, culture-specific uses of that tool.

The Developmental or Genetic Method

Vygotsky's second main idea refers to what is called the "developmental, or genetic method" (p. 5). As Berk and Winsler put it, "We can understand human behavior only by examining the development or history of behavior. To really know the essence of something, we must see how it was formed developmentally" (p. 5). This idea makes sense in any number of contexts. For example, if you really want to understand an automobile, you should follow the development of that automobile as it proceeds through the assembly line. In the same vein, to understand more fully a five-year-old child, you need to understand what has taken place developmentally during all the preceding weeks, months, and years of his life. This is one of the objectives of developmental psychology.

Two Lines of Development: The Natural Line and the Cultural Line

The third idea identifies two lines of development. Berk and Winsler refer to these as "two distinct planes on which child development takes place: the *natural line* and the *cultural line*" (p. 5, italics added). The natural line refers to biological growth and maturation of physical and mental structures. The cultural line refers to "learning to use cultural tools and to human consciousness, which emerges from engaging in cultural activity" (p. 5). Recall the discussion in Chapter 2 of the heredity versus environment (nature versus nurture) debate, which centers on the question of what is the primary source or cause of developmental change. One of the traditional answers to this question is that change comes from genetically determined processes of maturation, which subscribes to the nature side of the nature versus nurture debate. Vygotsky's cultural line overlaps the two remaining answers to the heredity versus environment debate: (1) developmental change is caused by experiences that come from the external environment (the nurture side of the debate), and (2) the source of developmental change comes from the interaction between the environment and the forces of maturation. Piaget, among others, took the second of these two positions.

But, as Berk and Winsler (1995) point out, "In most theories of cognition and cognitive development, the social and cognitive make contact only minimally. Rather than being truly joined and interactive, they are viewed as separate domains of functioning. At best, the social world is a surrounding context of cognitive activity, not an integral part of it" (p. 12). As these authors further state,

> Early childhood professionals have a long tradition of regarding what the young child knows and develops as personally rather than socially constructed—a tradition that flows from Piaget's massive contributions to our field. According to the strong Piagetian stance, as children independently explore their physical and social worlds, they build knowledge—a process located within and governed by the individual. If ways of understanding reality are similar across human beings, it is because all of us have the same biological equipment for interpreting experience: the human brain. (p. 12)

Vygotsky differs sharply from Piaget regarding the role and importance of the social context. Vygotsky believed that "social experience shapes the ways of thinking and interpreting the world available to individuals" (p. 12). Because of Vygotsky's emphasis on social and cultural influences on children's development, his theory is frequently referred to as a sociocultural theory.

Lower versus Higher Mental Functions

Berk and Winsler refer to Vygotsky's fourth main idea by the phrase *lower versus higher mental functions*. It is sufficient to say here only that lower mental functions are those shared with other species of mammals, whereas higher mental functions are unique to human beings. These higher functions entail the use of language and other cultural resources or tools that "guide or mediate cognitive activity" (Berk & Winsler, 1995, p. 5).

The General Genetic Law of Cultural Development

The fifth main idea Winsler and Berk refer to as the general genetic law of cultural development. This concept is an interesting one. Vygotsky invokes again the notion of development occurring on two planes. These planes emphasize the distinction between the individual and his culture or society. The first plane is the social, or interpersonal, plane; the second is the individual, or psychological, plane: "All higher mental functions have social origins that are eventually internalized" (Berk & Winsler, 1995, p. 12). This idea stresses the significance of the individual's social–cultural background and experiences, which contrasts sharply with Piaget's primary emphasis on the individual's contribution to his own development.

Language as Central

Vygotsky's sixth idea regards language as central. As Berk and Winsler (1995) write, "Language, the primary cultural tool used by humans to mediate their activities, is instrumental in restructuring the mind and informing higher-order, self-regulated thought processes" (p. 5). The authors' subsequent discussion of Vygotsky's view of language becomes a bit complicated, albeit not prohibitively so. Let us briefly summarize both Piaget's and Vygotsky's conceptions of the role of language in children's development.

Vygotsky and Piaget on Private Speech

"[F]or Piaget, private speech was an *important side effect, or a residual characteristic*, of the mind of the preoperational child—a *phenomenon that had no positive function in development*" (Berk & Winsler, 1995, p. 35, italics added). The significance of private speech forms the basis for the differences between Piaget and Vygotsky. Vygotsky differed sharply from Piaget with respect to the importance of children's private speech. One basic difference between their respective views is that Vygotsky conceptualized such speech as serving a purpose other than communicating with other people. This conclusion is based on Vygotsky's observation that "children use more private speech while working on difficult tasks than on either easy tasks or no task at all" (Berk & Winsler, 1995, p. 35). Vygotsky also observed that private speech becomes more frequent during the middle to end of the preschool years and then declines when "children's *overt* private speech is replaced by whispers and inaudible muttering" (Berk & Winsler, 1995, p. 35, italics added). A third difference between Piaget's and Vygotsky's interpretation of private speech is that "it does not become more social with age. Instead, it becomes less understandable to others as it is abbreviated and internalized" (p. 35).

The final difference between these two theorists is based on Vygotsky's observation "that the more opportunities for social interaction the child has, the more private speech that occurs. Rather than private speech giving way to social speech, social and private speech seem to go together" (Berk & Winsler, 1995, p. 35). Consequently, given all these findings, Vygotsky concluded that "the primary goal of private speech is not communication with others but *communication with the self* for the purpose of *self-regulation*, or guiding one's own thought processes and actions" (Berk & Winsler, 1995, p. 37, italics original). Berk (2006) confirms this perspective on children's private speech:

> He [Vygotsky] reasoned that children speak to themselves for self-guidance. Because language helps children think about mental activities and behavior and select courses of action, Vygotsky regarded it as a foundation for all higher cognitive processes, including controlled attention, deliberate memorization

and recall, categorization, planning, problem solving, abstract reasoning, and self-reflection. As children get older and find tasks easier, their self-directed speech is internalized as silent, inner speech—the verbal dialogues we carry on with ourselves while thinking and acting in everyday situations (p. 259).

This conclusion led Vygotsky to argue that

The most significant moment in cognitive development occurs when the preschool child begins to use language not only for communication with others but also as a tool of thought—a means to direct his or her own attention and behavior…. In sum, language is first used for social communication. It then turns inward, becoming a tool of the mind for speaking to the self and guiding behavior. This self-regulatory language is first overt (private speech) and then gradually becomes covert (inner speech or verbal thinking). In this way, language branches off from the social world and enters the individual cognitive world. Private speech is the intermediate stage in this internalization process. (Berk & Winsler, 1995, p. 37)

egocentric speech
Speech that does not take the other person into account and that, for all practical purposes, is private.

zone of proximal development
A concept found in Vygotsky's theory, the zone of proximal development (ZPD) refers to "space" or distance between what a child can do for herself and what she can do only with someone else's help. The purpose of the zone of proximal development in early child care and early childhood education is essentially to guide the caregivers and teachers—as well as parents—in their efforts to promote a child's cognitive development.

Let us look at the child's speech in terms of Piaget's concepts of egocentrism and **sociocentrism. Egocentric speech** is speech that does not take the other person into account; it is speech that, for all practical purposes, is private. There is no real effort to communicate with the other person; therefore, whatever is said is meaningful only to the speaker. Piaget identified three types of egocentric speech: (a) monologue, in which the individual talks only to himself and with no other persons present; (b) repetition, in which the individual repeats words and phrases over and over again as if to practice them or as if he simply enjoyed making the sounds; and (c) collective monologue, in which two or more persons are talking together but none of them is paying attention to what the others are saying. Each "conversation" is independent of the other conversation.

Socialized speech, on the other hand, is public speech. It is intended to communicate with someone, and each person takes into account what the others are saying and responds accordingly.

1. Does the child engage in egocentric or socialized speech? What are the circumstances under which these types of speech are used?

Vocabulary is the foundation of speech. We communicate by putting individual words together into properly constructed sentences and paragraphs. Presumably, the greater the number of words in our vocabularies, the greater the number and variety of sentences and ideas we can utter and transmit to others. Words have different meanings and serve different purposes. Moreover, words must be placed in the correct position within a sentence; thus, there are rules of grammar and syntax.

2. What do you observe about the child's vocabulary?

In particular, examine the child's speech for words that express relations and oppositions—for example, words such as *and, or, not, same, different, more, less, instead, if, then*, and *because*. Also, how varied or rich is the child's vocabulary when talking about the world and the people and things in it? Think in terms of general classes or categories of objects, persons, and events, and then assess how many different words the child uses to discuss those categories. For example, one can talk about animals, people, colors, shapes, vehicles, feelings, weather, food, and buildings, among many others. Each of these words (or concepts) represents a general class of phenomena. Therefore, how many different animals can the child specifically name or talk about: dog, cat, squirrel, tiger, fox, sheep, lamb, and so forth? The child may have only a few specific words representing members of the class known as animals. Assess the child's ability in the other categories in the same way.

Sentence structure is also an important aspect of speech. Structure refers to such things as the types of sentences the child uses: questions, imperatives (i.e., commands or directions), and sentences that contain a subject and an object. Does the child form compound sentences (two sentences separated by a conjunction), sentences containing a main clause and a subordinate clause (e.g., "I'll go with you if you play with me first"), and sentences containing relative clauses (e.g., "The boy who hit me is over there")?

3. Examine the child's speech for the type of sentences he uses. What is the apparent extent of such usage? That is, does the child have a wide or narrow variety of sentence types?

Finally, there is the area of syntactical forms. These refer to how various types of words are used within a sentence to convey meaning. Syntactical forms also refer to how various words in a sentence are positioned relative to one another to convey meaning. For example, we speak of forms of *to be*, as illustrated by sentences such as "Johnny *is* big" and "My mommy *was* here." There are also words that take the "ing" ending: "Sam is hitt*ing* Billy," and "The children were walk*ing* across the street." Then there are words that take the infinitive form, such as "I want *to watch* TV" and "He wanted *to go* with his mother." There are also the various tenses—past, present, and future, to mention only the simple tenses ("I *went* to the store"; "She *is playing* here with me"; "My mother *will go* to work on Monday").

4. What kinds of syntactical forms does the child use in his speech? What can you say about how he uses the various parts of speech, include the following?

   singular and plural forms: one bird and two birds; one man and two men
   possessive forms: my book; their house; his car
   verb forms (singular and plural): They don't eat here. He doesn't come very often. The boxers hit each other hard.
   pronouns: you, me, they, us, I, him

adverbs: She walked *slowly* across the room. He ate *quickly* and left.
adjectives: the *red* shoes; the *big* building
prepositional forms or phrases: He went *to* the blackboard. The cat hid *under* the couch.

Brief Summary

Vygotsky maintained that private speech undergoes four changes in the course of its development. First, it changes from distinctly overt private speech to increasingly internalized speech, the latter being thought or inner speech. Second, private speech becomes more frequent over the preschool years and then declines in frequency during the early years of elementary school. Third, structural/grammatical changes occur as private speech is abbreviated and internalized. And fourth, "speech moves from following behavior to preceding behavior, as it takes on a planning and regulatory function" (Berk & Winsler, 1995, p. 38).

Observation Objectives

To learn about the language production abilities of preschool children and how children of preschool age use language as a means of social interaction.

Procedure

In this exercise, you will most likely be performing a group observation. You are to choose two to three children who are playing together or are involved with one another in some way. (A legitimate exception to a group observation is any occasion when a child is talking to herself, such as in the case of self-regulation of behavior, or in language play [see Exercise 16-5 for a description of this kind of play], or in other circumstances in which the child is exhibiting language skills outside of a social context.) If the group breaks up during the observation session, complete your notes and then find a similar group and repeat the process. Your purpose is to observe and record the language behaviors of children who are engaging in social exchanges. You will be using the event sampling method to record instances of language use. You will also record the children's specific use of language to communicate with one another. As much as possible, record their speech word for word; also be sure to include data about the social and emotional aspects of the situation. (See Observation Exercise 16-4.)

EXERCISE 16-5: PLAY

Children engaged in parallel play—playing beside but not with each other.

Background Information

Play, as a concept, is probably very much like the concept of family or child: Most people think they know what play, family, and child are. Just as most people probably believe that family and children are very important, they also believe that play is extremely important in the lives of children. Indeed, some psychologists believe that play is the most important activity in which young children engage. Play activities pervade the lives of children from infancy throughout childhood. Some play seems obviously linked to the children's observation of adults; other play seems to stem from the children's fantasies and from experiences that they find particularly enjoyable.

Explanations of the major purposes of play are numerous. These range from play as getting rid of excess energy to play as a means of socioemotional expression. Play includes both group and individual activities. In principle, at least, play can be distinguished from nonplay behavior by its special characteristics, the most important of which are its voluntary nature and its complete structuring by the participants, with little regard for outside regulation. Although somewhat dated, Dworetzky's (1987) "five descriptors" of play are still relevant. The assumption is that "the greater number of descriptors that can be applied to any given situation, the more likely people are to call those circumstances play" (Dworetzky, 1987, p. 368). These five descriptors isolate different aspects of behavior that are considered to be indicative of play.

Dworetsky's Five Descriptors of Play

1. *Intrinsic motivation.* This simply means that behavior is motivated or prompted from within the individual, and it is "done for its own sake and not to satisfy social demands or bodily functions" (p. 369).

2. *Positive affect.* Play is pleasurable or fun to do.

3. *Nonlaterality.* This means that the behavior "does not follow a serious pattern or sequence"; it has a pretend quality about it (p. 369).

4. *Means/end.* Here the means are emphasized rather than the ends of the activity. Primary interest is in the behavior itself and not in any goals or outcomes that may be achieved.

5. *Flexibility.* This simply means that the behavior is not rigid but shows pliability in form and context across various situations.

Craig and Kermis (1995) identify six categories or forms of play, with each type having its own characteristics and functions. The authors note that these types of play overlap with one another and are not mutually exclusive or exhaustive.

Craig and Kermis's Six Categories of Play

1. *Sensory Pleasure.* "The aim of this kind of play," say Craig and Kermis, "is sensory experience in and for itself" (p. 402). This kind of play instructs children regarding their "bodies, senses, and the qualities of things in the environment" (p. 402).

2. *Play with Motion.* This is physical movement such as running, jumping, and skipping enjoyed for their own sake. As Craig and Kermis point out, "play with motion is often begun by an adult and provides infants with some of their earliest social experiences" (p. 255). The authors also point out that children do not share this kind of activity with other children much before the age of three (p. 402).

3. *Rough-and-Tumble Play.* Craig and Kermis note that although teachers and parents often discourage this kind of play, there is evidence that it is beneficial to children. Along with exercise (especially large-muscle exercise) and the release of energy, rough-and-tumble play teaches children how to "handle their feelings, to control their impulses, and to filter out negative behaviors that are inappropriate in a group" (p. 402).

4. *Play with Language.* This kind of play involves experimentation with language rhythms and cadences, the mixing up of words to make new meanings, the use of language "to poke fun at the world and to verify their grasp of reality"

(p. 402). There is no concern with using language to communicate; children concentrate on the language itself by manipulating its sounds, patterns, and meanings. Interestingly enough, Craig also notes that children use language play "as a buffer against expressions of anger" (p. 402).

5. *Dramatic Play and Modeling.* The taking on of roles or models is considered a major type of play. This involves such activities or behaviors as "playing house, imitating a parent going to work, pretending to be a firefighter, a nurse, an astronaut, or a truck driver" (p. 404). Entailed here is not just an "imitation of whole patterns of behavior, but also considerable fantasy and novel ways of interaction" (p. 404). The authors note further that "children come to understand various social relationships, rules, and certain other aspects of the culture through imitative play" (p. 404).

6. *Games, Rituals, and Competitive Play.* This last type of play is the most sophisticated. It involves rules and specific goals, decisions about taking turns, setting up guidelines about what is and is not allowed, and so on. These games and the activities they require help to develop cognitive skills such as "learning rules, understanding the sequence of cause-and-effect, realizing the consequences of various actions, learning about winning and losing, and learning to fit behavior to certain patterns and rules" (in Craig & Kermis, 1995, p. 404; see also Herron & Sutton-Smith, 1971; Kamii & DeVries, 1980).

Schwartz's Three Kinds of Language Play

Citing Judith Schwartz (1981), Craig and Kermis (1995) describe three kinds of language play:

1. There is the regular repetition of "letters and words in a steady beat: *La la la / Lol li pop / La la la / Lol li pop*" (p. 402).

2. There is a play consisting of patterns of words "as if they were practicing a grammatical drill or sentences using the same words: *Hit it. / Sit it. / Slit it. / Mit it*. And *There is the light. / Where is the light? / Here is the light*" (p. 402).

3. There is the less frequent kind of play in which "children play with the meaning of words or invent words to fit meanings" (p. 402). They give the examples of "*San Diego, Sandiego, Sandi Ego / San Diego, Sandi Ego / Eggs aren't sandy!*" (p. 402).

Craig and Kermis propose that children engage in language play because it is fun, it gives them the opportunity "to practice and master the grammar and words they are learning," and it allows them "to control their experiences" (pp. 402–404). They note that older children use language to structure their play, perhaps through the use of rituals, which, when followed, allow them to control the experience (p. 404).

Defining and Describing Play: Some Additional Considerations

Craig and Kermis's (1995) six forms of play will, for the purposes of this text, serve both to define and describe play. But other descriptions and definitions of *play* are available. Brewer (1998), for example, defines *play* that occurs in a school setting as falling on a continuum "that runs from free play to guided play to directed play" (p. 104). When children are allowed to choose the materials they want to play with and how they want to play with them, they are engaging in free play. If the teacher selects the materials from which the children may choose, and the teacher's intent is to help the children discover specific concepts, then the children are engaging in guided play. Directed play is play in which "the teacher instructs the children how to accomplish a specific task. Singing songs, engaging in fingerplays, and playing circle games are examples of directed play" (Brewer, 1998, pp. 104–105).

Recall the discussion in Chapter 7 of Parten's descriptions of social interactions, or what Brewer calls "levels of social play" (p. 105). Parten's descriptions entail different degrees of social interaction or involvement that children have with one another. Note that the first of Parten's classifications uses the term *behavior* rather than *play*, namely *unoccupied behavior* and *onlooker behavior*. The key characteristics of these two classifications consist of the fact that in unoccupied behavior, "the child is not engaging in any obvious play activity or social interaction," and in onlooker behavior, "the child spends most of her time watching other children play."

Berk (1998) discusses Parten's classifications in the context of "peer sociability." Parten described social development as occurring in a three-step sequence. The first step consists of unoccupied behavior, onlooker behavior, and solitary play (Berk, 1998, p. 251). These three categories are notable for the conspicuous absence of any kind of social interaction. The next step involves parallel play, in which the child plays near other children and with the same or similar materials, but again, there is no social interaction, nor does the child attempt to influence another child's behavior (1998, p. 251). True forms of play appear with associative play, in which "children engage in separate activities, but they interact by exchanging toys and commenting on one another's behavior... and cooperative play—a more advanced type of interaction in which children orient toward a common goal, such as acting out a make believe theme or working on the same product, such as a sand castle or a painting" (p. 251).

Berk (1998) further notes that associative play and cooperative play "emerge in the order suggested by Parten, but they do not form a neat developmental sequence in which later-appearing ones replace earlier ones.... Instead, all types coexist during the preschool years" (p. 251). Furthermore, even though nonsocial activity decreases in frequency with age, "it is still the most frequent form of behavior among 3- to 4-year-olds" (pp. 251–252). Berk indicates that during the years from three to six, "solitary and parallel play remain fairly stable... and together, these categories account for as much of the young child's play as highly social, cooperative interaction" (p. 252). What is of special interest is that the amount of solitary and parallel play—which are forms of nonsocial activity—changes less than the type of solitary and parallel play. Citing the 1994 work of Pan and the 1998 work of Rubin, Watson, and Jambor on preschoolers' play, Berk writes, "Within each of Parten's play types, older children displayed a more cognitively mature behavior than did younger children" (p. 252). She goes on to identify what she labels the "[d]evelopmental sequence of cognitive play categories" (p. 252). These categories are displayed in Table 16-5.

Brewer (1998) proposes an interesting modification of the description of onlooker behavior, which she calls "onlooker play" (p. 105). She defines such play as "[p]lay in which the child who is playing individually is simultaneously observing those playing in the same area" (p. 105). Brewer also notes that during onlooker play, "Children who watch each other play may alter their own play behavior after watching. Children engaged in onlooker play may seem to be sitting passively while children around them are playing, but they are very alert to the action around them" (p. 105). Brewer omits entirely the category of unoccupied behavior, most likely because it does not involve any kind of play. What appears to be the essential difference between onlooker behavior and onlooker play is that in the latter, the child is in fact engaging in play activity rather than simply passively watching other children play. This being so, there is no logical reason to discard Parten's onlooker behavior category if a child's actions conform to the category's definition.

Play with Objects

Piaget's Four Kinds of Play with Objects: Practice Play, Symbolic Play, Games with Rules, Games of Construction

Play does not take place only with other people—children also play with objects. Piaget identified four kinds of play with objects: practice play, symbolic play, games

Table 16-5 Developmental Sequence of Cognitive Play Categories			
Play Category	**Typical Age**	**Description**	**Examples**
Functional play	During first 2 years of life	Functional play consists of repetitive motor movements; child may or may not use objects	Manipulating an object (for example, "kneading clay") with no goal in mind; moving around a room for the sheer sake of the movement itself; "rolling a car back and forth"
Constructive play	Between 3 and 6 years	Making or building something	"Drawing a picture"; making a house with blocks or some other suitable material; working on a puzzle
Make-believe play	Between 2 and 6 years	Taking on "everyday and imaginary roles" (p. 252)	Pretending to be a parent, firefighter, or TV character; "playing house, school, or police officer"

Adapted from Berk, 2007, p. 262.

with rules, and games of construction. Practice play means pretty much what the term suggests—the exploration of materials and their possible uses and characteristics. This kind of play is similar to, or involves, what Piaget called functional or reproductive assimilation, in which the child learns about an object or toy by repeatedly interacting with it, thereby assimilating it into his or her cognitive scheme or structure. Symbolic play is play in which an object or toy stands for or represents something else, such as when a child pretends that a stick is a sword or a rocket ship. Games with rules occur when "children [might] play according to rules they have made up themselves or according to the rules that are generally agreed on for playing the game" (Brewer, 1998, pp. 106–107). Finally, Piaget believed that games of construction grow out of symbolic play "but tended later to constitute genuine adaptations (mechanical constructions, etc.) or solutions to problems and intelligent creations" (Piaget & Inhelder [1969], as cited in Brewer, 1998, p. 107).

Vygotsky's Views on Play

Brewer (1998) succinctly summarizes Vygotsky's ideas concerning play, and we defer to her for this present discussion. Vygotsky theorized that "play develops from the manipulative play of toddlers to the socially oriented play of older preschoolers and kindergartners and finally to games" (Brewer, 1998, p. 107). Brewer cites three ways in which Vygotsky believed play is important to the child's development:

■ **zone of proximal development**

A concept found in Vygotsky's theory, the zone of proximal development (ZPD) refers to "space" or distance between what a child can do for herself and what she can do only with someone else's help. The purpose of the zone of proximal development in early child care and early childhood education is essentially to guide the caregivers and teachers—as well as parents—in their efforts to promote a child's cognitive development.

1. *"Play creates the child's* ."**zone of proximal development**." In a play setting, a child can control behavior such as attending to a task before she is able to control that behavior in another setting.

2. *"Play facilitates the separation of thought from actions and objects*." In play, the child can pretend that a block is a boat; this separation of object from meaning is critical to the development of abstract thinking.

3. *"Play facilitates the development of self-regulation*." "In developing self-regulation, children in play are required to make their behavior match the role they have accepted. For example, a child playing a 'dog' can stop barking or sit still on command" (from Bodrova & Leong, 1996, p. 126, cited in Brewer, 1998, pp. 107–108).

The zone of proximal development (ZPD) is essentially the "space" between what children can do by themselves and what they can do only with someone's help. Therefore, the first of Vygotsky's benefits of play means that through play, children learn to do something they could not do before in another, nonplay setting. Play essentially moves them through that space between inability and ability, and they can subsequently express that newly acquired ability in situations other than the one in which they acquired it.

The second benefit of play is directly relatable to cognition. The primary accomplishment here is the children's recognition that an object's meaning can exist independently of the object itself. There is also an understanding that an object's meaning is not inherent in the object; its meaning is given to it by someone, and the meaning as well as the label applied to it are agreed upon by those who use the object and its label. The fact that objects have different meanings to different people attests to the rather arbitrary—conventionalized—nature of such meanings. Children also eventually learn this.

The third aspect or benefit of play—self-regulation—will not occur in every play situation because some play is characterized as voluntary and spontaneous. Indeed, play typically conjures up ideas of total disregard for any kind of regulation other than that imposed by the participants themselves. Therefore, to say "children in play are required to make their behavior match the role they have accepted" seemingly excludes spontaneity. Such matching sounds like imitation, although there are symbolic play and role-taking play, for example, both of which require self-regulation.

Observation Objectives

To study play behavior from a group or an individual perspective. To analyze children's behavior according to specific descriptive criteria and thereby determine whether that behavior is play or nonplay and to analyze the content of children's interaction patterns and determine into which of Parten's six classifications of play or social interaction those patterns can be put; to observe several children's behavior for evidence of Vygotsky's benefits or consequences of play, such as a child exhibiting behavior in play that she was unable to exhibit in some other, nonplay activity; and to observe examples of functional, constructive, or make-believe play.

Procedure

This exercise consists of two parts. In Part I you will be using a narrative description format. You may observe and record individuals, groups, or both. Observe at least three individual children, or two groups, for 10 to 15 minutes on each occasion. Then analyze your descriptive data and draw conclusions regarding whether the activity you have recorded is play or nonplay activity. Support your decisions by interpreting your data according to Craig's six types of play and Dworetzky's five descriptors. Indicate, where possible, the kind of play you have observed in each instance and which of the descriptors seem to apply to the behaviors you have recorded. If you believe a behavioral episode is not play, explain also why you reached that decision.

In Part II of this exercise you are given three options or purposes, and you may do one or all of them, depending upon the requirements of your situation. In the first option you will be using the event sampling technique. Observe two or three children over a period of 10 or 15 minutes, and look for examples of behavior that fit into any of

Parten's play/social interaction classifications. Try to observe children who exhibit play behaviors that fit into several of Parten's categories. In other words, if the children you first observe seem to be exhibiting the same kinds of play behavior, such as solitary play, observe other children who are exhibiting different play behaviors. The objective here is to gather data on several different play behaviors related to Parten's six classifications.

The second option might be a bit more complicated than the first. Here you are asked to use the event sampling technique and observe several—say, two or three—children's behavior for evidence of Vygotsky's proposed benefits or consequences of play. For example, are you able to observe a child exhibiting behavior in play that he or she apparently was unable to exhibit in some other, nonplay situation? You might possibly interpret the time spent in play as a practice or acquisition period, after which the child displays his or her newly acquired skill under different circumstances.

Because you are using the event sampling technique for this second option, you might need more time than you did for the first option. The event sampling technique requires you to wait for the target event to occur. However, do not spend an excessive amount of time trying to capture your target events. If the children you are observing do not exhibit the behaviors you want, try selecting different children who might be more likely to exhibit those behaviors.

For the third option you will again be using the event sampling technique. Select several children—again, perhaps two or three—as the focus for your observation. Review Table 16-5 depicting the developmental sequence of cognitive play categories. Based on that developmental sequence, look for examples of functional, constructive, or make-believe play.

These play categories cover the first six years of life, which means that the information in Table 16-5 is not restricted to the present observation exercise. It is also possible that you might observe a child between, let us say, three and six years of age exhibiting functional play that Berk describes as typical during the first two years of life. This would be similar to a child who is predominantly in Piaget's preoperational stage exhibiting sensorimotor behavior.

Your purpose is to look for behavioral events that fit into Parten's six categories of play or social interaction (see Table 7-3a p. 139). You will not necessarily observe particular preselected individual children or groups of children as you did in Part I. Rather than taking in all behavior as it occurs (narrative description), you will have to wait for the occurrence of a particular behavioral event that fits into one of Parten's categories (event sampling). Putting a behavior into a specific category will, for the purposes of this exercise, be the equivalent of making an interpretation. Consequently, there are no spaces specially designated for interpretive comments. (See Observation Exercise 16-5.)

EXERCISE 16-6: EMOTIONAL BEHAVIOR

Background Information

Emotions are such a basic part of our psychological being that we sometimes take them for granted. Some of our emotions are clearly identifiable by us. We know when we are angry, frightened, or joyous. At other times, however, we can have feelings that are not so clear; we may not be able to label what we feel. Whatever the case, emotions are internal experiences that are private and directly accessible only to the individual experiencing them. This being so, we cannot state with certainty what emotion another person is feeling. She must tell us, or we must infer the emotion on the basis of the individual's behavior, facial expressions, and the event that preceded and might have caused the feeling. A child's emotional behaviors become more refined and extensive as she matures. Therefore, a four- or five-year-old will typically be more emotionally expressive than a two-year-old. But what is the role of emotions? What is their significance? Let us examine for a moment the concept of emotions from a more developmental or perhaps theoretical perspective. Carroll Izard (1977), in his book *Human Emotions*, asks whether there is a need to study emotions. He notes that "there is a wide range of scientific opinion regarding the nature and importance of emotions" (p. 3). He goes on to give some of these scientific opinions, but very early on he reaches his own conclusion: "My view is that the emotions constitute the primary *motivational system* for human beings" (p. 3, italics added).

Regardless of your own specific opinion on this question, it is a fact that emotions are here to stay. It is also a fact that on a personal level, emotions—our own and those of children—are extremely important. They are also important on a professional level. Traditionally, for example, early childhood education programs emphasized children's social and emotional development, and the current stress on cognitive development is of relatively recent origin.

Stanley Greenspan, a practicing psychiatrist involved in research in infant and child development, and his wife Nancy Thorndike Greenspan, a health economist, wrote a book entitled *First Feelings* (1985), in which they deal with the emotional development of children from birth to age four years. Of interest to us are the six milestones that characterize or define children's emotional growth and development. In this chapter, we briefly discuss only the fifth and sixth emotional milestones, which begin at 18 months of age and go through 48 months of age. This span covers the preschool years, and we intend that you use them as guidelines for determining a child's approximate stage of emotional development or maturity. The earlier stages (one through four) are covered in Chapter 14 and Chapter 15. The Greenspans' six emotional milestones were arrived at by "closely observing babies' behavior, emotional reactions, and ways of relating to us" (pp. 3–4). You will be asked to do something similar, but in your case, the theoretical groundwork has already been laid. You will be asked only to put your observations into this theoretical framework and to draw some tentative conclusions regarding a child's level of emotional development.

However, let us point out again that our major purpose is not to provide you with a means of intervening in children's lives as therapists or even as teachers. Rather, in this exercise we want to give you a theoretical framework within which to observe and record children's actions in the particular area of emotional development and behavior.

Emotional Milestones during the Preschool Years

The Greenspan's Fifth Emotional Milestone

The fifth stage or milestone identified by the Greenspans occurs between 18 and 36 months of age. By the time children reach this stage, they have learned how objects work, and they continue to improve their ability to "organize complicated social and emotional patterns" (Greenspan & Greenspan, 1985, p. 5), an ability that becomes evident in stage 4. This stage 4 competence increases to enable the child to "create … objects in his own mind's eye" (p. 5). Mental images of his mother, for example, allow him to deal with her—and with objects—even in her absence. As the Greenspans also point out, this ability to form mental images and impressions (to "create [one's own] experiences" or "construct her own ideas," say the Greenspans) also gives the child the ability to dream "in an adult way" (p. 6). This occurs later than 15 months of age—perhaps by about two or two and one-half years of age. A child in this stage can also engage in pretend play.

The Greenspan's Sixth Milestone

The sixth and final milestone, which occurs between 30 and 48 months, takes children into what the Greenspans describe as "the emotional realms of pleasure and dependency, curiosity, anger, self-discipline or setting their own limits, even empathy and love" (p. 6). Additionally, children learn "to separate make-believe from reality and are able to work with ideas and to plan and anticipate" (p. 6). In this stage, according to the Greenspans, a three-and-a-half-year-old child can say such things as "I dreamed there were witches under my bed. Tonight I'm going to dream about kittens" (p. 6).

It is important to emphasize here that the child's emotional development and his intellectual development go hand in hand, so to speak. As the Greenspans put it, the child

will now begin to organize and manipulate his ideas into a cause-and-effect understanding of his own emotions and the world that *begins to take reality into account*

And

> [J]ust as your child learned to combine blocks to make an original house, now he can combine emotional ideas. He may create new feelings of shame and, eventually, guilt based on his own feelings about his "bad" wishes and behavior.

Further,

> He now emerges with the "cause-and-effect" logic at the level of emotional ideas that he developed earlier at the level of behavior. (p. 173, italics added)

The Greenspans' work reveals the developmental course of the emotions, and it gives a hint of some of the changing content or focus of a child's emotional behavior. Therefore, part of your observation task will be to identify the specific content, character, and developmental level of children's emotional responses.

There is a broad range of emotions that children are ultimately capable of displaying. Because we have relied on such a considerable proportion of the Greenspans' work on this critical aspect of development, we adopt for use the seven areas of emotional functioning that they identify. These areas of functioning are "dependency, pleasure, love and intimacy, curiosity, assertiveness and exploration, protest and anger, and self-discipline." Also noted are the emotions that are related to these areas: "[feelings of] loss, sadness, anxiety, fear, shame, and guilt" (Greenspan & Greenspan, 1985, p. 8).

We briefly discuss only a few of these emotions or areas of emotional functioning. We want to deal with aggression (which, in the context of the Greenspans' terminology, can be thought of as assertiveness, protest, and anger), dependency, and fear. We hesitate to focus on the negative feelings or behaviors, but they are usually of some concern to parents and adults. Inappropriate aggression may be of particular concern to parents and teachers, especially aggression that threatens the safety of others or that is directed against adults.

Aggression

Aggression, like some other types of behaviors, is used both to identify particular behaviors that have specific characteristics and to describe a particular personality **trait**. A trait is a tendency to behave in certain ways under certain circumstances. Each of these uses has accompanying problems. Aggressive behavior is frequently defined as behavior that is intended to physically or psychologically hurt another person (or oneself) or to damage or destroy property. An important issue is whether a behavior is

trait
A tendency or predisposition to behave in certain ways under certain circumstances.

intentionally aggressive or simply an accidental occurrence. Further, it is argued by some that for a behavior to be termed aggressive, the aggressor must feel anger or hostility toward the "victim" and must derive satisfaction from hurting the victim. This kind of aggression is called hostile aggression. In contrast to hostile aggression, there can be cases where the aggressor is interested only in getting some object from the victim or achieving some goal. This is called instrumental aggression, and it need not involve anger or hostility.

Be certain that you label as hostile aggression only those behaviors that you believe are purposely intended to hurt another person (include both physical and verbal aggression):

1. Observe the child's behavior for instances of aggression, either toward another child or an adult, or toward objects in the environment.

2. What kinds of situations or frustrations make the child angry? What behaviors by other people anger the child? How does she express her anger?

Dependency

Dependency consists of such behaviors as clinging or maintaining proximity to adults or other children; seeking approval, recognition, assistance, attention, and reassurance; and striving for affection and support. It is important to recognize that all of us are dependent. The issue is to what degree and under what circumstances we show our dependency. It is also useful to distinguish between two basic types of dependency: (a) instrumental dependency, which essentially is the necessary reliance we have on others for certain things that are beyond our capacity to do; and (b) emotional dependency, which is a need to be near others and to have their support, affection, and reassurance. It can also be the unwillingness or the self-perceived inability to do things for oneself that one can or should be able to do.

It is important that, where possible, you distinguish instrumental dependency from emotional dependency behaviors. It is also important to note that as children mature, the characteristics of their dependency behaviors change. Very young children are likely to show clinging and proximity-seeking behaviors, whereas older children, who also have greater cognitive abilities, will likely seek attention and approval.

3. In what situations or activities is the child dependent and, for example, seeks the presence, direction, or assistance of others? In what situations is the child independent and does not seek direction or assistance from others?

Fear

Fear is demonstrated by such behaviors as crying, withdrawing, seeking help, and avoiding the fear-producing situation. Fear can promote both dependency and

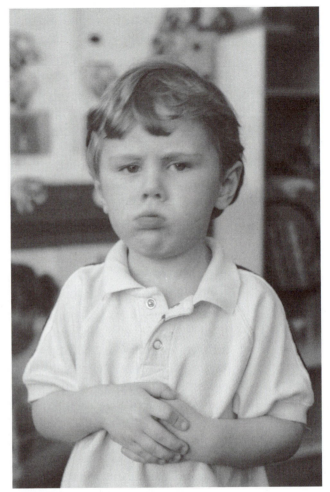

A face can say a lot to a teacher.

aggressive behaviors. Nonetheless, fear can be expressed in such a way that it, and not aggression or dependency, is the primary emotion.

4. What kinds of objects or situations appear to scare the child? In what ways does the child express his fears? How does he deal with his fears (e.g., by withdrawing, confronting the fearful situation, seeking help)?

In addition to the emotional behaviors just discussed, there are other feelings that children are capable of experiencing and expressing. You should be alert to as many of the child's affective states as possible. For example, there are the feelings of pleasure and displeasure, frustration, boredom, and sadness. Like adults, children will differ as to how accurately they can identify what they feel, and, like adults, children differ in how they explain their feelings. However, children may lack the ability to verbally express their feelings.

5. What kinds of things does the child appear to find pleasant? What activities, play materials, stories, games, and so on seem to be particularly attractive to the child? How does he express that pleasure?

6. What kinds of things are unpleasant or uncomfortable for the child? In what situations does the child appear to be ill at ease? How does she express her displeasure?

As a final topic, and one that pertains to all of the preceding, consider the following question:

7. Are all or most of the child's feelings expressed with equal strength, or does their intensity vary with the particular feeling or situation?

This exercise could get a bit complicated, essentially because you will be asked to attempt some conclusions regarding into which of the Greenspans' stages of development your particular child or children can be placed. Additionally, in this exercise you will be trying to gain some general understanding of the child's emotional behaviors, of the range of her emotions and the kinds of situations that prompt these behaviors. Again, you can only infer what the child is feeling from the overt behaviors you have witnessed; you cannot observe emotions directly.

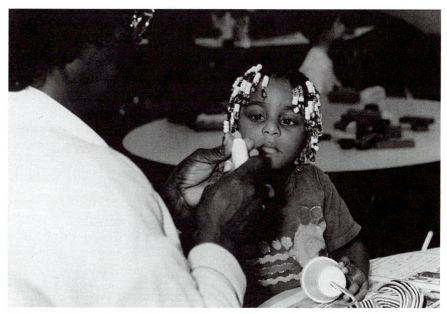

Instrumental dependency—this child relies on her teacher to complete a task she cannot handle herself.

Observation Objectives

To learn about the differences in children's emotional behaviors and the range of emotional responses in preschool children. To determine the level of a child's emotional development according to stages five and six of Greenspan and Greenspan's six milestones or stages of emotional development.

Procedure

There are two parts to this exercise. In Part I, select three children and, using the event sampling technique, watch for and record behaviors or patterns of behavior that would indicate or reflect at which milestone a child's emotional development can be located. Objectively describe those behaviors, and specify as precisely as you can why you think the behaviors you have recorded do in fact indicate a particular level of emotional development.

In Part II, staying with the same three children as in Part I, and using the narrative description technique, observe and record each child's behavior for a period of 10 to 15 minutes. Record in as much detail as possible, and be sure to include descriptions of the physical and social context as they apply to the emotional behaviors observed. Interpret or comment on each child, using the questions and background information provided as guides. Finally, compare the three children. Look at the range of emotional expression, intensity of expression, and what evokes emotional responses. In short, summarize how the children differ from one another in this area of functioning. (See Observation Exercise 16-6.)

EXERCISE 16-7: SOCIAL DEVELOPMENT AND PEER INTERACTIONS

Background Information

Some believe that social development should be the most important concern of the early education curriculum in particular and the early childhood years in general. It is during this period of life that the child's horizons are expanding dramatically, and his cognitive and emotional abilities are becoming more and more suited to interacting socially with others.

Social behaviors are behaviors that are oriented toward and influenced by other persons. A social interaction is a situation where two or more individuals take one another into account. So, for example, Alex and Thomas are in a social interaction when Alex influences Thomas and is also influenced by Thomas.

The concept of social skills is familiar to most of us. Social skills include such things as the ability to get along with others, to influence or persuade others without aggression, to resolve conflicts and disagreements in a socially approved way, and generally to be able to initiate and sustain friendships and social interactions. Social skills can involve the ability to be a leader in a group, as well as a follower who can work for the group's best interests.

Social skills are a product of decreasing egocentrism and increasing socio-centrism. Both of these are supported by increasing cognitive and intellectual skills, along with increased contact with others in social situations.

There are many areas of development and behavior that pertain to social behavior. It should also be noted that much of what the child does during the preschool day is done within a social context. Consequently, most if not all of your observation exercises in this chapter have a social component.

1. How does the child show awareness of and sensitivity to others? How does she express concern for others' feelings and needs?

2. How does the child respond in a situation in which he is a follower? Does he follow the directions of the leader, or does he refuse to cooperate? Is the child sensitive to the needs of the group, and is he willing to play a follower role where it is appropriate? In this regard, does the child follow whatever rules appear to be operating in the situation? Does the child share, take turns, and so on?

3. If the child is a leader, how does she behave in that role? Does she offer suggestions, or does she make demands on others? How do the other children respond to her efforts to lead? Does the child instill confidence in others, or does she tend to alienate them?

4. How does the child initiate contact with other children? That is, how does he try to join a group, start a new activity or participate in one already going on, or strike up a friendship? How do others respond to the child's efforts?

5. How does the child settle arguments or conflicts—with physical force, verbal threats, efforts to compromise, appeal to an adult, and so on?

Observation Objectives

To identify the social statuses of various children in a group. To learn about children's differing styles of social interaction.

Procedure

There are two parts to this exercise. In Part I, try to identify the leaders in particular social/peer interaction situations. Observe and record the behaviors of these leaders and the behaviors of the other children in the group. Do the following:

1. Compare and contrast the leadership styles or behaviors of the several different leaders you have observed. *Style* here simply refers to the way in which the

child asserts his or her leadership: through force, verbal persuasion, charisma, or sheer positive force of personality.

2. Compare and contrast the behaviors of the leaders with the behaviors of the followers or others in the group. How are they different? How are they alike? How do the leaders get the others to follow them? Is a child a leader in one group or situation and a follower in another?

In Part II, construct a chart or diagram (perhaps the best such diagram would be a **sociogram**) that will enable you to determine who are the most and the least popular children in the group—popular in the sense of such indications as the number of social interactions in which they engage, and the number of other children who seek them out or show signs of wanting to be with them. Then observe and record the behaviors of the most popular child and the least popular child in the group. Examine your data record, and compare the interaction styles and general behavioral characteristics of these children.

The sociogram was developed by a psychiatrist named J. L. Moreno. Sociograms, says sociologist Rodney Stark (1985), are "charts showing the social networks within a group" (p. 22). Networks are relationships within a group. Sociograms are often constructed by asking members of a group questions such as these: Who are your closest friends? Whom do you admire the most? With whom would you most like to take a trip? Asking such questions may not be possible or desirable with preschoolers;

sociogram
A graphic representation of how children in a group feel about one another. Children are often represented by circles, and their interactions with peers are represented by arrows that connect one circle (child) to another.

A child's emotional behaviors become more refined and extensive as she matures. A four- or five-year-old will typically be more emotionally expressive than a two-year-old.

therefore, you may have to observe the interactions and social exchanges that occur among the children and calculate a sociogram from that data. A sample sociogram is shown here. (See Observation Exercise 16-7.)

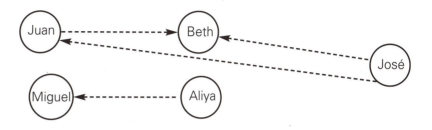

OBSERVATION EXERCISE **16-1**

PART I: The Preschool Child in the Physical Environment

Observer's Name _____

Child/Children Observed _____

Child's/Children's Age(s) _____ Child's/Children's Sex _____

Observation Context (home, child care center, preschool, school) _____

Date of Observation ___ Time Begun ___ Time Ended ___

Brief Description of Physical and Social Characteristics of Observation Setting:

Diagrams of the Physical Environment

Inside

Outside

PART II: The Preschool Child in the Physical Environment

Observer's Name _____

Child/Children Observed _____

Child's/Children's Age(s) _____ Child's/Children's Sex ___

Observation Context (home, child care center, preschool, school) _____

Date of Observation ___ Time Begun ___ Time Ended _____

Brief Description of Physical and Social Characteristics of Observation Setting:

OBSERVATION EXERCISE **16-1** (Continued)

Objective Behavioral Descriptions (OBDs) and Interpretations: *Narrative Description*

OBD Session 1: [Time begun _____ Time ended_____]

Interpretation 1: Location 1:

OBD Session 2: [Time begun _____ Time ended _____]

Interpretation 2: Location 2:

OBD Session 3: [Time begun _____ Time ended _____]

Interpretation 3: Location 3:

Continue with OBDs and interpretations for as long as needed.

Summary of Behavioral Differences:

PART THREE

OBSERVATION EXERCISE **16-2**

Physical Growth and Motor Functioning

Observer's Name _____

Child/Children Observed _____

Child's/Children's Age(s) _____Child's/Children's Sex ___

Observation Context (home, child care center, preschool, school) _____

Date of Observation ___ Time Begun ___ Time Ended _____

Brief Description of Physical and Social Characteristics of Observation Setting:

Objective Behavioral Descriptions (OBDs) and Interpretations: *Event Sampling*

OBD 1: Child 1 (age): [Time begun ___ Time ended ____]

Interpretation 1: Child 1:

OBD 2: Child 2 (age): [Time begun ___ Time ended ____]

Interpretation 2: Child 2:

Continue for as many OBDs as are needed or desired.

Comparison of Children's Motor Behaviors:

OBSERVATION EXERCISE **16-3**

Cognitive and Intellectual Development and Behavior

Observer's Name _____

Child/Children Observed _____

Child's/Children's Age(s) _____Child's/Children's Sex ___

Observation Context (home, child care center, preschool, school) _____

Date of Observation ___ Time Begun ___ Time Ended _____

Brief Description of Physical and Social Characteristics of Observation Setting:

Objective Behavioral Descriptions (OBDs) and Interpretations: *Narrative Description*

OBD 1: Child 1 (age): [Time begun ___ Time ended ____]
Interpretation 1: Child 1:

OBD 2: Child 2 (age): [Time begun ___ Time ended ____]
Interpretation 2: Child 2:

Continue for as many OBDs as are needed or desired.
Summary Child 1:

Summary Child 2:

Comparison: Child 1 with Child 2:

Contrast: Child 1 and Child 2:

OBSERVATION EXERCISE 16-4

Language Development

Observer's Name _____

Child/Children Observed _____

Child's/Children's Age(s) _____ Child's/Children's Sex ___

Observation Context (home, child care center, preschool, school) _____

Date of Observation ___ Time Begun ___ Time Ended _____

Brief Description of Physical and Social Characteristics of Observation Setting:

....

Objective Behavioral Descriptions (OBDs) and Interpretations: Event Sampling

OBD 1: [Time begun ___ Time ended ____]

Interpretation 1:

OBD 2: [Time begun ___ Time ended ____]

Interpretation 2:

Continue for as many OBDs as are needed or desired.

Descriptive and Interpretive Summary of Group's Language Behavior:

OBSERVATION EXERCISE 16-5

PART I: Play

Observer's Name _____

Child/Children Observed _____

Child's/Children's Age(s) _____Child's/Children's Sex ___

Observation Context (home, child care center, preschool, school) _____

Date of Observation ___ Time Begun ___ Time Ended _____

Brief Description of Physical and Social Characteristics of Observation Setting:

Objective Behavioral Descriptions (OBDs) and Interpretations: *Narrative Description*

OBD 1: [Time begun _____ Time ended _____]

Interpretation 1:

OBD 2: [Time begun _____ Time ended _____]

Interpretation 2:

OBD 3: [Time begun _____ Time ended _____]

Interpretation 3:

OBD 4: [Time begun _____ Time ended _____]

Interpretation 4:

Continue for as many OBDs as are needed or desired.

Summary of Interpretive Comments:

PART THREE

OBSERVATION EXERCISE 16-5

PART II: Play Option 1 (Parten's Play/Social Interaction Classifications):

Observer's Name _____

Child/Children Observed _____

Child's/Children's Age(s) _____ Child's/Children's Sex ___

Observation Context (home, child care center, preschool, school) _____

Date of Observation ___ Time Begun ___ Time Ended _____

Brief Description of Physical and Social Characteristics of Observation Setting:

Play Description and Classification (Parten's Six Categories—see Table 7-3a, p. 139): *Event Sampling*

Unoccupied Behavior:

Onlooker Behavior:

Solitary Play:

Parallel Play:

Associative Play:

Cooperative Play:

Summary of Interpretive Comments:

PART II: Play Option 2 (Vygotsky's benefits or consequences of play):

Observer's Name _____

Child/Children Observed _____

Child's/Children's Age(s) _____ Child's/Children's Sex ___

Observation Context (home, child care center, preschool, school) _____

Date of Observation ___ Time Begun ___ Time Ended _____

Brief Description of Physical and Social Characteristics of Observation Setting:

OBSERVATION EXERCISE **16-5** (Continued)

Objective Behavioral Descriptions (OBDs) and Interpretations: Event Sampling (see page 157 for a discussion of these consequences)

Observe and record play behaviors that properly fall under one or more of Vygotsky's benefits listed below. In each instance, record the child's name and the time the behavioral event began and the time it ended.

Play that creates the child's zone of proximal development:

Child: _____ [Time begun _____ Time ended _____]

Play that facilitates the separation of thought from actions and objects:

Child: _____ [Time begun _____ Time ended _____]

Play that facilitates the development of self-regulation:

Child: _____ [Time begun _____ Time ended _____]

Continue for as many OBDs as are needed or desired.

Summary of Interpretive Comments:

PART II: Play Option 3: Observing the Developmental Sequence of Cognitive Play Categories

Observer's Name _____

Child/Children Observed _____

Child's/Children's Age(s) _____ Child's/Children's Sex ___

Observation Context (home, child care center, preschool, school) _____

Date of Observation ___ Time Begun ___ Time Ended _____

Brief Description of Physical and Social Characteristics of Observation Setting:

OBSERVATION EXERCISE **16-5** (Continued)

Objective Behavioral Descriptions (OBDs) and Interpretations: *Event Sampling (see Table 17-5, page 408, for a review of these categories)*

Observe and record play behaviors that fall under one or more of the following play categories. In each instance, record the child's name and the time the behavioral event began and the time it ended.

Functional Play:

Child: _____ [Time begun _____ Time ended _____]

Constructive Play:

Child: _____ [Time begun _____ Time ended _____]

Make-Believe Play:

Child: _____ [Time begun _____ Time ended _____]

Continue for as many OBDs as are required or desired.

Summary of Interpretive Comments:

OBSERVATION EXERCISE **16-6**

PART I:
Emotional
Behavior
(Greenspan and
Greenspan's
Fifth and Sixth
Emotional
Milestones)

Observer's Name _____

Child/Children Observed _____

Child's/Children's Age(s) _____Child's/Children's Sex ___

Observation Context (home, child care center, preschool, school) _____

Date of Observation ___ Time Begun ___ Time Ended _____

Brief Description of Physical and Social Characteristics of Observation Setting:

....

Objective
Behavioral
Descriptions
(OBDs) and
Interpretations:
Event Sampling

Fifth Emotional Milestone:

Child 1: ____ [Time begun ____ Time ended ____]

Child 2: ____ [Time begun ____ Time ended ____]

Sixth Emotional Milestone:

Child 1: ____ [Time begun ____ Time ended ____]

Child 2: ____ [Time begun ____ Time ended ____]

Continue for as many OBDs as are needed or desired.

Summary of Interpretive Comments:

....

PART II:
Emotional
Behavior

Observer's Name _____

Child/Children Observed _____

Child's/Children's Age(s) _____Child's/Children's Sex ___

Observation Context (home, child care center, preschool, school) _____

Date of Observation ___ Time Begun ___ Time Ended _____

Brief Description of Physical and Social Characteristics of Observation Setting:

....

OBSERVATION EXERCISE **16-6** (Continued)

Objective Behavioral Descriptions (OBDs) and Interpretations: *Narrative Description*

OBD 1: Child 1: [Time begun _____ Time ended _____]

Interpretation 1:

OBD 2: Child 2: [Time begun _____ Time ended _____]

Interpretation 2:

OBD 3: Child 3: [Time begun _____ Time ended _____]

Interpretation 3:

Continue for as many OBDs as are required or desired.

Summary of Behavioral Differences:

Summary of Behavioral Similarities:

OBSERVATION EXERCISE 16-7

PART I: Social Development and Peer Interactions

Observer's Name _____

Child/Children Observed _____

Child's/Children's Age(s) _____ Child's/Children's Sex ___

Observation Context (home, child care center, preschool, school) _____

Date of Observation ___ Time Begun ___ Time Ended _____

Brief Description of Physical and Social Characteristics of Observation Setting:

Objective Behavioral Descriptions (OBDs) and Interpretations: *Narrative Description*

Leader 1: [Time begun ____ Time ended ____]

Interpretive Comments 1:

Leader 1: [Time begun ____ Time ended ____]

Interpretive Comments 2:

Leader 1: [Time begun ____ Time ended ____]

Interpretive Comments 3:

Followers Situation 1: [Time begun ___ Time ended ___]

Followers Situation 2: [Time begun ___ Time ended ___]

Followers Situation 3: [Time begun ___ Time ended ___]

Comparisons of Leaders:

Comparisons of Leaders and Followers:

Continue for as many OBDs and interpretations of leaders and followers as are needed or desired.

OBSERVATION EXERCISE **16-7** (Continued)

Part II: Social Development and Peer Interaction

Observer's Name _____

Child/Children Observed _____

Child's/Children's Age(s) _____ Child's/Children's Sex ___

Observation Context (home, child care center, preschool, school) _____

Date of Observation ___ Time Begun ___ Time Ended _____

Brief Description of Physical and Social Characteristics of Observation Setting:

Objective Behavioral Descriptions (OBDs) and Interpretations: *Narrative Description*

OBD 1 (Least Popular Child): [Time begun ___ Time ended ____]

Interpretation 1: (Least Popular Child):

OBD 2 (Most Popular Child): [Time begun ___ Time ended ____]

Interpretation 2: (Most Popular Child):

Continue for as many OBDs and interpretations as are needed or desired for least and most popular child.

Comparison of Least and Most Popular Child:

MIDDLE CHILDHOOD—
THE SCHOOL-AGE YEARS

INTRODUCTION AND PREPARATION

The National Association for the Education of Young Children (NAEYC) defines *early childhood* as comprising the years from birth through eight. The last three years in this age range typically would place children in the first, second, or third grades in the school system. Certainly six-, seven-, and eight-year-olds spend time in places other than the school classroom, but most would agree that, except for the summer, the majority of a school-age child's weekday is spent in the formal classroom setting. With regard to observation, therefore, we assume that at least some of the forthcoming observation exercises will be accomplished in some kind of formal education setting.

Although it depends on the particular school, it is also probable that observations done in a school classroom will be

Chapter 17:
The School-Age
Years: The Six-Year-
Old Child

Chapter 18:
The School-Age
Years: The Seven-
and Eight-Year-Old
Child

more structured and controlled than those performed in a preschool classroom or a child care center. This means that you will have less freedom to move around or participate in the children's activities than you would have in a preschool or child care setting. A possible exception to this, of course, is if you are a teacher, a student teacher, or are in some other way officially connected to the class, although regardless of your official or unofficial status, you will have to abide by the ethical standards that must govern all interactions with children. By all means, however, keep in mind that children of any age can be observed in settings of almost any number and description. Indeed, you have much to gain in your understanding of children of any age if you do observe them in many different kinds of settings and situations.

This extended coverage of the life span was first introduced in the fifth edition of *Seeing Young Children*. As then, we address most of the same functional behavioral areas that were addressed in the previous chapters. The years six through eight continue to see developmental changes in physical and motor abilities and behavior. Language and intellectual skills move along an inexorable path, barring any physical, emotional, or medical problems that would slow or interfere with their developmental course. Social and emotional behaviors change through the combination of experience and maturation. And yes, children of these ages even continue to play, although their play content and motivations are dramatically different from what they were just a few years earlier.

The general format for the following series of observation exercises—Chapters 17 and 18—will be similar to the format of the exercises in the previous chapters. There is one functional/behavioral area that we addressed previously that will not be dealt with in this section: the child's response to particular characteristics and requirements of the physical environment (refer to Observation Exercise 16-1).

The observation exercises will cover relevant behavioral and competency areas in a general way, which means that you are at liberty to apply them in whatever situations and in whatever manner suits your legitimate purposes. The premise is that, with regard to observation as observation, and leaving aside such aspects as language's social, pragmatic functions, language—to take just one behavioral domain—is language, whether it is displayed, observed, recorded, and interpreted during a classroom learning activity or during a pickup game of soccer in a school play yard. However, we acknowledge that you may be more interested in how the child talks about academic subject matter than in how he gives instructions to a teammate on how to score a goal. Nonetheless, in principle, not much will significantly change from one situation to the other with respect to the observation and recording skills that are required.

Chapter 17 deals only with the six-year-old child. The final chapter (Chapter 18) combines the years 7 and 8. This separation and combination have a precedent in other developmental texts. We cannot speak for other authors' rationales, but one motive guiding the present text rests on Piaget's assertion that the period of concrete operations begins at about 7 years of age (and ends at about 11 years of age). This means that, more or less technically, the six-year-old has not yet quite made the full transition out of the preoperational period. This statement must be put into the context of a general assumption that does not apply to all six-year-olds. Piaget's hypothesis simply provides one line of demarcation among many others. Although this text does not adopt Piaget as the ultimate authority on children's cognitive development, his ideas still have a prominent place in the developmental literature, a fact that should not be ignored despite the theories that are vying with his for attention and credibility.

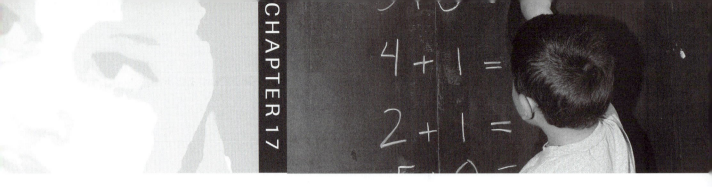

The School-Age Years: The Six-Year-Old Child

PHYSICAL GROWTH AND MOTOR FUNCTIONING

Background Information

This is a time of transitions and significant gains in all the developmental and behavioral areas. This transitional and time-of-improvement character can be discerned when one reads the child development literature. At least some authors describe the skills, abilities, and characteristics of school-age children by comparing and contrasting them with preschool children. Krantz (1994), for instance, provides us with a good summary of what physical growth and motor functioning are like during the general period of middle childhood. He notes that although "children's growth rate slows during the preschool years, significant changes in body size and proportion dramatically affect their motor skill development" (p. 371). This is a useful comparison that points out that even during the earlier preschool period, rapid changes influence the way a child looks and the way she functions or behaves. Growth slows even more after the preschool years, and children during the school-age years show significant ("extraordinary") gains in physical and motor development (Krantz, 1994, p. 371). As he states further, "Physical changes in size, proportion, strength, and endurance provide the foundation for significant improvements in children's motor skills" (p. 371).

Bukatko and Daehler (1995) also attest to the changes in motor skills and development that occur over a period of about two or three years. These changes are summarized in Table 17-1.

The tabular description is very brief, and it may not immediately suggest the scope of the behavioral differences that are displayed between the ages of four and six. Nonetheless, tying shoes and writing some numbers and words represent a rather significant jump in fine (small-muscle) motor ability.

Table 17-1 Summary of Changes in Motor Skills and Development	
Age	**Functional or Skill Area**
4–5 Years	The child ● can walk down steps by alternating his feet. ● can gallop and skip while leading with one foot and using the rear leg to propel himself forward. ● when throwing a ball, uses his body by transferring his weight forward to add force to the throw. ● tries to catch a ball with her hands instead of involving the arms and body. ● can eat with a fork. ● can engage in self-help skills such as dressing by himself.
5–6 Years	● has the ability to walk across a balance beam. ● can long jump about three feet, and he can jump vertically into the air for about a foot. ● can now throw and catch much like an adult.
6–7 Years	● can tie his shoes. ● can write some words and numbers.

Adapted from Bukatko and Daehler, 1995, p. 186.

Keep in mind, too, that six-year-olds retain all the skills they had before they were six, which demonstrates the cumulative nature of development.

Bukatko and Daehler (1995) also note that during middle childhood, motor skills improve with respect to the speed and complexity of movements. The child demonstrates more coordination and displays physical skills in a greater variety of situations and contexts than was possible at an earlier age (p. 187).

Berk's Four Basic Motor Capacities of School-Age Children: Flexibility, Balance, Agility, and Force of Movement

Berk (2005) identifies and describes four "basic motor capacities" in which school-age children show significant gains. The first of these is flexibility, which Berk describes through comparison and contrast. She notes that "[c]ompared with preschoolers, school-age children are physically more pliable and elastic, a difference that can be seen as they swing bats, kick balls, jump over hurdles, and execute tumbling routines" (p. 417). Balance is the second capacity to see improvement. Although some preschoolers can walk a balance beam, for example, the school-age child walks a narrower beam than the younger child. Better balance is important because, as Berk notes, "Improved balance supports many athletic skills, including running, hopping, skipping, throwing, kicking, and the rapid change of direction required in many team sports" (2005, p. 418). The third area of improvement is that of agility: "Quicker and more accurate movements are

Table 17-2 A Summary Description of Some Gross Motor Skills of a Six-Year-Old Child	
Motor Area	**Characteristics**
Running	Child's running speed is approximately 12 feet per second; has good balance while running; can change direction fairly easily; enjoys vigorous physical activity such as running, skipping, jumping, and so on.
Jumping and Variations	Can jump vertically about 4 inches; can long jump 3 feet from standing position. By age seven can jump with some accuracy from one square to another, as in hopscotch.
Throwing	Speed, accuracy, and distance in throwing increase more in boys than in girls. Differences in speed measured in feet per second (fps) are reflected by 39 fps for a ball thrown by a six-year-old boy versus 29 fps for a six-year-old girl. (Actual speed of throwing will not be possible to determine, but subjectively you should be able to detect differences when compared with a preschooler's throwing style and ability.)
Catching	Child can now catch smaller balls and over greater distances than when he or she was a preschooler.
Batting	"Batting motions become more effective with age, increasing in speed and accuracy and involving the entire body" (Berk, 2005, p. 417).
Dribbling	Arm movements in dribbling are more sophisticated—smoother, more controlled, and coordinated— than the earlier movements that are awkward and "slapping" in nature.

Adapted from Berk, 1993, p. 403, and 2005, p. 417.

evident in the fancy footwork of jump rope and hopscotch, as well as in the forward, backward, and sideways motions older children use as they dodge opponents in tag and soccer" (p. 418). Finally, the force with which children perform their movements increases dramatically from early childhood. Berk again notes that "older children throw and kick a ball harder and propel themselves farther off the ground when running and jumping than they could at earlier ages" (p. 418). Table 17-2 is a summary of some of Berk's descriptions.

COGNITIVE AND INTELLECTUAL DEVELOPMENT AND BEHAVIOR

Background Information: The "Cognitive Revolution"

From a cognitive and intellectual point of view, middle childhood is an interesting time. Piaget's theory claims that the period of concrete operational thinking, which is the third of his four stages of cognitive development, extends from 7 to about 11 years of age. Technically, therefore, the six-year-old is in the last phase of the preoperational period. This does not mean that no six-year-old can function in the period of concrete operations but that—at least if Piaget is correct—it is not typical for the six-year-old to function primarily in the later stage. Despite the possibility that the children you will observe will still be in the preoperational period, we give you some background information that goes beyond the preoperational 6 years of age and into Piaget's stage of concrete operational thinking.

Steinberg and Meyer (1995) refer to what they call the "cognitive revolution" that occurs between five and seven years of age. These authors identify some of the gains children make cognitively and intellectually during this period. These gains include a grasp of conservation, improved reasoning about causation, increasing classification skills, and an increasing ability to manipulate symbols (pp. 347–348).

According to Piaget, the preoperational child's reasoning is illogical and unsystematic, whereas the middle-childhood period allows just the opposite style of reasoning: the beginning of logical and systematic thinking and reasoning (e.g., see Krantz, 1994). However, it is important to note that moving from one kind of reasoning to the other involves a gradual shift or transition, not an abrupt one. Here, the term *cognitive revolution* can be replaced by the term **five-to-seven shift** or five-to-seven transition. Krantz (1994) points out that for Piaget, "children's reasoning during the five-to-seven shift [is] **intuitive**" (p. 397, emphasis original). As Krantz puts it, "With intuitive reasoning, children often get the right solutions to problems but without understanding the underlying principles" (p. 398). He describes two other characteristics of intuitive thought that are worth mentioning: It is inconsistent across situations, and it is tentative even when a solution is correct. The first characteristic means that a cognitive skill or decision breaks down or is abandoned if the original situation in which the child reasons correctly is changed. The second characteristic means that the child is easily persuaded from his or her decision about a solution to a problem. The child is insecure and uncertain about the correctness of his or her problem solution.

five-to-seven shift
The period of gradual transition from the illogical and unsystematic thinking of the preschooler to the more logical thinking of the school-age child.

intuitive
A substage of Piaget's preoperational stage of cognitive development. Intuitive thinking is the type of reasoning that takes place during the five-to-seven shift. (*See five-to-seven shift.*)

Information Processing and Sociocultural Theory

Piaget's theory is not the only one to try to explain children's cognitive development. Information processing theory and Vygotsky's sociocultural theory of cognitive development also compete for psychologists' attention and perhaps loyalty. Vygotsky's views are discussed in the text *Child Psychology* by Vasta, Haith, and Miller (1995). Note in this passage the brief but significant comparison with Piaget:

> For him [Vygotsky], the individual's development is a product of his or her culture. Development, in Vygotsky's theory, referred largely to mental development, such as thought, language, and reasoning processes. These abilities were assumed to develop through social interactions with others (especially parents) and thus represented the shared knowledge of the culture. Mental abilities and processes similarly were viewed in terms of the historical sequence of events that produced them. *Whereas Piaget believed that all children's cognitive development follows a very similar pattern of stages, Vygotsky saw intellectual abilities as being much more specific to the culture in which the child was reared.* (p. 23, italics added)

Vygotsky's emphasis on cultural influences on cognitive development is significant. Spodeck and Saracho (1994) discuss Vygotsky's distinction between natural development and cultural development. *Natural development*, as the term might suggest to you, is development that is the result of maturation, whereas *cultural development* "relates to language and reasoning ability" (p. 77). Spodeck and Saracho discuss the interaction between language and thought as follows:

[A]n individual's thinking patterns are products of the activities practiced in the culture in which the individual grows up. Moreover, advanced modes of thought (conceptual thinking) need to be verbally communicated to children; thus, language is an essential tool in determining a person's ability to learn to think. Children's informal and formal education, using a language medium, determines their conceptual thinking level. If children experience a language climate of direct speech and mass communication media that is dominated by simplistic or "primitive" language, then their thinking will be simplistic or primitive. On the other hand, if the children's language environment includes varied and complex concepts, the children's thinking will be diverse and intricate, provided that their biological equipment (the senses, central nervous system, and so on) is not disabled. (p. 77)

Vygotsky also proposed the concept of the zone of proximal development, which seems to be similar to what Hunt (1961) some years ago called the "problem of the match." The *zone of proximal development (ZPD)* refers to tasks that the child cannot master by himself but can eventually master with the help and guidance of an adult or an older, more skilled child (Santrock, 1993, p. 287). The ZPD further leads to the concept of **scaffolding**, which is the support or guidance offered by the adult and upon which the child builds—scaffolds—his own functional skills and competencies, eventually to be incorporated into his individual repertoire.

scaffolding
Related to the zone of proximal development, scaffolding is the process whereby an adult gives the child the necessary assistance to allow the child to function on her own. (See, e.g., Krantz, 1994.)

One implication or prediction from Vygotsky's theory is that children from different cultures show different rates of development and different contents in their thinking and reasoning. When observing children from different cultural backgrounds, awareness of these differences may require you to modify what you expect in the way of the child's behavior, attitudes, values, and performance in the various developmental areas.

Information processing theory has become rather popular because, say Bukatko and Daehler (1995), psychologists have become "disenchanted with learning, Piagetian, and other perspectives for explaining behavior" (p. 53). Information processing theory attempts to explain how the mind actually functions; it assumes that humans are really very much like computers. We deal with symbols just as computers do; we have cognitive structures such as short- and long-term memories. We can use various mental processes such as learning and memory strategies, rules, and plans that influence our "attention, decision-making, remembering" (p. 53).

One critical aspect of information processing theory's perspective is its assumption that humans have a limited capacity. This means that there are only so many mental resources at our disposal. Two important conditions stem from this limited capacity. First, engaging in one activity limits our ability to engage in another one; second, some mental activities need more mental resources than others. With development, practice, and experience, the child's mental functions become more efficient and effective (Krantz, 1994, pp. 407–408). Krantz identifies "three key aspects of children's cognitive functioning" (p. 408) that underlie the increases in this efficiency and effectiveness: (1) the child's increasing use of strategies, (2) his expanding knowledge base, and (3) an increasing awareness and control of his mental abilities.

Strategies

Briefly, Krantz (1994) defines *strategies* as "goal-directed operations that individuals use to deliberately facilitate their memory, attention, and problem solving" (p. 408). Rehearsal, which essentially is going over something again and again in one's mind, is a type of strategy. Organization is also a type of strategy, whereby the individual places objects or events into meaningful conceptual categories—for example, placing all things that can be eaten into the category "food," and so on. A third strategy is that of elaboration, which can be used "when items cannot be easily grouped into familiar categories" (p. 408). Elaboration involves "relating objects to one another with absurd or fanciful images" (p. 408). This involves creating in one's mind a mental image of various objects—that must be remembered or recalled—and that are in some kind of absurd, ridiculous relationship to one another. The example Krantz offers is that of a child having to memorize the words "book, boy, horse, field, rain." Through elaboration, the child could imagine "A boy riding his horse across a field, reading his book in the rain" (p. 408).

One might ask whether six-year-olds use such strategies. Apparently they do not, at least not consistently or spontaneously. Krantz (1994), for example, reports that children can be taught simple strategies to "facilitate attention and memory" by the time they reach kindergarten or first grade. However, they appear to stop using the strategies after the specific training sessions are ended, a phenomenon known as production deficiency (p. 409).

An Expanding Knowledge Base

An expanding knowledge base, most simply put, means that the middle-age child has more facts, information, and knowledge at his command than he did when he was younger, an accomplishment that stands to reason when considering the fundamental nature of developmental change. This expansion of knowledge can easily be determined simply by talking to a three- or four-year-old and seeing what he or she knows compared to a six-year-old. However, relatively extensive factual knowledge and expertise usually must wait for additional maturation, experience, and further improvements in the child's use of learning strategies.

Metacognition

metacognition
Thinking about thinking; being aware of one's cognitive abilities and exercising some control over them.

The third key aspect identified by Krantz also deserves some discussion, namely the child's increased awareness and control of his mental abilities. This new ability is called **metacognition** (Krantz, 1994). As Krantz describes the term, "It includes what you know, knowing what you do not know, and knowing what to do with what you know to solve problems" (p. 410). Put more simply, it is knowing both what you do and do not know and being able to benefit from that knowledge to solve problems, make decisions, and so on. It is important to note the two main components of metacognition. The first of these components is self-appraisal; this refers to an awareness of whether or not one knows or does not know something, the ability to determine what one needs to learn to accomplish a task (for instance), and the ability to reach a conclusion as to whether or not one has done the necessary work to perform adequately a given task or assignment (p. 411). Self-management, the second component of metacognition, involves the ability to perform the necessary behaviors that will enable one to succeed at a given task. So, for instance, does six-year-old Alyce realize that she does not adequately comprehend a playmate's instructions, that she must ask her friend questions, and does she know what she subsequently must do to successfully perform the desired actions or behaviors? This could also apply to a child's understanding a teacher's class assignment, and so on. Thinking about thinking, which is metacognition, is a significant addition to the child's store of intellectual resources.

A Little More about Piaget

Despite the growing popularity of competing theories, many texts still place heavy emphasis on Piaget's theory, which, the criticisms against some of his ideas and conclusions notwithstanding, still has merit and is worthy of continued consideration. In that light, we present Table 17-3, which summarizes some of the characteristics of the child's thought during the period of middle childhood. We are indebted to Harris's (1993) summary of these characteristics, from which we draw heavily for our own presentation of this topic.

Piaget's stage of concrete operations typically is said to begin at about seven years of age, which appears to make Table 17-3 irrelevant to the observation of six-year-olds. Nonetheless, our premise is that for the beginning student, learning firsthand what children cannot do can in some instances be as important as learning what they can do. Moreover, the age ranges that mark off the stages in any theory are never definitive or absolute, which leaves open the possibility that there are some six-year-olds who will be able to function at some level within the stage of concrete operations. Finally, the observer is not restricted to Piaget's theory for data on children's cognitive functioning, so, if necessary, Table 17-3 can be disregarded.

Table 17-3 Summary of Some Characteristics of Concrete Operational Thinking
Characteristics of Concrete Operational Thought (The School Years)

● Understands the general rules that underlie or lead to specific outcomes (idea of cause and effect).

● Has the ability to decenter, that is simultaneously take into account more than one feature or dimension of an object or situation.

● Understands the concept of mental and physical operations and the fact that they are reversible. (For example, the child understands that liquid poured from a short, wide jar into a tall, narrow one can be poured back into the short, wide container and that no amount of liquid is added or taken away during the "operation." The child is not as vulnerable to the appearance of things.)

● Can transfer learning (rules or principles) gained from solving concrete problems to solving problems in real life.

● Is not fooled by perceptions or by what appears to be true, but can rely on what he knows to be true.

● Is more logical and can reason inductively—can form hypotheses or educated guesses based on what he has experienced (he can reason from the specific case to a general theory, of sorts).

● Is more sociocentric than egocentric—can take someone else's viewpoint or perspective and is not restricted to his own point of view.

● "Change[s] the facts to fit their hypotheses rather than changing their hypotheses to fit the facts (a new egocentrism)" (Harris, 1993, p. 529).

Adapted from Harris, 1993, p. 529.

Summary of Cognitive Abilities

As one last source of information about the six-year-old child's cognitive–intellectual development and capabilities, we present in Table 17-4 some of the summarizing data found in Brewer's (1998) text *Introduction to Early Childhood Education: Preschool Through Primary Grades*. So that you can make some informative comparisons and contrasts, we also include information concerning the age ranges from four to five and from seven to eight, ages that immediately precede and immediately follow the target age of six years.

LANGUAGE

Background Information: Vygotsky on Language and Thought

We first want to comment very briefly on Vygotsky's views concerning language and its relation to thought, a relationship that has fostered some controversy or differences of opinion among theorists. Piaget believed that thought, and cognitive development in general, precedes language. Language, in this view, is essentially a vehicle for expressing one's thoughts or for manipulating one's ideas or intellectual content. Thus, for example, Piaget thought that a child did not use expressions such as "on top of" or "beside" until she understood what such words or phrases meant. Vygotsky conceptualized language and thought as developing independently of each other at first, but merging later on (see Santrock, 1993, p. 289).

Table 17-4 Summary of Cognitive Abilities and Characteristics of the Child from Three to Eight Years		
Three to Four Years	**Five to Six Years**	**Seven to Eight Years**
• Understands and follows instructions with as many as two commands.	• Attention span is lengthening; can attend to stimuli for longer, uninterrupted periods of time.	• "Differences in reading and language abilities widen" (Brewer, 2007, p. 17).
• Judgments are not thought out, and mistakes are frequent.	• Knows how to seriate objects—she can, for example, arrange objects according to their length.	• Begins transition to concrete operational thinking—Piaget's third stage of cognitive development.
• Vocabulary increases rapidly.	• Knows how to put objects into groups according to some predetermined criteria.	• Talking and discussion are important—uses language to solve problems and exchange ideas.
• Uses numbers but has no understanding of their meaning—lacks number concept.	• Thinking is more deliberate, judgments less impulsive; child can predict the outcome of his behavior before actually performing it.	• Knows how to plan, one of the characteristics of concrete operational thinking.
• Confuses fantasy and reality; may believe, for example, that dreams come into his head from the outside.	• Distinguishes between fantasy and reality; knows difference between dreams and actual experiences, for instance.	• Interest in activities endures over long periods of time.
• Has the beginning of classification, especially according to the function or purpose of an object.	• Uses language to categorize things, does so consciously.	• Cause and effect begin to be comprehensible.
• Has some use of abstract functional words.	• Has knowledge of the representational function of words and pictures (knows they stand for real objects).	• Understanding of time and money increases, which is abstract thinking.
• Incessant use of "why" questions; wants to know how things work, why they behave as they do.	• Shows interest in numbers and letters.	• Uses slang and profane language.
• Thinking is predominantly egocentric—i.e., it centers on the self; difficult for child to take another's point of view.	• Can name colors.	• Increased understanding and use of abstract terms.
	• In memory tasks, rehearsal is not a spontaneous strategy but must be induced or suggested.	• Demonstrates more awareness of the larger community, world.
	• Can follow three unrelated commands or instructions.	
	• Some children may start to demonstrate conservation of number and length.	

Adapted from Brewer, 1998, p. 13, and 2007, p. 17.

Vygotsky's views on cognitive development also stressed the importance of language. In discussing Vygotsky's theory and the role of culture in influencing cognitive development, Vasta, Haith, and Miller (1995) write about the "dialectical process," a process whereby learning takes place when the child shares problem-solving experiences with another person (p. 38). Interactions with other people are the dominant mechanism for cognitive growth, and although these interactions can take many forms, Vygotsky emphasized "language interchanges" (Vasta et al., 1995, p. 38). These authors' additional remarks are worth inclusion here:

> It is primarily through their speech that adults are assumed to transmit to children the rich body of knowledge that exists in the culture. As learning progresses, the child's own language comes to serve as his or her primary tool of intellectual adaptation. Eventually, for example, children can use internal speech to direct their own behavior in much the same way that the parents' speech once directed it. (p. 38)

Vygotsky called this transfer of control from parent to child internalization: "Bodies of knowledge and tools of thought at first exist outside the child, in the surrounding culture. Development consists of gradual internalization—primarily through language—of these forms of cultural adaptation" (Vasta et al., 1995, p. 38). These comments and citations help to explain why Vygotsky's theory is called a sociocultural or sociohistorical theory. Maybe the simplest and most understandable description of Vygotsky's view of the relationship between language and thought comes from Graves, Gardiulo, and Sluder (1996), who write that Vygotsky "viewed the language acquisition process as follows: Adults provide names for objects, give directions and suggestions, and gradually reduce the level of their language assistance as children gain more competence and confidence with language" (p. 297). It is here that the zone of proximal development comes into play, a concept discussed earlier.

Metalinguistic Awareness

Berk summarizes rather nicely the general characteristics of the school-age child's language achievements and her relative position on the language continuum:

metalinguistic awareness

the ability to attend and to understand the form that language takes, the structure by which meaning is conveyed.

> Vocabulary, grammar, and pragmatics continue to develop in middle-childhood, although less obviously than at earlier ages. In addition, children's attitude toward language undergoes a fundamental shift. They develop **metalinguistic awareness**, the ability to think about language as a system. (Berk, 2005, p. 451, emphasis original)

Santrock (1993), in addressing the same phenomenon, puts it this way:

> During the middle and late childhood, a change occurs in the way children think about words. They become less tied to the actions and perceptual dimensions associated with words, and they become more analytical in their approach to words.... The increasing ability elementary children have in analyzing words helps them to understand words that have no direct relationship to their own personal experiences. This allows children to add more abstract words to their vocabulary.... Also, children's increasing analytic abilities allow them to distinguish between words such as *cousin* and *nephew*, or *city*, *village*, and *suburb*. (p. 422, italics original)

Part of this achievement described by Berk and Santrock can be accounted for by the following explanation:

> They ... develop an intuitive awareness of how language works, known as *metalinguistic awareness*, that emerges about age 5 and develops throughout middle-childhood.... Metalinguistic awareness refers to intuitions about language that enable children to know, for example, whether a sentence is correct or detect that an ambiguous sentence has two meanings. (Zigler & Stevenson, 1993, p. 427, italics original)

Bukatko and Daehler (1995) also describe this awareness phenomenon: "Older children—for example, those in the first or second grade—show the ability to detect problems in the messages of others and can even suggest revisions" (p. 261). Schickedanz, Schickedanz, Hansen, and Forsyth (1993) add an important, clarifying piece to the meaning of metalinguistic awareness, noting that such awareness is being able to "pay attention to the form of language—to the structures used to convey meaning—instead of the meaning itself" (p. 484).

There are two components of metalinguistic awareness of interest to us: humor and metaphor. Humor might seem to be self-evident, but children of six have humor that differs significantly from that of older children and adults. Bukatko and Daehler (1995) use the term *language play* in discussing humor and metaphor. By language play, they mean "creating funny words, telling jokes or riddles, or using words in a figurative sense" (p. 263). Schickedanz and colleagues (1993) refer to one aspect of language play as **phonologically based ambiguity**, which is ambiguity or uncertainty about how words are pronounced. They offer an interesting, and to a six-year-old, humorous example of a phonologically ambiguous joke:

"Knock, knock."
"Who's there?"
"Duane."

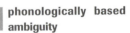

phonologically based ambiguity

Ambiguity in language based on how words sound or are pronounced.

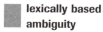
lexically based ambiguity

Ambiguity based on the different meanings of words—for example, *pen can refer to a writing tool or to an enclosure in which animals are kept.*

syntactically based ambiguity

Ambiguity based on different interpretations of a sentence. This ambiguity depends on the structure of the sentence itself and how that structure allows different meanings to be put on the sentence.

"Duane who?"

"Duane the tub ... I'm dwowning." (p. 485)

Schickedanz and associates also identify **lexically based ambiguity**, which is uncertainty about the meaning of words, and **syntactically based ambiguity**, which has to do with the actual structure of the sentence itself. These authors illustrate lexically based ambiguity by the following joke:

"Why did the farmer name his hog Ink?"

"Because he kept running out of the pen." (p. 484)

Syntactically based ambiguity is nicely illustrated by the following:

"Do you know how long cows should be milked?"

"How long?"

"As long as short ones, of course." (p. 485)

The ambiguity consists in the double meaning of the word *long*, which functions as either an adjective or an adverb.

Schickedanz and colleagues (1993) point out that understanding and using the various ambiguities follow a sort of stage-like progression: Children learn phonological ambiguity first at about 6 or 7, lexical ambiguity comes next, and syntactical ambiguity is not comprehended until about 11 or 12 years of age (p. 486).

Vocabulary and Some Syntax

The average six-year-old's vocabulary ranges between 10,000 and 14,000 words (see, e.g., Berk, 1993, 2005; Harris, 1993; Allen & Marotz, 2003, 2007). Despite this rather impressive number of usable words they have at their command, six-year-olds have not yet mastered all the facets of language usage. As Papalia, Olds, and Feldman (2007), for example, note, "Although grammar is quite complex by age 6, children during the early school years rarely use the passive voice (as in "The sidewalk is being shoveled"), verb tenses that include the auxiliary *have* ("I have already shoveled the sidewalk"), and conditional sentences ("If Barbara were home, she would help shovel the sidewalk") (p. 337).

Drawing on the work of Carol S. Chomsky (1969)—not to be confused with Noam Chomsky—Papalia and Olds (1992) cite three kinds of sentence structures, the difficult concepts they contain, and the age at which children typically acquire an understanding of these concepts. The information is presented in Table 17-5.

Metacommunication

We want to discuss one last aspect of language ability and functioning that is relevant to the forthcoming observation exercises. Our overall discussion of language has necessarily been very brief and incomplete. Indeed, fuller treatments of all the behavioral and developmental domains must be left to the human or child development textbooks. This last language topic is called *metacommunication*, which refers to an individual's understanding of the processes of communication. Papalia and

Table 17-5 Acquisition of Complex Syntactic Structures		
Structure	**Difficult Concept**	**Age of Acquisition**
The dog is easy to hear.	Who is doing the hearing?	5.6 to 9 years
Allen promised Fran to help.	Who is doing the helping?	5.6 to 9 years
Bill asked Anthony what to say.	Who is saying it?	Some 10-year-olds have not learned this (Papalia & Olds, 1992).
She knew that Amy would get into trouble.	Does the "she" refer to Amy?	5.6 years

Adapted from Papalia and Olds, 1992, p. 257.

Olds (1992) seem to have captured at least some of the essence of this concept and what it means to children and to adults who work with children:

> Young children do not understand all of what they see, hear, or read, but often they do not know that they do not understand. They may be so used to not understanding things in the world around them that this does not seem unusual. Adults therefore need to be aware that children's understanding cannot be taken for granted. For the sake of children's safety, well-being, and academic progress, we have to find some ways to determine whether children do, in fact, know what we want them to do. (p. 258)

A sound piece of advice, indeed. It is relevant to note here that sometimes children can fool us into believing that they know more than they actually do or are more sophisticated than they actually are because of the language they use. The deception, which is not deliberate on their part, is made possible by our failure to recognize the difference between a child saying particular words and her understanding the concepts that those words represent. Can you imagine, for example, a six-year-old saying to you, "I would like some milk, please, because I believe I am suffering from a calcium deficiency"? The point here is would a six-year-old really comprehend the meaning of "calcium deficiency"? The example need not be as esoteric as that just given. Put the issue in the context of a teacher giving a first-grade child an instruction or direction. Can the teacher be certain that the instruction or direction has been fully understood? The answer to this question is particularly critical if or when the child's safety and well-being are at stake.

SOCIAL AND EMOTIONAL DEVELOPMENT

This is the last functional/behavioral area to be covered. We have chosen to combine social and emotional behavior under a working assumption that much of an individual's emotional expression occurs in a social context of one kind or another. Moreover, the norm in developmental textbooks seems to be to make the same combination, treating social and emotional development within a one-chapter format. Furthermore, putting social and emotional development and behavior under one rubric emphasizes the interactive character of human growth and development.

This "interactive character" of the developmental and behavioral domains is nicely pointed out by Steinberg and Belsky (1991): "Middle childhood is a time of developing psychological and social competence in a world that is both expanding and demanding, and middle childhood is a time when psychosocial and cognitive development *strongly interact*" (p. 377, italics added). Thus it is that the many advances of the school-age child are made possible by the intellectual gains she has made. These authors also add that "cognitive gains provide impetus for social development, and social development, in turn, provides impetus for further cognitive gains" (Steinberg & Belsky, 1991, p. 377).

One important element of social and emotional development is **social role-taking ability,** which is defined by Schickedanz and associates (1993) as "[t]he ability to put oneself in someone else's place and anticipate what that person is likely to feel or do" (p. 504). These authors describe social role-taking ability as one of the significant milestones or hallmarks of the school-age child's social and emotional development. Furthermore, social role-taking ability "[l]eads children to a greater understanding of others as well as of themselves, since they can now think of themselves from the point of view of others." This ability involves such skills as "understanding emotions, understanding intentions, and understanding thinking" (p. 504). **Social cognition** is the concept used to explain this new social and intellectual skill; it is the ability to understand "a broad range of social and interpersonal events" (p. 504).

Social cognition also includes an ability to define oneself as well as others. In this regard, Bee (1995) writes that "by age 5 or 6, most children define themselves along a whole range of dimensions." Bee also notes that such early self-descriptions are strongly tied to the here and now (p. 296). With age and increasing developmental maturity, their descriptions move toward "a more abstract, more comparative, and more generalized self-definition" (p. 296). Children's descriptions of others also become more abstract, comparative, and generalized. As the term *social cognition* implies, social, interpersonal skills rely heavily on intellectual skills, thereby creating the occasion or opportunity for interaction between these two sets of abilities.

To keep the observation exercises within reasonable bounds, we focus on the six-year-old's relationship with peers, specifically friendships.

Relationships with Peers: Friendships

Middle childhood is a time when peer groups start to take on a singular importance. This importance is contributed to by the increasing influence of other, nonfamilial individuals and groups who assume significant roles in the child's socialization. The

social role-taking ability

The ability to understand another person's position or situation and what she might be feeling or thinking. It involves such things as understanding emotions, intentions, and thinking. (See, e.g., Schickedanz et al., 1993.)

social cognition

An ability to think about and understand social and interpersonal events of which one is a part. Social cognition includes such things as social role-taking ability (which see), empathy, identification, and vicarious experiencing, among others.

school-age child's social interactions are in sharp contrast to those of the preschooler, for example, whose circle of friends is usually limited to siblings, neighborhood children, classmates in his or her preschool or child care center, and so on. It is important to recognize that although preschool children's relationships are based at least in part on feelings, which makes friends more important than nonfriends, it is still the parents who meet most of the child's important emotional needs (Krantz, 1994, p. 438). This arrangement changes during middle childhood, however, in part because of the child's growing independence from her parents. Now the child is likely to choose as a friend someone who possesses personality characteristics that are able to fulfill her emotional needs (Krantz, 1994, p. 438).

Middle childhood is a time when peer groups start to take on a singular importance.

The school-age child also experiences greater physical mobility and more extensive contacts with other children, all of which result in an enlargement of his circle of potential friends (Krantz, 1994). School-age children choose friends largely on the basis of personality characteristics, but the criteria by which friends are selected change with age and maturity. Specific traits or characteristics come to be valued more than others. For instance, as Krantz (1994) reports, "Children in the early grades [i.e., first and second] select friends on the basis of self-serving needs: Who is a good, reliable play partner? Who is willing to share resources, such as toys and video games?" (p. 439). Other considerations apply as well, and some of these are gender-based. Although school-age children in general choose friends who are similar to themselves in terms of race, age, social class, sex, and social status (Krantz, 1994, p. 439; see also Ramsey & Myers, 1990, among others), "boys tend to emphasize similarity in superficial behaviors, such as interest in comic books or sports." Girls, on the other hand, emphasize "similarity in personality traits, such as kindness or friendliness" (Krantz, 1994, p. 439; see also Erwin, 1985).

Selman and Selman (1979), and later Selman (1981), have studied the progression of friendships. Selman and Selman (1979) depicted friendship as occurring in five stages, with some considerable overlap among the age ranges. Selman's (1981) later publication identifies four stages, and the ages are more precisely delineated. Their descriptions are interesting and informative, and both versions are presented in Table 17-6a and Table 17-6b.

However, Craig and Kermis (1995) hasten to point out that some researchers disagree with Selman and Selman's model. They write that "there is evidence that young children implicitly know more of the rules and expectations of being a friend than they are able to tell an interviewer" (p. 558). Also noted is the fact that "real friendships are quite complicated and are constantly changing" (p. 558).

Table 17-6a Three of Selman and Selman's (1979) Five Stages of Friendship		
Stage	**Ages**	**Characteristics**
"0 Momentary playmate-ship (undifferentiated)"	3 to 7	Child is egocentric and sees friendship primarily in terms of what he can get from it. Child defines or chooses friends in terms of how close they live; child also sees value in what a friend can offer in the way of material resources or possessions such as toys.
"1 One-way assistance (unilateral)"	4 to 9	Child defines a good friend as someone who is obedient to his wishes, who does what he wants the "friend" to do.
"2 Two-way, fairweather cooperation (reciprocal)"	6 to 12	Although there is some mutual reciprocity in the friendships at this age and stage, friends are still defined by each individual's self-interests rather than by common interests.

Adapted from Papalia and Olds, 1992, p. 284.

Table 17-6b Two of Selman's (1981) Four Stages in the Development of Friendship		
Stage	**Ages**	**Characteristics**
1	6 and under	Friendships are based on such things as where the child lives (geographical location) or on the other's physical characteristics or appearance. Child is egocentric (self-centered) and has difficulty seeing things from another person's perspective.
2	7 to 9	Child begins to form friendships based on others' feelings and on the principle of reciprocity—each doing for the other. Friendships also begin to be conducted on the basis of social behaviors and involve mutual evaluation by each other.

Adapted from Craig and Kermis, 1995, p. 558.

The cognitive and social skills needed by the school-age child to form and maintain friendships are considerably greater than (and are different from) the skills needed by the younger child to form and maintain his friendships. There are two specific elements involved in making and keeping friends: **social comparison** and **peer reputation** (Krantz, 1994, p. 439).

Social Comparison

social comparison
Describing, rating, and ranking peers on various characteristics and traits. Most simply put, social comparison involves comparing one's peers (or others) on various aspects of social and personal functioning and attributes.

peer reputation
The relatively stable and consistent way a child's peers perceive and describe or characterize him.

Social comparison is a cognitive skill that permits the individual to "describe, rate, and rank peers on various traits and attributes" (Krantz, 1994, p. 439). It is reported that school-age children devote substantial amounts of time comparing their peers. In doing so, they consider abstract qualities such as likes and dislikes, thoughts and feelings (Krantz, 1994, p. 439; see also Diaz & Berndt, 1982).

These social comparisons serve important functions and have some important consequences. Accurate comparisons enable children to assess how well they can meet their peers' needs and motivations; the ranking that takes place also guides children's social interactions. Furthermore, children hold a sort of mirror—or standard—up to other children by which they can judge their own competencies. These self-judgments also affect children's social behavior (see Krantz, 1994, pp. 439–440).

Peer Reputation

All of us know the importance of reputation and how effectively our own and others' reputations influence the way others deal with us and the way we deal with them. Krantz (1994) defines *peer reputation* as "the relatively stable characterization of a child shared by members of the peer group" (p. 441). It is significant that children learn how to influence their own reputation. They can do this by controlling the impression they make on others—through such things as personal grooming and dressing, displaying attributes that are valued by a peer, or by behaving in ways that contradict a negative reputation (p. 441).

Keeping Friends and the Emotions

In this area we briefly raise the topic of emotional behavior, an issue to which we have thus far given short shrift. It is one thing to establish a friendship, but it can be quite another to keep it alive and vital.

Required Skills to Meet Relationship Demands

Establishing a friendship requires certain social skills, which we have already discussed. Once it is established, however, other skills come into play because the relationship itself makes certain demands that are more or less continuous and that require careful monitoring and adjustments on the part of the participants. Krantz (1994) identifies as a critical skill the managing of one's emotions "in the context of increasingly intimate and reciprocal relationships" (p. 441). This management of the emotions involves several abilities or accomplishments. First, the child—let's call him Andrew—must be able to control emotional outbursts that might jeopardize the friendship by intimidating and overpowering Rebecca, his would-be friend. Second, Andrew must be sensitive to Rebecca's own changing emotions and adjust his behavior accordingly. Rebecca must reciprocate in this regard, of course, because sensitivity is a two-way street. Sensitivity to and understanding of the other person's feelings and their possible context paves the way for the expression of empathy and emotional support. A third aspect, which seems closely related to the second ability just mentioned, requires what Krantz describes as "learning to attune or to match their emotions and the tempo of their behavior to that of their friends" (Krantz, 1994, p. 442; see also Field et al., 1992). Thus, Rebecca may have to temper or tone down her excitement and joy at a good piece of news because Andrew's mood is less than joyous. As Krantz would put it, attunement might require Rebecca to be less buoyant in her emotional expression and Andrew to be a little more upbeat if their interaction is to go relatively smoothly (Krantz, 1994, p. 442). Finally, Andrew and Rebecca "must learn to avoid persistent nagging and complaining" that one or both may find annoying (p. 442).

When friendships are established, certain social skills can be observed.

Categories of Social Status That Reflect Children's Popularity

One more facet of friendship deserves some attention, namely that of popularity. Researchers have established categories they refer to as social status that reflect children's popularity among their peers. Citing such researchers as Bukowski and Hosa

PART FOUR

popular children
Children whom most peers like and no one dislikes.

rejected children
Children whom most peers dislike and very few like.

neglected children
Children who are essentially neutral on the scale of liked versus disliked. Their peers neither actively like or dislike them. It might be said that such children's peers are indifferent to them.

controversial children
Children who seem to strike a balance between being liked and disliked. Many of their peers like them, and many also dislike them.

average status children
Children whom some peers like and some dislike. Average status children appear to differ from the controversials in terms of the number of peers who have feelings one way or another toward them.

sociometry
A technique for studying children's popularity or social status among their peers. The technique can involve asking children to name their best friend or friends, or to identify the child or children who are most liked by the class or group.

stars
A classification that can be determined from a sociogram and that identifies or describes a child or children who are well liked and popular among their peers. Such children also have considerable status and influence in the peer group.

(1989) and Coie, Dodge, and Coppotelli (1982), Krantz (1994) discusses five such social categories and their respective characteristics.

The first of these categories is called **popular children**, described as children "who are liked by most of their peers and disliked by no one" (p. 443). **Rejected children** are those "who are disliked by most of their peers and liked by very few" (p. 443). Then there are **neglected children**, "who are neither actively liked nor disliked by anyone" (p. 443). There are children "who are liked by many of their peers and disliked by many others," and they are called **controversial children** (p. 443). Finally, there are so-called **average status children**, "who are liked by a few peers and disliked by some others" (p. 443).

There is yet one more set of descriptors that is associated with a method of studying relationships within a group, a method called **sociometry**. Steinberg and Meyer (1995) specify four groups that can be placed on a continuum of popularity via the use of this sociometric technique. The first of these groups contains children who are **stars**, described as children who "are very well liked and have considerable status and influence in the peer group." The authors add to this description by noting that stars, in addition to being "smart and attractive ... have better social skills and are more likely to act as leaders" (p. 421). They are socially active and tend to take charge of planning activities and initiating social events.

Amiables, the second group in order of popularity, are "liked by others, but they have less status and impact than the stars" (p. 421). Next in popularity are the **isolates**, who "are neither liked nor disliked; these children are often simply ignored" (p. 421). At the bottom of the popularity totem pole, so to speak, are the **rejects**, children who "are actively disliked by others and have a negative impact on their peer group" (p. 421). You might find it instructive to compare and contrast the two sets of categories for describing popularity. We return to them in the observation exercises on the social and emotional behavior of the six-year-old.

This ends our presentation of the background information on the four behavioral and developmental areas covered in this section of the text. We have discussed physical and motor development, cognitive and intellectual development, language development, and social and emotional development. All that remains are the observation exercises that accompany each of these domains.

OBSERVATION EXERCISE 17-1: PHYSICAL GROWTH AND MOTOR FUNCTIONING

Observation Objectives

In this exercise your objective will be to learn about the six-year-old's gross (large) and fine (small) motor abilities as well as his general physical characteristics.

amiables
Children who are "liked by others, but have less status and impact than the stars"; the second group in order of popularity.

isolates
Children who "are neither liked nor disliked; these children are often simply ignored."

rejects
Children at the bottom of the popularity scale, who "are actively disliked by others and have a negative impact on their peer group."

Procedure

As mentioned earlier in the presentation of background information, a great deal of discernment and understanding can be gained through the process of noting similarities (comparing) and differences (contrasting) between a six-year-old and a younger, preschool child. Therefore, your objective can be accomplished in one of two ways: (1) actually observe at least two, three- to four-year-olds and compare and contrast their physical characteristics and their motor abilities with those of at least two six-year-olds, or (2) observe at least two six-year-olds and compare and contrast their physical characteristics and motor abilities against written observation reports on preschoolers that you may have already completed for another assignment. If you can neither observe two preschoolers nor have access to observation reports already completed on some preschoolers, simply select at least two six-year-olds as the targets for your observation and recording.

Part I—Physical Characteristics of the Six-Year-Old

Using an event sampling format, do the following things: (1) describe in detail the preschoolers' general physical characteristics and the six-year-olds' general physical characteristics; (2) compare and contrast the older and the younger children's physical characteristics; in addition, however, compare and contrast the two six-year-olds with each other. The intent here is to observe any individual differences that might exist between the two children. Any such differences might be more apparent or pronounced if you observe a boy and a girl rather than two boys or two girls. In the former case, gender differences in motor skills and development will tend to be evident; in the latter case, non–gender-related individual differences among children will be manifested, if there are any.

Part II—Gross and Fine Motor Abilities of the Six-Year-Old

Using an event sampling format, follow the same pattern as explained for Part I, except now you will be observing and recording instances of large- and small-muscle abilities or skills, not physical characteristics. You might also want to refer to Chapter 16, Observation Exercise 16-2 ("Background Information"), for descriptions of various kinds of motor behaviors that you might observe. Be aware, however, that not all the descriptions found in Exercise 16-2 will apply to the six-year-old. Be discriminating when selecting examples of motor behavior that you want to apply to the children you observe in this exercise. By referring to these descriptions, you will again be engaging in a form of comparison and contrast; what does not fit the six-year-old's motor skill repertoire will be a reminder of how the child has changed since his preschool days. (See Observation Exercise 17-1.)

OBSERVATION EXERCISE 17-2: COGNITIVE AND INTELLECTUAL DEVELOPMENT AND BEHAVIOR

Observation Objectives

This overall exercise could have a number of objectives, primarily because this functional area is so rich in possibilities for observation and study. We have selected two objectives, designated as Parts I and II, leaving you or your instructor (if you are in a formal educational setting) to devise other practical exercises on your own if more are needed or desired. The two objectives are based on two of the three approaches to the study of cognitive development and functioning discussed earlier: Piaget's theory (Part I) and information processing theory (Part II).

PART I: Observation Objectives

To determine whether the children being observed display any of the characteristics of Piaget's concrete operational thought.

Procedure

For this first objective (Part I-A), we ask you to refer back to Chapter 16, Observation Exercise 16-3 ("Background Information"), for additional information on Piaget's theory of cognitive development, information that covers his stage of preoperational thinking. Observe at least two six-year-olds. You have several options open to you in this first objective. If you believe that merely observing the children, without intervening in any way, will yield you enough information, then use that approach. We believe that either the narrative description or the event sampling technique is the appropriate choice because they are the least selective of the techniques available and they provide the most raw data that can then be interpreted. You will have to depend on your own judgment and assessment of the observation setting to tell you which method will yield the most information in the most effective and efficient manner.

Bear in mind that the event sampling method relies more heavily than the narrative description on the target behavior occurring fairly frequently. You may simply want to casually watch the children for a short time to see whether they exhibit any of the behaviors or skills that are of interest to you. If they do, then naturalistic observation might suffice as a plausible approach to the exercise. If it appears that the children, or the particular conditions of your situation, will not lend themselves to naturalistic observation, then you may have to take what might be called a "testing approach" (Part I-B). But remember that to test is to interrupt the usual manner in which things are done in the children's environment. In a school setting, you may not interfere in any way with the official routine or activities that are taking place. Of course, if you are the teacher, or if you are a legitimate part of the classroom, you might have considerable latitude concerning what you are allowed to do. Otherwise, you may have to wait for recess or for some other occasion when your testing will not cause a disruption of normal routine.

Look at Table 17-3, which summarizes some of the characteristics of concrete operational thought. Observe the two children you have selected, and determine whether they exhibit any of the abilities described in Table 17-3. For example, does either or both of them understand the notion of cause and effect? Can either or both sort objects according to more than one criterion at a time, and so on? On the other hand, does either or both of them show more of the characteristics of preoperational thought than of concrete operational thought? What would you conclude regarding which stage of cognitive development predominates? (See Observation Exercise 17-2.)

PART II: Observation Objectives

The second objective emphasizes the information processing approach to understanding cognitive behavior. The purposes of this assignment are (1) to determine what, if any, strategies the child uses to "facilitate memory, attention, and problem solving" (such strategies include rehearsal, organization, and elaboration); and (2) to explore the child's knowledge base, which is to say, to find out the kinds of information and facts that the child has at his command.

Procedure

Select at least two children for the first objective of this exercise (Part II-A), but choose children who are different from the ones you observed for the previous exercise. You will use a combination of a modified checklist and the event sampling techniques. You should recognize that event sampling really also serves as a form of checklist, inasmuch as every time you observe and record the behaviors that make up the desired event, you are also keeping a running tab of the relative frequency with which those behaviors occur. This exercise is simply the first time in this text that you have specifically been asked to use the checklist. Simply place an "X" or a check mark in the box to the right of the strategy that you observe the child using. Then describe (as an Objective Behavioral Descriptions) how the child used the strategy—what she did specifically, under what circumstances or conditions, and so on.

Recall, also, that use of the event sampling method requires you to decide on the spot whether or not the child is using a strategy. If you were using the narrative description, of course, everything would be recorded, and only later would you have to determine whether or not the child employed strategic thinking. However, we recognize that learning frequently takes place silently and is not a publicly obvious affair. Consequently, you cannot know if a child is using a learning strategy if she is sitting at her seat and silently rehearsing information that she must remember at a later time. This being so, you may have to resort again to some sort of testing or interaction approach to accomplish this exercise's objective. The decision must be yours, of course, but remember that you are always to be as unobtrusive as possible, and you must always obey the ethical principles that govern our relationships with children.

For the second objective of this exercise (Part II-B), you will use the event sampling format. It might be informative and interesting if you were to pick two children who, although both being in their sixth year, were separated in age by a number of months. The purpose of this criterion for making your choice would be to see whether the age difference between the two children yielded any difference in how each functioned cognitively. The greatest difference, if there is any at all, might be in the amount of knowledge and information the older child has simply by virtue of her having acquired more life experiences. Perhaps the best approach here is simply to listen to what the children have to say to their teachers, to one another, or to you, if the occasion demands that you directly interact with them. Listen for such things as the kinds of information or general knowledge they have at their command; the accuracy of that information, if you can determine it; the kinds of special knowledge they possess, which is knowledge that is not necessarily common to or shared by many other children in the group, and so on. Although we are not necessarily recommending it, a tape recorder can be a useful tool in situations where recording speech word for word is desirable. However, we do not recommend that an electronic instrument replace the skills needed to observe and record speech behavior using only pencil and paper. (See Observation Exercise 17-2.)

OBSERVATION EXERCISE 17-3: LANGUAGE

Observation Objectives

There are three objectives to this overall exercise, and they deal with the three main topics discussed in the background information: (1) metalinguistic awareness, specifically, the child's use of metaphor and humor; (2) vocabulary and the child's practical understanding of syntax; and (3) metacommunication, but in the simplest terms of how well the child understands what is expected of her. These three objectives are designated as Parts I, II, and III.

PART I—Metalinguistic Awareness: Objectives

The major objective of Part I is to observe and record instances of the use of humor and metaphor. Humor may be the easier of the two to witness, although listening even to casual conversation will probably reveal some figurative speech if the child uses any. Put another way, metaphoric or figurative speech will generally not require special circumstances because people frequently speak in metaphors without taking special thought. Metaphor seems to be a rather natural linguistic occurrence. Humor should not be restricted only to specific instances of joke telling or asking the answers to riddles. We take the approach that anything children find funny is worth noting and perhaps analyzing for its content.

Procedure

Select several children, the exact number we leave to you based on how easily you are able to witness examples of humor or metaphor. It might be interesting to compare what different children think is funny and to compare how different children use figurative speech and under what circumstances. You may not be able to observe the use of both humor and metaphor. This is not critical; if you can get examples of only one or the other, that will suffice.

We suggest that you use the narrative description format. By so doing, you may also get an idea of the relative proportion of the children's speech that is humorous or metaphorical compared to that which is, let us say, more ordinary.

PART II—Vocabulary and Syntax: Objectives

The objectives of Part II are (1) to determine the extent and characteristics of the children's vocabulary, and (2) to determine the syntactical characteristics of the children's speech.

Procedure

For both objectives of Part II, select at least two children, and as nearly as you can, record verbatim the children's speech using the narrative description technique. Your goal is to obtain as much information as you need or desire and then analyze the speech content for vocabulary, for grammar—the use of such forms as past tense, adverbs, adjectives, verbs, and so on—and for sentence structure or syntax. If you have access to any observational records that you may have completed for preschool children, they will give you the opportunity to compare and contrast the language skills possessed by children within these two age periods.

This exercise will give you the opportunity to test Papalia and Old's (1992) assertion that "[d]uring the early school years, they [six-year-olds] rarely use the passive voice, verbs that include the form *have*, or conditional ('if ... then') sentences" (p. 257).

You may need to refresh your memory regarding examples of grammatical forms—parts of speech such as adverbs, prepositions, and adjectives—and issues concerning sentence structure and syntax.

PART III—Metacommunication: Objectives

The objective of this last part is to observe and record instances when the child must follow directions or instructions as given by a teacher, adult, or another child. We recognize that children much younger than six also have to learn to follow directions. Nonetheless, it is our working premise that if you are observing in a school classroom or other kind of formal academic setting, directions and instructions will be a common aspect of the teacher–child relationship. Furthermore, the consequences of following or not following such instructions will differ from those that might occur in a child care center, a preschool, or in the home. Additionally, comparatively speaking, the complexity of instructions given to a six-year-old is greater than those given, say, to a toddler or preschooler. Thus, cognitive, social, and emotional behaviors play a more sophisticated role with a six-year-old than with a younger child.

Procedure

Select two or three children, within a school setting, if possible. Using the event sampling format, look for occasions when the children are given specific directions or instructions. Observe and record how they carry out those instructions. How well do they understand what is expected of them? If they do not seem to understand, how do they deal with their misunderstanding? Do they ask questions, or do they move ahead anyway by experimenting, as it were, with a trial-and-error approach? You may also have the opportunity to compare and contrast the children's proficiency in this area of language functioning because it is likely that the children you observe will not all function at the same level of ability. (See Observation Exercise 17-3.)

OBSERVATION EXERCISE 17-4: SOCIAL AND EMOTIONAL DEVELOPMENT

General Observation Objectives

The overall objectives of this final exercise are, naturally enough, to learn how children of this age behave socially with adults and peers, and how they respond emotionally, either in the company of others or when alone and confronted by various circumstances. However, we put the primary emphasis on social development and behavior and ask you to deal with emotional behavior essentially in the context of social interactions—which is where many emotional expressions will occur anyway.

We have already stressed in the preceding presentation of background information the significance of social functioning for the school-age child. One of the areas that takes on special significance is that of peer relationships and friendships. It is on this facet of middle-childhood behavior and change that we base the concluding observation exercises. We leave to your creativity and imagination the devising of other exercises and recording formats that deal with the remaining aspects of social and emotional functioning, an approach that heretofore we have not used. However, it stands to reason that there are likely to be occasions when you will have to create a format for recording the behavior of children of various ages, for various purposes, and in various settings and situations. We give you an opportunity to do so now if it presently serves your best interests.

PART I—Children's Popularity (Social Status Categorization): Observation Objectives

The objective of Part I of this exercise is to observe and record children's social or interpersonal interactions and assess their relative popularity with their peers. These observations and assessments are based on Krantz's (1994) discussion of five categories of social status that indicate or reflect popularity among peers.

Procedure

Select three or four children, and using the event sampling format or technique, look for behaviors and interaction patterns that help identify into which social status category each child might be placed. You want to look for at least two things: (1) the responses of other children toward the target children you have selected for observation and (2) the behaviors of the target children that might help explain the other children's reactions toward them. Put another way, what might explain why Roxanne is a popular child, yet Jody is a rejected child, and so on? Read carefully the brief descriptions of these five categories provided in the background information. Identifying each child's respective category depends upon your understanding the behavioral characteristics associated with each category.

In this exercise, also look for examples of emotional expression, especially with respect to how each child responds emotionally to various situations and individuals in the setting. In your interpretations, comment on any differences in the emotional behavior of children you have placed in different social or popularity categories. That is, does the controversial child behave differently emotionally than, say, the neglected child or the average status child?

PART II—Sociometric Analysis of Children's Popularity and Friendships: Observation Objective

The objective of this final exercise is to observe and record children's interpersonal behaviors and, from the data gathered, construct a sociogram using Steinberg and Meyer's (1995) four popularity groupings: stars, amiables, isolates, and rejects. This may seem like a repetition of Part I, but it differs for two reasons: (1) it uses a slightly different set of popularity descriptors, and (2) it involves the method called sociometry. Sociograms are defined as "charts showing the social networks within a group" (Stark, 1985, p. 22). In a sociogram, each child is represented by a circle or a square—with his or her name written inside it. The circles or squares—children—are connected by lines or arrows that represent a contact with another child. The head or point of the arrow is drawn where the line touches the circle, and the arrowhead indicates the direction in which the contact occurred. Look at Figure 17-1 for a brief example.

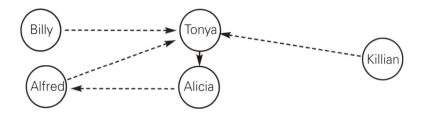

The arrow from Billy to Tonya indicates that Billy initiated social contact with Tonya, the arrow from Tonya to Alicia indicates that Tonya initiated a contact with Alicia, and so on with the remaining children and arrows. The figure with the greatest number of arrows going to it is the most popular child, provided that the popular child's social overtures were responded to in a positive way by the other children. There can be more than one very popular child, by the way, but the sociogram will reveal this fact.

Procedure

Using the narrative description format, observe and record the behavior of as many children as you can without being overburdened by the task. If the size of the group is rather large, you might want to do this exercise over the course of several days, where on successive days you observe a different subgroup of children. When your observation records are complete, analyze your data and from them construct a sociogram that depicts the children who are stars, amiables, isolates, or rejects. You might want to devise your own coding system by which you can tell not only who initiated contact with whom, but also how the child who was contacted first responded to the other child's efforts. Thus, in the preceding example, you know that Billy contacted Tonya, but did Tonya respond positively to Billy's overture? And so it is that a circle might have a lot of arrows going from it to other circles, but this is no evidence that the other children reacted positively to that child's initiations. Perhaps there are no arrows going back to that circle (child). (See Observation Exercise 17-4.)

OBSERVATION EXERCISE **17-1**

PART I: Physical Characteristics of the Six-Year-Old

Observer's Name _____

Child/Children Observed _____

Child's/Children's Age(s) _____ Child's/Children's Sex _____

Observation Context (home, child care center, preschool, school) _____

Date of Observation _____ Time Begun _____ Time Ended _____

Brief Description of Physical and Social Characteristics of Observation Setting:

Objective Behavioral Descriptions (OBDs) and Interpretations: *Event Sampling*

OBD 1 (six-year-old): [Time begun _____ Time ended _____]

Interpretation 1:

OBD 2 (six-year-old): [Time begun _____ Time ended _____]

Interpretation 2:

OBD A (preschooler): [Time begun _____ Time ended _____]

Interpretation A:

OBD B (preschooler): [Time begun _____ Time ended _____]

Interpretation B:

Continue with OBDs and interpretations for as many as possible or needed.

Comparison of six-year-olds and preschoolers:

Contrast of six-year-olds and preschoolers:

Comparison and contrasts of six-year-olds with each other:

Summary comments or descriptions:

(continues)

PART FOUR

OBSERVATION EXERCISE **17-1** (Continued)

PART II: Gross and Fine Motor Abilities of the Six-Year-Old

Observer's Name _____

Child/Children Observed _____

Child's/Children's Age(s) _____ Child's/Children's Sex _____

Observation Context (home, child care center, preschool, school) _____

Date of Observation _____ Time Begun _____ Time Ended _____

Brief Description of Physical and Social Characteristics of Observation Setting:

Objective Behavioral Descriptions (OBDs) and Interpretations: *Event Sampling*

OBD 1 (six-year-old): [Time begun _____ Time ended _____]

Interpretation 1:

OBD 2 (six-year-old): [Time begun _____ Time ended _____]

Interpretation 2:

OBD A (preschooler): [Time begun _____ Time ended _____]

Interpretation A:

OBD B (preschooler): [Time begun _____ Time ended _____]

Interpretation B:

Continue with OBDs and interpretations for as many as possible or needed.

Comparison of six-year-olds and preschoolers:

Contrast of six-year-olds and preschoolers:

Comparison and contrasts of six-year-olds with each other:

Summary comments or descriptions:

OBSERVATION EXERCISE **17-2**

PART I-A: Cognitive Functioning of the Six-Year-Old: Piaget's Theory (Naturalistic Observation)

Observer's Name _____

Child/Children Observed _____

Child's/Children's Age(s) _____ Child's/Children's Sex _____

Observation Context (home, child care center, preschool, school) _____

Date of Observation _____ Time Begun _____ Time Ended _____

Brief Description of Physical and Social Characteristics of Observation Setting:

Objective Behavioral Descriptions (OBDs) and Interpretations: *Narrative Description or Event Sampling*

OBD 1: [Time begun _____ Time ended _____]

Interpretation 1 (In what cognitive stage does the child appear to be functioning?):

OBD 2: [Time begun _____ Time ended _____]

Interpretation 2:

Continue for as long or for as many OBDs as are required.

Summary of Descriptive Data:

General Conclusions as to Children's Predominant Level of Cognitive Functioning:

PART FOUR

OBSERVATION EXERCISE **17-2** (Continued)

PART I-B: Cognitive Functioning of the Six-Year-Old: Piaget's Theory ("Testing" Approach)

Observer's Name _____

Child/Children Observed _____

Child's/Children's Age(s) _____ Child's/Children's Sex _____

Observation Context (home, child care center, preschool, school) _____

Date of Observation _____ Time Begun _____ Time Ended _____

Brief Description of Physical and Social Characteristics of Observation Setting:

Testing Method or Approach Used (Interaction) and Interpretation of Results

(Describe what you did to get child to respond, questions you asked, and so on.)

Interaction 1: [Time begun _____ Time ended _____]

Interpretation 1 (Level of Cognitive Functioning):

Interaction 2: [Time begun _____ Time ended _____]

Interpretation 2:

Continue for as long or for as many testing episodes as are required.

General Conclusions Regarding Children's Level of Cognitive Functioning:

(continues)

OBSERVATION EXERCISE **17-2** (Continued)

PART II-A: Cognitive Functioning of the Six-Year-Old (Information Processing Approach): Use of Strategies

Observer's Name _____

Child/Children Observed _____

Child's/Children's Age(s) _____ Child's/Children's Sex _____

Observation Context (home, child care center, preschool, school) _____

Date of Observation _____ Time Begun _____ Time Ended _____

Brief Description of Physical and Social Characteristics of Observation Setting:

Objective Behavioral Descriptions (OBDs) and Interpretations: *Checklist and Event Sampling or "Testing" Approach*

Rehearsal ☐ Organization ☐ Elaboration ☐

OBD 1: [Time begun _____ Time ended _____]

Rehearsal ☐ Organization ☐ Elaboration ☐

OBD 2: [Time begun _____ Time ended _____]

Rehearsal ☐ Organization ☐ Elaboration ☐

OBD 3: [Time begun _____ Time ended _____]

Continue for as long or for as many OBDs or events as are needed or desired.

Summary of Observations and Interpretations (summarize briefly the kinds of strategies that were used and under what circumstances each strategy was used):

(continues)

PART FOUR

OBSERVATION EXERCISE **17-2**(Continued)

PART II-B: Cognitive Functioning of the Six-Year-Old (Information Processing Approach): Extent of Children's Knowledge Base

Observer's Name _____

Child/Children Observed _____

Child's/Children's Age(s) _____ Child's/Children's Sex _____

Observation Context (home, child care center, preschool, school) _____

Date of Observation _____ Time Begun _____ Time Ended _____

Brief Description of Physical and Social Characteristics of Observation Setting:

....

Objective Behavioral Descriptions (OBDs) and Interpretations: *Event Sampling*

OBD 1: Child One's Age in Years and Months _____

[Time begun _____ Time ended _____]

Interpretation or Comments 1:

OBD 2: Child Two's Age in Years and Months _____

[Time begun _____ Time ended _____]

Interpretation or Comments 2:

Continue for as long or for as many OBDs as are needed or desired.

Summary Remarks (Comparisons and Contrasts of the Children):

OBSERVATION EXERCISE **17-3**

PART I: Metalinguistic Awareness

Observer's Name _____

Child/Children Observed _____

Child's/Children's Age(s) _____ Child's/Children's Sex _____

Observation Context (home, child care center, preschool, school) _____

Date of Observation _____ Time Begun _____ Time Ended _____

Brief Description of Physical and Social Characteristics of Observation Setting:

Objective Behavioral Descriptions (OBDs) and Interpretations: *Narrative Description*

OBD 1: [Time begun _____ Time ended _____]

Interpretation 1 (Did the child use metaphor—figurative speech—or humor? Into which of Schickedanz et al.'s categories of humor can you place the child's humorous speech?):

OBD 2: [Time begun _____ Time ended _____]

Interpretation 2:

Continue for as many OBDs as are needed or desired.

Summary Comments (Include the circumstances under which metaphor or humor was used):

(continues)

PART FOUR

PART II: Vocabulary and Syntax

Observer's Name _____

Child/Children Observed _____

Child's/Children's Age(s) _____ Child's/Children's Sex _____

Observation Context (home, child care center, preschool, school) _____

Date of Observation _____ Time Begun _____ Time Ended _____

Brief Description of Physical and Social Characteristics of Observation Setting:

....

Objective Behavioral Descriptions (OBDs) and Interpretations: *Narrative Description*

OBD 1: [Time begun _____ Time ended _____]

Interpretation 1 (an assessment of the child's speech with respect to vocabulary, sentence structure, and so on):

OBD 2: [Time begun _____ Time ended _____]

Interpretation 2 (same procedure as Interpretation 1):

Continue for as many OBDs as are needed or desired.

Summary Comments:

(continues)

OBSERVATION EXERCISE **17-3** (Continued)

PART III: Meta-communication

Observer's Name _____

Child/Children Observed _____

Child's/Children's Age(s) _____ Child's/Children's Sex _____

Observation Context (home, child care center, preschool, school) _____

Date of Observation _____ Time Begun _____ Time Ended _____

Brief Description of Physical and Social Characteristics of Observation Setting:

Objective Behavioral Descriptions (OBDs) and Interpretations: *Event Sampling*

OBD/Event/Child 1: [Time begun _____ Time ended _____]

Interpretation 1:

OBD/Event/Child 2: [Time begun _____ Time ended _____]

Interpretation 2:

OBD/Event/Child 3: [Time begun _____ Time ended _____]

Interpretation 3:

Continue for as many OBDs as are needed or desired.

Summary Comments (include any comparisons and contrasts between or among the children observed):

OBSERVATION EXERCISE **17-4**

PART I: Children's Popularity (Social Status Categorization)

Observer's Name _____

Child/Children Observed _____

Child's/Children's Age(s) _____ Child's/Children's Sex _____

Observation Context (home, child care center, preschool, school) _____

Date of Observation _____ Time Begun _____ Time Ended _____

Brief Description of Physical and Social Characteristics of Observation Setting:

Objective Behavioral Descriptions (OBDs) and Interpretations: *Event Sampling*

OBD 1 (Record observed child's behaviors and other children's responses to the child. Continue this procedure for each OBD.):

[Time begun _____ Time ended _____]

Interpretation 1 (Identify a possible social status category into which the child might be put, and include reasons why you believe the observed child falls into the category you have chosen.):

OBD 2: [Time begun _____ Time ended _____]

Interpretation 2:

OBD 3: [Time begun _____ Time ended _____]

Interpretation 3:

Continue for as many OBDs as are needed or desired.

Summary Comments (comparisons and contrasts among the observed children):

(continues)

OBSERVATION EXERCISE **17-4** (Continued)

PART II: Sociometric Analysis of Children's Popularity and Friendships

Observer's Name _____

Child/Children Observed _____

Child's/Children's Age(s) _____ Child's/Children's Sex _____

Observation Context (home, child care center, preschool, school) _____

Date of Observation _____ Time Begun _____ Time Ended _____

Brief Description of Physical and Social Characteristics of Observation Setting:

Objective Behavioral Descriptions (OBDs) and Interpretations: *Narrative Description*

OBD 1: [Time begun _____ Time ended _____]

Interpretation 1:

OBD 2: [Time begun _____ Time ended _____]

Interpretation 2:

Continue for as many OBDs as are needed or desired.

Summary Comments:

PART II (concluded): *Sociogram*

CHAPTER 18

The School-Age Years: The Seven- and Eight-Year-Old Child

KEY TERMS

self-esteem

self-concept

PHYSICAL GROWTH AND MOTOR DEVELOPMENT

Background Information

In Chapter 17 we sometimes presented data that did not always specifically pertain to the six-year-old. Some of what we discussed dealt with children younger than six and some with children older than six. This attests to the continuous quality of age, which is totally unlike counting the number of apples in a bag and coming up with a nice discrete whole number. It is not always easy or possible—indeed, it may be impossible—to define precisely where the gains of the sixth year of life end and those of the seventh year begin, and so on through the entire life span. (As you well know, changes are frequently reported within age ranges, even though efforts are sometimes made to attach changes to specific ages.) In any event, rather than repeat all this information when it applies to seven- and eight-year-olds, we refer you to the material that is relevant to those ages. In this chapter, although we present some of the physical changes that take place in seven- and eight-year-olds, we are not interested in physical changes for their own sake. We want to place such changes primarily in the context of the child's motor development and functioning.

As stated in Chapter 17, physical growth during this period is steady and sustained, much as it is during early childhood, and it is unlike the rapid growth that occurs during infancy. Many of the changes in physical characteristics and motor skills in the one to two years from six to eight appear to be increases in the sophistication of the child's chosen activities and improvements in such things as "agility, balance, control of motor skills, and endurance" (Allen & Marotz, 2007). Table 18-1 summarizes some of the physical and motor characteristics of the seven- and eight-year-old child.

Table 18-1 Summary of Physical and Motor Characteristics of the Seven- and Eight-Year-Old Child	
Physical Characteristics	**Motor Abilities**
• Gains an average of 5 to 7 pounds per year.	• Participates eagerly in competitive activities.
• Height gains of 2.5 inches per year on average; average height of girls is 46 to 49 inches, boys 48 to 52 inches.	• Enjoys such activities as dancing, skating, swimming, running, wrestling, and sports such as soccer and baseball.
• Arms and legs grow longer, thus giving child a thin, lanky appearance.	• Shows significantly more agility, balance, motor ability control, and endurance; is able to balance on one foot, jump rope, and catch a ball.
• Straighter, more erect posture.	
• Permanent teeth more prominent now than baby teeth.	• The tight grip on a pencil at seven years of age becomes more relaxed by eight.
• Suffers minor illnesses less frequently.	• Deliberate and confident writing of letters and numbers; character size becomes more consistent and uniform.
• Seven-year-old's "[e]nergy level comes and goes, fluctuating between spurts of high energy and intervals of temporary fatigue" (p. 176).	• Uses knife and fork when eating.
• Seven-year-old's "[b]aby teeth continue to be replaced by permanent teeth" (p. 176).	• Engages in repeated practice of newfound skills.

Adapted from Allen and Marotz, 2003, pp. 151–152, 158–159, and Allen and Marotz, 2007, pp. 176–177, 185–187.

In Chapter 17 we discussed play more in terms of its social implications and components than its physical or motor ones. In this chapter, we want to reverse this emphasis and treat play among seven- and eight-year-olds primarily in the context of their motor development. We remind the reader that the seven- and eight-year-old child's changing play is the product not only of his increased physical and motor skills but also of his equally increasing cognitive abilities and social and emotional maturity. As Berk (1996) puts it, "[G]reater cognitive and social maturity permits older children to use their new motor skills in more complex ways" (p. 409). We also want to discuss briefly the issue of sex differences in motor development, some of which, having begun in the preschool years, become more pronounced during middle childhood (see, e.g., Berk, 2005, especially p. 419ff). Let us begin with these differences.

Some Gender Differences in Motor Development

Berk (2005) writes that "[s]ex differences in motor skills that appeared during the preschool years extend into middle childhood and, in some instances, become more pronounced. Girls remain ahead of boys in the fine motor area, including handwriting and drawing" (p. 419). Interestingly enough, says Berk, girls "...continue to have

an edge in skipping, jumping, and hopping, which depend on balance and agility"
(p. 419). As for most other motor skills—running, throwing, catching, kicking, batting,
dribbling, and so on—boys confirm traditional thinking and perform better than girls.
Berk takes pains to point out, however, that it is not genetics alone that account for
boys' superior performance in gross motor activities. The environment, she believes,
"plays a larger role" (p. 419), an issue we do not take up here. As we note, girls and
boys also differ in the characteristics of their rough-and-tumble play.

Fine motor skills such as handwriting and drawing are well developed in this school-age
girl.

Games, Rules, and Motor Functioning

It is intuitively reasonable that with greater physical size and strength and constantly
improving motor skills, the physical activities of children in the middle-childhood years
should also become more sophisticated and more organized, characteristics contributed
to in no small way by the child's increasing cognitive and social skills. In this context,
we see an interaction between the quality of their play and the character of their
physical activities. Although not limited to the period from seven to eight years of age,
organized games with rules become more standard fare in children's daily lives, and
games demand different things from children than are demanded by the simpler forms
of play engaged in by younger, preschool children.

Not all games with rules, of course, are physically demanding; many make their
demands in the cognitive and social realms—board games, card games, and the like.

On the other hand, games such as kick the can, tag, hide-and-seek, leapfrog, and prisoner's base require physical–motor skills as well as their fair share of interpersonal skills, role and perspective-taking skills, and so on. The critical significance of play can be captured by Steinberg and Meyer's (1995) succinct assertion *"Play is the work of childhood:* When children play, they produce, whether it's a fantasy or a product" (p. 292, emphasis added). But again, our interest in play at this moment is in the opportunity it affords the child to exhibit her growing physical attributes and motor skills. Therefore, disregarding play's testimony to changing peer relations, cognitive abilities, and other dimensions of human behavior, let us look at the body–muscle aspects of play among seven- and eight-year-olds.

Rough-and-Tumble Play

There are many forms of play, but because we are concerned with play that makes demands on the child's motor abilities, the very name *rough-and-tumble* begs for attention. However, we should point out that rough-and-tumble play is not the only form of what can be called physical play. Berger (1991), for instance, discusses "three types of play that are especially well-suited to the development of motor skills." These are sensorimotor play, mastery play, and rough-and-tumble play (p. 254). We are concerned with the latter.

Bukatko and Daehler (1995) call rough-and-tumble play "a special form of play," which, they say, "emerges around age two years and becomes more visible during the elementary school years, especially among boys" (p. 566). Berk (2005) indicates that rough-and-tumble play "is a good-natured, sociable activity that is distinct from aggressive fighting" (p. 421). Berk further notes that "[s]chool-age children in many cultures engage in it with peers whom they like especially well, and they continue interacting after a rough-and-tumble episode rather than separating, as they do at the end of an aggressive encounter" (p. 421). Bukatko and Daehler make the same distinction: "[C]hildren do not intend to hurt one another and it often occurs between children who like each other" (p. 566). From this brief description, you can see the strong social components even of such a physically vigorous form of interaction.

Berk (2005) notes that boys of this age engage in rough-and-tumble play more than girls do, and their play "largely consists of playful wrestling, restraining, and hitting, whereas girls tend to engage in running and chasing, and only brief physical contact" (p. 42).

In the observation exercises that are to come, you will be asked to focus your attention on those activities children engage in that make special demands on their physical attributes and motor skills. We have chosen play as one vehicle for the exercise of these skills, but we advise you not to restrict yourself unnecessarily to play. There are many avenues for the display of motor behaviors, and you should take advantage of this fact. Put another way, the preceding discussion is necessarily limited in scope, but do not impose those same limitations on how you complete the exercises.

COGNITIVE AND INTELLECTUAL DEVELOPMENT AND BEHAVIOR

Background Information

If Piaget is correct, the typical seven- and eight-year-old child is in, or has progressed significantly toward, the period of concrete mental operations. In the preceding chapter we discussed several perspectives on children's intellectual behavior and development, and at least some of that information can be applied to the seven- and eight-year-old. We do not duplicate all that material in the present chapter. Table 18-2 outlines some of the characteristics of Piaget's period of concrete operational thought. Also as a reminder,

Table 18-2 Summary of Some Characteristics of Concrete Operational Thought
Characteristics of Concrete Operational Thought (The School Years)
• Understands the general rules that underlie or lead to specific outcomes (idea of cause and effect).
• Has the ability to decenter, i.e., simultaneously take into account more than one feature or dimension of an object or situation.
• Understands the concept of mental and physical operations and the fact that they are reversible. (For example, the child understands that liquid poured from a short, wide jar into a tall, narrow one can be poured back into the short, wide container and that no amount of liquid is added or taken away during the "operation." The child is not as vulnerable to the appearance of things.)
• Can transfer learning (rules or principles) gained from solving concrete problems to solving problems in real life.
• Is not fooled by perceptions or by what appears to be true, but can rely on what he knows to be true.
• Is more logical and can reason inductively—can form hypotheses or educated guesses based on what he has experienced (he can reason from the specific case to a general theory, of sorts).
• Is more sociocentric than egocentric—he can take someone else's viewpoint or perspective and is not restricted to his own point of view.
• "Change[s] the facts to fit their hypotheses rather than changing their hypotheses to fit the facts (a new egocentrism)" (Harris, 1993, p. 529).

Adapted from Harris, 1993, p. 529.

concrete here means that "children are bound by immediate physical reality and cannot transcend the here and now" (Vander Zanden, 1993, p. 302). In other words, much of the concrete operational child's thinking has to occur in the presence of the actual objects of thought, and she cannot deal easily with issues or events that are far from her own experiences, that are hypothetical, or that are too far in the future.

In Chapter 16 we addressed the issue of whether or not children in the period of early childhood could conserve such things as number, substance, or volume. That is, do children of this age understand, for example, that if there are two equal rows of pennies, and if one row is spread out so as to take up more space than the other row, there are still the same number of pennies in each row? This is a typical conservation-of-number task, and if the child answers that the number of pennies is unchanged, he has conserved number. Until fairly recently, the consensus was that children under six years of age could not conserve such things as number. Now research strongly suggests that very young children can perform some conservation tasks if the problem is presented in ways that are appropriate to their developmental level and prior experience. Bukatko and Daehler (1995), for instance, confirm that infants' and young children's abilities have indeed been underestimated. Reporting on the findings of various researchers, they note that if cognitive tasks are simplified and restructured and if children are observed under more naturalistic conditions than artificial laboratory settings, "they [children] display cognitive skills at much earlier ages than Piaget believed possible" (p. 296). Some of this research goes back to 1969, when Gelman demonstrated that five-year-olds could conserve number and length when they were tested for this ability through the use of different stimuli. Gelman (1972) later found that children as young as three and four could, with training, learn to conserve number (Bukatko & Daehler, 1995, p. 297).

In Table 18-3 we present the approximate ages at which children acquire various conservation abilities. Some of these go beyond the age parameters of early childhood, but we include them anyway to maintain a sense of continuity, as well as to provide for the possibility that your observations might disclose a child or children whose level of cognitive functioning is higher than their seven- and eight-year-old peers. However, it is more likely that Table 18-3 can serve as a guide to developmentally appropriate practice and developmentally appropriate expectations. You may recall from Chapter 13 the discussion of the concept of standards. There we wrote, "Selection of the standard ...is critical in many cases because the standard will determine whether the child's performance satisfies the adult's conception of what she can and should be able to do." Each of the conservation skills is a standard, and you would not expect a seven-year-old to be able to conserve weight or volume, skills that are ordinarily achieved between 9 and 14 years of age.

Other cognitive and intellectual functions applicable to seven- and eight-year-olds have been discussed in the previous chapter: information processing theory, Vygotsky's theory, Piaget's theory, and some of the major ideas that accompany those

Table 18-3 Order of Acquisition of Conservation Skills	
Conservation Skill	**Characteristics of Conservation Skill**
Number (Ages 5–7)	The number of objects is independent of how they are arranged in space, provided none is added or taken away.
Substance (Ages 7–8)	The amount of a substance—such as clay or play dough—remains unaffected by how that substance is shaped (e.g., the amount of clay in a ball does not increase or decrease if it is flattened out into the shape of a pancake).
Length (Ages 7–8)	The length, say, of a piece of string is not changed merely by changing how it is arranged (e.g., a string laid out in a straight line keeps its original length when it is formed into a circular shape).
Area (Ages 8–9)	The amount of total area of a space is not changed by rearranging any of the component parts of that total area (e.g., four one-foot square blocks arranged to form one large square comprising four square feet of area do not gain or lose any amount of area if the individual squares are rearranged to form a different geometric shape).
Weight (Ages 9–10)	The weight or heaviness of an object does not change merely by changing the shape of that object (e.g., four one-pound blocks stacked on top of one another, which weigh a total of four pounds, will still weigh a total of four pounds if they are placed side by side).
Volume (Ages 12–14)	The amount (volume) of liquid in a container, for example, does not depend on the shape of the container (e.g., a quart of water in a short, wide jar is still a quart of water when put into a tall, narrow jar).

Adapted from VanderZanden, 1993, p. 305.

perspectives. In the present chapter, we emphasize the concept of conservation because it can serve as one example of how the child's cognitive abilities become more and more sophisticated over the course of development.

Consequently, to complete this section of the chapter, we offer a brief tabular summary of some skills, behaviors, or abilities that appear to characterize the overall mental status of the seven- and eight-year-old child (Table 18-4). Keep in mind, though, that when it comes time to perform your observations, anything that is relevant to a child's cognitive functioning can be relevant.

LANGUAGE

Background Information

We have already written quite a lot about language and its developmental characteristics. In fact, language is one of those functional areas of such significance that it is hard to imagine saying too much about it, other than running the risk of prolonging discussion beyond a reasonable and tolerable length.

Table 18-4 Summary of Some Characteristics of Concrete Operational Thought
Some Activities and Interests Demonstrated by the Seven- and Eight-Year-Old Child Indicative of Cognitive Functioning

- Child collects things and organizes and displays them in accordance with a more complex system of classification than used when younger; also engages in bargaining with friends to acquire more items.

- Child can identify and name denominations of coins and paper currency.

- Child becomes more sociocentric or other-centered; that is, he takes an interest in what other people think and do, which is reflected in an interest in "different cultures, far away places" (Allen & Marotz, 2003, p. 159).

- Child can delay gratification as well as plan ahead (e.g., putting off doing something pleasant until a later, more appropriate time).

- Child can use some logic in efforts to understand how things work or to accomplish a goal (e.g., systematically searches for a lost object).

- Child can tell time and knows the correct day, month, and year.

- Child understands the idea of cause and effect; he knows how one event can affect or influence another event.

- Child is learning addition and subtraction of numbers.

- Child uses words to express ideas more efficiently and accurately.

- Child can recall details from stories and experienced events with considerable accuracy.

- Child now enjoys reading and does so more on his or her own without need for outside help or supervision.

Adapted from Allen and Marotz, 2003, pp. 153, 159–160; see also Allen and Marotz, 2007, pp. 178, 187.

Vocabulary

As a general premise, we can say that the seven- and eight-year-olds' language skills continue to improve beyond those held when they were six. In the area of vocabulary alone, marked increases seem to be the norm. Berk (1996), for example, asserts that

> Because the average six-year-old's vocabulary is already quite large (about 10,000 words), parents and teachers usually do not notice rapid gains during the school years. Between the start of elementary school and its completion, recognition vocabulary increases fourfold, eventually reaching about 40,000 words. On the average, about 20 new words are learned each day—a rate of growth that exceeds that of early childhood. (p. 446)

This rapid expansion of vocabulary is the result of gains in other related areas of functioning. For instance, Berk (2005) notes that "school-age children enlarge their vocabularies through an increasingly powerful ability to analyze the structure of complex words." She gives the example of the child being able to take words such as "happy" and "decide," and discern or derive "the meanings of 'happiness,' and 'decision'" (p. 451).

Another gain comes in the form of increased conceptual knowledge, which in turn forms the foundation for concomitant gains in vocabulary. As Berk (2005) reports, "Five- and 6-year-olds give concrete descriptions that refer to functions or appearance—for example, *knife*: 'when you're cutting carrots'; *bicycle*: 'it's got wheels, a chain, and handlebars'" (p. 451). But "by the end of elementary school synonyms and explanations of categorical relationships appear—for example, *knife*: 'something you could cut with. A saw is like a knife. It could also be a weapon'" (p. 451, italics original). Eventually, by fifth and sixth grade, children can acquire new vocabulary words merely by being given a definition (Berk, 2005, p. 452). Children also increasingly appreciate the multiple meanings of words. Such multiple meanings include psychological meanings as well as physical ones, which allows a richer, fuller use of the ambiguous character of language. This grasp of the double meanings of many words, of course, further allows the use of more sophisticated metaphors than was possible at an earlier age or level of language development. In turn, according to Berk (2005), children's humor changes rather dramatically, whereby "riddles and puns that go back and forth between different meanings of the same key word are common, as in: 'Hey, did you take a bath?' 'No! Why, is one missing?'" (p. 452).

Grammar

Another aspect of language development and functioning is that of grammar. We refer the reader to the lengthier discussion of language in Chapter 17, if and when more information is required than what is provided here.

Grammar, along with syntax, is what makes language—spoken or written—intelligible. Grammar is the rules governing the correct usage of words and their relationships to one another in sentences. *The American Heritage Talking Dictionary* (1994) defines *grammar* as "[t]he system of rules implicit in a language, viewed as a mechanism for generating all sentences possible in that language.... A normative or prescriptive set of rules setting forth the current standard of usage for pedagogical or reference purposes.... The study of how words and their component parts combine to form sentences."

One grammatical construction of some note is the use of the passive voice—"The ball *was hit* by Alonzo"—as opposed to the active voice—"Alonzo *hit* the ball." Berk (1996) writes that "full passives are rarely used by 3- to 6-year-olds" but that "they increase steadily over middle-childhood" (p. 447). Also noted by Berk is the fact that

"Older children also apply their understanding of the passive voice to a wider range of nouns and verbs" (p. 447).

Middle childhood also sees "advanced understanding of infinitive phrases, such as the difference between 'John is easy to please.' and 'John is eager to please'" (Berk, 2005, p. 452). All the above accomplishments are partly the result of increased cognitive skills and partly of an "improved ability to analyze and reflect on language" (Berk, 1996, p. 447), or what Berk later characterizes as "improved metalinguistic awareness, acquired during literacy activities" (2005, p. 452). The confusion arises over who exactly is doing what, or who exactly has what characteristics. In the sentence "John is eager to please," who is doing the pleasing, or who wants to please? It is difficult for children younger than five or six, which are the estimated beginning ages of acquisition of this syntactical structure, to distinguish between this sentence and the sentence "John is easy to please." Here, John is the potential recipient of actions that will please him, whereas before, John is the potential doer of actions that will please others.

A final aspect of language of concern to us is that of pragmatics, which has to do with what Berk (2005) calls "the communicative side of language" (p. 452). Here, the individual has to deal with the practical tasks associated with making herself understood by others. One such task is to take into account the particular needs or situation of the listener. For example, pragmatics would require the child to know what his conversational partner knows about the topic under discussion, or about the context of the conversation. Failure to take such matters into account might be partly explainable by invoking Piaget's concept of egocentrism. The younger, more egocentric child might fail to provide enough information for the other person to understand what is being communicated, or needed, in the situation. Giving instructions, for instance, will not result in meaningful action if those instructions are incomplete, vague, or ambiguous. The older child can realize or discern the gaps in her directions and adjust them accordingly, something the preschooler is unable to do.

This ability to give adequate instructions develops through a gradual progression. The older child just referred to probably is a child of about 10 or 11 years of age. Berger (1991), for instance, discusses this issue in the context of a study by Sonnenschein (1986) that involved first- and fourth-grade children giving instructions to a playmate on how to find a toy. As Berger (1991) reports the findings, "Only the fourth-graders' instructions were consistently well-suited to finding the toy; those of the first graders included both helpful and irrelevant additional information" (p. 380).

The relevance of these findings to your observations is that you can expect seven- and eight-year-olds to demonstrate at least some ability to provide a listener with meaningful information in particular situations.

Another important facet of pragmatics is the child's improved ability to understand "the distinctions between the form and meaning of utterances" (Berk, 1996, p. 447). This is an interesting phenomenon because it is an aspect of our daily interactions involving language that probably goes unnoticed by most of us. Think of it in terms of the following example of an eight-year-old. Josie's mother wants her to clean her room. Several times her mother has asked her to perform this household chore. She usually phrases her request as "Josie, clean your room." Josie has responded with "OK, Mom," but has left the job undone. Finally, in desperation and frustration, her mother says, "Josephine Markowitz, clean your room." Now Josie hops to it, knowing that her mother's rephrasing of her request signals some anger and urgency. And this realization on Josie's part was derived from her mother's simple use of Josie's full name, along with a probable rise in the volume and tone of her voice.

Berk (1996), again, provides an informative illustration of this communication skill:

> Even 3-year-olds know that a playmate who says "I need a pencil," is not just making a statement. She is asking for a pencil. But 8-year-olds understand more unconventional expressions of meaning. For example, the day after she forgot to take the garbage out, Lizzie knew that her mother's statement "The garbage is beginning to smell," really meant "Take that garbage out." Making subtle inferences about the relationship between an utterance and its context is beyond the ability of preschoolers. (p. 447)

Your observation exercises will, we hope, provide you the opportunity to witness and record some of these linguistic skills and to compare the seven- and eight-year-old's skills in this area with those of the younger child.

SOCIAL AND EMOTIONAL BEHAVIOR

Background Information

The school-age years (6–12) are when the child acquires and even masters certain basic competencies, many of which are functionally related to formal education. It is feasible to place these competencies and their accomplishments under the general rubric of personality changes. We take our lead in this assumption from Berk's (2005) statement, "According to Erikson (1950), the *personality changes* [emphasis added] of the school years build on Freud's *latency stage* [emphasis original]" (p. 470). The psychosocial crisis or task in Erikson's theoretical perspective of middle childhood is that of developing either a sense of industry or a sense of inferiority. It is the sense of industry that enables the child to accomplish the educational tasks associated with formal schooling, among other demands made in other contexts and situations. As Berk (1996) puts it, "In school, children engage in productive work beside and with other children" (p. 466). For our purposes, it is this engagement in meaningful, productive activity that captures the essence of industry.

A sense of inferiority can be captured by the ideas of pessimism or inadequacy, which interfere with the development of competence and mastery, critical components of industry. The concepts of both industry and inferiority lend themselves quite nicely to the concepts of, and issues associated with, **self-esteem**, **self-concept**, moral behavior and reasoning, and cooperation with others in such endeavors as accomplishing tasks. This latter set of issues goes to the heart of personality and social relationships.

Self-Concept and Self-Esteem

Self-concept should be distinguished from self-esteem. For our purposes, self-concept refers to the manner in which an individual describes herself—that is, what qualities or attributes does the child assign to herself? We may think of self-concept as a more or less objective assessment of who we are, our strengths and weaknesses, our personality characteristics, and so on. As Berk (2005) writes, "During the school years, children develop a much more refined *me-self*, or self-concept, organizing their observations of behaviors and internal states into general dispositions, with a major change taking place between ages 8 and 11" (p. 471, italics original). Berk offers an informative comparison between two children's descriptions of themselves, a 7-year-old boy and an 11-year-old girl. Note the rather significant differences between these two self-descriptions:

A boy age 7: I am 7 and I have brown hair and my hobby is stamp collecting. I am good at football and I am quite good at sums and my favorite game is football and I love school and I like reading books and my favorite car is an Austin. (Berk, 1996, p. 467; cited from Livesly & Bromley, 1973, p. 237)

A girl age 11 1/2: My name is A. I am a human being. I'm a girl. I'm a truthful person. I'm not pretty. I do so-so in my studies. I'm a very good cellist. I'm a very good pianist. I'm a little bit tall for my age. I like several boys. I like several girls. I'm old-fashioned. I play tennis. I am a very good swimmer. I try to be helpful. I'm always ready to be friends with anybody. Mostly I'm good, but I lose my temper. I'm not well-liked by some girls and boys. I don't know if I'm liked by boys or not. (Berk, 2005, p. 471, cited from Montemayor & Eisen, 1977, pp. 317–318)

Bukatko and Daehler (1995) discuss self-concept—or what they call "self-definition"—in terms of the categorical self. They note that "during the preschool years, knowledge of self extends beyond physical features to include activities the child likes and is good at, his possessions, and his relationship to others" (p. 441).

self-esteem
Self-esteem refers to one's sense of personal worth or value. It is distinguished from self-concept, although it is related to it.

self-concept
The more or less objective assessment of who we are, our strengths and weaknesses, our personality characteristics. Self-concept refers to the manner in which an individual describes himself—for example, the qualities or attributes that the child assigns to himself.

In developing a categorical self, children "classify themselves in terms of membership in certain groups based on their sex, age, skills, what they own, where they live, and who their friends are" (p. 441).

In rather sharp contrast to the preschooler and the 7-year-old, the 11-year-old moves beyond a listing of specific behaviors and describes general competencies and categories of characteristics. As Berk (1996) also points out, the younger child—as with younger children in general—does not identify any psychological traits, whereas the older child describes her personality (p. 467).

Self-esteem refers to one's sense of personal worth or value. So, for example, although the girl described earlier considers her academic abilities or performance only "so-so," she may still have a positive sense of personal worth that is essentially unaffected by her less than exemplary scholastic competence or accomplishments.

As Berk (2005) reports, "By age 7 to 8, children in diverse Western cultures have formed at least four separate self-esteems—academic competence, social competence, physical/athletic competence, and physical appearance. Within them are more refined categories that become increasingly distinct with age" (p. 472). This refinement consists in part of academic self-worth dividing into performance relative to different school subjects, social self-worth dividing into peer and parental relationships, and "physical/athletic competence into skill at various sports" (p. 472).

Conventional wisdom dictates that high or positive self-esteem contributes more to higher levels of confidence and performance than does low or negative self-esteem. But research also suggests that children's self-esteem becomes more realistic as they grow older and engage in more social comparisons with other individuals: "Self-esteem drops during the first few years of elementary school. This decline occurs as competence-related feedback becomes more frequent, children's performances are increasingly judged in relation to the performance of others, and children become cognitively capable of social comparison" (Berk, 2005, p. 472).

For the school-age child, there is an aspect of children's behavior that is particularly germane to academic performance, and it is an aspect that is, we think, fairly easily accessible to more or less direct observation. We are referring here to the reasons we—people in general—offer as explanations for our behavior. In the present context, they are reasons that are labeled by Berk (2005) as "achievement-related attributions" (p. 474ff). These attributions are among the influences that contribute to the child's self-esteem. Berk (2005) identifies two basic attributions that children make with respect to their academic self-esteem: (1) mastery-oriented attributions and (2) learned helplessness, which results in attributions that are made by the child himself and are critical and derogatory of his own abilities.

Children with high academic self-esteem, writes Berk, "...make **mastery-oriented attributions**, crediting their success to ability—a characteristic they can improve through trying hard and can count on when faced with new challenges" (2005, p. 475, emphasis original). And when failure occurs, they attribute it to

"...factors that can be changed and controlled, such as insufficient effort or a difficult task" (p. 475). In sharp contrast, the learned helpless child attributes her failures to the lack of ability, but, interestingly enough, she attributes her successes to luck rather than to ability (Berk, 2005, p. 475). In either circumstance, learned helpless children eventually "...hold a *fixed view of ability*—that cannot be changed. They do not think that competence can be improved by trying hard" (p. 475, emphasis original). Consequently, in their minds, effort does not count for much and will not have an appreciable effect on competence. As a further consequence, future difficult tasks merely increase their sense of incompetence and their feelings of loss of control, a condition that leads to Erikson's sense of inferiority (Berk, 2005, p. 475).

This concludes the background segment of this chapter. We have attempted to select developmental and behavioral occurrences in the lives of seven- and eight-year-olds that are either reasonably open or accessible to naturalistic observation or, where they are not, to some form of intervention or testing that might reveal the behaviors of interest. Again, constraints of time and space have forced us to make choices that might not have been made by others. You should always feel free to make your own decisions regarding what and how to observe. We can only offer a few guidelines to direct you down a few pathways among the many that exist in the context of young children's growth, development, and behavior.

Before getting into the observation exercises, we want to remind you that unless you are already officially associated with the school or other facility in which you will do your observations, prior permission is required to enter that facility and observe the children. Getting such permission must be one of the first tasks on your agenda. The actual process involved will undoubtedly already have been established by the appropriate authorities at the observation site. Consult with them before embarking on any of your assignments.

OBSERVATION EXERCISE 18-1: GENERAL PHYSICAL AND MOTOR SKILLS

Part I: Physical Growth and Motor Development: Observation Objectives

The purposes of this exercise are at least twofold: (1) to observe seven- and eight-year-olds' motor behavior in the context of their play activities and (2) to compare and contrast the characteristics of girls' and boys' play and motor functioning. Two factors are assumed to operate here. First, there is the assumption that children seven and eight years of age of both genders tend to play with more sophistication and complexity than they did when they were younger, characteristics that will influence the kind and quality of the motor behaviors that a child of either sex will exhibit during the course of play. Second, there is the assumption that girls play differently

During the school years, the development of advanced motor skills results in more complex play activities.

than boys, which means that the characteristics of each gender's physical/motor actions will be different from each other. It is these two general classes of differences that we want you to observe and record.

Procedure

In Part I of this exercise, you will use the event sampling format or technique. Find several children—at least two or three, if possible—who are playing together and whose play involves significant motor activity. Observe and record their behavior for as long as it lasts, unless its duration is too long and it becomes unfeasible for you to continue.

When you have gathered all your data, interpret them with respect to the overall characteristics of the children's motor functioning. Try to draw comparisons and contrasts between the kind and quality of these seven- and eight-year-olds' motor skills and preferences and what you know—or can find out—to be the kind and quality of a six-year-old's motor skills and preferences. You might be able to make such comparisons by using the information you acquired via your earlier observations of the six-year-old.

PART II: Gender-Related Differences in Motor Functioning: Observation Objectives

Part II of this exercise is concerned with discovering any differences that might exist between boys' and girls' motor behavior—that is, what kinds of games they play (or other activities they might participate in) and the differences in motor skills that these games or activities might require.

Procedure

You will again use the event sampling technique. This time, select a small group of girls and a similar group of boys who are engaged in some kind of activity that involves the use of their bodies and their motor skills and abilities.

Your focus here will be less on the individual child and more on how all of the individuals function as a group, but with respect to the physical–motor demands that the activity makes on the children. The assumption is that because the group as a whole has apparently gotten together to play in whatever game they happen to be playing, each individual child will have at least most of the prerequisite skills needed for that activity. If girls' games require different skills than boys' games, these differences should become apparent and accessible to your observation and recording. (See Observation Exercise 18-1.)

OBSERVATION EXERCISE 18-2: COGNITIVE AND INTELLECTUAL DEVELOPMENT AND BEHAVIOR

PART I: Concrete Operational Thinking: Observation Objectives

We have stressed Piaget's concrete operational stage of cognitive development both in Chapter 17 and again in the present one. You might recall that earlier in the text, we mentioned that although theory testing is not one of your usual tasks, in the course of your observations you might very well do just that—test a theory. Part of your assignment in Exercise 17-2 was to determine whether the six-year-old children you observed functioned significantly in the stage of concrete operations. At issue was the claim that the period of concrete operations does not "officially" begin until about age seven. One of the objectives of this present exercise is to compare and contrast the concrete operational thinking of some seven- and eight-year-olds with the concrete operational thinking of some six-year-olds. You are to decide which group of children, as identified by their ages, indeed better represents the cognitive functioning that is characteristic of this third stage in Piaget's theory.

Procedure

Therefore, for Part I of this exercise, select two or three children for observation. Use the event sampling format or technique, and look for examples of cognitive behavior that can be described as concrete operational thinking. Refer to Table 18-2 for more detailed information regarding the important characteristics of this stage. With the information you need at hand, compare your data on seven- and eight-year-olds' level of cognitive functioning with any data you have on six-year-olds' level of cognitive functioning. Are there any sharp differences or similarities between these two age groups? If you do not have prior observation data on six-year-olds, or if you are not able to observe children of this age before completing the present exercise, you may simply compare the information you do have against information available in a textbook or in this text. Although that information will not have come from your own personal observations, it will be the result of someone's observations, and that fact serves to attest to the importance of observation as a necessary and legitimate activity.

PART II: General Characteristics of Children's Cognitive Behavior: Observation Objectives

In Part II of this exercise, you focus on the overall characteristics of the children's cognitive functioning, with the goal of simply describing in more or less general terms how seven- and eight-year-olds think and process information, the kinds of knowledge they might possess and how they deal with or use this knowledge, and so on.

Procedure

Select at least three children, and, using the narrative description format, observe and record their behavior for what we simply call a reasonable length of time. However, we would add that you should select a situation and setting that lend themselves to witnessing the kinds of behaviors you want to observe. Refer to Table 18-4 for some guidelines regarding the types of cognitive behaviors that are relevant to this exercise. (See Observation Exercise 18-2.)

OBSERVATION EXERCISE 18-3: LANGUAGE

School-age children develop more advanced and interactive communication skills.

Observation Objectives

Although our background discussion of language presents rather specific information, the objectives for this exercise are purposely left somewhat open-ended. Your goal is simply to capture as much information about several children's language behavior as you possibly can and offer a general interpretive description of the basic characteristics of their language. The characteristics of major importance for this exercise are vocabulary, grammar, and pragmatics, as these are discussed earlier in the background information.

Procedure

Select at least two children as your targets. We recommend that both genders be represented, and if you observe, say, three children, two boys and a girl or two girls and a boy, rather than three boys or three girls, this would be the more desired gender composition of the group. Using the narrative description format, record verbatim as much of the children's speech as you can. Then interpret or discuss your data with respect to the children's vocabulary, the grammatical construction of their sentences, and whatever aspect of pragmatics you are able to discern.

Finally, compare and contrast the characteristics of the general language behavior exhibited by a child of each gender. For example, do girls talk about different things than boys? Can you detect significant differences in their respective vocabularies, grammatical constructions, and so on? Is it boys, girls, or neither gender who have the better verbal skills? Do boys and girls differ in their language usage when in the same setting and situation? That is, do boys use more assertive, aggressive, or authoritative language than girls when they are acting as leaders, for example? (See Observation Exercise 18-3.)

OBSERVATION EXERCISE 18-4: SOCIAL AND EMOTIONAL DEVELOPMENT AND BEHAVIOR

Observation Objectives

A primary objective of this exercise is to observe and record evidence of children's self-esteem as they express it in the course of their daily activities and interactions. Such expressions can be made with regard to one or more of the three kinds of self-esteem reported by Berk (1996) and discussed earlier in the background information: academic, physical, and social self-esteem. Coinciding with self-esteem is self-concept, which is how a child describes himself. You must understand and maintain the distinction between self-esteem and self-concept in order to complete this exercise successfully.

Procedure

This exercise may be difficult to complete through strictly naturalistic observation because it requires you to hear and record specifically what children say about themselves—descriptions in terms both of their self-concepts and their self-esteem. In view of this somewhat limiting condition, you may have to resort to some kind of intervention strategy, perhaps directly asking a child to talk about himself, to describe himself to you, to tell you something about himself. You may want to ask the child what he is or is not good at in school, for instance, or when playing with peers, and so on. You will have to try to get the child to evaluate himself with respect to his strengths and weaknesses; this evaluation will give you some notion of the worth or value the child places on himself with respect to his academic performance, social skills and status, and physical appearance, if you can tap into all those areas.

Whether you use naturalistic observation or a testing approach is a judgment you will have to make. In any event, use the following procedure if observation alone is feasible and it will give you the information you need to complete the assignment.

Select at least two children for this exercise. It might be desirable to observe a boy and a girl rather than two boys or two girls. Use the narrative description format because this technique yields the greatest amount of information per unit of time spent observing. The idea here is to try to witness the children's verbal and behavioral expressions concerning how they feel about themselves, along with how they rate themselves against various performance, social, and physical criteria, either in relation to themselves or in comparison to their peers.

If you are observing in a formal school setting, the children's academic self-esteem may be put in the context of mastery-oriented attributions or the attributions associated with learned helplessness. Whatever the specific context, try to obtain information about as many aspects of the children's self-esteem as you can, as well as descriptions of their self-concepts, or how they describe themselves and what qualities or characteristics they assign to themselves. We have been using the phrase *testing strategy* to indicate a means of obtaining information about children other than by naturalistic observation. Even though we have tried to recommend this approach very sparingly, *testing* may still not be quite the appropriate word because it could suggest a procedure that does not serve the child's best interests, or is too intrusive, or is not really observation in its purer form. In the present context, therefore, we offer the phrase *conversational strategy* or *conversational approach* to replace *testing strategy*. Apart from direct, nonintervening observation, and except for one possible alternative approach, it will be through conversation with children that you will have to get the information you need to complete this exercise.

Moreover, if you believe that a conversational approach is the better approach, even if only for part of the exercise, then we leave it up to you to devise an appropriate way of getting the data you need. But we must remind you that the sanctity of the child's feelings, the confidentiality of the information you obtain, and any other ethical issue or concern associated with the observation process have to be given top priority. This issue is of special relevance in this exercise because you are delving into children's perceptions of who they are and the value or worth they put on themselves as persons, as students, as physical beings, and as social partners with their teachers, friends, and peers.

Therefore, keep in mind that although the children may make judgments about themselves, you are not to make judgments about the children.

As a final task, it might be interesting to compare the self-concept statements your children make with the self-descriptive statements made by the 7-year-old boy and the 11-year-old girl reported by Berk. How close do the general characteristics of your children's self-concepts come to those of the children cited in the example?

There are those who would oppose the conversational approach for obtaining information about children's self-esteem and self-concept. If you or those in authority in the observational setting are opposed to such an approach, then out of respect for that point of view, let us suggest yet another possible way to get the data you need. If you are in a formal school setting, talk to a teacher or other appropriate staff member about a child's self-esteem and self-concept. What are that individual's perceptions or impressions of the child in that regard? Then observe the child and look for behavioral indications of the teacher's/staff member's impressions. For example, does the child persevere in the face of difficult tasks? Does the child blame himself or others for his success? His failures? Does the child describe himself in ways that correspond with the teacher's description of the child's self-concept? Instead of a teacher, a parent may be the person to give you this kind of information. (See Observation Exercise 18-4.)

Epilogue

There is only one more thing we have to say at this time: "Congratulations!" How far and how long you have traveled depends on how many of the observation exercises you have completed and how much you have involved yourself in the overall content of this text. We sincerely hope that your journey has been informative and interesting, even if at times it may have been difficult and time-consuming. We believe, nonetheless, that if not now, in the immediate present, then sometime in the future you will find that your hard work has paid off. If today you are a better, more astute observer of young children's behavior than you were just yesterday, and certainly before you first began, then we have accomplished our primary objective.

OBSERVATION EXERCISE **18-1**

PART I: General Physical and Motor Skills of the Seven- and Eight-Year-Old (in the Context of Play or Game)

Observer's Name _____

Child/Children Observed _____

Child's/Children's Age(s) _____ Child's/Children's Sex _____

Observation Context (home, child care center, preschool, school) _____

Date of Observation _____ Time Begun _____ Time Ended _____

Brief Description of Physical and Social Characteristics of Observation Setting:

....

Objective Behavioral Descriptions (OBDs) and Interpretations: *Event Sampling*

OBD 1: [Time begun _____ Time ended _____]

Interpretation 1:

OBD 2: [Time begun _____ Time ended _____]

Interpretation 2:

Continue for as many OBDs as are needed or desired.

Comparisons of Motor Skills of Seven- and Eight-Year-Olds with Those of Six-Year-Old:

Contrasts Between Motor Skills of Seven- and Eight-Year-Olds and Those of Six-Year-Old:

(continues)

OBSERVATION EXERCISE **18-1** (Continued)

**PART II:
Gender-Related
Differences
in Motor
Functioning**

Observer's Name _____

Child/Children Observed _____

Child's/Children's Age(s) _____ Child's/Children's Sex _____

Observation Context (home, child care center, preschool, school) _____

Date of Observation _____ Time Begun _____ Time Ended _____

Brief Description of Physical and Social Characteristics of Observation Setting:

**Objective
Behavioral
Descriptions
(OBDs) and
Interpretations:**
Event Sampling

Clearly indicate the gender composition of the respective groups for each OBD.

OBD 1: [Time begun _____ Time ended _____]

Interpretation 1:

OBD 2: [Time begun _____ Time ended _____]

Interpretation 2:

Continue for as many OBDs as are needed or desired.

Summary Comments Concerning General Characteristics of Boys' and Girls' Motor Functioning and Play:

Summary Comments Concerning Similarities and Differences Between Boys' and Girls' Motor Functioning and Play:

OBSERVATION EXERCISE 18-2

PART I: Cognitive Functioning in Piaget's Stage of Concrete Operational Thinking: A Comparison Between Six-Year-Olds and Seven- and Eight-Year-Olds

Observer's Name _____

Child/Children Observed _____

Child's/Children's Age(s) _____ Child's/Children's Sex _____

Observation Context (home, child care center, preschool, school) _____

Date of Observation _____ Time Begun _____ Time Ended _____

Brief Description of Physical and Social Characteristics of Observation Setting:

Objective Behavioral Descriptions (OBDs) and Interpretations: *Event Sampling*

OBD 1: [Time begun _____ Time ended _____]

Interpretation 1:

OBD 2: [Time begun _____ Time ended _____]

Interpretation 2:

OBD 3: [Time begun _____ Time ended _____]

Interpretation 3:

Continue for as many OBDs as are needed or desired.

Comparisons of the Two Groups of Children (with Respect to Stage of Cognitive Functioning):

Contrasts Between the Two Groups of Children (with Respect to Stage of Cognitive Functioning):

(continues)

PART FOUR

OBSERVATION EXERCISE 18-2 (Continued)

PART II: General Characteristics of Children's Cognitive Behavior

Observer's Name _____

Child/Children Observed _____

Child's/Children's Age(s) _____ Child's/Children's Sex _____

Observation Context (home, child care center, preschool, school) _____

Date of Observation _____ Time Begun _____ Time Ended _____

Brief Description of Physical and Social Characteristics of Observation Setting:

....

Objective Behavioral Descriptions (OBDs) and Interpretations: *Narrative Description*

OBD 1: [Time begun _____ Time ended _____]

Interpretation 1:

OBD 2: [Time begun _____ Time ended _____]

Interpretation 2:

OBD 3: [Time begun _____ Time ended _____]

Interpretation 3:

Continue for as many OBDs as are needed or desired.

Summary Remarks on Children's General Cognitive Characteristics:

OBSERVATION EXERCISE 18-3

Language

Observer's Name _____

Child/Children Observed _____

Child's/Children's Age(s) _____ Child's/Children's Sex _____

Observation Context (home, child care center, preschool, school) _____

Date of Observation _____ Time Begun _____ Time Ended _____

Brief Description of Physical and Social Characteristics of Observation Setting:

· ·

Objective Behavioral Descriptions (OBDs) and Interpretations: *Narrative Description*

OBD 1: Child's Sex □ Male □ Female [Time begun _____ Time ended _____]

Interpretation 1:

OBD 2: Child's Sex □ Male □ Female [Time begun _____ Time ended _____]

Interpretation 2:

OBD 3: Child's Sex □ Male □ Female [Time begun _____ Time ended _____]

Interpretation 3:

Continue for as many OBDs as are needed or desired.

Summary Comments on Children's General Language Behavior, Skills, etc.:

Comparisons and Contrasts Between Boys' and Girls' Language Behavior, Skills, etc.:

(continues)

OBSERVATION EXERCISE **18-3** (Continued)

OPTIONAL EXERCISE:

Comparison of Seven- and Eight-Year-Olds' Language Skills with Those of a

Six-Year-Old:

Five-Year-Old:

Three-Year-Old:

Please note that there is nothing wrong with comparing and contrasting seven- and eight-year-old children's language skills with, say, the language skills of nine-year-olds. Our assumption is that you may already have, from previous observation assignments, information on three-, five-, and six-year-olds' language abilities. Moreover, these younger ages fall within the definition of early childhood, and the nine-year-old does not.

OBSERVATION EXERCISE **18-4**

Social and Emotional Development and Behavior (Self-Esteem and Self-Concept)

Observer's Name _____

Child/Children Observed _____

Child's/Children's Age(s) _____ Child's/Children's Sex _____

Observation Context (home, child care center, preschool, school) _____

Date of Observation _____ Time Begun _____ Time Ended _____

Brief Description of Physical and Social Characteristics of Observation Setting:

Objective Behavioral Descriptions (OBDs) and Interpretations: *Narrative Description (with Naturalistic Observation)*

OBD 1: [Time begun _____ Time ended _____]

Interpretation 1:

OBD 2: [Time begun _____ Time ended _____]

Interpretation 2:

OBD 3: [Time begun _____ Time ended _____]

Interpretation 3:

Continue for as many OBDs as are needed or desired.

Summary Comments:

OPTIONAL EXERCISE 1:

Compare the self-concept statements you observed with the statements made by the children in Berk's example cited in the text:

(continues)

OBSERVATION EXERCISE **18-4** (Continued)

Alternate Version: Social and Emotional Development and Behavior-Testing Format (Self-Esteem and Self-Concept)

Observer's Name _____

Child/Children Observed _____

Child's/Children's Age(s) _____ Child's/Children's Sex _____

Observation Context (home, child care center, preschool, school) _____

Date of Observation _____ Time Begun _____ Time Ended _____

Brief Description of Physical and Social Characteristics of Observation Setting:

Objective Behavioral Descriptions (OBDs) and Interpretations: *Conversational Approach*

If direct questioning was used, indicate specifically the question(s) you asked the child. Do this for each OBD or whenever the form of the question changes.

Question Asked:

Response of Child 1:

Interpretive Comment 1:

Question Asked:

Response of Child 2:

Interpretive Comment 2:

Continue for as long as needed or desired.

Summary Remarks Regarding Children's Self-Esteem and Self-Concepts:

OBSERVATION EXERCISE **18-4** (Continued)

OPTIONAL EXERCISE 2:

Compare a teacher's or parent's description of perception of a child's self-concept and self-esteem with the child's behaviors that presumably reflect or confirm those descriptions or perceptions. In other words, does the child behave in ways that match the adult's perceptions of the child's self-concept and self-esteem?

Developmental Checklists

DEVELOPMENTAL CHECKLIST

Child's Name _____ Age _____

Observer _____ Date _____

	Yes	No	Sometimes
By three years, does the child:			
Run well in a forward direction?			
Jump in one place, two feet together?			
Walk on tiptoe?			
Throw ball (but without direction or aim)? Kick ball forward?			
String four large beads?			
Turn pages in book singly?			
Hold crayon: Imitate circular, vertical, horizontal strokes?			
Match shapes?			
Demonstrate number concepts of one and two? (Can select one or two; can tell if one or two objects.)			
Use spoon without spilling?			
Drink from a straw?			
Put on and take off coat?			
Wash and dry hands with some assistance?			
Watch other children; play near them; sometimes join in their play?			
Defend own possessions?			
Use symbols in play—for example, tin pan on head becomes a space ship?			
Respond to "Put ___ in the box," "Take the ___ out of the box"?			
Select correct item on request: big vs. little; one vs. two?			
Identify objects by their use: Show own shoe when asked, "What do you wear on your feet"?			
Ask questions?			
Tell about something with functional phrases that carry meaning: "Daddy go airplane." "Me hungry now"?			

DEVELOPMENTAL CHECKLIST

Child's Name _____ Age _____

Observer _____ Date _____

	Yes	No	Sometimes
By four years, does the child:			
Walk on line?			
Balance on one foot briefly? Hop on one foot?			
Jump over an object 6 inches high and land on both feet together?			
Throw ball with direction?			
Copy circles and crosses?			
Match 6 colors?			
Count to 5?			
Pour well from pitcher? Spread butter, jam with knife?			
Button, unbutton large buttons?			
Know own sex, age, last name?			
Use toilet independently and reliably?			
Wash and dry hands unassisted?			
Listen to stories for at least 5 minutes?			
Draw head of person and at least one other body part?			
Play with other children?			
Share, take turns (with some assistance)?			
Engage in dramatic and pretend play?			
Respond appropriately to "Put it beside," "Put it under"?			
Respond to two step directions: "Give me the sweater and put the shoe on the floor"?			
Respond by selecting the correct object—for example, hard vs. soft object?			
Answer "if," "what," and "when" questions?			
Answer questions about function: "What are books for"?			

DEVELOPMENTAL CHECKLIST

Child's Name _____ Age _____

Observer _____ Date _____

	Yes	No	Sometimes
By five years, does the child:			
Walk backward, heel to toe?			
Walk up and down stairs, alternating feet?			
Cut on line?			
Print some letters?			
Point to and name three shapes?			
Group common related objects: shoe, sock, and foot; apple, orange, and plum?			
Demonstrate number concepts to 4 or 5?			
Cut food with knife: celery, sandwich?			
Lace shoes?			
Read from story picture book—in other words, tell story by looking at pictures?			
Draw a person with three to six body parts?			
Play and interact with other children; engage in dramatic play that is close to reality?			
Build complex structures with blocks or other building materials?			
Respond to simple three step directions: "Give me the pencil, put the book on the table, and hold the comb in your hand"?			
Respond correctly when asked to show penny, nickel, and dime?			
Ask "How" questions?			
Respond verbally to "Hi" and "How are you"?			
Tell about event using past and future tense?			
Use conjunctions to string words and phrases together—for example, "I saw a bear and a zebra and a giraffe at the zoo"?			

DEVELOPMENTAL CHECKLIST

Child's Name _____ Age _____

Observer _____ Date _____

	Yes	No	Sometimes
By six years, does the child:			
Walk across a balance beam?			
Skip with alternating feet?			
Hop for several seconds on one foot?			
Cut out simple shapes?			
Copy own first name?			
Show well-established handedness; demonstrate consistent right- or left-handedness?			
Sort objects on one or more dimensions: color, shape, or function?			
Name most letters and numerals?			
Count by rote to 10; know what number comes next?			
Dress self completely; tie bows?			
Brush teeth unassisted?			
Have some concept of clock time in relation to daily schedule?			
Cross street safely?			
Draw a person with head, trunk, legs, arms and features; often add clothing details?			
Play simple board games?			
Engage in cooperative play with other children, involving group decisions, role assignments, rule observance?			
Use construction toys, such as Legos, blocks, to make recognizable structures?			
Do 15-piece puzzles?			
Use all grammatical structures: pronouns, plurals, verb tenses, conjunctions?			
Use complex sentences; carry on conversations?			

DEVELOPMENTAL CHECKLIST

Child's Name _____ Age _____

Observer _____ Date _____

	Yes	No	Sometimes
By seven or eight years, does the child:			
Participate in competitive activities?			
Show significant improvement from earlier age in agility, balance, control of motor abilities, and so on?			
Produce letters and numbers deliberately and confidently?			
Cut food with knife and fork?			
Name denominations of coins and currency?			
Plan ahead?			
Tell time and know the correct day, month, and year?			
Comprehend cause and effect in developmentally appropriate situations?			
Show some knowledge of addition and subtraction of numbers?			
Recall stories in considerable detail?			
Use adult-like sentences?			
Use gestures to make a point in a conversation?			
Play with two or three close friends of the same age?			
Like to talk with friends on the telephone?			
Want to belong to groups; like to talk in secret code; strongly desire peer acceptance?			

Adapted from Allen and Marotz, 2003, pp. 151–162.

Social-Emotional Checklist

1. Initiation of Activity:

   ___ Almost always involves self in constructive activity of own choice; often rejects suggestions.

   ___ Occasionally needs help in initiating activity; accepts it readily.

   ___ Frequently spends long period before initiating activity; sometimes may reject suggestions.

   ___ Rarely initiates activities, or usually rejects suggestions.

2. Attention Span:

   ___ Can stay with a chosen activity for very long periods, even returning the next day.

   ___ Can remain with an age-appropriate task until it is finished.

   ___ Needs encouragement to stay with task until complete.

   ___ Rarely finishes task. Moves rapidly from one to another.

3. Curiosity:

   ___ Interested in new ideas—words and relationships as well as things.

   ___ Actively explores any new things in the room.

   ___ Can be intrigued by really exciting things, but usually uninterested.

   ___ Shows little or no interest in anything new.

4. Frustration Tolerance:

   ___ Is inventive in solving practical problems. If he is completely blocked, shows mature behavior.

   ___ Usually tries hard and accepts failure well, but if severely frustrated may behave immaturely.

   ___ Sometimes reacts to mild frustrations by giving up, crying, or behaving aggressively.

   ___ Unable to tolerate any level of frustration; gives up, cries, or behaves aggressively.

5. Relationship with Teacher:

   ___ Self-sufficient; may volunteer help or support to teacher.

   ___ Warm relationship, but asks for help or attention when appropriate.

___ Sometimes requires unusual amount of help or physical contact; or seeks attention through silly or wild actions; or is occasionally aggressive toward teacher.

___ Continually seeks help, contact, or attention; or frequently behaves aggressively; or ignores teacher entirely (but clings to avoid some situations).

6. Acceptance of Routines and Limits:

___ Understands and obeys intelligently even when teacher is not present.

___ Usually conforms to limits and routines but can deviate easily when appropriate.

___ Frequently tests limits; or fails to follow routines; or somewhat anxious about changes in routine.

___ Testing of limits and resisting of routines continuous problem; or compulsive about routine—becomes anxious at any deviation from schedule.

7. Reactions to Adults Other Than Teacher:

___ Interested in new adults; will take lead in conversation but not try to monopolize.

___ Does not initiate contact but will accept it and leave room with adult if teacher tells him to do so.

___ Will not respond to initiation; or refuses to leave room until he knows person well; or overly eager for attention from strangers.

___ Cries or hides when stranger approaches; or makes immediate demands for exclusive attention from new adults.

8. Interaction with Other Children:

___ Initiates cooperative play regularly.

___ Occasionally initiates play and usually accepts initiation from others.

___ Often rejects advances of others; or plays more alone than with others.

___ Avoids other children most of the time.

Reprinted, by permission, from Helen Chauvin, Director, Head Start Program, Plattsburgh State University College.

Areas for Notice in Observing an Individual Child

Physical Appearance

What are the child's general physical features?

Does he seem in good physical health?

Body Movements and Use of Body

Does he move quickly or slowly?

Does he seem at ease with his body, or is he stiff or unsure?

Are his small- and large-muscle skills and movements about equally developed or is one area more developed than the other?

Does he express his feeling through his body—slouching shoulders, drooping head, slow movements; or quick, jaunty pace, chest puffed out, marked arm swing?

Facial Expressions

Does she use her face to express feelings?

Does her face register her minute-by-minute reactions to what she is experiencing and what is occurring around her?

Does her face show only intense feelings?

Does she typically show a "deadpan" expression?

Speech

How much of his feelings does he express through his tone of voice?

Does he generally keep his voice under control, or does it express changing moods?

When upset, does he talk more or less than usual?

Is speech an important means of communication to the child, or does he seldom speak, preferring to communicate in other ways?

Does he play with speech by making up chants, songs, puns, stories?

Is his speech fluent, average, inarticulate?

Emotional Reactions

How and when does she exhibit happiness, anger, sadness, doubt, enthusiasm, fear?

Does she seem to have too much control over her feelings, too little control, or a good balance?

Play Activities

What activities does he get involved in?

How does he become involved; how do the activities progress; what does he go to next?

Does he play for a long time at one thing or does he move from one activity to another?

Does he play only briefly in some activities but show prolonged attention in others?

Does she avoid any activities?

What does she seem to derive from an activity—the pleasure of being with other children, sensory stimulation or pleasure, a feeling of mastery or problem solving, a sense of creative expression of ideas and feelings?

Do any aspects of an activity seem to especially frustrate or especially please her?

Does the tempo or pace of his play remain even? Speed up? Slow down? Under what circumstances?

Does he prefer to play alone—never, always, sometimes? Under what circumstances?

Does she express fantasy in her play verbally, through gestures, through play materials?

If she engages in dramatic play, what kind of roles does she like to take—mother, baby, father, dog?

Does he try new things?

Does he show curiosity about his environment, equipment, people?

Does she prefer to confine her play to a relatively small space, or does she expand over a large area?

Does he seem more comfortable playing indoors or outdoors?

Does she have special skills (music, painting, puzzles, dramatic play)?

Basic Needs

Do you notice anything in particular about his habits and feelings about food? Elimination? Sexuality? Sleep? Rest?

Emotional Dependency Behavior: Time Sample Procedure

APPENDIX 4

Observer's Name _____

Observation Setting (home, child care center, etc.) _____

Date _____ Time _____ Activity _____

Brief Description of Setting/Situation:

_____

Recording Intervals	1	2	3	4	5	6

CHILD BEHAVIOR SIGNS

Proximity-Seeking

FT   Follows teacher

FC   Follows child

CT   Cries when teacher leaves area

RS   Resists strangers

CT   Clings to teacher

Positive Attention-Seeking

AT   Seeks approval from teacher for specific acts done, work accomplished

AC   Seeks approval from child, for acts done, work accomplished

GT   Seeks general acknowledgment from teacher—no specific focus of efforts

GC   Seeks general acknowledgment from child—no specific focus of efforts

Negative Attention-Seeking

WA   Whines for attention

CA   Cries for attention

TT   Temper tantrum for attention, or if does not get attention

DG   Disrupts group activities to get attention

Definitions of Behavior Signs and Procedure

Proximity-seeking consists of behaviors that (1) serve to keep the child physically close to the teacher or another child, or (2) indicate anxiety or displeasure at being apart from the teacher or other child. "Clings to teacher" (or child) involves actual physical contact, whereas "follows" indicates being close without actually touching. "Resists strangers" implies stranger anxiety and an accompanying desire on the part of the child to be near a familiar adult or child. Proximity is sought for its own sake and for the emotional security it provides the child.

Positive and negative attention-seeking are more specific in their focus, even though they usually require the child to be at least momentarily close to the adult or another child. "General acknowledgment" refers to attention-seeking that has no specific focus or intent; the child simply wants an adult or another child to know he is there or that he has done something. He does not demand actual approval for his accomplishment, so a mere "I see" from the teacher may be sufficient. Approval-seeking demands a more specific kind of acknowledgment from the teacher or another child—"Yes, John, that's *very good!*" may be the response John wants to hear.

Negative attention-seeking behaviors are behaviors that adults (and sometimes children) usually define as unpleasant or unacceptable. Whining, crying, temper tantrums, and generally disruptive behaviors are usually considered negative. The child who displays such behaviors often does so for their attention-getting value; he will even risk punishment, if that is a form of attention he is willing to accept, or if it seems to him to be the only way he can get attention when he wants or feels he needs it. These behaviors can be viewed as attention-seeking if the child stops the behavior when he receives the attention.

Procedure

Observe for 10 seconds and note whether the child is displaying any of the behaviors listed on the observation sheet. Record the behavior using the coding abbreviations; give yourself 20 seconds to make the recording. Then move on to the next child; stay in column 1 until all the children have been observed once. Repeat this process until you have a total of 6 separate recordings for each child. If you observe 10 children, it will take you 5 minutes to complete the first round of observations.

Always record the most complex behavior displayed by the child. For example, if the child follows the teacher to get her approval of a drawing she has just completed, mark the incident as AT, because the proximity-seeking served only the primary purpose of getting approval of the drawing.

Observation Record (Social Skills)

Date

Frequency of Participation

Activities	9:00	9:15	9:30	9:45	10:00	10:15	10:30	10:45	11:00	11:15	Total
Easel-Markers turtle, printing, playdough											
Housekeeping											
Blocks Large Small											
Manipulative toys dominoes counting bears											
Calendar Weather											
Finger plays "8 pigs" "This little cow"											
Pig puppets art (group)											
Name bingo (group)											
Trikes Sand (group)											
Books Music											
Making snack											
Game: Guess Who's tapping											

Reprinted, with permission, from Susan Benzon.

Comments

Observational Records

Totals:
Observational Record I
Date:

Social Situations

	Name	1	2	3	4	5	6	7	8	9	10	11	12
ART													
MUSIC													
SAND & WATER													
HOUSEKEEPING													
DRAMA PLAY													
BLOCKS													
BOOKS													
PUZZLES													

Reprinted, with permission, from Susan Benzon.

Observational Record II

Date:

Group Activities

Name	Large Groups		%		Large Groups		%

Reprinted, with permission, from Susan Benzon.

Comments:

Note:

Appendices 5 and 6 are used with permission of Susan Benzon, former Director, Humpty Dumpty Preschool, Plattsburgh Air Force Base, Plattsburgh, New York.

Summary of Piaget's First Two Stages of Cognitive Development

Stage 1	Sensorimotor	Child learns to control his body in space. Behaves intelligently, but without use of language; uses his physical senses and his motor capacities to interact with and learn about the environment. Object permanence the capstone achievement of this stage.
Stage 2	Preoperational	Judgments of quantity based on perceptions. Various cognitive operations begin—seriation; classification; concepts of space, time, causality. Egocentric in some thinking and behavior. Language used to express thoughts. Still needs practical, concrete experiences; cannot reason hypothetically. Reasons from particular to particular; cannot reason from the general to the particular.

Havighurst's Development Tasks— Infancy through Middle-Childhood

Havighurst (1953, p. 2) defined *developmental task* as "a task which arises at or about a certain period in the life of an individual, successful achievement of which leads to his happiness and to success with later tasks while failure leads to unhappiness in the individual, disapproval by society, and difficulty with later tasks."

Infancy and Early Childhood (first 5 years)

1. Learning to walk
2. Learning to take solid food
3. Learning to talk
4. Learning to control elimination of body wastes
5. Learning sex differences and sexual modesty
6. Achieving physiological stability
7. Forming simple concepts of social and physical reality
8. Learning to relate oneself emotionally to parents, siblings, and other people
9. Learning to distinguish right and wrong, and developing a conscience

Middle Childhood (from 6 to 12 years)

1. Learning physical skills necessary for ordinary games
2. Building wholesome attitudes toward oneself as a growing organism
3. Learning to get along with agemates
4. Learning an appropriate masculine or feminine social role
5. Developing fundamental skills in reading, writing, and calculating
6. Developing concepts necessary for everyday living
7. Developing a conscience, morality, and a scale of values
8. Achieving personal independence
9. Developing attitudes toward social groups and institutions

A

accommodation—A mental process in which the person changes his cognitive structure or sensorimotor scheme to deal successfully with a new situation; for example, a child accommodates when he comes to understand that not every four-legged animal is a doggie.

action fragment—A sample of behavior that is not representative and therefore supplies no information about the larger behavior stream; the behavior sample is thus only a fragment of the total action that occurred.

actions—Behaviors; actions form a class or set of items that are recorded by checklists, what Brandt (1972) called action checklists.

activity versus passivity in development—Two opposing points of view regarding the extent to which the child participates in his own development. The passive view holds that the child is primarily a *reactor* to the environment and soaks up stimulation like a sponge; the active view sees the child as an *actor* who seeks stimulation rather than passively waits for it to occur.

alert activity (also called active alert, waking activity)—One of the six states or relative levels of infant arousal first identified by Wolff (1966). Alert activity is characterized by such things as irregular breathing and vigorous body movements.

amiables—Children who are "liked by others, but have less status and impact than the stars;" the second group in order of popularity.

anecdotal record—An informal observation method often used by teachers as an aid to understanding the child's personality or behavior. It provides a running account of behavior that is either typical or unusual for the child being observed.

animism—A belief that nonliving objects are actually alive and behave like humans.

artificialism—The belief that everything that exists has been created by human beings or by a god who builds things the way people do according to a plan or blueprint.

assimilation—A mental process in which the person attempts to make a stimulus or piece of information fit into what she already knows.

attachment—A condition process in which one person is dependent on another for emotional satisfaction and support; attachment forms with specific other persons and is enduring over time.

average status children—Children whom some peers like and some dislike. Average status children appear to differ from the controversials in terms of the number of peers who have feelings one way or another toward them.

B

behavior—Anything an individual does that can be directly observed by one or more of the five physical senses.

behavior sampling—This is the general objective and characteristic of all observation; sampling involves taking some portion (sample) of the behaviors out of an individual's behavior stream. Different methods of observing and recording take different sized samples with different amounts and kinds of information.

behavior stream—A metaphor used by Herbert Wright to capture the continuous quality of behavior; behavior is a lifelong continuum, a stream that can never be seen in its entirety.

behavioral schemes—Organized patterns of behavior.

bias—A particular perspective or point of view; biases can be personal or based on a theory or philosophy.

C

category system—A type of coding system in which the categories of behavior chosen for observation are both mutually exclusive and exhaustive; that is, each category excludes all other categories, and the categories include the total range of behaviors that a child can exhibit.

causality—The comprehension of cause-and-effect relationships.

cephalocaudal principle—The principle that describes motor development as progressing in a head-to-foot direction; the child first gains control over the head and neck and proceeds down the body to finally gain control over the legs and feet.

checklist—An information observation method that denotes the presence or absence of something. In studying children, checklists record whether specific behaviors have occurred.

classical conditioning—A form of learning in which a neutral stimulus—one that evokes no response—becomes paired with a stimulus that does. Eventually, the neutral stimulus evokes the response—for example, a puff of air on the eye causes the individual to blink; a soft tone does not. If the tone and the puff of air are both administered very close together in time, eventually the tone by itself will cause the individual to blink.

classification—A process of sorting objects into groups according to perceived similarities—for example, putting all green things into one group and all red things into another group. Objects (and ideas) can be classified according to a number of dimensions at the same time—for example, according to shape, size, and color.

closed method—A characteristic of any method that does not preserve descriptions of behavior and events as they originally occurred.

coding scheme—A means of reducing complex, detailed descriptions of behavior to a simple mark or tally on an observation sheet; coding schemes often record categories of behavior, such as aggression, dependency, or quarrels.

cognitive schemes—Mental representations or concepts of the environment.

cognitive structure—Piaget's concept referring to one's mental organization of ideas and facts; an individual's cognitive structure determines his intellectual behavior and abilities at any given stage of development.

collective monologue—A form of egocentric speech in which two or more persons are talking together but none of them is paying attention to what the others are saying; each conversation is independent of the other conversations.

complexity—Directional development that results in more sophisticated and refined behavior, emotion, ability, and language.

concept—A mental representation or memory of something. Concepts bring together attributes that are common to several different events—for example, the concept "dog" represents the attributes of fur-bearing, four-legged, mammal, and domesticated carnivore that characterize collies, terriers, German shepherds, and all other breeds of dog.

concrete operational thinking—The kind of intellectual ability possible for the child in Piaget's stage of concrete operations. Concrete operational thinking allows the child to adapt to various aspects of his environment through the use of systematic logic. Such thinking is characterized by the ability to (1) reverse mental actions, (2) move away from the appearance of things to their reality, (3) attend to several aspects of a situation at a time rather than just one, and (4) see others' points of view—that is, there is a decline in egocentrism.

confidentiality—A condition of research and observation in which the observer or researcher does not reveal information about any individual to anyone.

conservation—A general principle that the physical appearance of a substance does not necessarily affect its quantity. The principle applies to such things as substance, volume, number, area, and length—for example, the principle of conservation of number dictates that the physical arrangement of a group of coins has no effect on their number.

conservation of number—One of several conservation tasks or abilities, conservation of number refers to the fact that two numerically equal quantities of something remain equal even when one of them is changed in some way, provided that nothing has been added or taken away. Changes that do not affect the quantity of something are called irrelevant transformations.

constructivist theory—A theory of human development that is organismic in its basic orientation. Constructionist theory assumes that the developing child participates in the developmental process and literally constructs his or her own reality. This reality undergoes a series of reconstructions that bring it more and more into line with the reality assumed by most adults in a given culture or society. This theory most appropriately falls within the broader organismic view. (See **organismic view**.)

context—A term that combines setting and situation to include all aspects of an environment—time, space, circumstances, other people, and physical and psychological conditions.

contextualism—A concept most notably associated with the Russian psychologist Lev Vygotsky, who argued that a child's development cannot be studied, understood, or take place outside of some cultural context or other. In other words, all development change—as well as, for that matter, all current behavior—has to be seen as part of, or as taking place within, a larger social/cultural environment.

control—Related to structure, control also refers to observing young children's behavior in a patterned, systematic way. The observer controls the observation by knowing her purpose and being able, for the most part, to accomplish her objectives.

controversial children—Children who seem to strike a balance between being liked and disliked. Many of their peers like them, and many also dislike them.

cumulative change—A characteristic of development in which behaviors build on one another and contribute to the overall character and direction of the developmental process.

D

degree of observer inference required—A characteristic of observation and recording methods involving the amount of inference that is required in using a particular method; inference is also discussed in terms of when in the observation process it is needed. Narrative descriptions (specimen records) require no inferences at the time of initial recording; time sampling using a coding scheme does require inferences at the time of recording.

degree of selectivity—A characteristic of observation and recording methods that determines how many behaviors are targeted for observing and recording. Methods vary from completely unselective (specimen record) to highly selective (such as the event sample).

describe—To tell or write about; to give a word picture of some object, event, or idea.

development—Change over time in the structure, thoughts, and behaviors of an individual due to biological and environmental influences.

diary description—An informal observation method in which records are made daily of selected aspects of a child's growth and development. The topical diary restricts itself to new behaviors exhibited by the child in a particular developmental area, such as language, social behavior, and emotional behavior; the comprehensive diary records in order as much of everything new as it can.

differentiation—A process in which behaviors that are initially expressed in a diffuse, nonspecific way eventually separate out and become more skilled, specific, and independent of one another. Also refers to learning a new skill and, during that process, having to practice only that skill, isolating it from other skills already mastered.

directional—Development that moves toward a greater complexity or ideal goal.

duration record—A variation of the frequency count in which the observer times how long a particular behavior lasts.

E

ego—That part of the personality in Sigmund Freud's theory that has the function of keeping the child in touch with reality and with the demands made on the child by the family and other individuals and groups in his larger social community. The ego is also that part of the personality that gives the individual a sense of identity.

egocentric speech—Speech that does not take the other person into account and that, for all practical purposes, is private.

egocentrism—The cognitive inability to take other people's points of view and to recognize their needs and interests; a preoccupation with one's own view of the world.

elaboration—In information processing theory, elaboration is a memory device that forms absurd associations or connections among items to be remembered. It is the absurdity of the associations that makes remembering the items easier.

emergent properties—A term used in connection with qualitative change, emergent properties are traits or characteristics that are not present at an earlier stage of development but emerge as the individual moves from one developmental stage to another. Walking, for example, can be thought of as a behavior that emerges out of the earlier behaviors of crawling and creeping.

emotional dependency—A need to be near others and to have their support, affection, and reassurance; it can also involve the unwillingness or self-perceived inability to do things for oneself that one can or should be able to do.

empirical—Having to do with things that can be seen, heard, touched, smelled, and tasted; data obtained by direct observation and not through abstract thought processes or theory; tied to the "real" world.

empirical data—Data that are connected to the real world by having been observed through one or more of the five physical senses.

environmentalism—A point of view that stresses the role of the environment in determining behavior and development, in contrast with the role of heredity.

errors of commission—Errors in which you include more information than is actually present in the situation; reporting behaviors and interactions that did not occur or persons as present who were not.

errors of omission—Errors in which you leave out information that is helpful or necessary for understanding the child's behavior.

errors of transmission—Errors in which you record observed behaviors in the wrong order.

evaluation—The application of your own values and attitudes to the child's behavior, characteristics, and personality; generally, placing a value on or judging the worth of something.

event—Behaviors that can be placed into particular categories—for example, hitting to get a toy away from another child is a behavior that can be put into the category "instrumental aggression."

event sampling—A formal method that observes and records specific kinds of behaviors (events) whenever they occur. It is a sampling technique because it takes out of the behavior stream only preselected behaviors or categories of behaviors.

explain—To give the meaning or interpretation of; to make clear or plain; to show the relationship among facts or ideas.

F

filter—A term used metaphorically to illustrate the idea that things and events pass through our personalities, through our individual experiences, values, attitudes, and knowledge; these act as filters that allow certain information to get through to us, while excluding or screening out certain other information.

five-to-seven shift—The period of gradual transition from the illogical and unsystematic thinking of the preschooler to the more logical thinking of the school-age child.

formal observation method—A method of observing and recording behavior that is highly structured and controlled; it typically involves a great deal of prior preparation, including the construction of elaborate data forms and training of observers. Formal methods are often used in research studies.

formal operational thinking—The name Piaget gave to his fourth and final stage of cognitive development. An individual who is in the formal operational stage is able to think abstractly, deal with hypothetical situations, and understand the concept of conservation of number, area, volume, length, and so on.

frequency count—An informal observation method in which the observer simply makes a mark or tally on an observation sheet every time a particular behavior occurs.

G

group—A collection of individuals who are organized around a common purpose. Some groups are organized by an outside agency or authority—a school system or church, for example—and these are called institutional groups. Other groups form spontaneously on the basis of mutual interests and common characteristics; these are called peer groups.

group observation—Observations in which (1) the individual is observed in the context of a group, and changes in her behavior as she participates in different groups are documented, or (2) the group itself is considered a single entity or unit, and its behavior is observed and recorded.

growth—Increase in size, function, or complexity to some point of optimal maturity; associated with quantitative change.

H

habituation—After being exposed to a physical stimulus that originally evokes a response, the individual ceases paying attention to it; getting used to stimulus and losing interest in it.

hierarchic integration—A process in which skills and behaviors that are initially separate and independent of one another are combined and can work together as a harmonious unit (for example, the skill of grasping an object and the skill of moving the hand toward an object are combined to form the integrated skill of reaching and grasping).

hostile aggression—Aggression in which the aggressor feels anger or hostility toward the victim and derives satisfaction from hurting the victim.

I

id—That part of the personality in Sigmund Freud's theory that functions from the moment of birth. The id operates according to what Freud called the pleasure principle. In essence, the id is concerned with meeting the child's needs and desires, but perhaps most frequently the id can be thought of as contributing to the child's self-centeredness. The id's guiding theme is "I want what I want when I want it."

inconspicuous observation—Observation that imposes or introduces nothing into the observation setting and situation (context) beyond what is required to achieve legitimate objectives.

inference—A conclusion based on directly observable data, premises, or evidence, but that is not itself directly observable. The conclusion is reached through a mental process.

informal observation method—A method of observing and recording behavior that lacks the strict research format of formal methods; it is less structured than a formal method and is suitable for immediate use by teachers and others who can use the method for day-to-day program operation and interactions with children.

information processing theory—A model of cognitive functioning that assumes that (1) the mind is similar to a computer in that it stores and processes information;

(2) processed information is also transformed by the individual, for example, from a visual to a verbal or conceptual form; and (3) the individual's ability to process information is limited. (*See*, e.g., Zigler and Stevenson, 1993.)

instrumental aggression—Aggression in which the aggressor is interested only in getting an object from the victim or in achieving some goal, and he uses aggression to do so; it need not involve anger or hostility.

instrumental dependency—The necessary reliance we all have on others for certain things that are beyond our own capacities to do.

integration—Combining a newly learned skill with existing skills to form an integrated whole. The skills can be not only physical motor skills but also verbal or cognitive skills.

inter-observer reliability—The degree to which two or more observers agree with one another as to what occurred during an observation session. High inter-observer reliability indicates minimal disagreement and relatively few differences in observers' judgments and inferences.

interpretation—Going beyond objective descriptions and trying to explain or give them meaning; relating something that is directly observable to something that is not directly observable but that is perhaps based on a theory or hypothesis.

intra-observer reliability—Repeated use of a checklist by the same individual will yield the same results if the checklist categories have been carefully defined and the observer knows the definitions of behavior and recognizes the behavior as such.

intuitive—A substage of Piaget's preoperational stage of cognitive development. Intuitive thinking is the type of reasoning that takes place during the five-to-seven shift. (*See* **five-to-seven shift.**)

invisible displacement—Taking an object from one place of concealment (such as under a piece of cloth) and moving it to another, but not allowing the child to watch you make the change; this is a technique used to test a child's concept of object permanence.

isolates—Children who "are neither liked nor disliked; these children are often simply ignored."

L

learning history—An individual's life experiences, which form a unique set of learned associations or stimulus-response bonds; these constitute that person's distinctive history and make her different from everyone else.

lexically based ambiguity—Ambiguity based on the different meanings of words—for example, *pen* can refer to a writing tool or to an enclosure in which animals are kept.

linguistic—Vocalizations that include actual words.

M

maturation—Developmental changes over time that are the result of heredity; changes built into the individual that unfold naturally and sequentially with time.

mechanistic view—A theoretical or philosophical perspective that conceptualizes human beings and other living creatures as being like machines in that they are essentially passive and act primarily as responders to environmental stimuli. (*See* **organismic view.**)

metacognition—Thinking about thinking; being aware of one's cognitive abilities and exercising some control over them.

metacommunication—Similar to metacognition, metacommunication is communicating about communication. It is the ability, for instance, to talk about what makes a particular communication style effective or ineffective, or to consider how best to communicate a message to someone so that its meaning will not be lost or distorted.

metalinguistic awareness—The ability to attend to and understand the form that language takes, the structure by which meaning is conveyed. The meaning itself is of secondary importance.

method—A set of instructions that specifies what one must do to accomplish some task; it may also describe how to do what needs to be done.

middle childhood—That period of the life span that comprises the period from 6 through 12 years of age. It is also frequently called the school-age years.

monologue—A form of egocentric speech in which the individual talks only to herself, with no one else present.

N

narrative description—A formal method of observation and recording in which you continuously record in as much detail as possible what the child does and says, by herself and in interaction with other persons or objects. (*See* **specimen record.**)

natural unit—A sequence of behaviors that forms a logical whole or segment within the overall behavior stream; the unit has a distinct beginning, behaviors in the middle that constitute a specific event, and a distinct ending. Event sampling structures the observation environment into natural units (Wright, 1960).

neglected children—Children who are essentially neutral on the scale of liked versus disliked. Their peers neither actively like or dislike them. It might be said that such children's peers are indifferent to them.

O

object permanence—The understanding that objects continue to exist even when out of sight or hearing; this is the most important achievement of the sensorimotor period.

objective description—Description of behavior and events that does not contain interpretations, subjective impressions, or speculations, but describes only what you see and hear in such a way that another observer would agree with your report.

observation—Noting and recording facts and events; looking for something in a controlled, structured way.

observation plan—A plan that guides all phases of the observation process. The plan determines what behaviors will be observed, how much of the behavior stream will be sampled, and which observation method will be used to achieve the other steps in the plan.

observe—The ability to take in information through one or more of the five physical senses and to make sense of that information so that it can be used in meaningful ways.

one-to-one correspondence—A matching of two groups of objects in which one object of one group is paired with one and only one object of the other group—for example, a child who has this ability can give each child at the snack table one cookie and one napkin.

open method—A characteristic of any method that preserves descriptions of behavior and events as they originally occurred.

operant conditioning—A form of learning in which the consequences of a response determine whether that response is likely to be repeated under the same or similar circumstances—for example, if a child's whining gets her the attention from the teacher that she desires, the child is likely to whine in future situations when she wants attention.

operational definition—Defining something according to behavioral criteria. A psychologist, for example, might define as aggressive any behavior that involves one child hitting another child. An operational definition of aggressive behavior, in this example, requires that certain predetermined behaviors or actions have to occur in order for a behavior to be defined as aggressive.

organismic view—A theoretical or philosophical perspective that conceptualizes human beings as active participants in their own development rather than as passive reactors to the world around them. (*See* **mechanistic view.**)

organization—A strategy for remembering things by placing them into larger categories—for example, putting all things that can be eaten into the category "food," or all things that one wears into the category "clothing." Remembering the broad category supposedly helps one to remember the specific items in that category.

orienting response—A response in which the individual turns toward the source of a sound or other stimulus.

P

participant observation—When an observer becomes part of the group she is observing and participates in as many of its activities as is appropriate, with the objective of reducing the effects of observation on the group's behavior.

peer—A companion who is approximately the same age and developmental level.

peer reputation—The relatively stable and consistent way that a child's peers perceive and describe or characterize him.

perception—Taking in information through one or more of the five physical senses and organizing it in a meaningful way.

phonologically based ambiguity—Ambiguity in language based on how words sound or are pronounced.

playscapes—A relatively recent term to describe contemporary playground structures that are innovative by combining "a variety of material" (Essa, 1996).

popular children—Children whom most peers like and no one dislikes.

pragmatics—Pragmatics has to do with the practical, communicative side of language. Here, the individual has to deal with the practical tasks associated with making herself understood by others. One such task is to take into account the particular needs or situation of the listener.

prelinguistic—Vocalizations that occur prior to actual speech (cooing and babbling, for example).

preoperational period—The second stage in Piaget's theory of cognitive development. It is defined primarily by the child's ability to use language and otherwise engage in symbol manipulation (what Piaget called the "symbolic function"). Unlike the later stages, however, the preoperational child is not able to engage in true operational thinking.

process (noun)—A series of related activities that require time to accomplish.

process (verb)—To think about, give a verbal label to, or to put a fact into some meaningful relationship with other facts.

production deficiency—A term used to describe the case in which a child knows how to use a particular strategy but does not spontaneously do so in situations where it would help him solve a problem.

professional ethics—Standards of conduct that serve to protect the privacy, confidentiality, rights, and safety of anyone who is the subject of observation or research.

proximodistal principle—The principle that describes motor development as progressing from the midline of the body outward to the extremities; thus, chest, shoulders, and upper arms come under control before the hands and feet.

psychosocial crisis—A concept in Erikson's theory of personality development; a crisis is a conflict, a turning point, or time of special sensitivity to particular social influences.

Q

qualitative change—Change in psychological functions such as speech, emotions, and intelligence; involves change in the fundamental organization of behaviors and behavior patterns; change in the child's cognitive structure.

quantitative change—Growth; changes in the amount, number, or quantity of something (for example, increases in height and weight).

R

raw data—Descriptions of behavior and events as they originally occurred.

raw stimuli—Stimuli—such as perceptions, data acquired through observation, and the like—that have not been interpreted or processed in any way, thus the term "raw." When using the narrative description method of recording behavior, for example, one is gathering raw data or stimuli that must subsequently be interpreted and given some meaning if the observation is to have any significance.

reflex—A built-in, preprogrammed pattern of involuntary motor behavior that is elicited by a specific form of stimulation—for example, the startle reflex is elicited by a sudden loud noise.

rehearsal—A strategy that involves going over information again and again in order to remember it at a later time. In information processing theory, rehearsal aids the storage and retrieval processes.

reinforcement—A condition in which an individual's response to a stimulus has rewarding or satisfying consequences; those consequences provide reinforcement of the response, thus increasing the probability that, in the future, the individual will respond in similar fashion to a similar stimulus.

rejected children—Children whom most peers dislike and very few like.

rejects—Children at the bottom of the popularity scale, who "are actively disliked by others and have a negative impact on their peer group."

repetition—A form of egocentric speech in which the individual repeats words and phrases over and over again as if to practice them or as if he simply enjoyed making the sounds.

representativeness—A desirable feature of behavior samples; representative samples are those that exemplify or reflect the typical characteristics of the larger population or class of behaviors of which the sample is a part.

role—Recurring behaviors and behavior patterns that are associated with specific statuses; teachers' role behaviors include teaching, grading, and counseling students, for example; parents' role behaviors include nurturing, protecting, and socializing the child.

rough-and-tumble play—Play that involves a lot of strenuous physical activity such as wrestling, running, and pushing. However, it is good-natured, prosocial activity that is very different from aggressive fighting. In this kind of play, there is no intent to hurt the other, and it is frequently engaged in by children who like each other.

S

scaffolding—Related to the zone of proximal development, scaffolding is the process whereby an adult gives the child the necessary assistance to allow the child to function on her own. (*See*, e.g., Krantz, 1994.)

schema—Piaget's term for a concept or mental representation of events in the world.

self-concept—The more or less objective assessment of who we are, our strengths and weaknesses, our personality characteristics. Self-concept refers to the manner in which an individual describes himself—for example, the qualities or attributes that the child assigns to himself.

self-esteem—Self-esteem refers to one's sense of personal worth or value. It is distinguished from self-concept, although it is related to it.

sensorimotor period—The first stage in Piaget's theory of cognitive development. In this stage, the infant learns about his environment by active manipulation of the objects in it; learning and intellectual development are accomplished by use of the physical senses and motor abilities.

sensorimotor schemes—Organized actions or sequences of actions that permit the individual to interact with the environment.

sequential change—Change that occurs in a lawful, orderly fashion and according to a predetermined series of steps or stages; stage theories hold that change is sequential.

seriation—A process of arranging objects in some order according to a particular dimension; seriation requires the ability to compare and coordinate differences between objects—for example, arranging a collection of rocks in order of increasing weight, from the lightest to the heaviest.

setting—The physical environment in which an observation takes place; it includes such factors as physical space, objects in that space, and opportunities and resources that permit people to behave in certain ways.

sign system—A type of coding system in which the categories of behavior chosen for observation are mutually exclusive; that is, no given behavior can be put into more than one category because each category excludes all others.

situation—The social and psychological characteristics and conditions that exist in a particular setting—the nature of the children's play, events that occur that may change the character of the ongoing activities, and so on.

social—An interaction or situation in which each participant takes the others into account, or in which each participant influences and is influenced by the others.

social autonomy—The ability to rely on oneself for the satisfaction of various needs and desires; self-sufficiency.

social behavior—Behavior between two or more persons who take one another into account and influence one another in some way.

social cognition—An ability to think about and understand social and interpersonal events of which one is a part. Social cognition includes such things as social role-taking ability (which see), empathy, identification, and vicarious experiencing, among others.

social comparison—Describing, rating, and ranking peers on various characteristics and traits. Most simply put, social comparison involves comparing one's peers (or others) on various aspects of social and personal functioning and attributes.

social role-taking ability—The ability to understand another person's position or situation and what she might be feeling or thinking. It involves such things as understanding emotions, intentions, and thinking. (*See*, e.g., Schickedanz et al., 1993.)

sociocentric (or **socialized**) **speech**—Public speech; speech that is intended to communicate with someone; each person takes into account what the other says, and each responds accordingly.

sociocentrism—The opposite of egocentrism; the ability to take others' points of view and to recognize their needs and interests.

sociocultural theory (also **sociohistoric theory**)—The name given to Vygotsky's theory of mental development in which the emphasis is shifted away from the child in explaining development and to the influence of the individual's social or cultural environment.

sociogram—A graphic representation of how children in a group feel about one another. Children are often represented by circles, and their interactions with peers are represented by arrows that connect one circle (child) to another.

sociometry—A technique for studying children's popularity or social status among their peers. The technique can involve asking children to name their best friend or friends, or to identify the child or children who are most liked by the class or group.

soothability—The ability of a crying or upset infant to be quieted by such adult responses as rocking, holding, swaddling, or giving a pacifier.

spatial definition—The concept that physical spaces or environments have particular meanings associated with them, and these meanings or definitions determine what one may do when in that space or environment.

specimen record—A formal method of observation and recording in which you continuously record in as much detail as possible what the child does and says, by herself and in interaction with other persons or objects. (*See* **narrative description.**)

spontaneous behaviors—Behaviors that are internally generated and not responses to outside stimuli; they include behaviors such as random startles, fleeting smiles, and erections.

stage theory—A theory that holds that development occurs in a step-like fashion, with each step or level qualitatively distinct from, and more complex than, previous levels.

stars—A classification that can be determined from a sociogram and that identifies or describes a child or children who are well liked and popular among their peers. Such children also have considerable status and influence in the peer group.

states—Levels of arousal such as asleep, alert, drowsy, and crying; they are behavioral conditions that (1) are stable over a period of time, (2) occur repeatedly in an individual infant, and (3) are encountered in similar form in other individuals.

static descriptor—A descriptive item that pertains to a highly stable characteristic of research subjects or settings (Brandt, 1972); age, sex, race, and socioeconomic are examples of static descriptors. These descriptors are often recorded by a checklist.

status—A position within a social group or organization; teacher, student, child, adult, president, and parent are examples of statuses.

stimulus-response bond—A connection or association between an environmental stimulus and an individual's response to that stimulus; the connection is established because the consequences of the response are rewarding or reinforcing to the individual.

strategies—Mental operations that are used to enhance memory, attention, and problem solving.

structure—In the context of observation, structure refers to observing and recording behavior in a systematic, patterned way such that the observer knows why he or she is in the observation setting and by what method the behaviors of interest will be recorded.

superego—That part of the personality in Sigmund Freud's theory that develops out of the id and the ego and essentially acts as the individual's conscience. (*See* **id** and **ego**.)

syntactically based ambiguity—Ambiguity based on different interpretations of a sentence. This ambiguity depends on the structure of the sentence itself and how that structure allows different meanings to be put on the sentence.

T

temperament—A child's characteristic ways of responding to various situations; temperament is described by the child's responses on six personality dimensions: activity level, rhythmicity, approach/withdrawal, adaptability, intensity of reaction, and quality of mood.

theory—A formal set of general statements or propositions that are supported by data and that attempt to explain a particular phenomenon.

time sampling—A formal method of observation and recording in which you record selected behaviors during preset uniform time periods and at regularly recurring or randomly selected intervals.

trait—A tendency or predisposition to behave in certain ways under certain circumstances.

trust versus mistrust—The first crisis in Erikson's theory; the infant's experiences with his environment and the people in it will determine whether he resolves the crisis or conflict by establishing a stronger sense of trust than of mistrust. A sense of trust will enable the infant to see his world as a predominantly safe, nurturing, and trustworthy place.

V

validity—Pertaining to the accuracy and soundness of an observation or interpretation; the degree to which something measures what it claims to.

vicarious punishment—Similar to vicarious reinforcement, vicarious punishment is punishment a child experiences indirectly when he or she observes another child being punished and reacts as though he or she had been punished. (*See* **vicarious reinforcement**.)

vicarious reinforcement—Reinforcement that an individual experiences indirectly through observing someone else being reinforced or rewarded for his behavior. The concept of vicarious reinforcement is usually associated with social learning theory. (*See* **vicarious punishment**.)

visible displacement—Taking an object from one place of concealment (such as under a cloth) and moving it to another, allowing the child to watch you make the change. This is a technique used to test a child's concept of object permanence.

Z

zone of proximal development—A concept found in Vygotsky's theory, the zone of proximal development (ZPD) refers to "space" or distance between what a child can do for herself and what she can do only with someone else's help. The purpose of the zone of proximal development in early child care and early childhood education essentially is to guide the caregivers and teachers—as well as parents—in their efforts to promote a child's cognitive development.

Ahola, D., & Kovacik, A. (2007). *Observing and understanding child development: A child study manual.* Clifton Park: Thomson Delmar Learning.

Ainsworth, M. (1967). *Infancy in Uganda: Infant care and the growth of love.* Baltimore: Johns Hopkins University Press.

Ainsworth, M. O. (1973). The development of mother–infant attachment. In B. Caldweel & H. Ricciuti (Eds.), *Review of child development research* (Vol. 3). Chicago: University of Chicago Press.

Allen, K. E., & Marotz, L. (2003). *Developmental profiles: Prebirth through eight* (4th ed.). Clifton Park: Thomson Delmar Learning.

Allen, K. E., & Marotz, L. (2007). *Developmental profiles: Prebirth through twelve* (5th ed.). Clifton Park: Thomson Delmar Learning.

Almy, M., & Genishi, C. (1979). *Ways of studying children* (rev. ed.). New York: Teachers College Press.

Ault, R. (1977). *Children's cognitive development.* New York: Oxford University Press.

Barker, R. G., & Wright, H. F. (1951). *One boy's day.* New York: Harper and Row.

Beaty, J. J. (2002). *Observing development of the young child* (5th ed.). Columbus: Merrill. (4th ed. 1998).

Bee, H. (1995). *The growing child.* New York: HarperCollins. (2nd ed., 1999).

Berger, K. S. (1980). *The developing person.* New York: Worth. (4th ed., 1998).

Berger, K. S. (1991). *The developing person: Through childhood and adolescence* (3rd ed.). New York: Worth. (5th ed., 1999).

Berk, L. E. (1989). *Child development.* Needham Heights: Allyn and Bacon. (5th ed., 2000).

Berk, L. E. (1993). *Infants, children, and adolescents.* Boston: Allyn and Bacon. (3rd ed., 1999).

Berk, L. E. (1996). *Infants, children, and adolescents* (2nd ed.). Boston: Allyn and Bacon. (3rd ed., 1999).

Berk, L. E. (1998). *Development through the lifespan.* Boston: Allyn and Bacon.

Berk, L. E. (2005). *Infants, children, and adolescents* (5th ed.). Boston: Pearson Allyn and Bacon.

Berk, L. E. (2006). *Child development* (7th ed.). Boston: Pearson Allyn and Bacon.

Berk, L. E. (2007). *Development through the lifespan* (4th ed.). Boston: Pearson Allyn and Bacon.

Berk, L. E., & Winsler, A. (1995). *Scaffolding children's learning: Vygotsky and early childhood education.*

Washington, DC: National Association for the Education of Young Children.

Berndt, T. J. (1997). *Child development* (2nd ed.). Chicago: Brown and Benchmark.

Berns, R. M. (1994). *Topical child development.* Clifton Park: Thomson Delmar Learning.

Bigner, J. J. (1983). *Human development: A life-span approach.* New York: Macmillan.

Bjorklind, D. F. (1987). How age changes in knowledge base contribute to the development of children's memory: An interpretive review. *Developmental Review, 7,* 93–130.

Bower, T. G. R. (1977). *A primer of infant development.* San Francisco: W. H. Freeman.

Bowlby, J. (1969). *Attachment and loss: Volume 1. Attachment.* New York: Basic.

Brainerd, C. J. (1978). *Piaget's theory of intelligence.* Englewood Cliffs: Prentice-Hall.

Brandt, R. M. (1972). *Studying behavior in natural settings.* New York: Holt, Rinehart and Winston.

Bredekamp, S., & Copple, C. (Eds.). (1997). *Developmentally appropriate practice in early childhood programs* (rev. ed.). Washington, DC: National Association for the Education of Young Children.

Brewer, J. A. (1998). *Introduction to early childhood education* (3rd ed.). Boston: Allyn and Bacon.

Brewer, J. A. (2007). *Introduction to early childhood education: Preschool through primary grades* (6th ed.). Boston: Pearson Allyn and Bacon.

Bruner, J. (1975). From communication to language. *Cognition, 3,* 255–287.

Bukatko, D., & Daehler, M. W. (1995). *Child development: A thematic approach.* Boston: Houghton Mifflin.

Bukowski, W. M., & Hosa, B. (1989). Popularity and friendship: Issues in theory, measurement, and outcome. In T. J. Berndt & G. W. Ladd (Eds.), *Peer relationships in child development.* New York: Wiley.

Carpenter, G. (1974). Mother's face and the newborn. *New Scientist, 61,* 742–744.

Charlesworth, R. (2008). *Understanding child development* (7th ed.). Clifton Park: Thomson Delmar Learning.

Chomsky, C. S. (1969). *The acquisition of syntax in children from five to ten.* Cambridge: MIT Press.

Coie, J. D., Dodge, K. A., & Coppotelli, H. (1982). Dimensions and types of social status: A cross-age perspective. *Developmental Psychology, 18,* 557–570.

Coombs, C. H. (1964). *A theory of data.* New York: Wiley.

Craig, G. J. (1989). *Human development* (5th ed.). Englewood Cliffs: Prentice-Hall. (8th ed., 1999).

Craig, G. J., & Kermis, M. D. (1995). *Children today.* Englewood Cliffs: Prentice-Hall.

De Mause, L. (1974). The evolution of children. In De Mause, L. (Ed.), *The history of childhood.* New York: Pyschohistory Press.

Diaz, R. M., & Berndt, T. J. (1982). Children's knowledge of a friend: Fact or fancy? *Developmental Psychology, 18,* 787–794.

Dreikers, R. (1964). *Children: The challenge.* New York: Hawthorne.

Dworetzky, J. P. (1987). *Introduction to child development* (3rd ed.). New York: West. (6th ed., 1996).

Elkind, D. (1981). *The hurried child: Growing up too fast too soon.* Reading: Addison-Wesley. (revised 1989).

Erwin, P. G. (1985). Similarity of attitudes and constructs in children's friendships. *Journal of Experimental Child Psychology, 40,* 470–485.

Essa, E. (2007). *Introduction to early childhood education* (5th ed.). Clifton Park: Thomson Delmar Learning.

Fantz, R. L. (1963). Pattern vision in newborn infants. *Science, 140,* 296–297.

Faw, T., & Belkin, G. S. (1989). *Child psychology.* New York: McGraw-Hill.

Federico, R. C. (1979). *Sociology* (2nd ed.). Reading: Addison-Wesley.

Field, T. M., Greenwald, P., Morrow, C., Healy, B., Foster, T., Guthertz, M., & Frost, P. (1992). Behavior state matching during interactions of preadolescent friends versus acquaintances. *Developmental Psychology, 28,* 242–250.

Fogel, A. (1984). *Infancy: Infant, family, and society.* New York: West. (3rd ed., 1997).

Gander, M. J., & Gardner, H. W. (1981). *Child and adolescent development.* Boston: Little, Brown.

Gardner, D. B. (1973). *Development in early childhood* (2nd ed.). New York: Harper and Row.

Gaver, D., & Richards, H. C. (1979, Jan./Feb.). Dimensions of naturalistic observation for the prediction of academic success. *Journal of Educational Research.*

Gelman, R. (1969). Conservation acquisition: A problem of learning to attend to relevant attributes. *Journal of Experimental Child Psychology, 7,* 167–187.

Gelman, R. (1972). Logical capacity of very young children: Number invariance rules. *Child Development, 43,* 75–90.

Gibson, J. J. (1966). *The senses considered as perceptual systems.* Boston: Houghton Mifflin.

Gonzalez-Mena, J. (1997). *Multicultural issues in child care* (2nd ed.). Mountain View: Mayfield.

Gonzalez-Mena, J. (1998). *Foundations: Early childhood education in a diverse society.* Mountain View: Mayfield.

Gonzalez-Mena, J. (2005). *Foundations of early childhood education: Teaching children in a diverse society* (3rd ed.). Boston: McGraw-Hill.

Goodwin, W. R., & Driscoll, L. A. (1980). *Handbook for measurement and evaluation in early childhood education.* San Francisco: Jossey-Bass.

Graves, S. B., Gardiulo, R. M., & Sluder, L. C. (1996). *Young children: An introduction to early childhood education.* New York: West.

Greenspan, S., & Greenspan, N. T. (1985). *First feelings: Milestones in the emotional development of your baby and child.* New York: Viking Penguin.

Hansen, N. R. (1958). *Patterns of discovery.* Cambridge: Cambridge at the University Press.

Harris, A. C. (1993). *Child development* (2nd ed.). New York: West.

Havighurst, R. J. (1953). *Human development and education.* New York: Longmans, Green.

Herron, R. E., & Sutton-Smith, B. (1971). *Child's play.* New York: Wiley.

Hunt, J. McV. (1961). *Intelligence and experience.* New York: Ronald.

Hutt, S. J., Lenard, H. G., & Prechtl, H. E. R. (1969). Psychophysiology of the newborn. *Advances in child development and behavior.* New York: Academic Press.

Ihde, D. (1977). *Experimental phenomenology: An introduction.* New York: Paragon.

Irwin, D. M., & Bushnell, M. M. (1980). *Observational strategies for child study.* New York: Holt, Rinehart and Winston.

Izard, C. E. (1977). *Human emotions.* New York: Plenum.

Jalongo, M. R., & Isenberg, J. P. (2000). *Exploring your role: A practitioner's introduction to early childhood education.* Columbus: Merrill.

Kagan, J. (1971). *Personality development.* New York: Harcourt Brace Jovanovich.

Kagan, J. (1984). *The nature of the child.* New York: Basic.

Kamii, C., & DeVries, R. (1980). *Group games in early education.* Washington, DC: National Association for the Education of Young Children.

Kamii, C., & DeVries, R. (1977). Piaget for early education. In M. S. Day & R. K. Parker (Eds.), *The preschool in action: Exploring early childhood programs* (2nd ed.). Boston: Allyn and Bacon.

Krantz, M. (1994). *Child development: Risk and opportunity.* Belmont: Wadsworth.

Krogh, S. L. (1994). *Educating young children: Infancy to grade three.* New York: McGraw-Hill.

Lay-Dopyera, M., & Dopyera, J. E. (1982). *Becoming a teacher of young children* (2nd ed.). Lexington: Heath. (5th ed., 1993).

Lefrancois, G. R. (2001). *Of children: An introduction to child and adolescent development.* Belmont: Wadsworth.

Lerner, R. (1976). *Concepts and theories of human development.* Reading: Addison-Wesley. (2nd ed., 1997).

Lively, W. J., & Bromley, D. B. (1973). *Person perception in childhood and adolescence.* London: Wiley.

Martin, P. Y., & O'Connor, G. G. (1989). *The social environment: Open systems application.* New York: Longman.

Miller, P. H. (1993). *Theories of developmental psychology* (3rd ed.). New York: W. H. Freeman.

Montemayor, R., & Eisen, M. (1977). The development of self-conceptions from childhood to adolescence. *Developmental Psychology, 13*, 314–319.

Morrison, G. S. (1995). *Early childhood education today* (6th ed.). Englewood Cliffs: Merrill.

Mussen, P. H., Conger, J. J., & Kagan, J. (1979). *Child development and personality* (5th ed.). New York: Harper and Row.

Mussen, P. H., Conger, J. J., Kagan, J., & Huston, A. (1984). *Child development* (6th ed.). Philadelphia: Harper and Row. (8th ed., 1996).

Nelson, K. (1973). Structure and strategy in learning to talk. *Monographs of Society for Research in Child Development, 38*, 182.

Neuman, W. L. (1994). *Social research methods: Qualitative and quantitative approaches* (2nd ed.). Needham Heights, MA: Allyn and Bacon. (3rd ed., 1997).

Nilsen, B. A. (2001). *Week by week: Plans for observing and recording young children* (2nd ed.). Clifton Park: Thomson Delmar Learning.

Papalia, D. E., & Olds, S. W. (1987). *A child's world: Infancy through adolescence* (4th ed.). New York: McGraw-Hill. (8th ed., 1999).

Papalia, D. E., & Olds, S. W. (1992). *Human development* (5th ed.). New York: McGraw-Hill. (7th ed., 1998).

Papalia, D. E., & Olds, S. W. (1993). *A child's world: Infancy through adolescence* (6th ed.). New York: McGraw-Hill. (8th ed., 1999).

Papalia, D. E., Olds, S. W., and Feldman, R. D. (1999). *A child's world: Infancy through adolescence* (8th ed.). New York: McGraw-Hill.

Papalia, D. E., Olds, S. W., & Feldman, R. D. (2006). *A child's world: Infancy through adolescence* (10th ed.). New York: McGraw-Hill.

Papalia, D. E., Olds, S. W., & Feldman, R. D. (2007). *Human development* (10th ed.). New York: McGraw-Hill.

Parten, M. B. (1932). Social participation among pre-school children. *Journal of Abnormal and Social Psychology, 27*, 243–269.

Pillari, V. (1998). *Human behavior in the social environment: The developing person in a holistic context* (2nd ed.). New York: Brooks/Cole.

Ramsey, P. G., & Myers, L. C. (1990). Salience of race in young children's cognitive, affective, and behavioral responses to social environments. *Journal of Applied Developmental Psychology, 11*, 49–67.

Richarz, A. S. (1980). *Understanding children through observation*. New York: West.

Salkind, N. (1981). *Theories of human development*. New York: Van Nostrand.

Santrock, J. W. (1993). *Children* (3rd ed.). Madison: Brown and Benchmark. (6th ed., 1999).

Saunders, R., & Bingham-Newman, A. M. (1984). *Piagetian perspective for pre-schools: A thinking book for teachers*. Englewood Cliffs: Prentice-Hall.

Schiamberg, L. B. (1985). *Human development* (2nd ed.). New York: Macmillan.

Schickedanz, J. A., Schickedanz, D. I., Hansen, K., & Forsyth, P. D. (1993). *Understanding children* (2nd ed.). Mountain View: Mayfield. (3rd ed., 1998).

Schwartz, J. I. (1981). Children's experiments with language. *Young Children, 36*, 16–26.

Seifert, K. L., & Hoffnung, R. J. (1987). *Child and adolescent development*. Boston: Houghton Mifflin. (4th ed., 1997).

Selman, R. L. (1981). The child as a friendship philosopher. In S. R. Asher & J. M. Gorman (Eds.), *The development of children's friendships*. Cambridge, UK: Cambridge University Press.

Selman, R. L., & Selman, A. P. (1979). Children's ideas about friendship: A new theory. *Psychology Today, 13* (4), 71–80, 114.

Shaffer, D. R. (1996). *Developmental psychology: Childhood and adolescence* (4th ed.). Pacific Grove: Brooks/Cole.

Shaffer, D. R., & Kipp, K. (2007). *Developmental psychology: Childhood and adolescence* (7th ed.). Belmont: Thomson Learning.

Sonnenschein, S. (1986). Development of referential communication skills: How familiarity with a listener affects a speaker's production of redundant messages. *Developmental Psychology, 22*, 549–552.

Spodeck, B., & Saracho, O. N. (1994). *Right from the start: Teaching children ages three to eight*. Boston: Allyn and Bacon.

Sroufe, L. A., & Cooper, R. G. (1988). *Child development: Its nature and course.* New York: Knopf.

Stark, R. (1985). *Sociology.* Belmont: Wadsworth. (7th ed., 1998).

Steinberg, L., & Belsky, J. (1991). *Infancy, childhood, and adolescence: Development in context.* New York: McGraw-Hill.

Steinberg, L., & Meyer, R. (1995). *Childhood.* New York: McGraw-Hill.

Stern, V., & Cohen, D. (1958). *Observing and recording the behavior of young children.* New York: Teachers College. (Revised 1978).

Stone, L. J., & Church, J. (1979). *Childhood and adolescence: A psychology of the growing person* (4th ed.). New York: Random House.

Stone, L. J., & Church, J. (1984). *Childhood and adolescence: A psychology of the growing person* (5th ed.). New York: Random House.

Thomas, A., Chess, S., & Birch, H. (1968). *Temperament and behavior disorders in children.* New York: New York University Press.

Thomas, A., Chess, S., & Birch, H. (1970). The origin of personality. *Scientific American, 232*(2), 102–109.

Thorndike, R. L., & Hagan, E. P. (1977). *Measurement and evaluation in psychology and education* (4th ed.). New York: Wiley. (6th ed., 1997).

Travers, J. F. (1982). *The growing child* (2nd ed.). Dallas: Scott, Foresman.

Vander Zanden, J. W. (1993). *Human Development* (4th ed.). New York: Knopf. (7th ed., 1999).

Vasta, R., Haith, M. M., & Miller, S. A. (1995). *Child psychology: The modern science* (2nd ed.). New York: Wiley. (3rd ed., 1999).

Wadsworth, B. J. (1984). *Piaget's theory of cognitive and affective development* (3rd ed.). New York: Longman. (5th ed., 1996).

Willemsen, E. (1979). *Understanding infancy.* San Francisco: W. H. Freeman.

Wolff, P. H. (1973). The classification of states. In L. J. Stone, H. Smith, & L. B. Murphy (Eds.), *The competent infant: Research and commentary.* New York: Basic.

Wright, H. F. (1960). Observational child study. In P. H. Mussen (Ed.), *Handbook of research methods in child development.* New York: Wiley.

Zigler, E. F., & Stevenson, M. F. (1993). *Children in a changing world: Development and social issues* (2nd ed.). Pacific Grove: Brooks/Cole.

ANNOTATED BIBLIOGRAPHY

Children with Developmental Problems or at High Risk for Developmental Problems (Identification and Intervention)

Adler, S., & King, D. (Eds.). (1986). *A Multidisciplinary treatment program for the preschool exceptional child.* Springfield: Charles C. Thomas.

This text is a comprehensive, interdisciplinary manual on the care, education, and treatment of young children with developmental problems; it is directed toward professionals, child care providers, and parents.

Allen, K. E., & Schwartz, I. (2001). *The exceptional child: Inclusion in early childhood education.* (4th ed.). Clifton Park: Thomson Delmar Learning.

This text provides a comprehensive overview of early intervention and early childhood education for children with developmental problems, as well as their inclusion in the integrated (mainstreamed) classroom.

Blackman, J. A. (1984). *Medical aspects of developmental disabilities in children birth to three.* Rockville: Aspen. (3rd ed., 1997).

This is an outstanding book for early childhood personnel as it provides well-illustrated and readily understood information about medical issues that affect the developmental progress of young children; it is highly recommended.

Fallen, N. F., & Umansky, W. (1985). *Young children with special needs.* Columbus: Merrill.

This text is especially useful for its focus on the developmentally different child as being in need of a holistic approach to early care and education, just as is the normally developing child.

Hanson, M. J., & Harris, S. R. (1986). *Teaching the young child with motor delays.* Austin: Pro-Ed.

This easy-to-read handbook bridges the gap between parents and professionals who work with motor-impaired children, birth to three, and includes teaching strategies and therapy activities to be used in the home and in the infant center.

Haslam, R. H. A., & Valletutti, P. J. (1985). *Medical problems in the classroom.* Austin: Pro-Ed.

This book provides teachers and professionals from other disciplines with clues to early identification and points out ways that teachers can assist in the management of these problems.

Krajicek, M. J., & Tomlinson, A. I. T. (1983). *Detection of developmental problems in children.* Baltimore: University Park Press.

Practical and readable, this is a highly acclaimed pediatric nursing text that focuses on early identification, screening, and beginning intervention strategies with children with potential or identified developmental problems.

498

McCormick, L., & Schiefelbusch, R. L. (1984). *Early language intervention*. Columbus: Merrill.

A good introduction to both typical and atypical language development and overall communication development with practical examples of programs, procedures, and materials for fostering communication skills in young children.

Peterson, N. L. (1987). *Early intervention for handicapped and at-risk children*. Denver: Love.

This is an excellent text for students and professionals in early childhood special education and related disciplines who are working with young children with developmental problems; it gives an invaluable perspective on what early intervention actually entails.

Infants, Toddlers, and Parents

Apgar, V., & Beck, J. (1972). *Is my baby all right? A guide to birth defects*. New York: Trident.

This continues to be one of the best sources for information about genetic and environmental causes of developmental problems and what the progress and treatment of a problem is from birth on; it is sensitive and readable.

Brazelton, T. B. (1969). *Infants and mothers: Differences in development*. New York: Dell.

Although this book was published a number of years ago, it remains one of the best descriptions of the first year of life. It is written by a sensitive and observant pediatrician who has remained at the forefront of developmental pediatrics.

Brazelton, T. B. (1974). *Toddlers and parents*. New York: Dell.

Like Brazelton's infant book, this is an exceptionally good book for parents and caregivers of young children; just as sensitively written as the earlier book, this one also is a treasury of good advice and sensible suggestion about toddlers.

Bricker, D. D. (1986). *Early education of at-risk and handicapped infants, toddlers, and preschool children*. Glenview: Scott, Foresman.

Written by one of the leading infant specialists, this text offers both students and practitioners a contemporary view of the field, with examples of application for those working with atypical infants and children.

Bromwich, R. M. (1981). *Working with parents and infants*. Austin: Pro-Ed.

This remains one of the best books in the field for helping parents learn to work with their handicapped or high-risk children; particularly noteworthy is the inclusion of case histories covering successful, partly successful, and unsuccessful interventions; it is invaluable for those working with parents.

Caplan, F., & Caplan, T. (1982). *The first twelve months of life* and *The second twelve months of life*. New York: Putnam.

Very readable books that provide excellent descriptions of normal growth and development, although their emphasis on month-to-month changes rather than on developmental sequence may contribute to some undue anxiety in new parents. These books include many practical suggestions for dealing with daily behaviors and routines.

Hanson, M. J. (1984). *Atypical infant development*. Austin: Pro-Ed.

This interdisciplinary text presents students and professionals with a current review of research and literature on both typical and atypical infant developmental problems.

Leach, P. (1986). *Your baby and child from birth to age five*. New York: Knopf.

This book offers parents and caregivers excellent developmental explanations as well as practical suggestions for daily caregiving routines, appropriate play equipment, and behavior management.

Marotz, L., Rush, J., & Cross, M. (2001). *Health, safety and nutrition for the young child* (5th ed.). Clifton Park: Thomson Delmar Learning.

This book provides a comprehensive overview of the factors that contribute to maximizing the growth and development of each child. It includes some of the most current research information and knowledge concerning each of these areas and is especially useful for teachers, caregivers, and parents.

Wilson, L. C., Watson, L., & Watson, M. (2003). *Infants and toddlers* (5th ed.). Clifton Park: Thomson Delmar Learning.

Parents and caregivers will find this book particularly useful in understanding developmental sequences, creating enriching environments, and providing appropriate learning experiences for infants and toddlers based on their developmental needs.

INDEX

Developmental environment, 62
Developmental method, 356
Developmental milestones, 35t, 36t
Developmental theories. *See also* growth
  and development; Piaget; Vygotsky
  cephalocaudal principle, 34
  classical conditioning, 40, 46t
  cognitive domain, 33
  cognitive view, 42–44, 47t. *See also*
    Piaget; Vygotsky
  domains of behavior, 20, 24, 33, 39t
  ego, 37
  emotional domain, 33
  Erikson, Erik, 37, 39
  Freud, Sigmund, 36–37
  human nature, 30–31, 33, 38t, 39t
  id, 37
  importance of, 30
  language domain, 33
  learning, definition, 40
  learning view, 40–42, 46t, 47t. *See
    also* mechanistic view
  locomotion, 35t, 36t
  manual control, 35t, 36t
  modeling, 41
  nature of development, 33–34
  nature *versus* nurture, 32–33, 36–37,
    38t, 39, 40–44
  observational learning, 41
  operant conditioning, 40–41, 46t
  physical domain, 33
  physical-motor development, 34
  postural control, 35t, 36t
  proximodistal principle, 34
  psychoanalytic view, 36–37, 39, 46t
  psychosocial crisis, 37, 39
  psychosocial domain, 33
  qualitative *versus* quantitative,
    31–32, 38t
  reinforcement, 41
  social domain, 33
  social learning theory, 41–42, 47t
  sociocultural theory, 43–44, 47t
  sociohistorical theory. *See* sociocultural
    theory
  stage theory, 33–34, 37, 39
  summary of, 46t, 47t
  superego, 37
  vicarious punishment, 41, 47t
  vicarious reinforcement, 41, 47t
  Vygotsky, Lev, 43–44
Development areas, focusing on, 57
DeVries, Rheta, 15–16
Dialectical process, 405
Diary description. *See also* methods of
  observing and recording

advantages, 167
anecdotal record, 172–173
versus case study, 168–170
comprehensive diaries, 166–167,
  167, 171
definition, 167
degree of inference, 168
degree of selectivity, 167
disadvantages, 167
versus event sampling, 172–173
exercise, 174–175
forms, 169t, 170t
versus narrative description, 166
new behaviors, 172
objective, 166
open *versus* closed, 167
purpose, 166
versus running record, 172–173
summary of, 215t
topical diaries, 166, 167, 171
Differentiation, 23, 24, 25–26
Difficult temperament in newborns, 262
Directional development, 23
Directionality, 23
Discomfort, effect on observation, 70–71
Dishabituation, 270–271
Diversity. *See* multiculturalism
Domains of behavior, 20, 24, 33, 39t
Dramatic play, 15, 364
Drowsiness state, 260t
Duration records. *See also* frequency
  counts; methods of observing
  and recording
  advantages, 190–192
  definition, 189
  degree of inference, 190
  degree of selectivity, 190
  disadvantages, 192
  exercise, 193–194
  forms, 193t
  graphing data, 191
  open *versus* closed, 189
  summary of, 215t
  uses for, 192–194

E

Early reaching period, 301–302
Easy temperament in newborns, 262
Ego, 37
Egocentric speech, 359–361
Egocentrism
  definition, 9–10, 349–350
  language development, 443
  role in development, 9–10, 349–350
Elaboration, 401

Electronic recording
  audiotaping, rating scales, 221
  narrative description, 112
  videotaping, 78–79, 218–221
Elkind, David, 293
Emergent properties, 28, 29t
Emotional development. *See under age
  groups*
Emotional dialogue, 323
Emotional domain, 33
Emotional functioning of newborns,
  273–274, 283t
Emotive skills, 290. *See also under age
  groups*
Empirical data, 12
Environmental influences, 21, 24. *See also*
  context; nature *versus* nurture
Episodes, group component, 83
Erikson, Erik, 34, 37, 39, 306–307
Errors in recording, 73–74
Ethics. *See* professional ethics
Evaluation, description, 76
Events, 59, 155, 160–161
Event sampling. *See also* methods of
  observing and recording
  advantages, 158–159
  versus anecdotal record, 180
  baseline data, 162
  coding schemes, 155, 159
  definition, 155
  degree of inference, 158
  degree of selectivity, 158
  description, 154–156, 158
  versus diary description, 172–173
  disadvantages, 159–160
  exercise, 162–163
  forms, 157t, 158t
  guidelines, 160
  versus narrative description, 156, 158
  with narrative description, 155, 159
  natural units, 159
  open *versus* closed, 158
  recording technique, 155–156
  space/equipment events, 160–161
  summary of, 214t
  versus time sampling, 156
  uses for, 160–162
Evidence, 225
Evolutionary explanation, 51
Exclusive categories, 133–134
Exercises. *See under age groups*
Exhaustive categories, 133–134
Expanding knowledge base, 401
Explaining behavior, 45, 48–51. *See also*
  degree of inference; interpretation

Spontaneous behaviors in newborns, 261–262
Stage theory, 33–34, 35t, 36t, 37, 39. *See also* Erikson; Piaget
Standardized testing, appropriateness, 8
Standards, comparing results to, 247–249
Standing, infancy, 295, 298
Stars, 414
Startle reflex. *See* Moro reflex
States, of newborns, 259–261, 260t, 276t
Static descriptors, 198
Status, 98
Stepping reflex, 266, 267t
Streams of behavior, 95–96
Stress, 7–9
Subgroups, 79–80
Subjects
  right to withdraw, 69
  selecting, 58
Superego, 37
Supervision, 65
Symbolic play, 366–367
Symbolic skills. *See* representational/symbolic skills
Syntactical ambiguity, 407
Syntactical forms, 360–361
Syntax, 407, 419
Systematic change, 27

T

Techniques for recording behavior. *See* methods of observing and recording
Temperament, 261–262, 263t, 264t, 309t, 310t, 311t
Testing, 7–8, 66
Testing strategies, 453
Test-taking *versus* observation, 7–8
Theoretical bias, 231–232
Theory, relationship to observation, 9–13. *See also* developmental theories
Thinking skills. *See* conceptual/thinking skills
Time
  allotment, 57
  concepts, cultural significance, 245
  considerations, narrative description, 123–124
  intervals, specifying, 134, 136, 137–138
  learning concept of, 352
Time sampling. *See also* methods of observing and recording
  advantages, 143–144
  behaviors, 132, 133, 138–140, 143–145, 146
  category coding schemes, 133–134

coding schemes, 133–134, 146
context, 149–150
degree of inference, 143
degree of selectivity, 143
description, 130–131
disadvantages, 144–146
economy, 144
versus event sampling, 156
exclusive categories, 133–134
exercise, 138–142, 150–151
exhaustive categories, 133–134
forms, 135t, 136t, 137t, 141t, 147t, 148t, 149t
inter-observer reliability, 144
and narrative description, 122t, 143
note expansion, 143
note taking, 143
open *versus* closed, 142–143
play, classifications of, 138–140
predetermined categories, 146
recording techniques, combining, 144
representativeness, 131, 146–148
sampling behavior *versus* describing, 131
sign system coding schemes, 133–134, 135t
social interactions, classifications of, 138–140
structure, 133
summary of, 214t
time intervals, specifying, 134, 136, 137–138
uses for, 146–150
variations of, 133
when to use, 141, 146–150
Toddlers. *See* infancy
Tonic neck reflex, 267t
Tool-using skills. *See* sensorimotor/tool-using skills
Topical diaries, 166, 167, 171
Touch, cultural significance, 245
Trained *versus* untrained observers, 6
Traits, 372
Transmission errors, 74
Trust *versus* mistrust, 39, 306–307

U

Unnecessary testing, 66
Unoccupied behavior, 139, 365

V

Validity (accuracy), 14, 204–206
Vicarious punishment, 41, 47t
Vicarious reinforcement, 41, 47t
Videotaping
  advantages, 219

checklists, 218–221
disadvantages, 220
group observation, 78–79
limitations, 219
permissions, 220
purpose of, 219
rating scales, 218–221
rights of the taped, 220–221
"soft eyes," 220
usefulness, 219
Vietnamese, smiling, 244
Visible displacement, 320
Vision, newborns, 269–270
Vocabulary, 360, 407, 419, 441–442
Vygotsky, Lev
  cognitive/intellectual development, 292, 399–400
  contextual theory, 43–44
  language development, 354–355, 356–357, 358–361, 403, 405
  play, 367–368
  sociocultural theory, 43–44, 399–401

W

Waking activity state, 260t
Walking, infancy, 300
Walking reflex, 267t
Wright, Herbert F., 95, 97–98
Written recording, 112

Y

Young children (2 to 5 years). *See also* infancy; newborns; school age
  cognitive/intellectual development, 349–354, 383
  emotional development, 370–375, 376, 389–390
  language development, 354–361, 384
  physical environment, 339–340, 380–381
  physical/motor development, 340–345, 343t, 344t, 345t, 345–349, 382
  play, 362, 363–364, 365–366, 366t, 366–369, 385–388
  playscapes, 339–340
  social/emotional development, 376–379, 391–392

Z

Zone of proximal development, 367–368, 400